ISRAEL
THE CHOSEN
— *or* —
THE ENEMY?

DR. BRUCE CALDWELL

Copyright © 2020 by Dr. Bruce Caldwell

ISBN   Softcover   978-1-951469-43-6

All rights reserved. No part of this book may be reproduced or transmitted in any form or by any means, electronic or mechanical, including photocopying, recording, or by any information storage and retrieval system without express written permission from the author, except in the case of brief quotations embodied in critical reviews and certain other non-commercial uses permitted by copyright law.

Printed in the United States of America.

To order additional copies of this book, contact:
Bookwhip
1-855-339-3589
https://www.bookwhip.com

CONTENTS

Preface 1
Prologue 3

Chapter 1   The Seed of Abraham 11
Chapter 2   Has Israel Been "On Hold" for 2000 Years? 18
Chapter 3   Key Signals Regarding the "End Times" 23
Chapter 4   You Are His Chosen and Holy People 29
Chapter 5   The Messiah In The Old Testament 34
Chapter 6   God's Love And Mercy Towards The Jews 50
Chapter 7   The "Scattering" and "Gathering" of the Jews 68
Chapter 8   Peace and Safety 72
Chapter 9   The Unmistakable Events That Chronicle the Tribulation .. 75
Chapter 10 The Messiah and Then the Tribulation Or the Tribulation and Then the Messiah? 83
Chapter 11 The Rapture Of The "Body Of Believers" 100
Chapter 12 Defining The Body Of Believers 121
Chapter 13 The Two Witnesses—Drought and Fiery Judgment 126
Chapter 14 Prepare To Flee The Final Exodus 143
Chapter 15 The Prince Of Peace Or The Prince—Good And Evil Personified 152
Chapter 16 The Mark Of The Beast—A Choice For Eternity 157
Chapter 17 The Battle Of Armageddon—The Prelude To A Restored Kingdom 174
Chapter 18 How Does One Define The Remnant? 179
Chapter 19 The Restoration And Cleansing Of The Promised Land 186
Chapter 20 Satan Bound For 1000 Years 201
Chapter 21 The Rebuilding Of The Temples—#3 And #4 204
Chapter 22 The Kingdom Restored 219
Chapter 23 These Bones Are Going To "Walk Around" Again—David As King 222

Chapter 24	The Lame – The Deaf And Those Who Are "Last" Will Emerge As "First"	227
Chapter 25	The Enemy Is Defeated—The Messiah Establishes "New Jerusalem"	238
Chapter 26	Why Would God Be Angry With His People?	245
Chapter 27	How Could A Loving God Allow His Children To Die?	256
Chapter 28	The New Covenant	273
Chapter 29	Omnipotence—Omniscience—Omnipresence	287
Chapter 30	Failing To Revere His Word An Opportunity Lost – A Critical Error	294
Chapter 31	Life – One Two-Sided Page	299
Chapter 32	God Has Revealed Himself To Every Man	304
Chapter 33	The Unpardonable Sin	312
Chapter 34	Sanctification—A Result Of God's Grace	317
Chapter 35	I've Been A Sinner My Entire Life—Salvation Is Too Late For Me	326
Chapter 36	My Sins Are Such That God Would Never Allow Me To Enter Into His Presence	329
Chapter 37	The Grace Of God—Our Only Hope	337
Chapter 38	The Firstborn	345
Chapter 39	The Holy Spirit	355
Chapter 40	Fear Should Bring Us To Our Knees—It Will	372
Chapter 41	Die Twice Or Be Born Twice—Your Choice	378
Chapter 42	How Terrible Will It Be To Be "Separate" From God And Those You Love?	380
Chapter 43	If There Is One God—Why So Many Different Bodies Of Believers?	384
Chapter 44	Why Hasn't "Fulfilled Prophecy" Led To Repentance?	392
Chapter 45	The Fruit Of Righteousness—A Fig Tree Does Not Give Off Olives!	404
Chapter 46	Repent—Serve The Lord—Not Satan	409
Chapter 47	The Word—The Very Essence Of Truth— A Permanent Promise	429

Epilogue: Got Eternity? 447

PREFACE

On May 14, 1948, Israel became a nation. Now, 63 years later, many nations of the world have declared that Israel must be wiped from the map. God is not surprised. He told us that all nations would turn against Israel.

Are you surprised at this development? Did you ever think the United States and Great Britain, et al, would turn against Israel? The tiny nation of Israel, God's chosen people, has or soon will become the enemy of all nations.

Prophecy, fulfilled, is confirmation of the authenticity of the Bible. Now it is time to turn to prophecies which detail the "final events" prior to God's unleashing His righteous judgment on the enemies of Israel.

Recall that after the great flood only 8 persons survived. Why was nearly all mankind wiped out during that event? God was angered with the attitudes and actions of the people. Sin was rampant. Disobedience documented the lifestyle of people who had become self-centered and self-righteous. The people of the world ignored the commands of God.

Is history about to repeat itself? Are we approaching a time of sinful self-indulgence never before equaled? Are we sliding toward Armageddon at a precipitous pace?

PROLOGUE

Zechariah 14:1, 2 NKJV
1 Behold, the day of the LORD is coming…
2 For I will gather all the nations to battle against Jerusalem;

When this specific prophecy is fulfilled, the entire world will have decided that Israel is the "enemy". It is incredible, given the size of Israel, that mighty nations will have decided that the nation of Israel must be dismantled. How could such a small nation have become the fulcrum upon which major international calamitous events could pivot?

How could God's chosen people have become the enemy of all the nations? Doesn't the following prophecy by Ezekiel feel like it just came from the front page of the newspapers of the nations?

Ezekiel 25:6-7 NKJV
6 'For thus says the Lord God: "Because you clapped your hands, stamped your feet, and rejoiced in heart with all your disdain for the land of Israel,
7 indeed, therefore, I will stretch out My hand against you, and give you as plunder to the nations; I will cut you off from the peoples, and I will cause you to perish from the countries; I will destroy you, and you shall know that I am the Lord."

Has the world not seen people celebrating in the streets as the enemies of Israel rejoice when the Jews are killed or injured?

Why did God choose Israel? Listen to the word of God as transmitted by Moses:

Deuteronomy 7:6-9 NKJ
6 "For you are a holy people to the LORD your God; the LORD your God has chosen you to be a people for Himself, a special treasure above all the peoples on the face of the earth.
7 "The LORD did not set His love on you nor choose you because you were more in number than any other people, for you were the least of all peoples;
8 "but because the LORD loves you, and because He would keep the oath which He swore to your fathers, the LORD has brought you out with a mighty hand, and redeemed you from the house of bondage, from the hand of Pharaoh king of Egypt.
9 "Therefore know that the LORD your God, He is God, the faithful God who keeps covenant and mercy for a thousand generations with those who love Him and keep His commandments;

At this time, many nations have decided that Israel is the "enemy". Even the United States, one of Israel's closest allies, is telling Israel to "return to its 1967 borders" if they expect to achieve peace with the Palestinians. Prime Minister Benjamin Netanyahu, and the Israeli Parliament, is feeling pressure from many nations all over the world, including the United Nations General Assembly, to cede territory to the Palestinians in order to establish a Palestinian state along side Israel.

Are the "Chosen People" about to become the enemy of all nations? Perhaps not all nations have decided to declare Israel the enemy, yet, but Zechariah 14:2 says that "all nations" will do so. The most outspoken so far have been members of "far left" movements and the Muslim nations

Those who "will surely assemble" against Israel is not an unexpected event. Listen:

Isaiah 54:14-15 NKJV
14 In righteousness you shall be established; You shall be far from oppression, for you shall not fear; And from terror, for it shall not come near you.
15 Indeed they shall surely assemble, but not because of Me. Whoever assembles against you shall fall for your sake.

King David said the following:

Psalm 2:1-9 NKJV
1 Why do the nations rage, And the people plot a vain thing?
2 The kings of the earth set themselves, And the rulers take counsel together, Against the Lord and against His Anointed, saying,
3 "Let us break Their bonds in pieces And cast away Their cords from us."
4 He who sits in the heavens shall laugh; The Lord shall hold them in derision.
5 Then He shall speak to them in His wrath, And distress them in His deep displeasure:
6 "Yet I have set My King On My holy hill of Zion."
7 "I will declare the decree: The Lord has said to Me, 'You are My Son, Today I have begotten You.
8 Ask of Me, and I will give You The nations for Your inheritance, And the ends of the earth for Your possession.
9 You shall break them with a rod of iron; You shall dash them to pieces like a potter's vessel.'"

Listen to what the prophet Obadiah said, regarding those who rejoice over the destruction of Israel:

Obadiah 1:12-15 NKJV
12 "But you should not have gazed on the day of your brother In the day of his captivity; Nor should you have rejoiced over the children of Judah In the day of their destruction; Nor should you have spoken proudly In the day of distress.
13 You should not have entered the gate of My people In the day of their calamity. Indeed, you should not have gazed on their affliction In the day of their calamity, Nor laid hands on their substance In the day of their calamity.
14 You should not have stood at the crossroads To cut off those among them who escaped; Nor should you have delivered up those among them who remained In the day of distress.
15 "For the day of the Lord upon all the nations is near; As you have done, it shall be done to you; Your reprisal shall return upon your own head.

The Holy Scriptures indicate that being an enemy of Israel is a risky endeavor!

In the Book of Genesis, the Lord said to Abraham:

Genesis 12:3 NKJV
3 I will bless those who bless you, And I will curse him who curses you; And in you all the families of the earth shall be blessed."

Notice the last sentence "...in you all the families of the earth will be blessed." It seems like a non-sequitur to say that God will curse those who curse you yet in you all families will be blessed. The Holy Scriptures frequently speak in the present and simultaneously reference the future.

God does not only warn the enemies of Israel but He also warns the false prophets of Israel who say "peace when there is no peace". Listen to the words of the prophet Ezekiel:

Ezekiel 13:3, 6-10 NKJV
3 Woe to the foolish prophets, who follow their own spirit and have seen nothing!
6 They have envisioned futility and false divination, saying, 'Thus says the Lord!' But the Lord has not sent them; yet they hope that the word may be confirmed.
7 Have you not seen a futile vision, and have you not spoken false divination? You say, 'The Lord says,' but I have not spoken."
8 Therefore thus says the Lord God: "Because you have spoken nonsense and envisioned lies, therefore I am indeed against you," says the Lord God.
9 "My hand will be against the prophets who envision futility and who divine lies; they shall not be in the assembly of My people, nor be written in the record of the house of Israel, nor shall they enter into the land of Israel. Then you shall know that I am the Lord God.
10 "Because, indeed, because they have seduced My people, saying, 'Peace!' when there is no peace.

Notice the sentence, "…people who envision futility." Those who feel that it is useless to embrace God's plan for Israel shall not be rewarded. God's hand will be against them.

Today, at the highest levels of government among many nations, there are movements whose sole purpose is to eliminate Israel (Zionism). This news article below focuses on the Prime Minister of Israel but it is indicative of the boldness coming forth from world leaders depicting Israel and her leaders as the enemy.

In another recent article, November 25, 2011, Islamic activists proclaim that "One day we will kill all the Jews"

Cairo rally: One day we'll kill all Jews

Sarkozy Calls Netanyahu a 'Liar'

By Géraldine Amiel

PARIS—French President Nicolas Sarkozy described Israeli Prime Minister Benjamin Netanyahu as a "liar" during a recent conversation with President Barack Obama that was overheard by reporters, according to a French website's report of the incident.

"I can't stand him anymore, he is a liar," Mr. Sarkozy told Mr. Obama as the two were preparing to start a news conference during a summit of the Group of 20 world's largest economies in Cannes, France, last week.

"You may be sick of him, but me, I have to deal with him every day," Mr. Obama replied, according to the French site, Arrêt sur Images.

A spokesman for Mr. Sarkozy, a spokesman for Mr. Netanyahu and a White House official declined to comment.

Senior French government officials have criticized Mr. Netanyahu in recent months over his refusal to freeze Israeli settlement construction in Palestinian territories.

The Associated Press on Tuesday said one of its reporters overheard the comments but didn't initially report them because the agency thought they "were deemed private under French media traditions."

The website said the Cannes conversation was overheard by several reporters because, even though the two presidents were still in a separate room, they were already wearing microphones for the news conference and aides to Mr. Sarkozy had distributed translating devices to a small group of journalists.

Reporters were told not to connect headphones until the news conference started. Those who did, however, heard the exchange, according to Arrêt sur Images.

During the conversation, Mr. Obama asked Mr. Sarkozy to help persuade Palestinians not to seek membership at the United Nations.

Mr. Obama also blamed the French president for not warning him that France would support the Palestinian Authority's application to Unesco, the United Nations Educational, Scientific and Cultural Organization.

Unesco members approved the application, despite U.S. lobbying efforts against the bid and the threat that Palestinian membership would legally oblige the U.S.—the largest contributor to the organization—to withdraw funding.

White House spokesman Jay Carney said he had no comment on the substance of the overheard remarks. But he said it is well known that the U.S. and France disagree on the Palestinian efforts at the U.N.

—Joshua Mitnick and Carol E. Lee contributed to this article.

Sarkozy and Obama at a lunch on Nov. 3 in Cannes, France.

Muslim Brotherhood holds venomous anti-Israel rally in Cairo mosque Friday; Islamic activists chant: Tel Aviv, judgment day has come

Arab hate: A Muslim Brotherhood rally in Cairo's most prominent mosque Friday turned into a venomous anti-Israel protest, with attendants vowing to "one day kill all Jews."

Muslim Brotherhood spokesmen, as well as Palestinian guest speakers, made explicit calls for Jihad and for liberating the whole of Palestine. Time and again, a Koran quote vowing that "one day we shall kill all the Jews" was uttered at the site... Throughout the event, Muslim Brotherhood activists chanted: "Tel Aviv, Tel Aviv, judgment day has come."

At a program called The World without Zionism, in preparation for an annual anti-Israel demonstration held on the last Friday of the holy month of Ramadan, Mahmoud Ahmadinejad, told a group of students that Israel must be "wiped off the map". More recently similar radical statements have been made.

At the end of WW II, Hitler, in his final political statement said, ""Above all I charge the leaders of the nation and those under them to scrupulous observance of the laws of race and to merciless opposition to the universal poisoner of all peoples, international Jewry."

Not much has changed. Hitler's charge to the leaders of the nations is beginning to sound like a prophecy fulfilled. It is most perplexing to know that prophecies of our Lord, being fulfilled by man, make His chosen people the enemy of all.

One final Biblical perspective on this matter provided by the prophet Ezekiel:

Ezekiel 30:3-5 NKJV
3 For the day is near, Even the day of the Lord is near; It will be a day of clouds, the time of the Gentiles.
4 The sword shall come upon Egypt, And great anguish shall be in Ethiopia, When the slain fall in Egypt, And they take away her wealth, And her foundations are broken down.

5 "Ethiopia, Libya, Lydia, all the mingled people, Chub, and the men of the lands who are allied, shall fall with them by the sword."

When the Holy Scriptures refer to "Egypt", the land of the Americas was not yet discovered, thus if you look at Egypt as a typology, rather than a nation, you will see the nations of the Americas may also be the object of Ezekiel's prophecy. It is true that modern weapons of war did not exist when Ezekiel wrote, so we read of swords where in fact, such ancient weapons are representative of what is to come.

Here, Jeremiah speaks from the heart, expressing his concern over the spiritual state of Israel:

Jeremiah 8:18-22 NIV
18 O my Comforter in sorrow, my heart is faint within me.
19 Listen to the cry of my people from a land far away: "Is the Lord not in Zion? Is her King no longer there?" "Why have they provoked me to anger with their images, with their worthless foreign idols?"
20 "The harvest is past, the summer has ended, and we are not saved."
21 Since my people are crushed, I am crushed; I mourn, and horror grips me.
22 Is there no balm in Gilead? Is there no physician there? Why then is there no healing for the wound of my people?

Though Jeremiah was referring to events of the past, does it not seem applicable to the current forecast? The plan of Israel's enemies is to crush them.

This book explores these points in detail, citing the key signals, pointing to the coming tribulation, the rapture of the Church, the anti-Christ and the Millennium. These are indeed perilous times. Israel is both heralded as God's chosen people and yet they are cursed by many as "the enemy." When the nations decide to attack Israel, to erase their country from the map, God will act and the tribulation will commence.

Now, to the fundamental teaching of this book:

CHAPTER 1

THE SEED OF ABRAHAM

As we hear about the impending disaster wherein the principal enemy of Israel is the nation of Islam, it would be useful to consider the fact that the nation of Israel and the nations of Islam both had their origins in Abraham. The Bible establishes the basis for that fact.

As God prepared to call out this nation, eventually to be called Israel, He called Abram (Abraham) to move from the land of Ur to a place God would reveal to him. To put this event in perspective, Adonai (called Adonai due to reverence for the name of God, written as G_D in many cases) called Abraham to form a new nation (not called Israel because Jacob whose name was changed to Israel had not yet been born). This event occurred two years after Noah died. The Bible does not say that any person but Abraham was called to fulfill the purpose of establishing a new nation. In fact Abraham had to move away from "his people" in Ur in obedience to God's command.

This historical timeframe is so important that I will quote exactly what happened.

Genesis Chapters 16 and 17

Genesis 16:1-16 NKJV
1 Now Sarai, Abram's wife, had borne him no children. And she had an Egyptian maidservant whose name was Hagar.
2 So Sarai said to Abram, "See now, the Lord has restrained me from bearing children. Please, go in to my maid; perhaps I shall obtain children by her." And Abram heeded the voice of Sarai.

3 Then Sarai, Abram's wife, took Hagar her maid, the Egyptian, and gave her to her husband Abram to be his wife, after Abram had dwelt ten years in the land of Canaan.

4 So he went in to Hagar, and she conceived. And when she saw that she had conceived, her mistress became despised in her eyes.

5 Then Sarai said to Abram, "My wrong be upon you! I gave my maid into your embrace; and when she saw that she had conceived, I became despised in her eyes. The Lord judge between you and me."

6 So Abram said to Sarai, "Indeed your maid is in your hand; do to her as you please." And when Sarai dealt harshly with her, she fled from her presence.

7 Now the Angel of the Lord found her by a spring of water in the wilderness, by the spring on the way to Shur.

8 And He said, "Hagar, Sarai's maid, where have you come from, and where are you going?"
She said, "I am fleeing from the presence of my mistress Sarai."

9 The Angel of the Lord said to her, "Return to your mistress, and submit yourself under her hand."

10 Then the Angel of the Lord said to her, "I will multiply your descendants exceedingly, so that they shall not be counted for multitude."

11 And the Angel of the Lord said to her: "Behold, you are with child, and you shall bear a son. You shall call his name Ishmael, Because the Lord has heard your affliction.

12 He shall be a wild man; His hand shall be against every man, And every man's hand against him. And he shall dwell in the presence of all his brethren."

13 Then she called the name of the Lord who spoke to her, You-Are-the-God-Who-Sees; for she said, "Have I also here seen Him who sees me?"

14 Therefore the well was called Beer Lahai Roi; observe, it is between Kadesh and Bered.

15 So Hagar bore Abram a son; and Abram named his son, whom Hagar bore, Ishmael.

16 Abram was eighty-six years old when Hagar bore Ishmael to Abram.

Genesis 17:1-27 NKJV

1 When Abram was ninety-nine years old, the Lord appeared to Abram and said to him, "I am Almighty God; walk before Me and be blameless.
2 And I will make My covenant between Me and you, and will multiply you exceedingly."
3 Then Abram fell on his face, and God talked with him, saying:
4 "As for Me, behold, My covenant is with you, and you shall be a father of many nations.
5 No longer shall your name be called Abram, but your name shall be Abraham; for I have made you a father of many nations.
6 I will make you exceedingly fruitful; and I will make nations of you, and kings shall come from you.
7 And I will establish My covenant between Me and you and your descendants after you in their generations, for an everlasting covenant, to be God to you and your descendants after you.
8 Also I give to you and your descendants after you the land in which you are a stranger, all the land of Canaan, as an everlasting possession; and I will be their God."
9 And God said to Abraham: "As for you, you shall keep My covenant, you and your descendants after you throughout their generations.
10 This is My covenant which you shall keep, between Me and you and your descendants after you: Every male child among you shall be circumcised; 11 and you shall be circumcised in the flesh of your foreskins, and it shall be a sign of the covenant between Me and you.
12 He who is eight days old among you shall be circumcised, every male child in your generations, he who is born in your house or bought with money from any foreigner who is not your descendant.
13 He who is born in your house and he who is bought with your money must be circumcised, and My covenant shall be in your flesh for an everlasting covenant.
14 And the uncircumcised male child, who is not circumcised in the flesh of his foreskin, that person shall be cut off from his people; he has broken My covenant."
15 Then God said to Abraham, "As for Sarai your wife, you shall not call her name Sarai, but Sarah shall be her name.

16 And I will bless her and also give you a son by her; then I will bless her, and she shall be a mother of nations; kings of peoples shall be from her."

17 Then Abraham fell on his face and laughed, and said in his heart, "Shall a child be born to a man who is one hundred years old? And shall Sarah, who is ninety years old, bear a child?"

18 And Abraham said to God, "Oh, that Ishmael might live before You!"

19 Then God said: "No, Sarah your wife shall bear you a son, and you shall call his name Isaac; I will establish My covenant with him for an everlasting covenant, and with his descendants after him.

20 And as for Ishmael, I have heard you. Behold, I have blessed him, and will make him fruitful, and will multiply him exceedingly. He shall beget twelve princes, and I will make him a great nation.

21 But My covenant I will establish with Isaac, whom Sarah shall bear to you at this set time next year."

22 Then He finished talking with him, and God went up from Abraham.

23 So Abraham took Ishmael his son, all who were born in his house and all who were bought with his money, every male among the men of Abraham's house, and circumcised the flesh of their foreskins that very same day, as God had said to him.

24 Abraham was ninety-nine years old when he was circumcised in the flesh of his foreskin.

25 And Ishmael his son was thirteen years old when he was circumcised in the flesh of his foreskin.

26 That very same day Abraham was circumcised, and his son Ishmael;

27 and all the men of his house, born in the house or bought with money from a foreigner, were circumcised with him.

This chapter is entitled, The Seed of Abraham. As you just read, both Isaac and Ishmael are of the seed of Abraham. Only Isaac was the son of the covenant. As strange as it may sound, given the current situation, there will eventually be reconciliation between the Arabs and the Jews, both being the seed of Abraham. This quotation from Isaiah clarifies the issue:

Isaiah 19:19-25 NKJV
19 In that day there will be an altar to the Lord in the midst of the land of Egypt, and a pillar to the Lord at its border.

20 And it will be for a sign and for a witness to the Lord of hosts in the land of Egypt; for they will cry to the Lord because of the oppressors, and He will send them a Savior and a Mighty One, and He will deliver them.
21 Then the Lord will be known to Egypt, and the Egyptians will know the Lord in that day, and will make sacrifice and offering; yes, they will make a vow to the Lord and perform it.
22 And the Lord will strike Egypt, He will strike and heal it; they will return to the Lord, and He will be entreated by them and heal them.
23 In that day there will be a highway from Egypt to Assyria, and the Assyrian will come into Egypt and the Egyptian into Assyria, and the Egyptians will serve with the Assyrians.
24 In that day Israel will be one of three with Egypt and Assyria — a blessing in the midst of the land,
25 whom the Lord of hosts shall bless, saying, "Blessed is Egypt My people, and Assyria the work of My hands, and Israel My inheritance."

None of us are in a position to declare God's intention regarding other nations and other faiths. We do know that Adonai is a God of Love, declaring that we are to respond to that love with great dedication to His principles, expectations and laws. I thank God that His expectations are crystal clear and I pray for forgiveness of sin, mine and yours, among all people everywhere. The Scriptures say that the Mercy Seat sits above the Ark of the Covenant and I pray, hopefully with you, for God's mercy for every creature created in His image. This is what God told Abraham:

Genesis 12:1-3 CJB
Now Adonai said to Avram, "Get yourself out of your country, away from your kinsmen and away from your father's house, and go to the land that I will show you. I will make of you a great nation, I will bless you, and I will make your name great; and you are to be a blessing. I will bless those who bless you, but I will curse anyone who curses you; and by you all the families of the earth will be blessed."

Notice the last sentence of the quotation. "…by you all the families of the earth will be blessed." All means all, thus Abraham is the father of a new nation, a nation that was to become the oracle of God to the world. Thus

Abraham is father to many nations, transmitting God's Word to the entire world. It was God's will that Israel, His chosen people, receive and preserve the Holy Scriptures for all mankind.

That brings us to a question that begs an answer: If God created man in His own image and if the Holy Scriptures state that it His express will is that no man perish, how can we who are so imperfect ever rise to the perfection of the Prophet, the Messiah, the One sent by God to redeem those who are sons of the living God? How can we stand, as a sinner in the presence of our Creator?

The answer is that we cannot, as an uncleansed sinner, stand in the presence of God. From the beginning to the present, God's people were told to look forward to the moment in time where a Deliverer, Yeshua, the Messiah would enter history and change things forever. The Scriptures promise that no longer would God measure the condition of the soul by adherence to the Law and sacrifices of animals that were to be a "stand in", an atoning sacrifice for the sinner. It was the shed blood of animals, sacrificed to cover the sins of the people, that was initially commanded by God.

If the sacrifice of animals was to atone for the sins of Israel, then what atonement for sin is available now? Even with the movement, by some in Israel, to rebuild the Temple, there is talk of "virtual sacrifice". Those persons want to obey the law but they do not want to actually return to the practice laying their hands on the head of animal to be sacrificed for their sins. Whether that attitude is one of mercy towards the animal or convenience to oneself, it matters not. The ultimate sacrifice has already been made and the only sacrifice needed now are "sacrifices of righteousness" not to cover our sin because certainly the sacrifice of animals cannot atone, ultimately, for the sins of man.

Every person created in the image of God should be asking themselves, "What will allow me to stand in the presence of God, one who will not look upon sin?" Certainly not our own worthiness, our own perfection and our own righteousness qualifies us for entry. There is only One who is able to reconcile us with the Father, there is only One who provided for our atonement and that One, along with His angels will, on Judgment Day, separate the saints from the sinners, the sheep from the goats. That One is our only hope. I doubt that a single person reading this feels that they are a saint. And we are not! Only by being cloaked in the righteousness of Jesus Christ, the Messiah, the promised Yeshua, the One who gives meaning to A.D. and B.C. (Anno Domini and Before Christ), can we be delivered into the Presence of the Holy Father.

Fortunately, God provided the perfect sacrifice for sinners. His unblemished Son, the Messiah, Yeshua, went to the cross as a final and ultimate sacrifice for the sins of Man. From that time forward, no further sacrifices for sin are needed or wanted by the Father. By the sacrifice of one Man, the sins of a repentant person, committed to turning away from sin and obeying God, are forgiven. It seems too good to be true that an act of sincere repentance followed by acts of love and kindness to all persons will allow you to enter into the presence of the Holy Father, for eternity.

It is critical that Christians and others acknowledge that they are not the chosen people but as a result of Jewish history, have been "grafted into" the root of Israel. Christians, in particular, see what they see, in light of the God of the Jews, whose message, delivered by the Jews, shape the views of all worshippers of God. Without the Jews, our faith would not be based on the facts of the Old Testament. God's relationship to Abraham, Isaac and Joseph form the basis of our understanding of the Scriptures. Prophecies, precisely fulfilled, and prophecies yet to be fulfilled, shed light on the past and give us a roadmap and hope for the future.

The title of this chapter is the seed of Abraham and the blessing is assured:
...and in thee shall all families of the earth be blessed. Genesis 12:3 NKJ

CHAPTER 2

HAS ISRAEL BEEN "ON HOLD" FOR 2000 YEARS?

I believe that the first 2000 years of the history of Israel, up to the birth of Jesus Christ, were essentially years in which God was dealing with His chosen people. He intervened in their lives, He led them, loved them and disciplined them. He spoke through Moses and the prophets, He established kingdoms and He gave the Jewish people the Word of God. The history of Israel, its past, present and future was made manifest. He promised a Messiah and He promised to establish His kingdom in the promised land.

I believe the Messiah did come as promised and that the subsequent 2000 year period has been a period without the sort of Divine Revelation previously provided to the nation of Israel. Why would God have done this? Read on.

Isaiah 6:10 (NKJ)
10 "Make the heart of this people dull, and their ears heavy, and shut their eyes; lest they see with their eyes, and hear with their ears, and understand with their heart, and return and be healed."

This verse has long puzzled many readers, Jew and Gentile alike. Why did God tell Isaiah to speak these things? First, any thoughtful response covers more ground that I can cover here. The entire Bible provides answers. But there is one particular answer that I want to quote because it seems to be the simplest explanation. It is an explanation of hope. It's an explanation of how God first scattered His people; then said that He plans to gather them and restore the Kingdom to them. But He sustained them "as a nation" without a king, without prophets, and without a Temple in Jerusalem. Listen.

Romans 11:7-10, 25-29 (NKJ)
7 Just as it is written: "God has given them a spirit of stupor, eyes that they should not see and ears that they should not hear, to this very day.
8 "And David says: "Let their table become a snare and a trap, a stumbling block and a recompense to them.
9 Let their eyes be darkened, so that they do not see, and bow down their back always.
10 "I say then, have they stumbled that they should fall? Certainly not! But through their fall, to provoke them to jealousy, salvation has come to the Gentiles...
25 For I do not desire, brethren, that you should be ignorant of this mystery, lest you should be wise in your own opinion, that blindness in part has happened to Israel until the fullness of the Gentiles has come in.
26 And so all Israel will be saved, as it is written: "The Deliverer will come out of Zion, and He will turn away ungodliness from Jacob;
27 For this is My covenant with them, when I take away their sins."
28 Concerning the gospel they are enemies for your sake, but concerning the election they are beloved for the sake of the fathers.
29 For the gifts and the calling of God are irrevocable.

Here the Apostle Paul has quoted David in a letter to the Romans and a quote from Isaiah makes the point that "in part" Israel's blindness has happened "until the fullness of the Gentiles has come in". But do not miss the other key points in verses 26 and 27. "All Israel will be saved... The Deliverer will come out of Zion... and take away their sins". Verse 29 says "the gifts and the calling of God are irrevocable". When God made promises to Abraham, Moses, Isaac, Jacob and Joseph and many others about His love for His people, He also promised to keep those promises. He said the Messiah would redeem them.

Deuteronomy 18:18 (NKJ)
18 I will raise up for them a Prophet like you from among their brethren, and will put My words in His mouth, and He shall speak to them all that I command Him.

What prophet? Notice the capitalization of Prophet, His, He and Him. This is a reference to our Lord. Moses was told by God that a Prophet would be raised up, from among the brethren. Listen to the prophecy of Isaiah.

Isaiah 11:1 (NKJ)
"There shall come forth a Rod from the stem of Jesse, and a Branch shall grow out of his roots."

The expected Prophet from among the brethren, from Jesse, from the tribe of Judah, the father of David, is the lineage from which the Messiah was to come. And He did, and here in the Gospel of John, Jesus speaks and the recorder, John, quotes Isaiah.

John 12:36-41 (NKJ)
36 "While you have the light, believe in the light, that you may become sons of light." These things Jesus spoke, and departed, and was hidden from them.
37 But although He had done so many signs before them, they did not believe in Him,
38 that the word of Isaiah the prophet might be fulfilled, which he spoke: "Lord, who has believed our report? And to whom has the arm of the Lord been revealed?"
39 Therefore they could not believe, because Isaiah said again:
40 "He has blinded their eyes and hardened their hearts, lest they should see with their eyes, lest they should understand with their hearts and turn, so that I should heal them."
41 These things Isaiah said when he saw His glory and spoke of Him.

Here, the physician, Luke, who accompanied the apostles during the years in which the Messiah was with them, quotes Paul, the apostle, who was formerly a Jewish Pharisee.

Israel the Chosen or the Enemy?

Acts 28:25-29 (NKJ)
25 So when they did not agree among themselves, they departed after Paul had said one word: "The Holy Spirit spoke rightly through Isaiah the prophet to our fathers,
26 "saying, 'Go to this people and say: "Hearing you will hear, and shall not understand; and seeing you will see, and not perceive;
27 For the hearts of this people have grown dull. Their ears are hard of hearing, and their eyes they have closed, lest they should see with their eyes and hear with their ears, lest they should understand with their hearts and turn, so that I should heal them."'
28 "Therefore let it be known to you that the salvation of God has been sent to the Gentiles, and they will hear it!"
29 And when he had said these words, the Jews departed and had a great dispute among themselves.

I do not know how the Word of God can be more clear. Israel has been "on hold", in terms of their understanding and for one specific reason and perhaps many corollary reasons. That "reason" was to allow the Gentiles access to the God of Israel. The blindness and the hardness of heart refer specifically to the Messiah and the gospel message.

The fact that the Jews have remained "a people" this past 2000 years, even in dispersion, is a miracle that distinguishes them from any other nation. God has not forgotten His people nor has His Arm been shortened that He can not heal and restore His chosen people. The Jewish nation is at the very center of God's plan and every prophecy concerning the Jews will be fulfilled.

These past 2000 years are often referred to as the "Church Age". The New Testament, the Gospel, the chronology of the early church, the letters and the Revelation of John, all were given to the Gentiles by the grace of God, who sent His only begotten Son, as promised, that those who believe on Him might have eternal life.

There are many signs that we are quickly moving toward the Kingdom Age, a time of joyous reunion for Israel and for the souls of the faithful. Listen to the circumstances:

Revelation 20:1-6 (NKJ)
(Satan bound 1000 Years)

1 Then I saw an angel coming down from heaven, having the key to the bottomless pit and a great chain in his hand.

2 He laid hold of the dragon, that serpent of old, who is the Devil and Satan, and bound him for a thousand years;

3 and he cast him into the bottomless pit, and shut him up, and set a seal on him, so that he should deceive the nations no more till the thousand years were finished. But after these things he must be released for a little while.

4 The Saints Reign with Christ 1000 Years And I saw thrones, and they sat on them, and judgment was committed to them. Then I saw the souls of those who had been beheaded for their witness to Jesus and for the word of God, who had not worshiped the beast or his image, and had not received his mark on their foreheads or on their hands. And they lived and reigned with Christ for a thousand years.

5 But the rest of the dead did not live again until the thousand years were finished. This is the first resurrection.

6 Blessed and holy is he who has part in the first resurrection. Over such the second death has no power, but they shall be priests of God and of Christ, and shall reign with Him a thousand years.

CHAPTER 3

KEY SIGNALS REGARDING THE "END TIMES"

What will be the most obvious sign leading us into what is called the "End times?" I believe It will be the fulfillment of a very specific prophecy which states that the Temple in Jerusalem will be rebuilt. The events leading up to the restoration of the Kingdom will start with the rebuilding of the Temple in Jerusalem. From that day forward, prophecy is very precise and very clear. The assertions listed below are based on the fulfillment of these end times prophecies and each assertion is addressed in the chapters of this book. This information is written with total respect toward all God's people and in admiration of Israel. It is intended to strengthen the relationship that all Jews have with our Creator, our Lord. I pray that God's hand is upon these words and that His will is being fulfilled.

Assertions:

1. All of Israel is God's chosen people yet it is often stated that only a remnant will be saved.
2. The Temple in Jerusalem will be rebuilt soon, offerings and sacrifice will occur, again.
3. Israel will seek and find treaties of peace and new agreements with its neighbors prior to the rebuilding of the Temple
4. Peace and safety will be achieved as the Temple is rebuilt. The Antichrist will play the role of counselor, and peacemaker.

5. The initial time period for #'s 2, 3, and 4 to be fully accomplished will be a period of 3½ years.
6. At the end of 3½ years, the Antichrist will declare that sacrifices have ended and the Temple will be destroyed.
7. During this latter 3½-year period, if you are alive, you will be required to accept the mark of the beast in order to buy and sell. No mark on the right hand or forehead will mean, no transactions of any kind.
8. These 3½ years will be marked by persecution, such as never before seen, of all worshipers of God. The scriptures will be destroyed and all visible worship of God shall cease. The Antichrist will demand subservience.
9. God will send "two witnesses." They will have the power to cause the rain to cease and will do remarkable things to oppose the Antichrist. They will be hated by the people and killed by the Antichrist. The world will celebrate their death and they both will rise again, after lying dead in the streets for three days.
10. During this 3½-year period of time, those not accepting the mark of the Beast will face death. Many thousands will be beheaded.
11. Those refusing the mark will flee to the mountains and valleys in order to preserve their lives. God will provide for them as He did in the exodus from Egypt.
12. God's anger with Satan and his servants, the political leaders and the Antichrist, will lead to the Battle of Armageddon.
13. At this time, great earthquakes will occur, lightning and huge hailstones will besiege the earth and islands shall disappear. The earth will become a very different political, physical and spiritual place.
14. After the siege, it will take all those who survive, 7 months to bury the dead and cleanse the land. The ruined weapons of war will provide fuel for a period of 7 years. No trees will be cut for these 7 years.
15. The Messiah and His Saints will come and establish His Kingdom on earth for a period of 1000 years.
16. The millennium Temple will be rebuilt in Jerusalem, not by man, but by God (the 4th and final Temple). Sacrifices, not for sin, but

"of righteousness" will occur. Rivers of living water will flow from the base of the Temple to the east and west, purifying the Dead Sea, where fish will be abundant.

17. At the outset of the millennium, the bones of the Jews will be resurrected and His Saints, including King David, will reign with Him in a restored Jerusalem, here on earth.
18. All of the seed of Abraham will be saved but only the pure blooded Jews will enter the 4th temple. The others, of the seed of Abraham, will serve them.
19. During the millennium, the Feast of Tabernacles will be celebrated annually, in Jerusalem. All nations will come, or in failing to do so, their land will receive no rain.
20. Satan will be bound for 1000 years. There will be no "tempter" or accuser among men for these 1000 years.
21. During this millennium, all will be herbivorous, not carnivorous. All animals will be vegetarians as well.
22. An elevated Highway of Holiness will be built spanning all of Israel, stretching from the Nile to the Euphrates. The Promised Land shall be fully restored.
23. The "oppressed" shall lead "other nations." The last shall be first and the first shall be last.
24. Lives will be long and fruitful, it will be a period marked by peace and by righteousness. Jerusalem will be as the "Garden of Eden."
25. The "New Covenant" will be a reality for all of Abraham's children.
26. At the end of 1000 years, Satan will be loosed to tempt and to claim, as his followers (enemies of Israel), whomever he can.
27. God will wage one final war against Satan and his followers. They, and this world, will be destroyed, forever.
28. The sheep will be separated from the goats, saints from sinners, at the Great White Throne Judgment.
29. New Jerusalem will descend from the heavens and those who love God and have experienced His grace and mercy will join Him.
30. Heaven will be a place of peace and beauty beyond the imagination of man, where God will be worshipped constantly and joy will reign eternally.
31. There will be no day and night there. The Lord will be the light.

32. You will be neither young nor old.
33. The sea will no longer exist.
34. You and the Lord will be called by a new name. We will all speak one language.

No other individual, institution, organization or association is responsible for the contents of this book. I feel unqualified to proclaim to a Jew what God's Word says; yet when the Holy Spirit seems to be leading, it is best to obey. I feel a little like Ezekiel must have felt some 2600 hundred years ago when he heard God say,

EZEKIEL 33:7-8 (NKJ)
7 "So you, son of man: I have made you a watchman for the house of Israel; therefore you shall hear a word from My mouth and warn them for Me.
8 "When I say to the wicked, 'O wicked man, you shall surely die!' and you do not speak to warn the wicked from his way, that wicked man shall die in his iniquity; but his blood I will require at your hand.

It is absurd and very presumptuous to use my name in the same context as Ezekiel. I am not a watchman of Israel and I have no idea why God put this task upon my heart. I am trying to serve Him and I feel that this is what God wants me to do. I also believe that failing to speak when God puts a message on your heart is a mistake. I believe this is God's message, not mine.

Very recently, God has shown me, in a fresh and exciting way, what I believe are truths about the Millennium and the Kingdom Age, which I have never understood before. As I search the commentaries of Bible expositors, I find that some of the points of view I am going to share with you are considered by scholars to be extreme. Therefore, be forewarned that what I sense to be the truth places some, not all, of these points of view, outside the mainstream. If I am wrong, I am wrong and I am accountable to God. I share these words in all love, praying that every soul will be redeemed. I do so with a sincere sense of humility and unworthiness.

I have often thought to myself that I wish God would give me a "sign" as he did others in the Bible. But then, isn't the Word full of "signs." Don't we have access to prophecy "fulfilled" which the prophets only spoke of, but did not see. Yes, we are sitting on a treasury of signs. The Word of God is full of signs. Forgive us God for suggesting that we need more evidence upon which to act.

Evil and good contend for our souls, constantly. Because of the sin of Adam, we are born with a "default setting" of the "flesh." But God put His Spirit within each of us, ready to be awakened at our own volition. The Scripture says that if we resist the devil, he will flee from us and if we draw near to God, He will draw near to us. How does one "flee" from the devil? Satan would have you stop thinking about the issues raised in this book, right now. But know that the "Word of God" is Satan's greatest enemy and as you turn to it, Satan will try to give you the special attention that he reserves for those who seek a personal relationship with God. Expect his attack, sometimes in the subtlest ways, and arm yourself with the only force on earth greater than Satan. That is, arm yourself with the Spirit of God, His Holy Word. Only He can overcome the evil that is in you, in me and in the world.

If you say, "I am without sin, my flesh is not evil," you are making a grave error and if you feel you can, in your own strength, resist evil, you are compounding the error. The Scriptures clearly teach that all have sinned and come short of the glory of God, you and I included. Your spirit can not contend with Satan's power. The Holy Spirit in you is your only hope in resisting evil. The Holy Scriptures, the inspired Word of God, preserved for us these centuries, is the starting point. The words of men may be useful and interesting but they are trite in comparison to God's Word.

If you heard God's voice saying "come, I want to speak to you." Would you hesitate to come and listen? No, you would be awe struck. The Scriptures present a constant opportunity to listen to God. Do you listen? You are, if you are not listening to God, denying yourself access to the only enduring Truth that exists. That may seem like an extreme statement, but I say to you in all certainty, God is the only truth that exists. Not listening to Him is worse than foolish. Absent a personal relationship with the Lord, you serve, perhaps unwittingly, Satan. There is no middle ground. The Scriptures say, "Choose, this day, whom you will follow." As to the level of certainty regarding the statements in this presentation, the Scripture says that we know in part and prophesy, in part and that we now see in a mirror, dimly, but some day, face to face.

The points made in this book rest on the view that Israel will be redeemed. God has not forsaken His chosen people. Knowing what is going to happen is not enough. I encourage you, after looking at all of the evidence, to consider taking action. What action? Listen to the words of Ezekiel, one of Israel's prophets.

EZEKIEL 18:30-32 (NKJ)
30 "Therefore I will judge you, O house of Israel, every one according to his ways," says the Lord GOD. "Repent, and turn from all your transgressions, so that iniquity will not be your ruin."
31 "Cast away from you all the transgressions which you have committed, and get yourselves a new heart and a new spirit. For why should you die, O house of Israel?"
32 "For I have no pleasure in the death of one who dies" says the Lord God. "Therefore turn and live!"

God's patience with His chosen people is well documented, but it is time to "turn and live" says the Lord, God. The prophesied events, in whatever order, will occur. This book is not intended to "inform you" but to call you to action. Pray that God will reveal to you His will for your life and that He will direct you, as only He can.

CHAPTER 4

YOU ARE HIS CHOSEN AND HOLY PEOPLE

As we approach the end times, we approach that moment in history wherein God has promised his chosen people, the Jews, that the Messiah will come and restore the Kingdom. Focus first on God's word. He repeatedly teaches how important the Jew is in His eyes and how He has chosen to intervene in the affairs of the nation of Israel.

Deuteronomy 7:6-9 (NKJ)
6 "For you are a holy people to the LORD your God; the LORD your God has chosen you to be a people for Himself, a special treasure above all the peoples on the face of the earth.
7 "The LORD did not set His love on you nor choose you because you were more in number than any other people, for you were the least of all peoples;
8 "but because the LORD loves you, and because He would keep the oath which He swore to your fathers, the LORD has brought you out with a mighty hand, and redeemed you from the house of bondage, from the hand of Pharaoh king of Egypt.
9 "Therefore know that the LORD your God, He is God, the faithful God who keeps covenant and mercy for a thousand generations with those who love Him and keep His commandments;

Exodus 19:5-6 (NKJ)
5 'Now therefore, if you will indeed obey My voice and keep My covenant, then you shall be a special treasure to Me above all people; for all the earth is Mine.
6 'And you shall be to Me a kingdom of priests and a holy nation.' These are the words which you shall speak to the children of Israel."

Deuteronomy 14:2 (NKJ)
2 For you are a holy people to the LORD your God, and the LORD has chosen you to be a people for Himself, a special treasure above all the peoples who are on the face of the earth.

Deuteronomy 28:9 (NKJ)
9 The LORD will establish you as a holy people to Himself, just as He has sworn to you, if you keep the commandments of the LORD your God and walk in His ways.

Psalm 33:12 (NKJ)
12 Blessed is the nation whose God is the LORD, the people He has chosen as His own inheritance.

Psalm 105:6-10 (NKJ)
6 O seed of Abraham His servant, you children of Jacob, His chosen ones!
7 He is the LORD our God; his judgments are in all the earth.
8 He remembers His covenant forever, the word which He commanded, for a thousand generations,
9 The covenant which He made with Abraham, and His oath to Isaac,
10 And confirmed it to Jacob for a statute, to Israel as an everlasting covenant,

Psalm 105:43-45 (NKJ)
43 He brought out His people with joy, His chosen ones with gladness.
44 He gave them the lands of the Gentiles, and they inherited the labor of the nations,
45 That they might observe His statutes and keep His laws. Praise the LORD!

Psalm 132:13-16 (NKJ)
13 For the LORD has chosen Zion; He has desired it for His dwelling place:
14 "This is My resting place forever; here I will dwell, for I have desired it.
15 I will abundantly bless her provision; I will satisfy her poor with bread.
16 I will also clothe her priests with salvation, and her saints shall shout aloud for joy.

Isaiah 41:8-10 (NKJ)
8 "But you, Israel, are My servant, Jacob whom I have chosen, the descendants of Abraham My friend.
9 You whom I have taken from the ends of the earth, and called from its farthest regions, and said to you, 'You are My servant, I have chosen you and have not cast you away:
10 Fear not, for I am with you; be not dismayed, for I am your God. I will strengthen you, yes, I will help you, I will uphold you with My righteous right hand.'

Isaiah 43:1-5 (NKJ)
1 But now, thus says the LORD, who created you, O Jacob, and He who formed you, O Israel: "Fear not, for I have redeemed you; I have called you by your name; you are Mine.
2 When you pass through the waters, I will be with you; and through the rivers, they shall not overflow you. When you walk through the fire, you shall not be burned, nor shall the flame scorch you.
3 For I am the LORD your God, the Holy One of Israel, your Savior; I gave Egypt for your ransom, Ethiopia and Seba in your place.
4 Since you were precious in My sight, you have been honored, and I have loved you; therefore I will give men for you, and people for your life.
5 Fear not, for I am with you; I will bring your descendants from the east, and gather you from the west;

Jeremiah 2:3 (NKJ)
3 Israel was holiness to the LORD, the firstfruits of His increase. All that devour him will offend; disaster will come upon them," says the LORD.'"

Malachi 3:17 (NKJ)
17 "They shall be Mine," says the LORD of hosts, "On the day that I make them My jewels. And I will spare them as a man spares his own son who serves him."

There are many more references in the Scriptures that make the same point over and over again. God has chosen Israel as His special people, the firstfruits of His increase. Again, every non-Jew is a Gentile. I am a Gentile. One of the leaders of the Jews who persecuted Jesus Christ and all of His followers was Saul of Tarsus, a student of Gamaliel, the great Jewish teacher of the time. Saul's heart was changed as God taught Him the truth regarding His Son. Saul became known as Paul. The Holy Spirit witnessed to his spirit and he, a Jew of renown, became God's messenger to the Gentiles, after his Jewish counterparts rejected him. As a Jew, he knew that the Jews were God's chosen people but he also knew, because the Holy Spirit revealed it to him, that the Gentiles too, were called to love, honor and obey God.

Listen carefully to Paul's instruction to the Gentiles concerning their relationship to the Jews. Remember, you, a Jew, are the root and Paul was a Jew. We Gentiles are the branches, grafted in, by the Grace of God.

Romans 11:16-25 (NKJ)
16 For if the firstfruit is holy, the lump is also holy; and if the root is holy, so are the branches.
17 And if some of the branches were broken off, and you, being a wild olive tree, were grafted in among them, and with them became a partaker of the root and fatness of the olive tree,
18 do not boast against the branches. But if you do boast, remember that you do not support the root, but the root supports you.
19 You will say then, "Branches were broken off that I might be grafted in."
20 Well said. Because of unbelief they were broken off, and you stand by faith. Do not be haughty, but fear.
21 For if God did not spare the natural branches, He may not spare you either.

22 Therefore consider the goodness and severity of God: on those who fell, severity; but toward you, goodness, if you continue in His goodness. Otherwise you also will be cut off.

23 And they also, if they do not continue in unbelief, will be grafted in, for God is able to graft them in again.

24 For if you were cut out of the olive tree which is wild by nature, and were grafted contrary to nature into a cultivated olive tree, how much more will these, who are natural branches, be grafted into their own olive tree?

25 For I do not desire, brethren, that you should be ignorant of this mystery, lest you should be wise in your own opinion, that blindness in part has happened to Israel until the fullness of the Gentiles has come in.

Read chapters 1-12 in the book of Romans. Your personal position with the Lord is "in process." Until the moment that we die, we make choices. God's forgiveness for our bad choices exceeds our understanding. We deserve retribution yet we are offered mercy instead. Israel, God truly has chosen you. Have you sought Him with all of your heart, mind, strength and soul? The Word is a treasure, full of instruction, love and wisdom and a gift directly from God.

CHAPTER 5

THE MESSIAH IN THE OLD TESTAMENT

I realize that when writing to Israel, we must deal with the question, "Who was Jesus Christ?" while standing in the Light of the New Testament and while maintaining the integrity of the Old Testament. The answer to the question is the fulcrum upon which the history of the world turns. If so, and as the world looks to each new Millennium and beyond, those who honor the Jewish calendar would seem to be well served by doing some research on this Messianic topic. Seeking answers, and God's direction as you do so, is a reasonable endeavor. Surely those of Abraham's seed and who love God are not the enemy, myself included. Perhaps misled or unenlightened, but not the enemy.

The chapter we are dealing with here is best studied, in my opinion, by first considering the words of the One to which the Old Testament points. If that seems too difficult a starting point, please just try to bear with me as we transition to the Old Testament. This quotation is one of many that place the Old Testament and its prophecies in perspective.

Numbers 24:16-19 (NKJ)
16 The utterance of him who hears the words of God, and has the knowledge of the Most High, who sees the vision of the Almighty, who falls down, with eyes wide open:
17 "I see Him, but not now; I behold Him, but not near; a Star shall come out of Jacob; a Scepter shall rise out of Israel, and batter the brow of Moab, and destroy all the sons of tumult.

18 "And Edom shall be a possession; Seir also, his enemies, shall be a possession, while Israel does valiantly.
19 Out of Jacob One shall have dominion, and destroy the remains of the city."

John 5:2-43 (NKJ)
2 Now there is in Jerusalem by the Sheep Gate a pool, which is called in Hebrew, Bethesda, having five porches.
3 In these lay a great multitude of sick people, blind, lame, paralyzed, waiting for the moving of the water.
4 For an angel went down at a certain time into the pool and stirred up the water; then whoever stepped in first, after the stirring of the water, was made well of whatever disease he had.
5 Now a certain man was there who had an infirmity thirty-eight years.
6 When Jesus saw him lying there, and knew that he already had been in that condition a long time, He said to him, "Do you want to be made well?"
7 The sick man answered Him, "Sir, I have no man to put me into the pool when the water is stirred up; but while I am coming, another steps down before me."
8 Jesus said to him, "Rise, take up your bed and walk."
9 And immediately the man was made well, took up his bed, and walked. And that day was the Sabbath.
10 The Jews therefore said to him who was cured, "It is the Sabbath; it is not lawful for you to carry your bed."
11 He answered them, "He who made me well said to me, 'Take up your bed and walk.'"
12 Then they asked him, "Who is the Man who said to you, 'Take up your bed and walk'?"
13 But the one who was healed did not know who it was, for Jesus had withdrawn, a multitude being in that place.
14 Afterward Jesus found him in the temple, and said to him, "See, you have been made well. Sin no more, lest a worse thing come upon you."
15 The man departed and told the Jews that it was Jesus who had made him well.
16 For this reason the Jews persecuted Jesus, and sought to kill Him, because He had done these things on the Sabbath.

17 But Jesus answered them, "My Father has been working until now, and I have been working."

18 Therefore the Jews sought all the more to kill Him, because He not only broke the Sabbath, but also said that God was His Father, making Himself equal with God.

19 Then Jesus answered and said to them, "Most assuredly, I say to you, the Son can do nothing of Himself, but what He sees the Father do; for whatever He does, the Son also does in like manner.

20 "For the Father loves the Son, and shows Him all things that He Himself does; and He will show Him greater works than these, that you may marvel.

21 "For as the Father raises the dead and gives life to them, even so the Son gives life to whom He will.

22 "For the Father judges no one, but has committed all judgment to the Son,

23 "that all should honor the Son just as they honor the Father. He who does not honor the Son does not honor the Father who sent Him.

24 "Most assuredly, I say to you, he who hears My word and believes in Him who sent Me has everlasting life, and shall not come into judgment, but has passed from death into life.

25 "Most assuredly, I say to you, the hour is coming, and now is, when the dead will hear the voice of the Son of God; and those who hear will live.

26 "For as the Father has life in Himself, so He has granted the Son to have life in Himself,

27 "and has given Him authority to execute judgment also, because He is the Son of Man.

28 "Do not marvel at this; for the hour is coming in which all who are in the graves will hear His voice

29 "and come forth– those who have done good, to the resurrection of life, and those who have done evil, to the resurrection of condemnation.

30 "I can of Myself do nothing. As I hear, I judge; and My judgment is righteous, because I do not seek My own will but the will of the Father who sent Me.

31 "If I bear witness of Myself, My witness is not true.

32 "There is another who bears witness of Me, and I know that the witness which He witnesses of Me is true.
33 "You have sent to John, and he has borne witness to the truth.
34 "Yet I do not receive testimony from man, but I say these things that you may be saved.
35 "He was the burning and shining lamp, and you were willing for a time to rejoice in his light.
36 "But I have a greater witness than John's; for the works which the Father has given Me to finish– the very works that I do– bear witness of Me, that the Father has sent Me.
37 "And the Father Himself, who sent Me, has testified of Me. You have neither heard His voice at any time, nor seen His form.
38 "But you do not have His word abiding in you, because whom He sent, Him you do not believe.
39 "You search the Scriptures, for in them you think you have eternal life; and these are they which testify of Me.
40 "But you are not willing to come to Me that you may have life.
41 "I do not receive honor from men.
42 "But I know you, that you do not have the love of God in you.

Here we will focus on the last 4 verses. In these 4 verses, what writings was Jesus referring to? The Old Testament is full of quotations that point to Jesus and the promised Messiah, the Christ. Let's look at only a few.

Moses in Numbers, Chapters 22-24 recorded one of the strangest stories in the Bible, where a donkey spoke to his master, Baalam and Baalam subsequently prophesied as follows:

Numbers 24:16-19 (NKJ)
16 The utterance of him who hears the words of God, and has the knowledge of the Most High, who sees the vision of the Almighty, who falls down, with eyes wide open:
17 "I see Him, but not now; I behold Him, but not near; a Star shall come out of Jacob; a Scepter shall rise out of Israel, and batter the brow of Moab, and destroy all the sons of tumult.
18 "And Edom shall be a possession; Seir also, his enemies, shall be a possession, while Israel does valiantly.

19 Out of Jacob One shall have dominion, and destroy the remains of the city."

I believe that the Bible properly capitalizes references to the Deity. Note verse 17. The Star out of Jacob refers to the Messiah, the one coming out of Jacob and the tribe of Judah as prophesied in other Old Testament references we will consider. The Scepter shall rise out of Israel refers to the Messiah as Judge. To put this assertion in perspective, listen to what Jacob said as he called his sons together.

Genesis 49:8-10 (NKJ)
8 "Judah, you are he whom your brothers shall praise; your hand shall be on the neck of your enemies; your father's children shall bow down before you.
9 Judah is a lion's whelp; from the prey, my son, you have gone up. He bows down, he lies down as a lion; and as a lion, who shall rouse him?
10 The scepter shall not depart from Judah, nor a lawgiver from between his feet, until Shiloh comes; and to Him shall be the obedience of the people.

Shiloh, though a city, also means "sent" and thus would be capitalized either way, but here I believe it means the One who is sent, who will come and to Him shall be the "obedience of the people." The "scepter" is not capitalized here because it is an implement in the hand of "Shiloh," the Judge.

Now, let's look at some of the most clearly stated promises in the Old Testament regarding who the Messiah is to be and what evidence will be present that we should know it is Him.

Isaiah 7:10-14 (NKJ)
10 Moreover the LORD spoke again to Ahaz, saying,
11 "Ask a sign for yourself from the LORD your God; ask it either in the depth or in the height above."
12 But Ahaz said, "I will not ask, nor will I test the LORD!"
13 Then he said, "Hear now, O house of David! Is it a small thing for you to weary men, but will you weary my God also?

14 "Therefore the Lord Himself will give you a sign: Behold, the virgin shall conceive and bear a Son, and shall call His name Immanuel.

Biblical references call this "The Immanuel Prophecy." Immanuel means God with us. Read verse 14 very carefully and know this prophecy was fulfilled. No Jew needs to wonder about the dispersion and gathering of Israel. It is a historical fact, well documented and experienced by generations. Listen.

Isaiah 8:8-10 (NKJ)
8 He will pass through Judah, he will overflow and pass over, he will reach up to the neck; and the stretching out of his wings will fill the breadth of Your land, O Immanuel.
9 "Be shattered, O you peoples, and be broken in pieces! Give ear, all you from far countries. Gird yourselves, but be broken in pieces; gird yourselves, but be broken in pieces.
10 Take counsel together, but it will come to nothing; speak the word, but it will not stand, for God is with us.

Then we read that a Child is born, the Prince of Peace.

Isaiah 9:6-7 (NKJ)
6 For unto us a Child is born, unto us a Son is given; and the government will be upon His shoulder. And His name will be called wonderful, **Counselor, Mighty God, everlasting Father, Prince of Peace.** (My emphasis)
7 Of the increase of His government and peace there will be no end, upon the throne of David and over His kingdom, to order it and establish it with judgment and justice from that time forward, even forever. The zeal of the LORD of hosts will perform this.

Then we see that the Child becomes a Rod, from the stem of Jesse.

Isaiah 11:1-5 (NKJ)
1 There shall come forth a **Rod from the stem of Jesse**, and a Branch shall grow out of his roots. (My emphasis)

2 The Spirit of the LORD shall rest upon Him, the Spirit of wisdom and understanding, the Spirit of counsel and might, the Spirit of knowledge and of the fear of the LORD.
3 His delight is in the fear of the LORD, and He shall not judge by the sight of His eyes, nor decide by the hearing of His ears;
4 But with righteousness He shall judge the poor, and decide with equity for the meek of the earth; he shall strike the earth with the rod of His mouth, and with the breath of His lips He shall slay the wicked.
5 Righteousness shall be the belt of His loins, and faithfulness the belt of His waist.

Perhaps a Jewish reader is thinking, "Yes, this is all about the Messiah, but it is about a Messiah yet to come." That is true. It is about the Messiah yet to come but it is also completely in sync with the birth, life and mission of Jesus Christ, right down to the smallest detail. The Messiah came, born of a virgin. This Messiah, in order to be the Messiah yet to come, would again have to come as a child, born of a virgin, in the town of Bethlehem, from the tribe of Judah, be crucified as the Lamb of God, and atone for the sins of all men, as well as fulfill numerous other prophetic details. Does Israel really look for another One, who will fulfill prophecy as Jesus Christ did, to yet come? It has already happened! Prophecy has been fulfilled. Read on.

Isaiah 28:16-23 (NKJ)
16 Therefore thus says the Lord GOD: "Behold, I lay in Zion a stone for a foundation, a tried stone, a precious cornerstone, a sure foundation; whoever believes will not act hastily.
17 Also I will make justice the measuring line, and righteousness the plummet; the hail will sweep away the refuge of lies, and the waters will overflow the hiding place.
18 Your covenant with death will be annulled, and your agreement with Sheol will not stand; when the overflowing scourge passes through, then you will be trampled down by it.
19 As often as it goes out it will take you; for morning by morning it will pass over, and by day and by night; it will be a terror just to understand the report."
20 For the bed is too short to stretch out on, and the covering so narrow that one cannot wrap himself in it.

21 For the LORD will rise up as at Mount Perazim, he will be angry as in the Valley of Gibeon– that He may do His work, His awesome work, and bring to pass His act, His unusual act.
22 Now therefore, do not be mockers, lest your bonds be made strong; for I have heard from the Lord GOD of hosts, a destruction determined even upon the whole earth.
23 Give ear and hear my voice, listen and hear my speech.

Isaiah 33:10 (NKJ)
10 "Now I will rise," says the LORD; "Now I will be exalted, now I will lift Myself up.

Isaiah 42:1-9 (NKJ)
1 "Behold! My Servant whom I uphold, my Elect One in whom My soul delights! I have put My Spirit upon Him; He will bring forth justice to the Gentiles.
2 He will not cry out, nor raise His voice, nor cause His voice to be heard in the street.
3 A bruised reed He will not break, and smoking flax He will not quench; He will bring forth justice for truth.
4 He will not fail nor be discouraged, till He has established justice in the earth; and the coastlands shall wait for His law."
5 Thus says God the LORD, who created the heavens and stretched them out, who spread forth the earth and that which comes from it, who gives breath to the people on it, and spirit to those who walk on it:
6 "I, the LORD, have called You in righteousness, and will hold Your hand; I will keep You and give You as a covenant to the people, as a light to the Gentiles,
7 To open blind eyes, to bring out prisoners from the prison, those who sit in darkness from the prison house.
8 I am the LORD, that is My name; and My glory I will not give to another, nor My praise to graven images.
9 Behold, the former things have come to pass, and new things I declare; before they spring forth I tell you of them."

Isaiah 48:16 (NKJ)
16 "Come near to Me, hear this: I have not spoken in secret from the beginning; from the time that it was, I was there. And now the Lord GOD and His Spirit have sent Me."

Isaiah 49:1-7 (NKJ)
1 "Listen, O coastlands, to Me, and take heed, you peoples from afar! The LORD has called Me from the womb; from the matrix of My mother He has made mention of My name.
2 And He has made My mouth like a sharp sword; in the shadow of His hand He has hidden Me, and made Me a polished shaft; in His quiver He has hidden Me."
3 "And He said to me, 'You are My servant, O Israel, in whom I will be glorified.'
4 Then I said, 'I have labored in vain, I have spent my strength for nothing and in vain; yet surely my just reward is with the LORD, and my work with my God.'"
5 "And now the LORD says, who formed Me from the womb to be His Servant, to bring Jacob back to Him, so that Israel is gathered to Him (for I shall be glorious in the eyes of the LORD, and My God shall be My strength),
6 Indeed He says, 'It is too small a thing that You should be My Servant to raise up the tribes of Jacob, and to restore the preserved ones of Israel; I will also give You as a light to the Gentiles, that You should be My salvation to the ends of the earth.'"
7 Thus says the LORD, the Redeemer of Israel, their Holy One, to Him whom man despises, to Him whom the nation abhors, to the Servant of rulers: "Kings shall see and arise, princes also shall worship, because of the LORD who is faithful, the Holy One of Israel; and He has chosen You."

Isaiah 50:6-9 (NKJ)
6 I gave My back to those who struck Me, and My cheeks to those who plucked out the beard; I did not hide My face from shame and spitting.
7 "For the Lord GOD will help Me; therefore I will not be disgraced; therefore I have set My face like a flint, and I know that I will not be ashamed.

8 He is near who justifies Me; Who will contend with Me? Let us stand together. Who is My adversary? Let him come near Me.
9 Surely the Lord GOD will help Me; Who is he who will condemn Me? Indeed they will all grow old like a garment; the moth will eat them up.

Isaiah 52:13-15 (NKJ)
13 Behold, My Servant shall deal prudently; He shall be exalted and extolled and be very high.
14 Just as many were astonished at you, so His visage was marred more than any man, and His form more than the sons of men;
15 So shall He sprinkle many nations. Kings shall shut their mouths at Him; for what had not been told them they shall see, and what they had not heard they shall consider.

Isaiah 53:1-12 (NKJ)
1 Who has believed our report? And to whom has the arm of the LORD been revealed?
2 For He shall grow up before Him as a tender plant, and as a root out of dry ground. He has no form or comeliness; and when we see Him, there is no beauty that we should desire Him.
3 He is despised and rejected by men, a Man of sorrows and acquainted with grief. And we hid, as it were, our faces from Him; he was despised, and we did not esteem Him .
4 Surely He has borne our griefs and carried our sorrows; yet we esteemed Him stricken, smitten by God, and afflicted.
5 But He was wounded for our transgressions, he was bruised for our iniquities; the chastisement for our peace was upon Him, and by His stripes we are healed
6 All we like sheep have gone astray; we have turned, every one, to his own way; and the LORD has laid on Him the iniquity of us all.
7 He was oppressed and He was afflicted, yet He opened not His mouth; he was led as a lamb to the slaughter, and as a sheep before its shearers is silent, so He opened not His mouth.
8 He was taken from prison and from judgment, and who will declare His generation? For He was cut off from the land of the living; for the transgressions of My people He was stricken.

9 And they made His grave with the wicked– but with the rich at His death, because He had done no violence, nor was any deceit in His mouth.
10 Yet it pleased the LORD to bruise Him; he has put Him to grief. When You make His soul an offering for sin, he shall see His seed, He shall prolong His days, and the pleasure of the LORD shall prosper in His hand.
11 He shall see the labor of His soul, and be satisfied. By His knowledge My righteous Servant shall justify many, for He shall bear their iniquities.
12 Therefore I will divide Him a portion with the great, and He shall divide the spoil with the strong, because He poured out His soul unto death, and He was numbered with the transgressors, and He bore the sin of many, and made intercession for the transgressors.

The prophecy of Isaiah 53:1-12 could not be more clear. What possible fulfillment of this prophecy exists than that which is before you?

Isaiah 59:14-20 (NKJ)
14 Justice is turned back, and righteousness stands afar off; for truth is fallen in the street, and equity cannot enter.
15 So truth fails, and he who departs from evil makes himself a prey. Then the LORD saw it, and it displeased Him that there was no justice.
16 He saw that there was no man, and wondered that there was no intercessor; therefore His own arm brought salvation for Him; and His own righteousness, it sustained Him.
17 For He put on righteousness as a breastplate, and a helmet of salvation on His head; he put on the garments of vengeance for clothing, and was clad with zeal as a cloak.
18 According to their deeds, accordingly He will repay, fury to His adversaries, recompense to His enemies; the coastlands He will fully repay.
19 So shall they fear the name of the LORD from the west, and His glory from the rising of the sun; when the enemy comes in like a flood, the Spirit of the LORD will lift up a standard against him.
20 "The Redeemer will come to Zion, and to those who turn from transgression in Jacob," says the LORD.

Isaiah 61:1-3 (NKJ)
1 "The Spirit of the Lord GOD is upon Me, because the LORD has anointed Me to preach good tidings to the poor; he has sent Me to heal the brokenhearted, to proclaim liberty to the captives, and the opening of the prison to those who are bound;
2 To proclaim the acceptable year of the LORD, and the day of vengeance of our God; to comfort all who mourn,
3 To console those who mourn in Zion, to give them beauty for ashes, the oil of joy for mourning, the garment of praise for the spirit of heaviness; that they may be called trees of righteousness, the planting of the LORD, that He may be glorified."

This One, upon whom the Spirit of the Lord God rests, will yet console those who mourn in Zion and those in Zion will be called trees of righteousness, the planting of the Lord.

Job 19:25-27 (NKJ)
25 For I know that my Redeemer lives, and He shall stand at last on the earth;
26 And after my skin is destroyed, this I know, that in my flesh I shall see God,
27 Whom I shall see for myself, and my eyes shall behold, and not another. How my heart yearns within me!

Job, whose writings are considered the oldest in the Old Testament, said that he knew that his Redeemer lives and that upon death he would see God. You and I both know that his Redeemer was the Messiah. The only question is "Has he come or shall we look for another?"

Job 33:14-25 (NKJ)
14 For God may speak in one way, or in another, yet man does not perceive it.
15 In a dream, in a vision of the night, when deep sleep falls upon men, while slumbering on their beds,
16 Then He opens the ears of men, and seals their instruction.
17 In order to turn man from his deed, and conceal pride from man,

18 He keeps back his soul from the Pit, and his life from perishing by the sword.
19 "Man is also chastened with pain on his bed, and with strong pain in many of his bones,
20 So that his life abhors bread, and his soul succulent food.
21 His flesh wastes away from sight, and his bones stick out which once were not seen.
22 Yes, his soul draws near the Pit, and his life to the executioners.
23 "If there is a messenger for him, a mediator, one among a thousand, to show man His uprightness,
24 Then He is gracious to him, and says, 'Deliver him from going down to the Pit; I have found a ransom';
25 His flesh shall be young like a child's, he shall return to the days of his youth.

Please read verses 22-24 again carefully. Life is finite. Job misestimated the situation here, in terms of how much time he had left. Here we have in these last few verses the answer to his question about a messenger, mediator, one who would deliver him from the pit. He says, "I have found a ransom." When you consider the Prince of Peace as Messiah, know that He broke the power of death, He provided the ransom for each of our souls.

The Old Testament is full of references to the Messiah. Again, this book is intended to point you towards God's Word. There is no authority outside of God's Word upon which you should rely. Listen again, and consider memorizing, one of the most powerful verses in the Bible concerning the Word of God.

Hebrews 4:12 (NKJ)
12 For the word of God is living and powerful, and sharper than any two-edged sword, piercing even to the division of soul and spirit, and of joints and marrow, and is a discerner of the thoughts and intents of the heart.

Before I leave the issue of the circumstances and mission of the Messiah, as prophesied in the Old Testament, let's look at some of the Messianic Psalms.

Psalm 2:6-7 (NKJ)
6 "Yet I have set My King on My holy hill of Zion."
7 "I will declare the decree: the LORD has said to Me, 'You are My Son, today I have begotten You.

Psalm 16:8-10 (NKJ)
8 I have set the LORD always before me; because He is at my right hand I shall not be moved.
9 Therefore my heart is glad, and my glory rejoices; my flesh also will rest in hope.
10 For You will not leave my soul in Sheol, nor will You allow Your Holy One to see corruption.

Psalm 22:1-18 (NKJ)
1 My God, My God, why have You forsaken Me? Why are You so far from helping Me, and from the words of My groaning?
2 O My God, I cry in the daytime, but You do not hear; and in the night season, and am not silent.
3 But You are holy, enthroned in the praises of Israel.
4 Our fathers trusted in You; they trusted, and You delivered them.
5 They cried to You, and were delivered; they trusted in You, and were not ashamed.
6 But I am a worm, and no man; a reproach of men, and despised of the people.
7 All those who see Me ridicule Me; they shoot out the lip, they shake the head, saying,
8 "He trusted in the LORD, let Him rescue Him; let Him deliver Him, since He delights in Him!"
9 But You are He who took Me out of the womb; you made Me trust while on My mother's breasts.
10 I was cast upon You from birth. From My mother's womb you have been My God.
11 Be not far from Me, for trouble is near; for there is none to help.
12 Many bulls have surrounded Me; strong bulls of Bashan have encircled Me.
13 They gape at Me with their mouths, like a raging and roaring lion.

14 I am poured out like water, and all My bones are out of joint; my heart is like wax; it has melted within Me.
15 My strength is dried up like a potsherd, and My tongue clings to My jaws; you have brought Me to the dust of death.
16 For dogs have surrounded Me; the congregation of the wicked has enclosed Me. They pierced My hands and My feet;
17 I can count all My bones. They look and stare at Me.
18 They divide My garments among them, and for My clothing they cast lots.

Psalm 96:13 (NKJ)
13 For He is coming, for He is coming to judge the earth. He shall judge the world with righteousness, and the peoples with His truth.

Psalm 118:22 (NKJ)
22 The stone which the builders rejected has become the chief cornerstone.

If you would like to compare Messianic prophecy with New Testament fulfillment, go to Scripture Topics on the Gospel Global Vision Website (https://gospelglobalvision.com) and review the three topics which do so, Messiah Part 1, Part 2, and Part 3. The Sola Scriptura Project is an assembly of 85 "topics" such as The Story of Abraham, The End Times, Faith, Marriage, Godly Habits, God's Children and so on. Each topic consists of direct quotations from the Old and New Testament, without commentary. Please read this quotation.

Matthew 15:22-28 (NKJ)
22 And behold, a woman of Canaan came from that region and cried out to Him, saying, "Have mercy on me, O Lord, Son of David! My daughter is severely demon-possessed."
23 But He answered her not a word. And His disciples came and urged Him, saying, "Send her away, for she cries out after us."
24 But He answered and said, "I was not sent except to the lost sheep of the house of Israel."
25 Then she came and worshiped Him, saying, "Lord, help me!"

26 But He answered and said, "It is not good to take the children's bread and throw it to the little dogs."
27 And she said, "Yes, Lord, yet even the little dogs eat the crumbs which fall from their masters' table."
28 Then Jesus answered and said to her, "O woman, great is your faith! Let it be to you as you desire." And her daughter was healed from that very hour.

These verses make a point that I wish to amplify and it is not a point most Gentiles will love to hear. Jesus said, "I was not sent except to the lost sheep of the house of Israel."

Now, one could argue that this was a sentence lifted out of the context of a situation wherein the disciples were annoyed with the persistence of a Gentile woman. They were annoyed, true, but Jesus taught them a lesson that reinforces something not often taught by Gentiles. The ministry of Jesus was focused on the Jews.

We Gentiles, as a result of the grace of God and our faith in Jesus Christ have chosen (actually responded to God's invitation to accept His Grace) to be attached to the God of the Jews, not the gods of the Gentiles, to the Lion of the tribe of Judah, Jesus Christ. We Gentiles are not the root, but the branch, and a grafted branch, at that! The history of man pivots upon the Jewish nation, as does the immediate future of man. Again, the entire history of man pivots on the relationship of God to His chosen people.

This earth and all of the flesh upon it shall perish. God will first return it to a "Garden of Eden" situation for 1000 years, and the Messiah will reign and the nation of Israel shall enter into His rest. What a perfect ending for Judaism and a perfect beginning, thereafter, for eternity. This glory, this grace, is not of yourselves but of God, who sent His Lamb to redeem you and cleanse you, forever. Me too, thank God. Thank you Israel for preserving the Word and for being the Oracle of God.

CHAPTER 6

GOD'S LOVE AND MERCY TOWARDS THE JEWS

Before we look at the rest of the signs pertaining to the rebuilding of the 3rd Temple, most of which are very specific, let's deal with the question of God's promises to Israel. God's promises are certain. On the one hand we will see references to all Israel being saved and yet there are other references that say a remnant will be saved. If you are among the "remnant" that has remained faithful, in the eyes of God, you are assured of eternal salvation. Listen to God's Word regarding the remnant.

Isaiah 10:21-22 (NKJ)
21 The remnant will return, the remnant of Jacob, to the Mighty God. 22 For though your people, O Israel, be as the sand of the sea, a remnant of them will return; the destruction decreed shall overflow with righteousness.

Ezra 9:8 (NKJ)
8 "And now for a little while grace has been shown from the LORD our God, to leave us a remnant to escape, and to give us a peg in His holy place, that our God may enlighten our eyes and give us a measure of revival in our bondage. (NKJ)

Ezra 9:15 (NKJ)
15 "O LORD God of Israel, You are righteous, for we are left as a remnant, as it is this day. Here we are before You, in our guilt, though no one can stand before You because of this!"

Isaiah 11:10-11 (NKJ)
10 "And in that day there shall be a Root of Jesse, who shall stand as a banner to the people; for the Gentiles shall seek Him, and His resting place shall be glorious."
11 It shall come to pass in that day that the LORD shall set His hand again the second time to recover the remnant of His people who are left, from Assyria and Egypt, from Pathros and Cush, from Elam and Shinar, from Hamath and the islands of the sea.

Isaiah 11:16 (NKJ)
16 There will be a highway for the remnant of His people who will be left from Assyria, as it was for Israel in the day that he came up from the land of Egypt.

Isaiah 28:5 (NKJ)
5 In that day the LORD of hosts will be for a crown of glory and a diadem of beauty to the remnant of His people,

Isaiah 46:3-4 (NKJ)
3 "Listen to Me, O house of Jacob, and all the remnant of the house of Israel, who have been upheld by Me from birth, who have been carried from the womb:
4 Even to your old age, I am He, and even to gray hairs I will carry you! I have made, and I will bear; even I will carry, and will deliver you.

Jeremiah 23:1-8 (NKJ)
1 "Woe to the shepherds who destroy and scatter the sheep of My pasture!" says the LORD.
2 Therefore thus says the LORD God of Israel against the shepherds who feed My people: "You have scattered My flock, driven them away, and not attended to them. Behold, I will attend to you for the evil of your doings," says the LORD.
3 "But I will gather the remnant of My flock out of all countries where I have driven them, and bring them back to their folds; and they shall be fruitful and increase.

4 "I will set up shepherds over them who will feed them; and they shall fear no more, nor be dismayed, nor shall they be lacking," says the LORD.

5 "Behold, the days are coming," says the LORD, "That I will raise to David a Branch of righteousness; a King shall reign and prosper, and execute judgment and righteousness in the earth.

6 In His days Judah will be saved, and Israel will dwell safely; now this is His name by which He will be called: THE LORD OUR RIGHTEOUSNESS.

7 "Therefore, behold, the days are coming," says the LORD, "that they shall no longer say, 'As the LORD lives who brought up the children of Israel from the land of Egypt,'

8 "but, 'As the LORD lives who brought up and led the descendants of the house of Israel from the north country and from all the countries where I had driven them.' And they shall dwell in their own land."

Jeremiah 31:7 (NKJ)
7 For thus says the LORD: "Sing with gladness for Jacob, and shout among the chief of the nations; proclaim, give praise, and say, 'O LORD, save Your people, the remnant of Israel!'

Ezekiel 6:7-8 (NKJ)
7 "The slain shall fall in your midst, and you shall know that I am the LORD.
8 "Yet I will leave a remnant, so that you may have some who escape the sword among the nations, when you are scattered through the countries.

Ezekiel 11:13-21 (NKJ)
13 Now it happened, while I was prophesying, that Pelatiah the son of Benaiah died. Then I fell on my face and cried with a loud voice, and said, "Ah, Lord GOD! Will You make a complete end of the remnant of Israel?"
14 Again the word of the LORD came to me, saying,
15 "Son of man, your brethren, your relatives, your countrymen, and all the house of Israel in its entirety, are those about whom the inhabitants of Jerusalem have said, 'Get far away from the LORD; this land has been given to us as a possession.'

16 "Therefore say, 'Thus says the Lord GOD: "Although I have cast them far off among the Gentiles, and although I have scattered them among the countries, yet I shall be a little sanctuary for them in the countries where they have gone."'
17 "Therefore say, 'Thus says the Lord GOD: "I will gather you from the peoples, assemble you from the countries where you have been scattered, and I will give you the land of Israel."'
18 "And they will go there, and they will take away all its detestable things and all its abominations from there.
19 "Then I will give them one heart, and I will put a new spirit within them, and take the stony heart out of their flesh, and give them a heart of flesh,
20 "that they may walk in My statutes and keep My judgments and do them; and they shall be My people, and I will be their God.
21 "But as for those whose hearts follow the desire for their detestable things and their abominations, I will recompense their deeds on their own heads," says the Lord GOD.

Ezekiel 14:22 (NKJ)
22 "Yet behold, there shall be left in it a remnant who will be brought out, both sons and daughters; surely they will come out to you, and you will see their ways and their doings. Then you will be comforted concerning the disaster that I have brought upon Jerusalem, indeed all that I have brought upon it.

Joel 2:32 (NKJ)
32 And it shall come to pass that whoever calls on the name of the LORD shall be saved. For in Mount Zion and in Jerusalem there shall be deliverance, as the LORD has said, among the remnant whom the LORD calls.

Amos 5:14-15 (NKJ)
14 Seek good and not evil, that you may live; so the LORD God of hosts will be with you, as you have spoken.
15 Hate evil, love good; establish justice in the gate. It may be that the LORD God of hosts will be gracious to the remnant of Joseph.

Micah 2:12 (NKJ)
12 "I will surely assemble all of you, O Jacob, I will surely gather the remnant of Israel; I will put them together like sheep of the fold, like a flock in the midst of their pasture; they shall make a loud noise because of so many people.

Micah 5:2-3 (NKJ)
2 "But you, Bethlehem Ephrathah, though you are little among the thousands of Judah, yet out of you shall come forth to Me the One to be Ruler in Israel, whose goings forth are from of old, from everlasting."
3 Therefore He shall give them up, until the time that she who is in labor has given birth; then the remnant of His brethren shall return to the children of Israel.

Micah 5:7-8 (NKJ)
7 Then the remnant of Jacob shall be in the midst of many peoples, like dew from the LORD, like showers on the grass, that tarry for no man nor wait for the sons of men.
8 And the remnant of Jacob shall be among the Gentiles, in the midst of many peoples, like a lion among the beasts of the forest, like a young lion among flocks of sheep, who, if he passes through, both treads down and tears in pieces, and none can deliver.

Micah 7:18-19 (NKJ)
18 Who is a God like You, pardoning iniquity and passing over the transgression of the remnant of His heritage? He does not retain His anger forever, because He delights in mercy.
19 He will again have compassion on us, and will subdue our iniquities. You will cast all our sins into the depths of the sea.

Zechariah 8:12-15 (NKJ)
12 'For the seed shall be prosperous, the vine shall give its fruit, the ground shall give her increase, and the heavens shall give their dew— I will cause the remnant of this people to possess all these.
13 And it shall come to pass that just as you were a curse among the nations, O house of Judah and house of Israel, so I will save you, and you shall be a blessing. Do not fear, let your hands be strong.'

14 "For thus says the LORD of hosts: 'Just as I determined to punish you when your fathers provoked Me to wrath,' says the LORD of hosts, 'And I would not relent,
15 So again in these days I am determined to do good to Jerusalem and to the house of Judah. Do not fear.

Romans 11:2-5 (NKJ)
2 God has not cast away His people whom He foreknew. Or do you not know what the Scripture says of Elijah, how he pleads with God against Israel, saying,
3 "Lord, they have killed Your prophets and torn down Your altars, and I alone am left, and they seek my life?"
4 But what does the divine response say to him? "I have reserved for Myself seven thousand men who have not bowed the knee to Baal."
5 Even so then, at this present time there is a remnant according to the election of grace.

I offered extensive quotations on the issue of the "remnant being saved," because it is a very significant issue. Are you part of the remnant? Only God knows the answer but you either have comfort and peace in your relationship with Him or you do not.

The question arises, who will, in the end, judge you? Who will decide if you are part of the remnant? We know that the Father, The Son and The Holy Spirit are one, yet function in different ways. We know that sinners, uncleansed, will not enter into the Holy Presence of God, our Father. How then can you and I as sinners be in His presence? We are cleansed by the redeeming Blood of Jesus. There is only one way to stand in the presence of the Father. Our sins must be atoned for. It is Jesus Christ, the Son of God, who will judge us because He is the one who took your sins and mine upon Himself. Listen to the Scriptures as this issue is addressed.

John 5:22-27 (NKJ)
22 "For the Father judges no one, but has committed all judgment to the Son,
23 "that all should honor the Son just as they honor the Father. He who does not honor the Son does not honor the Father who sent Him.

24 "Most assuredly, I say to you, he who hears My word and believes in Him who sent Me has everlasting life, and shall not come into judgment, but has passed from death into life.

25 "Most assuredly, I say to you, the hour is coming, and now is, when the dead will hear the voice of the Son of God; and those who hear will live.

26 "For as the Father has life in Himself, so He has granted the Son to have life in Himself,

27 "and has given Him authority to execute judgment also, because He is the Son of Man.

Matthew 16:27 (NKJ)
27 "For the Son of Man will come in the glory of His Father with His angels, and then He will reward each according to his works.

Matthew 25:31-46 (NKJ)
31 "When the Son of Man comes in His glory, and all the holy angels with Him, then He will sit on the throne of His glory.

32 "All the nations will be gathered before Him, and He will separate them one from another, as a shepherd divides his sheep from the goats.

33 "And He will set the sheep on His right hand, but the goats on the left.

34 "Then the King will say to those on His right hand, 'Come, you blessed of My Father, inherit the kingdom prepared for you from the foundation of the world:

35 'for I was hungry and you gave Me food; I was thirsty and you gave Me drink; I was a stranger and you took Me in;

36 'I was naked and you clothed Me; I was sick and you visited Me; I was in prison and you came to Me.'

37 "Then the righteous will answer Him, saying, 'Lord, when did we see You hungry and feed You, or thirsty and give You drink?

38 'When did we see You a stranger and take You in, or naked and clothe You?

39 'Or when did we see You sick, or in prison, and come to You?'

40 "And the King will answer and say to them, 'Assuredly, I say to you, inasmuch as you did it to one of the least of these My brethren, you did it to Me.'

41 "Then He will also say to those on the left hand, 'Depart from Me, you cursed, into the everlasting fire prepared for the devil and his angels:
42 'for I was hungry and you gave Me no food; I was thirsty and you gave Me no drink;
43 'I was a stranger and you did not take Me in, naked and you did not clothe Me, sick and in prison and you did not visit Me.'
44 "Then they also will answer Him, saying, 'Lord, when did we see You hungry or thirsty or a stranger or naked or sick or in prison, and did not minister to You?'
45 "Then He will answer them, saying, 'Assuredly, I say to you, inasmuch as you did not do it to one of the least of these, you did not do it to Me.'
46 "And these will go away into everlasting punishment, but the righteous into eternal life."

2 Corinthians 5:6-10 (NKJ)
6 So we are always confident, knowing that while we are at home in the body we are absent from the Lord.
7 For we walk by faith, not by sight.
8 We are confident, yes, well pleased rather to be absent from the body and to be present with the Lord.
9 Therefore we make it our aim, whether present or absent, to be well pleasing to Him.
10 For we must all appear before the judgment seat of Christ, that each one may receive the things done in the body, according to what he has done, whether good or bad.

Even though Jesus will judge us, the Word frequently makes it clear that mercy triumphs over judgment.

Zechariah 3:8-9 (NKJ)
8 'Hear, O Joshua, the high priest, you and your companions who sit before you, for they are a wondrous sign; for behold, I am bringing forth My Servant the BRANCH.
9 For behold, the stone that I have laid before Joshua: upon the stone are seven eyes. Behold, I will engrave its inscription,' says the LORD of hosts, 'And I will remove the iniquity of that land in one day.

Zechariah 8:14-15 (NKJ)
14 "For thus says the LORD of hosts: 'Just as I determined to punish you when your fathers provoked Me to wrath,' says the LORD of hosts, 'And I would not relent,
15 So again in these days I am determined to do good to Jerusalem and to the house of Judah. Do not fear.

Perhaps the one thing that stands out in the Scriptures regarding God's love and mercy for Israel is His determination to do good to Jerusalem. His will is for Israel to glorify His name and to be glorified and His will cannot be resisted by any force, anywhere. God is determined to good to Jerusalem.

Micah 7:18-20 (NKJ)
18 Who is a God like You, pardoning iniquity and passing over the transgression of the remnant of His heritage? He does not retain His anger forever, because He delights in mercy.
19 He will again have compassion on us, and will subdue our iniquities. You will cast all our sins into the depths of the sea.
20 You will give truth to Jacob and mercy to Abraham, which You have sworn to our fathers from days of old.

Zechariah 10:6-8 (NKJ)
6 "I will strengthen the house of Judah, and I will save the house of Joseph. I will bring them back, because I have mercy on them. They shall be as though I had not cast them aside; for I am the LORD their God, and I will hear them.
7 Those of Ephraim shall be like a mighty man, and their heart shall rejoice as if with wine. Yes, their children shall see it and be glad; their heart shall rejoice in the LORD.
8 I will whistle for them and gather them, for I will redeem them; and they shall increase as they once increased.

In these next verses, Isaiah is talking about a 3-year period, in which the remnant that escaped shall survive, having taken root downward and born fruit upward. If this is referring to the last 3½ years of the tribulation, it appears that within a 6-month period following the cessation of the newly commenced Temple rites, a remnant will flee, survive and serve the Lord.

Isaiah 37:30-32 (NKJ)
30 "This shall be a sign to you: you shall eat this year such as grows of itself, and the second year what springs from the same; also in the third year sow and reap, plant vineyards and eat the fruit of them.
31 And the remnant who have escaped of the house of Judah shall again take root downward, and bear fruit upward.
32 For out of Jerusalem shall go a remnant, and those who escape from Mount Zion. The zeal of the LORD of hosts will do this.

In many places, the Bible indicates that "all" of the Jews will be saved and restored to righteousness. This is a difficult teaching, not because it isn't good news, but because it must be contrasted with the many verses where the sins of Israel (and every one else!) have greatly grieved your Lord and mine. Listen to a precise point regarding Israel's salvation.

Romans 11:25-27 (NKJ)
25 For I do not desire, brethren, that you should be ignorant of this mystery, lest you should be wise in your own opinion, that blindness in part has happened to Israel until the fullness of the Gentiles has come in.
26 And so all Israel will be saved, as it is written: "The Deliverer will come out of Zion, and He will turn away ungodliness from Jacob;
27 For this is My covenant with them, when I take away their sins."

Judgment clearly belongs to the Lord, and no reader of this book doubts his or her own sin. The scriptures tell us that "all have sinned and come short of the glory of God." Referencing and emphasis hardly seems necessary whether we are speaking of King David or of ourselves. The fact of our sin is undisputed. We live with it daily. It is the righteousness of God, which we seek. Read on.

Isaiah 45:22-25 (NKJ)
22 "Look to Me, and be saved, all you ends of the earth! For I am God, and there is no other.

23 I have sworn by Myself; the word has gone out of My mouth in righteousness, and shall not return, that to Me every knee shall bow, every tongue shall take an oath.
24 He shall say, 'Surely in the LORD I have righteousness and strength. To Him men shall come, and all shall be ashamed who are incensed against Him.
25 In the LORD all the descendants of Israel shall be justified, and shall glory.'"

Notice that it says "all the descendants of Israel shall be justified." Yet earlier, we read of the remnant that will be saved. Which is it? First, only God knows the answer to that question and the uncertainty of our individual circumstance with God should bring us to a position where we seek certainty. Jeremiah lamented, perhaps more than any other prophet, over Israel's stubbornness and sin. Could these verses be directed to you personally? The Word is truth and placing it in your heart will help you strengthen your sense of resolve to serve Him.

Jeremiah 6:16-19 (NKJ)
16 Thus says the LORD: "Stand in the ways and see, and ask for the old paths, where the good way is, and walk in it; then you will find rest for your souls. But they said, 'We will not walk in it.'
17 Also, I set watchmen over you, saying, 'Listen to the sound of the trumpet!' But they said, 'We will not listen.'
18 Therefore hear, you nations, and know, O congregation, what is among them.
19 Hear, O earth! Behold, I will certainly bring calamity on this people–the fruit of their thoughts, because they have not heeded My words, nor My law, but rejected it.

Here Samuel scolds Saul, for his sins and the sins of the people.

1 Samuel 15:22-23 (NKJ)
22 Then Samuel said: "Has the LORD as great delight in burnt offerings and sacrifices, as in obeying the voice of the LORD? Behold, to obey is better than sacrifice, and to heed than the fat of rams.

23 For rebellion is as the sin of witchcraft, and stubbornness is as iniquity and idolatry. Because you have rejected the word of the LORD, he also has rejected you from being king."

If, for some reason, you are not among the remnant that will be saved, then it looks like judgment awaits. But what is the remnant? Is it that small proportion of Israel's people, who have in fact placed their love and trust in God? Is it that portion of Israel that has not rejected the Word, and what is rejection except turning one's back on what God wants to tell you?

You know yourself whether you love God with all your heart, mind, soul and strength and whether you are obedient to His laws. You can see from those saints in history what constitutes real love and obedience. Are you part of the remnant? Will you endure the great tribulation and remain faithful to God? If so, you and all those who have died, in the faith, blessed of God, will reign together with the Messiah, Jesus Christ during the Millennium, the Kingdom Age, that time in history in which the promises of God to the faithful of Israel will be fulfilled.

Who is included in the remnant? First, let us agree again that not one of us knows, except where God has already revealed it, such as those persons listed in Hebrews, chapter 11. That list includes Abel, Enoch, Noah, Abraham, Sarah, Isaac, Jacob, Joseph, Moses, Samuel, David and many others. But we do not truly know about God's judgment of others except where He has revealed it. God teaches us that only He knows the hearts and minds of men.

1 Chronicles 28:9 (NKJ)
9 "As for you, my son Solomon, know the God of your father, and serve Him with a loyal heart and with a willing mind; for the LORD searches all hearts and understands all the intent of the thoughts. If you seek Him, He will be found by you; but if you forsake Him, He will cast you off forever.

It is a fact that God knows your heart and understands all the intent of your thoughts, but that is why you ought to be reading the Bible instead of this book. God wants to feed you "directly," every day. God's Word "interacts" with you. As you listen, you learn.

Man can not improve upon what God has revealed nor stand between God and other men. Your faith must be in God and in no other and you must love Him with all your heart, mind, soul and strength. I would guess that the kind of love stated here would dictate a sense of urgency in your heart that would drive you to prayer and to the study of His Word. What possible excuse will we be able to offer regarding our lack of familiarity with the Word or of our spirit being distanced from His Spirit?

Listen to this wonderful quote:

Jeremiah 29:11-13 (NKJ)
11 For I know the thoughts that I think toward you, says the LORD, thoughts of peace and not of evil, to give you a future and a hope.
12 Then you will call upon Me and go and pray to Me, and I will listen to you.
13 And you will seek Me and find Me, when you search for Me with all your heart.

If the scriptures are the truth, most of the world has their priorities completely upside down. The Word is far down the list of those things to which men dedicate their time and their lives. Are you certain that you are residing in the presence and peace of God, right now and forever?

Many of those who know they are outside of God's will for their lives are gambling that death will be the end. They think that somehow, their failure to seek and to serve God will result in death, period. According to the scriptures, physical death will not be the end. It is the beginning of eternity, to be spent either in His Presence or outside His Presence. The motivation behind this book is that it serves as a warning first and a "pointer" second.

The warning is clear enough. Prophecy says that when the Temple is rebuilt, the clock will start running. It appears that only those, whose faith is so strong that they would rather die than accept the mark of the beast, will enter the Kingdom. Do you have that kind of faith?

The "pointer" is to fulfilled prophecy, which when attended to, will take you to the foot of the Cross. You have already learned how God desires obedience and mercy not sacrifice. Here Micah teaches you one of the most important concepts in the Old Testament. Read carefully.

Micah 6:1-16 (NKJ)
1 Hear now what the LORD says: "Arise, plead your case before the mountains, and let the hills hear your voice.
2 Hear, O you mountains, the LORD'S complaint, and you strong foundations of the earth; for the LORD has a complaint against His people, and He will contend with Israel.
3 "O My people, what have I done to you? And how have I wearied you? Testify against Me.
4 For I brought you up from the land of Egypt, I redeemed you from the house of bondage; and I sent before you Moses, Aaron, and Miriam.
5 O My people, remember now what Balak king of Moab counseled, and what Balaam the son of Beor answered him, from Acacia Grove to Gilgal, that you may know the righteousness of the LORD."
6 With what shall I come before the LORD, and bow myself before the High God? Shall I come before Him with burnt offerings, with calves a year old?
7 Will the LORD be pleased with thousands of rams, ten thousand rivers of oil? Shall I give my firstborn for my transgression, the fruit of my body for the sin of my soul?
8 He has shown you, O man, what is good; and what does the LORD require of you but to do justly, to love mercy, and to walk humbly with your God?
9 The LORD'S voice cries to the city– wisdom shall see Your name: "Hear the Rod! Who has appointed it?
10 Are there yet the treasures of wickedness in the house of the wicked, and the short measure that is an abomination?
11 Shall I count pure those with the wicked scales, and with the bag of deceitful weights?

12 For her rich men are full of violence, her inhabitants have spoken lies, and their tongue is deceitful in their mouth.
13 "Therefore I will also make you sick by striking you, by making you desolate because of your sins.
14 You shall eat, but not be satisfied; hunger shall be in your midst. You may carry some away, but shall not save them; and what you do rescue I will give over to the sword.
15 "You shall sow, but not reap; you shall tread the olives, but not anoint yourselves with oil; and make sweet wine, but not drink wine.
16 For the statutes of Omri are kept; all the works of Ahab's house are done; and you walk in their counsels, that I may make you a desolation, and your inhabitants a hissing. Therefore you shall bear the reproach of My people."

As hard as it is to read of the judgment that will be brought upon man for failing to honor and obey God, the "solution" lies before you. You can not redeem yourself with burnt offerings, rivers of oil nor by giving the fruit of your body, your firstborn, as an offering to cover the sin of your soul. How then can you be redeemed? Even the life of your precious child, the supreme sacrifice cannot redeem you. But unlike Abraham, you are not asked to give your most precious lamb, your child to God, as an act of obedience.

Doesn't it strike you as ironic that God, in fact, told you in many Messianic prophecies that His Son would come and redeem you? How else can your sins be forgiven if the blood of bulls and goats won't redeem you? It is only by the shed blood of the perfect Lamb of God, His only begotten Son, promised beforehand, that you and I can be cleansed, forgiven and redeemed. Jesus, the Christ, atoned for our personal, individual sins.

The sin described in verses 10-16 is not atypical of your sin and mine. We need to repent and God's mercy awaits. The fact that God continues to extend His Hand to us, even in our sin, by offering us access to the heart and mind of the Messiah, in us, is grace that defies logic. It is simply a gift, an undeserved gift. It makes no sense to mankind, at all, that a simple confession of faith offered in humility and contrition and a promise to repent can reverse a lifetime of sin. Yet that is the deal! Choose today whom you will serve, Satan, the flesh, or God, in Spirit and Truth.

If you are struggling with that decision, go off to a private, quiet place, be alone with God and pray for His guidance, His strength, and His peace. Everything you see around you is perishing, including your flesh. Only the spirit, the Spirit in you survives. Your spirit will survive. But where will it reside?

I much prefer the Holy Scriptures to anything I have to say, for every thought I have is from Him, or at least I pray that is so. How else could one be so bold? Certainly not in their own righteousness! Read these verses carefully. The Bible is full of this kind of revelation. You must start reading it with a sense of urgency, never before felt. Redeem the time while there is time.

Romans 8:26-28 (NKJ)
26 Likewise the Spirit also helps in our weaknesses. For we do not know what we should pray for as we ought, but the Spirit Himself makes intercession for us with groanings which cannot be uttered.
27 Now He who searches the hearts knows what the mind of the Spirit is, because He makes intercession for the saints according to the will of God.
28 And we know that all things work together for good to those who love God, to those who are the called according to His purpose.

1 Corinthians 2:14-16 (NKJ)
14 But the natural man does not receive the things of the Spirit of God, for they are foolishness to him; nor can he know them, because they are spiritually discerned.
15 But he who is spiritual judges all things, yet he himself is rightly judged by no one.
16 For "who has known the mind of the Lord that he may instruct Him?" But we have the mind of Christ.

Philippians 2:1-11 (NKJ)

1 Therefore if there is any consolation in Christ, if any comfort of love, if any fellowship of the Spirit, if any affection and mercy,
2 fulfill my joy by being like-minded, having the same love, being of one accord, of one mind.
3 Let nothing be done through selfish ambition or conceit, but in lowliness of mind let each esteem others better than himself.
4 Let each of you look out not only for his own interests, but also for the interests of others.
5 Let this mind be in you which was also in Christ Jesus,
6 who, being in the form of God, did not consider it robbery to be equal with God,
7 but made Himself of no reputation, taking the form of a bondservant, and coming in the likeness of men.
8 And being found in appearance as a man, He humbled Himself and became obedient to the point of death, even the death of the cross.
9 Therefore God also has highly exalted Him and given Him the name which is above every name,
10 that at the name of Jesus every knee should bow, of those in heaven, and of those on earth, and of those under the earth,
11 and that every tongue should confess that Jesus Christ is Lord, to the glory of God the Father.

As to the tendency we all have to think we have "arrived" and that we "know," the following excerpt from a presentation by Paul to the Philippians makes it very clear that the "journey" for all of life is one of "seeking, not apprehending." Apprehension awaits, but not while we reside in the flesh.

Philippians 3:8-15 (NKJ)

8 Yet indeed I also count all things loss for the excellence of the knowledge of Christ Jesus my Lord, for whom I have suffered the loss of all things, and count them as rubbish, that I may gain Christ
9 and be found in Him, not having my own righteousness, which is from the law, but that which is through faith in Christ, the righteousness which is from God by faith;
10 that I may know Him and the power of His resurrection, and the fellowship of His sufferings, being conformed to His death,

11 if, by any means, I may attain to the resurrection from the dead.

12 Not that I have already attained, or am already perfected; but I press on, that I may lay hold of that for which Christ Jesus has also laid hold of me.

13 Brethren, I do not count myself to have apprehended; but one thing I do, forgetting those things which are behind and reaching forward to those things which are ahead,

14 I press toward the goal for the prize of the upward call of God in Christ Jesus.

15 Therefore let us, as many as are mature, have this mind; and if in anything you think otherwise, God will reveal even this to you.

As Paul, we seek to apprehend perfection, but until we are there, it remains a lifelong pursuit. The process is called sanctification . . .

CHAPTER 7

THE "SCATTERING" AND "GATHERING" OF THE JEWS

There has, up to now, been a 2000 year period in which the Temple has not existed and the prophets, to whom God formerly spoke, have been silent. The scriptures are also quite silent on the circumstances of the Jews during this 2000 year period, other than their being "scattered," only to be "gathered" again.

Deuteronomy 30:1-6 (NKJ)
1 "Now it shall come to pass, when all these things come upon you, the blessing and the curse which I have set before you, and you call them to mind among all the nations where the LORD your God drives you,
2 "and you return to the LORD your God and obey His voice, according to all that I command you today, you and your children, with all your heart and with all your soul,
3 "that the LORD your God will bring you back from captivity, and have compassion on you, and gather you again from all the nations where the LORD your God has scattered you.
4 "If any of you are driven out to the farthest parts under heaven, from there the LORD your God will gather you, and from there He will bring you.
5 "Then the LORD your God will bring you to the land which your fathers possessed, and you shall possess it. He will prosper you and multiply you more than your fathers.

6 "And the LORD your God will circumcise your heart and the heart of your descendants, to love the LORD your God with all your heart and with all your soul, that you may live.

The "scattering" and "gathering" of Israel is a pattern repeated in history, but this prophecy, uttered by Moses seems to include the possession of all the land your fathers possessed. What land is "promised?" Listen.

Genesis 15:18 (NKJ)
18 On the same day the LORD made a covenant with Abram, saying: "To your descendants I have given this land, from the river of Egypt to the great river, the River Euphrates

This granting of the Promised Land to the Jews will be preceded by an event that foreshadows the establishment of the Kingdom. There will be a gathering, but first the lawless one, Satan, will be revealed. Listen to what Paul said to the Thessalonians regarding the "gathering" of God's people. When I say, God's people, I am referring to those Paul was referring to, namely those who look forward to the coming of the Messiah, which in this case definitely included Jewish believers.

2 Thessalonians 2:1-12 (NKJ)
1 Now, brethren, concerning the coming of our Lord Jesus Christ and our gathering together to Him, we ask you,
2 not to be soon shaken in mind or troubled, either by spirit or by word or by letter, as if from us, as though the day of Christ had come.
3 Let no one deceive you by any means; for that Day will not come unless the falling away comes first, and the man of sin is revealed, the son of perdition,
4 who opposes and exalts himself above all that is called God or that is worshiped, so that he sits as God in the temple of God, showing himself that he is God.
5 Do you not remember that when I was still with you I told you these things?
6 And now you know what is restraining, that he may be revealed in his own time.

7 For the mystery of lawlessness is already at work; only He who now restrains will do so until He is taken out of the way.
8 And then the lawless one will be revealed, whom the Lord will consume with the breath of His mouth and destroy with the brightness of His coming.
9 The coming of the lawless one is according to the working of Satan, with all power, signs, and lying wonders,
10 and with all unrighteous deception among those who perish, because they did not receive the love of the truth, that they might be saved.
11 And for this reason God will send them strong delusion, that they should believe the lie,
12 that they all may be condemned who did not believe the truth but had pleasure in unrighteousness.

In verse 6, Paul says, "And now you know what is restraining." What was he referring to? He was referring to verse 1 when he said, "Now, brethren, concerning the coming of our Lord Jesus Christ and our gathering together to Him."

And verse 3 "Let no one deceive you by any means; for that Day will not come unless the falling away comes first, and the man of sin is revealed, the son of perdition."

These verses were written to believers, Jewish and Gentile, who wanted to know what signs they should look for regarding the Messiah's return. But, in addition, it is clear enough that the gathering of the Jews for the establishment of the Kingdom in the Promised Land will follow the revealing of the son of perdition. At some point, Christians and Jews will embrace the Messiah in unison and what we see as differences will disappear. The Messiah will be the One in whom we unite and none of this will happen until the Antichrist is revealed.

The Kingdom "gathering" will be marked by spiritual renewal on a scope never before seen in Israel. There will be no false gods and no idols among the Jews. There will be no temptation by Satan. It will be as the Garden of Eden restored.

What will have changed? Why will Israel suddenly be empowered to love and obey, as God intended? It will be because of the following "enabling" prophecy stated by Jeremiah:

Jeremiah 31:33-34 (NKJ)
33 "But this is the covenant that I will make with the house of Israel after those days, says the LORD: I will put My law in their minds, and write it on their hearts; and I will be their God, and they shall be My people.
34 "No more shall every man teach his neighbor, and every man his brother, saying, 'Know the LORD,' for they all shall know Me, from the least of them to the greatest of them, says the LORD. For I will forgive their iniquity, and their sin I will remember no more."

Our Lord, Our God, Our Messiah will reign eternally, beginning with the Millennium and Satan will finally be cast out as New Jerusalem, the eternal Kingdom will be established. The "gathering" will be complete. The dispersion will be behind us and all of God's people will rejoice.

CHAPTER 8

PEACE AND SAFETY

The most wonderful part about prophecy is that it provides verification. You would think that all of the prophecy that has been fulfilled would "seal the deal," so to speak. The fact that it has not testifies to the power of evil present in this world and to the hardness of the hearts of many that do not serve nor love God.

The scriptures indicate that a pronouncement of "Peace and Safety" in Israel will precede the beginning of the tribulation period. This will require new treaties, some of which are under negotiation at this moment. Watch the newspapers to see how the placement of the Temple foundation is resolved and who plays the lead arbiter roles. The treaties will necessarily allow Israel to rebuild the Temple in an air of compromise, through peaceful negotiations.

Actually, when I started writing this book, I said, "may be under negotiation." Certainty on this issue now abounds. Whether these treaties link directly to the rebuilding of the Temple, we will see. I think you know that they will.

If this prophecy were fulfilled before your eyes, I would think you would be startled at first and then secondly, you would be placed on alert. Peace and safety will not endure in Jerusalem, according to the scriptures, not until the Messiah returns.

1 Thessalonians 5:2-3 (NKJ)
2 For you yourselves know perfectly that the day of the Lord so comes as a thief in the night.
3 For when they say, "Peace and safety!" then sudden destruction comes upon them, as labor pains upon a pregnant woman. And they shall not escape.

Jeremiah speaks of a time where the Word of God will not be regarded and the leadership will be speaking of "peace and safety." Listen.

Jeremiah 6:10-14 (NKJ)
10 To whom shall I speak and give warning, that they may hear? Indeed their ear is uncircumcised, and they cannot give heed. Behold, the word of the LORD is a reproach to them; they have no delight in it.
11 Therefore I am full of the fury of the LORD. I am weary of holding it in. "I will pour it out on the children outside, and on the assembly of young men together; for even the husband shall be taken with the wife, the aged with him who is full of days.
12 And their houses shall be turned over to others, fields and wives together; for I will stretch out My hand against the inhabitants of the land," says the LORD.
13 "Because from the least of them even to the greatest of them, everyone is given to covetousness; and from the prophet even to the priest, everyone deals falsely.
14 They have also healed the hurt of My people slightly, saying, 'Peace, peace!' When there is no peace.

Jeremiah goes on to say:

Jeremiah 8:15 (NKJ)
15 "We looked for peace, but no good came; and for a time of health, and there was trouble!

Jeremiah 9:12-14 (NKJ)
12 Who is the wise man who may understand this? And who is he to whom the mouth of the LORD has spoken, that he may declare it? Why

does the land perish and burn up like a wilderness, so that no one can pass through?
13 And the LORD said, "Because they have forsaken My law which I set before them, and have not obeyed My voice, nor walked according to it, 14 "but they have walked according to the dictates of their own hearts…

Such prophecy seems too transparent not to be heeded. But what does one do to "pay heed." Go to all of the Word of God and seek a personal relationship with the only One who can offer you true peace and safety. Everything around you will perish, only your soul and spirit will survive. But I must say, because God's word says it, turn now from your sins of the flesh, repent and seek to know and to be known by God the Father, The Son and The Holy Spirit.

All prophecy will be fulfilled. The Messiah has come and will come again. Only He can present you to the Holy Father, blameless. There is no peace and safety that will endure until the Messiah returns and establishes the Kingdom here on earth for 1000 years and even then, this earth will perish in the end along with everyone who serves evil.

CHAPTER 9

THE UNMISTAKABLE EVENTS THAT CHRONICLE THE TRIBULATION

The Word of God states that the temple in Jerusalem will be rebuilt. This will be the third Temple and it will be located on a site that God has foreordained. Many faithful Jews are in advanced stages of planning for the rebuilding of the third Temple and strongly believe that the Temple will be rebuilt soon. The governance of the Temple Mount is now a matter of great debate and importance. The media is focused on the pivotal role of the governance of Jerusalem as the leaders of the world seek to establish peaceful relations between Israel and her neighbors.

There are disputes among all interested parties as to the exact location of Solomon's Temple. There are at least three possibilities and each of them have supporters who persuasively argue their case. One group places the original temple site on the area now occupied by the AL Aqsa mosque. Another group supports a location alongside the Mosque, meaning the Temple could be rebuilt without tearing down the mosque. Another group believes the location is as far as a quarter mile away from the mosque site. In my opinion, it does not matter. The Scriptures say the temple will be rebuilt under peaceful circumstances and as a result of treaties.

As mentioned below, the one who negotiates the treaty, which will cover many more issues than the rebuilding of the Temple, will be greatly respected and heralded. That person, according to Scripture, is the anti-Christ and the victory of a rebuilt Temple will be short-lived. In 3 ½ years it will be torn down and the persecution will begin.

As of this writing, the primary issue is one of governance. The Palestinian's are demanding sovereignty over all of the eastern part of Jerusalem, including the Old City and its holy sites. The United States has proposed complex sovereignty arrangements, including placing some areas under "divine sovereignty" to enable both sides to save face in accepting the compromise. The Pope has proposed ideas of shared governance.

At this time, both the rhetoric and the aggression have intensified. It appears that severe hostility may necessarily precede any formal resolution regarding the governance of the holy sites in Jerusalem. This ten year old December 2001 quote, from an Arutz-7 news report, characterizes what remains as the Arab position: Arafat… said the Palestinian Authority would hold steadfast to its goals for a Palestinian state that has Jerusalem as its capital. "We frankly want a Palestinian state … in the full sense of the word … with Jerusalem being its capital, alongside Israel," he said. And subsequent to that remark, Arafat has died and trust levels have diminished even further. A storm may have to occur before the air clears. Hopefully it will not completely destroy Jerusalem and Scripture seems to point in that direction.

Scripture makes it clear that the placement of the foundation for the third Temple will be resolved through negotiations. Then he (the prince) shall confirm a covenant with many for one week. Covenants are generally preceded by disagreements and the decision to rebuild the third Temple will not be made unilaterally. There will be negotiations. The individual who plays the lead role in resolving this pivotal dispute between Muslims and Jews is of great significance. The treaties between Israel and her neighbors will necessarily allow Israel to rebuild the Temple in an air of compromise.

The following complex prophecy by Daniel is relied upon by many as a Messianic prophecy, with mysterious mathematical properties. Read "weeks," as "years" and you will see why.

Daniel 9:24-27 (NKJ)

24 "Seventy weeks are determined for your people and for your holy city, to finish the transgression, to make an end of sins, to make reconciliation for iniquity, to bring in everlasting righteousness, to seal up vision and prophecy, and to anoint the Most Holy.

25 "Know therefore and understand, that from the going forth of the command to restore and build Jerusalem until Messiah the Prince, there shall be seven weeks and sixty-two weeks; the street shall be built again, and the wall, even in troublesome times.

26 "And after the sixty-two weeks Messiah shall be cut off, but not for Himself; and the people of the prince who is to come shall destroy the city and the sanctuary. The end of it shall be with a flood, and till the end of the war desolations are determined.

27 Then he shall confirm a covenant with many for one week; but in the middle of the week he shall bring an end to sacrifice and offering. And on the wing of abominations shall be one who makes desolate, even until the consummation, which is determined, is poured out on the desolate."

Daniel said that "until Messiah the Prince" there will be 7 weeks and 62 weeks until the street and the wall (the Temple wall) is rebuilt. This is a designation of two "rebuildings." The first was based on the decree of King Cyrus. His decree to rebuild is the starting point of the time line prophesied by Daniel. Understand that Daniel's prophecy concerning the first rebuilding was fulfilled and that event set the calendar for the Messiah's return and crucifixion. The flood mentioned is not one of water, but of sin, since God promised that no flood would ever destroy man again. "Then," that is, after the flood of sin which led to the destruction of the 2nd Temple, he, the prince (Antichrist), will confirm a covenant for one week (read 7 years) and in the middle of that week (read 3½ years) he shall bring an end to sacrifice and offering.

In order to consider Daniel's prophecy more carefully, read of the event that Daniel is referring to in verse 25, above:

Ezra 6:1-15 (NKJ)

1 Then King Darius issued a decree, and a search was made in the archives, where the treasures were stored in Babylon.

2 And at Achmetha, in the palace that is in the province of Media, a scroll was found, and in it a record was written thus:

3 In the first year of King Cyrus, King Cyrus issued a decree concerning the house of God at Jerusalem: "Let the house be rebuilt, the place where they offered sacrifices; and let the foundations of it be firmly laid, its height sixty cubits and its width sixty cubits,

4 with three rows of heavy stones and one row of new timber. Let the expenses be paid from the king's treasury.

5 Also let the gold and silver articles of the house of God, which Nebuchadnezzar took from the temple which is in Jerusalem and brought to Babylon, be restored and taken back to the temple which is in Jerusalem, each to its place; and deposit them in the house of God"–

6 Now therefore, Tattenai, governor of the region beyond the River, and Shethar-Boznai, and your companions the Persians who are beyond the River, keep yourselves far from there.

7 Let the work of this house of God alone; let the governor of the Jews and the elders of the Jews build this house of God on its site.

8 Moreover I issue a decree as to what you shall do for the elders of these Jews, for the building of this house of God: Let the cost be paid at the king's expense from taxes on the region beyond the River; this is to be given immediately to these men, so that they are not hindered.

9 And whatever they need– young bulls, rams, and lambs for the burnt offerings of the God of heaven, wheat, salt, wine, and oil, according to the request of the priests who are in Jerusalem– let it be given them day by day without fail,

10 that they may offer sacrifices of sweet aroma to the God of heaven, and pray for the life of the king and his sons.

11 Also I issue a decree that whoever alters this edict, let a timber be pulled from his house and erected, and let him be hanged on it; and let his house be made a refuse heap because of this.

12 And may the God who causes His name to dwell there destroy any king or people who put their hand to alter it, or to destroy this house of God which is in Jerusalem. I Darius issue a decree; let it be done diligently.

13 Then Tattenai, governor of the region beyond the River, Shethar-Boznai, and their companions diligently did according to what King Darius had sent.

14 So the elders of the Jews built, and they prospered through the prophesying of Haggai the prophet and Zechariah the son of Iddo. And they built and finished it, according to the commandment of the God of Israel, and according to the command of Cyrus, Darius, and Artaxerxes king of Persia.
15 Now the temple was finished on the third day of the month of Adar, which was in the sixth year of the reign of King Darius.

This rebuilding of the Temple establishes the starting point of the 70 weeks mentioned in Daniel 9:25. The temple was rebuilt and Daniel's prophecy says that 62 weeks would pass before the Messiah would be "cut off" (this prophecy says the Messiah will have been rejected and killed). If the 62 weeks represent one year periods, given the Roman calendar of 360 days in a year, the Messiah did come, triumphantly riding into Jerusalem on a donkey, right on schedule (173,380 days after the decree) and then was "cut off."

Of course this 2nd Temple was destroyed by the Romans in 70 AD. Read verse 12 above and you will understand that those who alter or destroy the house of God and His Temple will be destroyed. Those who destroyed the 2nd Temple and those who will yet destroy the 3rd Temple will be dealt with very harshly.

The crucifixion of Jesus completed the first 62 "week" period. That would leave the completion of a one-week period (7 years) until the Messiah will return again. The prophecy (Daniel 9:24-27) pointing to the "rebuilding of the Temple," for the 3rd time, will, according to the beliefs of many, commence the final 7 year period. This event is clearly linked to the return of the Messiah.

When Daniel says "in the middle of the week" sacrifices and offerings will cease, they would, of course, had to have commenced. This prophecy is not about a time in the past, but it is focused on the future until Messiah the Prince. The Messiah will come and His millennium kingdom will be established and it will "follow the consummation," which will be poured out on the desolate, the battle of Armageddon.

The rebuilding of the temple and the re-institution of sacrifices will be the preamble to the period of tribulation described in Daniel. There is not one prophecy yet to be fulfilled, in my opinion, more pivotal than this prophecy. Seven years is not a very long period of time and the events that are prophesied will shake the earth to its foundation, setting in motion the millennium.

As I write this, the leadership of Israel and the world has become totally focused on the fate of Jerusalem and its Holy sites. You are witnessing the events leading to the rebuilding of the 3rd Temple. It will happen sooner or later and peace will appear to have come to Israel. But listen to Daniel: and the people of the prince who is to come shall destroy the city and the sanctuary….. in the middle of the week he shall bring an end to sacrifice and offering.

The prince referred to is going to deceive many. He shall even deceive some of the chosen people, the elect. Many will buy into the belief that peace and safety has come to Israel and for a brief time it will be true. But this very powerful and very attractive and very persuasive prince will, "in the middle of the week" destroy the Temple and assert that he is to be worshipped and followed. Obedience and cooperation will be required and you will agree to participate (accept the mark of the beast) or you will be persecuted.

For those of you doubting that Daniel's prophecy of weeks should be interpreted as years, do the math that makes the decree of Cyrus accurate regarding the rebuilding of the 2nd Temple. I believe that you will agree that the destruction of the Temple is in the middle of a period of 7 years, in order for these prophecies to be consistent.

I have capitalized the Temple in Jerusalem as "The Temple," although I want to say it is not capitalized in Scripture. I am treating it as a proper noun but I am not attributing Deification to the Temple. In New Jerusalem, heaven, there will be no temple. Referring to heaven the Scripture says:

Revelation 21:22 (NKJ)
22 But I saw no temple in it, for the Lord God Almighty and the Lamb are its temple.

Our focus in our worship will be God, then, and should be now. We do not worship a temple built with human hands. We worship at such temples but our praise and our joy is directed to the Father, Son and Holy Spirit, not pillars nor statues or furnishings. We worship a true and living God and celebrate together His presence in such places as synagogues, churches and temples. The very ground we stand upon when communing with God is Holy ground. Listen:

Exodus 3:1-5 (NKJ)
1 Now Moses was tending the flock of Jethro his father-in-law, the priest of Midian. And he led the flock to the back of the desert, and came to Horeb, the mountain of God
2 And the Angel of the LORD appeared to him in a flame of fire from the midst of a bush. So he looked, and behold, the bush was burning with fire, but the bush was not consumed
3 Then Moses said, "I will now turn aside and see this great sight, why the bush does not burn."
4 So when the LORD saw that he turned aside to look, God called to him from the midst of the bush and said, "Moses, Moses!" And he said, "Here I am."
5 Then He said, "Do not draw near this place. Take your sandals off your feet, for the place where you stand is holy ground."

Yes, the temple will be rebuilt, but let's not ever forget what the temple is and what it is not. It is Holy ground because the Spirit of God is there but it is not a place in which we worship any item in it. We worship our Lord and Savior and our relationship is a personal one, with Him, whether in a temple or in a place where you have gone to be alone with Him. The worship of icons is an error, in my opinion. It was an error made by Aaron when he made the molded, golden calf and it is an error that persists in many quarters today. Listen to the admonition of our Lord.

Exodus 20:4-5 (NKJ)
4 "You shall not make for yourself a carved image, or any likeness of anything that is in heaven above, or that is in the earth beneath, or that is in the water under the earth;

5 you shall not bow down to them nor serve them. For I, the LORD your God, am a jealous God, visiting the iniquity of the fathers on the children to the third and fourth generations of those who hate Me, ..."

Yes, the temple will be rebuilt and it will be a time for joyous celebration because our Lord will be glorified. But, listen to the prophecy of Daniel stated above. It is a temple that will be destroyed in a short time. Do not let the events surrounding the construction and destruction of the temple confound you. Be ready. Turn and live. Get the "new heart" that Ezekiel told you to seek.

Ezekiel 18:30-32 (NKJ)
30 "Therefore I will judge you, O house of Israel, every one according to his ways," says the Lord GOD. "Repent, and turn from all your transgressions, so that iniquity will not be your ruin
31 "Cast away from you all the transgressions which you have committed, and get yourselves a new heart and a new spirit. For why should you die, O house of Israel?
32 "For I have no pleasure in the death of one who dies," says the Lord GOD. "Therefore turn and live!"

God wants you to turn to Him as these calamitous events unfold. He will judge "each one" according to his ways."

CHAPTER 10

THE MESSIAH AND THEN THE TRIBULATION OR THE TRIBULATION AND THEN THE MESSIAH?

If I have not lost you as a reader after all these references to Jesus Christ, praise God. But let's go to the question of those Jews who will survive what is called the great tribulation and will enter into the Kingdom and reign with the Messiah. If you do not yet understand the tribulation, you will. You may believe the Messiah is coming to set up His Kingdom and to restore Jerusalem. He is! But first comes the tribulation.

Which Jews will survive the tribulation? Will the Holy Spirit come upon those Jews that do survive the tribulation? What is the Holy Spirit except the Spirit that Jesus said He would ask the Father to send following His ascension? Will the Jews who survive the tribulation think of themselves as "Christians" and thus enter into salvation? That does not seem to be the scenario.

The term Christians means followers of Jesus Christ. In scripture they are referred to as the "body of believers," the Church. Believers are those who the scriptures say will have, by the Grace of God, through faith, received eternal salvation. There is no controversy among New Testament scholars as to whether the Body of Believers, the Church, will have been raptured at some point prior to the battle of Armageddon.

The Church includes those individuals (not persons identified as members of some particular organization) who have received the gift of the Holy Spirit. It is more likely that the Jews surviving the tribulation will think of themselves as Jews, obedient to God during this terrible time. They will not have taken the mark of the beast and their faithfulness will be counted unto them for righteousness, just as it was with Abraham. I pray that you personally, in failing to accept the Messiah now, have the faith to endure the persecution you are about to experience.

By now, you may be asking, what is the true motive behind your writing this book? Aside from the "warning and pointing," referred to earlier, there are two additional reasons I am writing this book. First, I pray that you receive the gift of eternal life right now, by accepting Jesus Christ as the Messiah, your personal Savior and that you accept the cleansing that entails. That cleansing, that renewal of a right relationship with the Father, is made possible by the sacrifice of Jesus, wherein your sins are as "separate from you from the east is from the west," never to be remembered against you again.

If that is your desire, confess your sins to Jesus, ask for forgiveness, thank Jesus for taking your sins from you by the shedding of His blood, ask to be filled with the Holy Spirit, and seek a moment by moment relationship with Him every day, and be obedient and faithful to His Word.

The second reason is, if you decide not to act on the first reason, at least understand that what lies ahead is both glorious and frightening. It will only be glorious if you choose to obey God during this upcoming period of severe persecution and punishment. Only your personal faith in God will provide you with the strength, His strength, to endure. It is frightening because of what will be required of you if you refuse to accept the mark of the beast, your only means of proving your faithfulness when that moment in time occurs.

Now, listen to Isaiah and allow for the possibility that the Old Testament prophecies applied to a people and times of the past and to a people and times of the future, simultaneously. You will have to arrive at that point anyway with some yet unfulfilled prophecy, but if understanding the

Word of God was entirely that simple, why, for centuries have we lived in darkness? The scriptures say "God has given them a spirit of stupor, eyes that they should not see and ears that they should not hear, to this very day." But listen to what Isaiah says about the Light of Israel.

Isaiah 10:17-22 (NKJ)
17 So the Light of Israel will be for a fire, and his Holy One for a flame; it will burn and devour his thorns and his briers in one day.
18 And it will consume the glory of his forest and of his fruitful field, both soul and body; and they will be as when a sick man wastes away.
19 Then the rest of the trees of his forest will be so few in number that a child may write them.
20 And it shall come to pass in that day that the remnant of Israel, and such as have escaped of the house of Jacob, will never again depend on him who defeated them, but will depend on the LORD, the Holy One of Israel, in truth.
21 The remnant will return, the remnant of Jacob, to the Mighty God.
22 For though your people, O Israel, be as the sand of the sea, a remnant of them will return; the destruction decreed shall overflow with righteousness.

The Light of Israel, His Holy One, I say the Messiah, Jesus Christ, will burn and consume in one day, the thorns and briers, the fruitful field, both soul and body and there will be so few left that even a child may "write them." Notice that the "destruction decreed shall overflow with righteousness." Whose righteousness? Not yours and not mine. It is God who is righteous and our faith in Him shall cause Israel to be "overflowing" with righteousness, even during the great destruction. Righteousness is an attitude, a cloak of salvation that will envelop you during this time of tribulation. Your heart will be at peace because of His righteousness in you.

Then Ezra makes it clear that even the remnant stands before God in guilt, needing a redeemer. If you retain your guilt, you cannot attain His righteousness.

Ezra 9:15 (NKJ)
15 "O LORD God of Israel, You are righteous, for we are left as a remnant, as it is this day. Here we are before You, in our guilt, though no one can stand before You because of this!"

No man can stand before God because of his guilt. The scripture says God hates sin, it grieves Him when His children sin. Does it grieve you when your children sin? Of course it does. It also says every man has sinned. None is "righteous," no not one. Every name is written either in the Book of Life or in "other books." Your soul, your spirit is being sustained, awaiting judgment. Listen.

Revelation 20:12 (NKJ)
12 And I saw the dead, small and great, standing before God, and books were opened. And another book was opened, which is the Book of Life. And the dead were judged according to their works, by the things which were written in the books.

The Book of Life is defined in this verse.

Revelation 3:5 (NKJ)
5 "He who overcomes shall be clothed in white garments, and I will not blot out his name from the Book of Life; but I will confess his name before My Father and before His angels.

These are great teachings from His scriptures. It implies, and this is broadly supported in scriptures, that every name, including yours and mine, is in the Book of Life. How else could it be blotted out, except that it be there first? It is God's will that every man be saved, that none perish. It states that those who "overcome" will be clothed in white garments. Listen to a description of one group of "overcomers" and what will have happened to them.

Revelation 20:4 (NKJ)
4 And I saw thrones, and they sat on them, and judgment was committed to them. Then I saw the souls of those who had been beheaded for their witness to Jesus and for the word of God, who had not worshiped the

beast or his image, and had not received his mark on their foreheads or on their hands. And they lived and reigned with Christ for a thousand years.

During the tribulation, your personal sacrifice, at the hands of God's enemy, will be the price you pay as you seek to obey God, provided that you understand that there is not one thing you can do to earn salvation except to be obedient to God, and to, by grace, accept His gift of life. Stated another way, even the sacrifice of your physical body must be a decision you make that is based upon faith and obedience to the Father, not some macho "I can take anything you can dish out," attitude.

I used the word "enemy" in the singular, because there is only one enemy that you cannot, in your own strength, ever overcome. Satan is the enemy, the fallen angel who is the ruler of this world. Understand that from the day that Adam sinned until now, man's heart is on a "default" setting. We are born with a heart of flesh. We serve that heart our entire lives unless we are able, not in our own power, but by the grace of God, to have a new heart.

You cannot, in and of yourself, overcome the desires of the flesh. Those desires will overcome you, again and again. God provided relief that only He could have envisioned and delivered. He sent the Messiah to provide a means for us to have a new heart, one that is first broken, then replaced. If one does not, by absolute contrition understand how fruitless it is to seek to be like God, absent the empowerment of the Holy Spirit, that one is destined to die in their pride.

Yes, we should work hard, study, contribute and share in the bounty of this world, but this world is perishing and all the bounty and bodies with it. Life must be about more than what you can do during your three score and ten allotments, if it is to be "redemptive;" or else, all really is vanity. Death is the victor and your achievements, trophies, assets and "record" will soon perish. If you think life is about a physical life only, your God either does not exist or is so infinitesimally small as to be of no consequence. Our physical bodies are finite. If you don't think this is true, then listen to the comment of the thief on the cross and the response of the Messiah.

Then one of the criminals who were hanged blasphemed Him, saying, "If You are the Christ, save Yourself and us."

But the other, answering, rebuked him, saying, "Do you not even fear God, seeing you are under the same condemnation? And we indeed justly, for we receive the due reward of our deeds; but this Man has done nothing wrong." Then he said to Jesus, "Lord, remember me when You come into Your kingdom." And Jesus said to him, "Assuredly, I say to you, today you will be with Me in Paradise." Luke 23:39-43 NKJV

Notice that Jesus said to the man being condemned, you will be in Paradise, not someday; He said, "today".

The only victory you have over the grave is the spiritual victory made accessible by the Holy Father who sent His only begotten Son to redeem you and me. But the choice remains yours, right up until your last breath.

I have often wondered what the greatest single cause of failure is, as men seek to obey God. I will estimate that "pride" is the answer. It seems, especially after reading Solomon's writings. We strive to attain, to possess, to control, to satisfy our physical needs, in vain. After all of the "trying" comes the end and the end is not a pretty sight. I would remind you of what happens to our physical bodies but it is just too gross.

Does man have to be "at the end of his rope" either in age or in circumstance to finally recognize that life is vanity when lived as if "that is all there is?"

The sacrifice of your life, during the tribulation, if that is required of you, as you stand steadfast in the declaration of your faith, will be an act of incomparable faith and obedience. Are you capable of that kind of faith? Do you have the strength to endure this test? The answer is yes, at least in some cases, but why would one do that? In hope, in hope that God will honor their faith, that God really exists, that there is a heaven and that life is eternal to those whom "obey." But obedience to death is a large order. Not so large, again, that you can't handle it, in the strength of God, but an ordeal that God foresaw.

God sent His only begotten Son, Jesus, to provide a means of escape, that you might be able to bear the pain of temptation, that you might depend on the power of the Holy Spirit in getting through the dilemmas that life in the flesh presents. Listen please. The redeeming blood of Jesus, the Messiah, was a foreordained condition for the "final" sacrifice, at least final in the sense that any future sacrifices are offerings of gifts of righteousness, not for the forgiveness of sin. The perfect redemptive power of the sacrifice of Jesus, the sinless Lamb of God, sets aside any further pursuit of sacrifice aimed at cleansing yourself of sin. Otherwise, Jesus gave His life for nothing.

If we seek "another way" to redeem our souls, we make a mockery of God's plan of redemption. For instance, does anyone think the blood of bulls or goats can redeem a soul? Do you believe that great financial gifts to honorable causes or the dedication of one's life to serving God can secure your redemption? Of course not. If those acts could redeem you, again Jesus went to the cross for nothing. If you ignore God's gift of redemption, what gift will you offer? Even the gift of your sinful self, as an act of contrition, done in faith, pales by comparison with the Gift of God. If we try to circumvent the shed blood of Jesus, who knew no sin, then the Messiah is not yet our Redeemer. Every dedicated Jew believes God will provide a Redeemer, a perfect, unblemished sacrifice.

It is a fundamental scriptural truth that without the shedding of blood there is no remission of sin. The only sacrifice that is going to matter is the One that permanently cleanses you, wherein you have triumph over sin by the power of the Holy Spirit and by your faith in the eternal love and grace of God.

Hebrews 9:22 (NKJ)
22 And according to the law almost all things are purified with blood, and without shedding of blood there is no remission.

Isaiah 48:17-18 (NKJ)
17 Thus says the LORD, your Redeemer, the Holy One of Israel: "I am the LORD your God, who teaches you to profit, who leads you by the way you should go.

18 Oh, that you had heeded My commandments! Then your peace would have been like a river, and your righteousness like the waves of the sea.

Following the period of great tribulation, there will be 144,000 Jewish martyrs who will have been beheaded for asserting their faith in God and refusing the mark of the beast. There will be a multitude without number who will stand in white robes with them, in God's eternal kingdom. Listen.

Revelation 7:1-17 (NKJ)
1 After these things I saw four angels standing at the four corners of the earth, holding the four winds of the earth, that the wind should not blow on the earth, on the sea, or on any tree.
2 Then I saw another angel ascending from the east, having the seal of the living God. And he cried with a loud voice to the four angels to whom it was granted to harm the earth and the sea,
3 saying, "Do not harm the earth, the sea, or the trees till we have sealed the servants of our God on their foreheads."
4 And I heard the number of those who were sealed. One hundred and forty-four thousand of all the tribes of the children of Israel were sealed:
5 of the tribe of Judah twelve thousand were sealed; of the tribe of Reuben twelve thousand were sealed; of the tribe of Gad twelve thousand were sealed;
6 of the tribe of Asher twelve thousand were sealed; of the tribe of Naphtali twelve thousand were sealed; of the tribe of Manasseh twelve thousand were sealed;
7 of the tribe of Simeon twelve thousand were sealed; of the tribe of Levi twelve thousand were sealed; of the tribe of Issachar twelve thousand were sealed;
8 of the tribe of Zebulun twelve thousand were sealed; of the tribe of Joseph twelve thousand were sealed; of the tribe of Benjamin twelve thousand were sealed.
9 After these things I looked, and behold, a great multitude which no one could number, of all nations, tribes, peoples, and tongues, standing before the throne and before the Lamb, clothed with white robes, with palm branches in their hands,
10 and crying out with a loud voice, saying, "Salvation belongs to our God who sits on the throne, and to the Lamb!"

11 All the angels stood around the throne and the elders and the four living creatures, and fell on their faces before the throne and worshiped God,
12 saying: "Amen! Blessing and glory and wisdom, thanksgiving and honor and power and might, be to our God forever and ever. Amen."
13 Then one of the elders answered, saying to me, "Who are these arrayed in white robes, and where did they come from?"
14 And I said to him, "Sir, you know." So he said to me, "These are the ones who come out of the great tribulation, and washed their robes and made them white in the blood of the Lamb.
15 "Therefore they are before the throne of God, and serve Him day and night in His temple. And He who sits on the throne will dwell among them.
16 "They shall neither hunger anymore nor thirst anymore; the sun shall not strike them, nor any heat;
17 "for the Lamb who is in the midst of the throne will shepherd them and lead them to living fountains of waters. And God will wipe away every tear from their eyes."

Notice it says, "These are the ones who come out of the great tribulation, and washed their robes and made them white in the blood of the Lamb." Therefore they are before the throne of God…

Know that the "therefore" that places them before the throne of God, is based upon their having been washed in the blood of the Lamb. If you miss that point, you miss the entire basis of your being able to stand before God. Neither you nor I will ever stand in the presence of God on the basis of our worthiness. Our righteousness is as filthy rags. Only the blood of the sinless Lamb, the Son of God, can make us worthy. We stand in His presence because of His righteousness and mercy. We do not stand there based on our merit.

I have always want to ask a Jewish friend, "would you like to be judged by the Law?" I know that I do not want to be judged by the Law. The Law chronicles our sins. It is the straight edge by which we can be measured. The scriptures teach that if you are guilty of breaking even the smallest of the Laws, you are guilty of breaking the whole Law. No, we do not want to be judged by the Law. We much prefer to receive mercy, not judgment. The scriptures say that "Mercy triumphs over judgment." Thank our Holy Father that is true.

The scriptures teach that there is a 1000-year period in which the kingdom will be restored here on earth. Verse 15, above, is a Millennium scenario where God's people serve Him "day and night" (thus this verse does not refer heaven where there is no day and night) and in verse 16 the scene moves on to eternal heaven where there is no sun, only the light of the Lord. Some will argue that you can't jump in and out of scenarios that way, but if you have read the scriptures, you find prophecy does exactly that. Everything is not in a "straight line," but everything fits.

God's truth is neither contradictory nor false. Literalism is a very narrow place in which to stand but which of you would like the responsibility of saying "God did not mean what He said?" Once you start down that path, instead of "believing" and seeking discernment, you end up "interpreting" and laying man's limited thinking on the analysis of the truth. God sums it up for us when He says,

Isaiah 55:1-13 (NKJ)
1 "Ho! Everyone who thirsts, come to the waters; and you who have no money, come, buy and eat. Yes, come, buy wine and milk without money and without price.
2 Why do you spend money for what is not bread, and your wages for what does not satisfy? Listen carefully to Me, and eat what is good, and let your soul delight itself in abundance.
3 Incline your ear, and come to Me. Hear, and your soul shall live; and I will make an everlasting covenant with you– the sure mercies of David.
4 Indeed I have given him as a witness to the people, a leader and commander for the people.
5 Surely you shall call a nation you do not know, and nations who do not know you shall run to you, because of the LORD your God, and the Holy One of Israel; for He has glorified you."
6 Seek the LORD while He may be found, call upon Him while He is near.

7 Let the wicked forsake his way, and the unrighteous man his thoughts; let him return to the LORD, and He will have mercy on him; and to our God, for He will abundantly pardon.
8 "For My thoughts are not your thoughts, nor are your ways My ways," says the LORD.
9 "For as the heavens are higher than the earth, so are My ways higher than your ways, and My thoughts than your thoughts.
10 "For as the rain comes down, and the snow from heaven, and do not return there, but water the earth, and make it bring forth and bud, that it may give seed to the sower and bread to the eater,
11 So shall My word be that goes forth from My mouth; it shall not return to Me void, but it shall accomplish what I please, and it shall prosper in the thing for which I sent it.
12 "For you shall go out with joy, and be led out with peace; the mountains and the hills shall break forth into singing before you, and all the trees of the field shall clap their hands.
13 Instead of the thorn shall come up the cypress tree, and instead of the brier shall come up the myrtle tree; and it shall be to the LORD for a name, for an everlasting sign that shall not be cut off."

Daniel 10:21 (NKJ)
Daniel said, "But I will tell you what is noted in the Scripture of Truth."

Jesus, in responding to those who doubted He was the Messiah, said "the scripture can not be broken." I believe the reason that people who take the Scriptures "literally" are willing to get chastised so often is that they take this quotation by Jesus very seriously. We may not understand what was said or what was meant by what was said, but that does not make it false. It simply means we don't understand everything all the time. Here is the context in which Jesus made that statement.

John 10:22-38 (NKJ)
22 Now it was the Feast of Dedication in Jerusalem, and it was winter.
23 And Jesus walked in the temple, in Solomon's porch.
24 Then the Jews surrounded Him and said to Him, "How long do You keep us in doubt? If You are the Christ, tell us plainly."

25 Jesus answered them, "I told you, and you do not believe. The works that I do in My Father's name, they bear witness of Me.

26 "But you do not believe, because you are not of My sheep, as I said to you.

27 "My sheep hear My voice, and I know them, and they follow Me.

28 "And I give them eternal life, and they shall never perish; neither shall anyone snatch them out of My hand.

29 "My Father, who has given them to Me, is greater than all; and no one is able to snatch them out of My Father's hand.

30 "I and My Father are one."

31 Then the Jews took up stones again to stone Him.

32 Jesus answered them, "Many good works I have shown you from My Father. For which of those works do you stone Me?"

33 The Jews answered Him, saying, "For a good work we do not stone You, but for blasphemy, and because You, being a Man, make Yourself God."

34 Jesus answered them, "Is it not written in your law, 'I said, "You are gods" '?

35 "If He called them gods, to whom the word of God came (and the Scripture cannot be broken),

36 "do you say of Him whom the Father sanctified and sent into the world, 'You are blaspheming,' because I said, 'I am the Son of God'?

37 "If I do not do the works of My Father, do not believe Me;

38 "but if I do, though you do not believe Me, believe the works, that you may know and believe that the Father is in Me, and I in Him."

Here, in this next quotation, the apostle Peter offers a very important teaching about the interpretation of scripture. After reading this, consider laying this presentation aside, which is only a hint of the breadth of God's Word, and take up His Word with all urgency, storing it in your heart. Seek His Face, His Holy Presence, His Wisdom and His Guidance now, before another day passes. Here is what Peter said about interpreting prophecy.

2 Peter 1:16-21 (NKJ)

16 For we did not follow cunningly devised fables when we made known to you the power and coming of our Lord Jesus Christ, but were eyewitnesses of His majesty.

17 For He received from God the Father honor and glory when such a voice came to Him from the Excellent Glory: "This is My beloved Son, in whom I am well pleased."
18 And we heard this voice which came from heaven when we were with Him on the holy mountain.
19 And so we have the prophetic word confirmed, which you do well to heed as a light that shines in a dark place, until the day dawns and the morning star rises in your hearts;
20 knowing this first, that no prophecy of Scripture is of any private interpretation,
21 for prophecy never came by the will of man, but holy men of God spoke as they were moved by the Holy Spirit.

I realize this is a lot of reading, but if you can't wade through what seems like a lot, how will you ever get through the Bible? When the Messiah returns there will be no time to "catch up." Do everything you can, right now, to equip yourself for the moment in time where you will meet Him face to face. I can personally relate to the following verses.

Psalm 119:123 (NKJ)
123 My eyes fail from seeking Your salvation and Your righteous word.

Psalm 119:81-82 (NKJ)
81 My soul faints for Your salvation, but I hope in Your word.
82 My eyes fail from searching Your word, saying, "When will You comfort me?"

Psalm 130:5-6 (NKJ)
5 I wait for the LORD, my soul waits, and in His word I do hope.
6 My soul waits for the Lord more than those who watch for the morning– yes, more than those who watch for the morning.

Psalm 143:8 (NKJ)
8 Cause me to hear Your loving kindness in the morning, for in You do I trust; cause me to know the way in which I should walk, for I lift up my soul to You.

Seeking God may take on many forms, but I do not know how you can anticipate standing before your Maker without having "listened intently" to Him. Could a person spend a lifetime in pursuit of knowledge, power, wealth and fame and have missed the opportunity to have God speak, directly to him? Of course you could avoid listening to God but why listen to the words of mere men? To whom do you listen all day? We are "choosing" to be an audience to someone or something. Time is running very short. Seek Him now. What else is more important? Certainly not a ball game, your garden, a good novel, or whatever else has your attention.

The scriptures say that the greatest commandment is to love God with all your heart, mind, soul and strength. How does your love manifest itself? It is excellent to love your neighbor as yourself. That is the second greatest commandment, but don't miss number one as you pursue number two. The first great commandment, a summary of the first 4 of the 10 commandments, is "Love God with all your heart, mind, soul and strength." This is the enabling commandment that makes the second 6 commandments (love toward others) "work," to the glory of God. If you simply pursue the last 6 commandments, you will have done well, but not well enough, according to scripture.

There is no redemptive power in good deeds. If you fail to understand that fact, you fail to understand why any sacrificial law was ever instituted or why the Messiah had to suffer and die for our sins. If one could "earn" their salvation by good deeds, neither faith nor sacrifice would be required. Your love for the Father, the Son and the Holy Spirit and your understanding of the redemptive power of the Messiah and the enabling power of the Holy Spirit equip you to serve Him as you serve others.

True love will require "forgiveness" every time. Not one of us is perfect and the love that we extend to others, if it is to be truly genuine, ignores the unrighteousness, on occasion, of the recipient. When each of us reflects on our own past sins (and all sin is of equal importance before God, there is no hierarchy of sin) we know that if God can forgive us, by the shed blood of Jesus, then He can forgive everyone else too. The scriptures say that "if you say you love God but you say you hate your brother, you are a liar and the truth is not in you."

Loving the unlovely and the unlovable is only possible when you see in them, the image of God. You know that you were created in the image of God and so was every person. God would that no man perish and He expects we who have been cleansed and forgiven to convey His message of salvation. Listen.

2 Peter 3:9 (NKJ)
9 The Lord is not slack concerning His promise, as some count slackness, but is longsuffering toward us, not willing that any should perish but that all should come to repentance.

That sentence could not be more clear. Repentance is the key to life. No repentance, no forgiveness; No repentance, no empowerment by the Holy Spirit. Repentance is the step you take in response to God's invitation to enter into His Holy Presence.

Isaiah 57:15 (NKJ)
15 For thus says the High and Lofty One who inhabits eternity, whose name is Holy: "I dwell in the high and holy place, with him who has a contrite and humble spirit, to revive the spirit of the humble, and to revive the heart of the contrite ones.

I pray that my Jewish friends take solace in the fact that only some of their ancestors missed recognizing the Messiah. A great many Jews knew that Jesus Christ was the promised Messiah. The New Testament that we have is largely a record prepared by and preserved by the Jews. The Messiah was a Jew, sent by God. God said the following words to the prophet Isaiah, some 700 years before the birth of the Messiah, His Elect one. Read this and Chapter 53 of Isaiah and ask your self, "Who could this be but the Messiah?"

Isaiah 42:1-9 (NKJ)
1 "Behold! My Servant whom I uphold, my Elect One in whom My soul delights! I have put My Spirit upon Him; he will bring forth justice to the Gentiles.
2 He will not cry out, nor raise His voice, nor cause His voice to be heard in the street.

3 A bruised reed He will not break, and smoking flax He will not quench; he will bring forth justice for truth.
4 He will not fail nor be discouraged, till He has established justice in the earth; and the coastlands shall wait for His law."
5 Thus says God the LORD, who created the heavens and stretched them out, who spread forth the earth and that which comes from it, who gives breath to the people on it, and spirit to those who walk on it:
6 "I, the LORD, have called You in righteousness, and will hold Your hand; I will keep You and give You as a covenant to the people, as a light to the Gentiles,
7 To open blind eyes, to bring out prisoners from the prison, those who sit in darkness from the prison house.
8 I am the LORD, that is My name; and My glory I will not give to another, nor My praise to graven images.
9 Behold, the former things have come to pass, and new things I declare; before they spring forth I tell you of them."

God has taken steps to reveal Himself to us in so many unmistakable ways. Prophecy is one way, miracles are another. How in the light of fulfilled prophecy could one doubt? How could men watch a miracle of God, performed before their very eyes, and then return to their sin?

Here is one answer.

Jeremiah 17:9-10 (NKJ)
9 "The heart is deceitful above all things, and desperately wicked; who can know it?
10 I search the heart, I test the mind, even to give every man according to his ways, according to the fruit of his doings.

The heart that is deceitful and wicked is the heart of man. God wants to give you a new heart.

Jeremiah 24:6-7 (NKJ)
6 'For I will set My eyes on them for good, and I will bring them back to this land; I will build them and not pull them down, and I will plant them and not pluck them up.

7 'Then I will give them a heart to know Me, that I am the LORD; and they shall be My people, and I will be their God, for they shall return to Me with their whole heart.

A "new heart" is a gift from God. Perhaps my favorite verse in the entire Bible, written by Paul, a devout Jew, is embodied in this quotation.

Galatians 2:19-21 (NKJ)
19 ...I through the law died to the law that I might live to God.
20 "I have been crucified with Christ; it is no longer I who live, but Christ lives in me; and the life which I now live in the flesh I live by faith in the Son of God, who loved me and gave Himself for me.
21 "I do not set aside the grace of God; for if righteousness comes through the law, then Christ died in vain."

I write to you, not in my righteousness, but His. When you can say I live, yet not I, but Christ lives in me, you are able to draw upon His unending reserve of grace and mercy and to thereby witness the crucifixion of your own flesh. Listen again.

"I have been crucified with Christ; it is no longer I who live, but Christ lives in me;"

This leaves no room for pride. There is plenty of room for joy, which I must admit sometimes appears self indulgent, but again, if Christ is going to bless you and use you, rejoice, not in your own accomplishments but in being His servant.

CHAPTER 11

THE RAPTURE OF THE "BODY OF BELIEVERS"

A Clear Signal You Must Not Miss

What will be one of the most visible signs of the Messiahs coming? Most Biblical students agree that the Book of Daniel teaches that there will be a period known as the tribulation period in which the Antichrist, the prince of the earth, will reign for 7 years. Then the Messiah, the Prince, shall come. Listen to Daniel's prophecy.

Daniel 9:24-27 (NKJ)
24 "Seventy weeks are determined for your people and for your holy city, to finish the transgression, to make an end of sins, to make reconciliation for iniquity, to bring in everlasting righteousness, to seal up vision and prophecy, and to anoint the Most Holy.
25 "Know therefore and understand, that from the going forth of the command to restore and build Jerusalem until Messiah the Prince, there shall be seven weeks and sixty-two weeks; the street shall be built again, and the wall, even in troublesome times.
26 "And after the sixty-two weeks Messiah shall be cut off, but not for Himself; and the people of the prince who is to come shall destroy the city and the sanctuary. The end of it shall be with a flood, and till the end of the war desolations are determined.
27 Then he shall confirm a covenant with many for one week; but in the middle of the week he shall bring an end to sacrifice and offering. And

on the wing of abominations shall be one who makes desolate, even until the consummation, which is determined, is poured out on the desolate."

The final seven weeks in verse 25 (read as 7 years) are referred to as the Great Tribulation. Most also agree that this 7-year period will probably be preceded by the rapture of the "Church," the body of believers. (I capitalize "Church," not because it ranks with the Deity, but because there is only one Church although there are many churches). Listen to the words of Jesus as He taught his disciples what was going to happen.

Luke 17:34-37 (NKJ)
34 "I tell you, in that night there will be two men in one bed: the one will be taken and the other will be left.
35 "Two women will be grinding together: the one will be taken and the other left.
36 "Two men will be in the field: the one will be taken and the other left."
37 And they answered and said to Him, "Where, Lord?" So He said to them, "Wherever the body is, there the eagles will be gathered together."

The question is not "whether the Church will be raptured," but exactly when it will occur. Listen to God's word regarding when it will occur.

Matthew 24:42 (NKJ)
42 "Watch therefore, for you do not know what hour your Lord is coming.

The answer to when the Church will be raptured is "you do not know." Now the apostle Paul explains both the rapture and the resurrection of the dead in more detail.

1 Corinthians 15:35-57 (NKJ)
35 But someone will say, "How are the dead raised up? And with what body do they come?"
36 Foolish one, what you sow is not made alive unless it dies.
37 And what you sow, you do not sow that body that shall be, but mere grain– perhaps wheat or some other grain.
38 But God gives it a body as He pleases, and to each seed its own body.

39 All flesh is not the same flesh, but there is one kind of flesh of men, another flesh of beasts, another of fish, and another of birds.
40 There are also celestial bodies and terrestrial bodies; but the glory of the celestial is one, and the glory of the terrestrial is another.
41 There is one glory of the sun, another glory of the moon, and another glory of the stars; for one star differs from another star in glory.
42 So also is the resurrection of the dead. The body is sown in corruption, it is raised in incorruption.
43 It is sown in dishonor, it is raised in glory. It is sown in weakness, it is raised in power.
44 It is sown a natural body, it is raised a spiritual body. There is a natural body, and there is a spiritual body.
45 And so it is written, "The first man Adam became a living being." The last Adam became a life-giving spirit.
46 However, the spiritual is not first, but the natural, and afterward the spiritual.
47 The first man was of the earth, made of dust; the second Man is the Lord from heaven.
48 As was the man of dust, so also are those who are made of dust; and as is the heavenly Man, so also are those who are heavenly.
49 And as we have borne the image of the man of dust, we shall also bear the image of the heavenly Man.
50 Now this I say, brethren, that flesh and blood cannot inherit the kingdom of God; nor does corruption inherit incorruption.
51 Behold, I tell you a mystery: We shall not all sleep, but we shall all be changed–
52 in a moment, in the twinkling of an eye, at the last trumpet. For the trumpet will sound, and the dead will be raised incorruptible, and we shall be changed.
53 For this corruptible must put on incorruption, and this mortal must put on immortality.
54 So when this corruptible has put on incorruption, and this mortal has put on immortality, then shall be brought to pass the saying that is written: "Death is swallowed up in victory."
55 "O Death, where is your sting? O Hades, where is your victory?"
56 The sting of death is sin, and the strength of sin is the law.

57 But thanks be to God, who gives us the victory through our Lord Jesus Christ.

Paul, in a different letter, makes the same point again.

1 Thessalonians 4:13-17 (NKJ)
13 But I do not want you to be ignorant, brethren, concerning those who have fallen asleep, lest you sorrow as others who have no hope.
14 For if we believe that Jesus died and rose again, even so God will bring with Him those who sleep in Jesus.
15 For this we say to you by the word of the Lord, that we who are alive and remain until the coming of the Lord will by no means precede those who are asleep.
16 For the Lord Himself will descend from heaven with a shout, with the voice of an archangel, and with the trumpet of God. And the dead in Christ will rise first.
17 Then we who are alive and remain shall be caught up together with them in the clouds to meet the Lord in the air. And thus we shall always be with the Lord.

1 Thessalonians 5:1-2 (NKJ)
1 But concerning the times and the seasons, brethren, you have no need that I should write to you.
2 For you yourselves know perfectly that the day of the Lord so comes as a thief in the night.

These verses describe the circumstance of the resurrection of the Body of Believers who have died and the rapture of those believers who are alive when the trumpet sounds. When one is taken and the other is left, the one taken will have confessed their faith in Jesus Christ as their personal Redeemer and they will by the grace of God have entered into a saving relationship with Him.

There are other instances in the Bible in which individuals have been taken up to be with the Lord. Listen.

2 Kings 2:1-12 (NKJ)

1 And it came to pass, when the LORD was about to take up Elijah into heaven by a whirlwind, that Elijah went with Elisha from Gilgal.

2 Then Elijah said to Elisha, "Stay here, please, for the LORD has sent me on to Bethel." But Elisha said, "As the LORD lives, and as your soul lives, I will not leave you!" So they went down to Bethel.

3 Now the sons of the prophets who were at Bethel came out to Elisha, and said to him, "Do you know that the LORD will take away your master from over you today?" And he said, "Yes, I know; keep silent!"

4 Then Elijah said to him, "Elisha, stay here, please, for the LORD has sent me on to Jericho." But he said, "As the LORD lives, and as your soul lives, I will not leave you!" So they came to Jericho.

5 Now the sons of the prophets who were at Jericho came to Elisha and said to him, "Do you know that the LORD will take away your master from over you today?" So he answered, "Yes, I know; keep silent!"

6 Then Elijah said to him, "Stay here, please, for the LORD has sent me on to the Jordan." But he said, "As the LORD lives, and as your soul lives, I will not leave you!" So the two of them went on.

7 And fifty men of the sons of the prophets went and stood facing them at a distance, while the two of them stood by the Jordan.

8 Now Elijah took his mantle, rolled it up, and struck the water; and it was divided this way and that, so that the two of them crossed over on dry ground.

9 And so it was, when they had crossed over, that Elijah said to Elisha, "Ask! What may I do for you, before I am taken away from you?" Elisha said, "Please let a double portion of your spirit be upon me."

10 So he said, "You have asked a hard thing. Nevertheless, if you see me when I am taken from you, it shall be so for you; but if not, it shall not be so."

11 Then it happened, as they continued on and talked, that suddenly a chariot of fire appeared with horses of fire, and separated the two of them; and Elijah went up by a whirlwind into heaven.

12 And Elisha saw it, and he cried out, "My father, my father, the chariot of Israel and its horsemen!" So he saw him no more…

When you read the letters of Paul, you are amazed at his wisdom and insight. Read this excerpt and understand why Paul had insights into God's will for our lives.

2 Corinthians 12:2-5 (NKJ)
2 I know a man in Christ who fourteen years ago– whether in the body I do not know, or whether out of the body I do not know, God knows– such a one was caught up to the third heaven.
3 And I know such a man– whether in the body or out of the body I do not know, God knows–
4 how he was caught up into Paradise and heard inexpressible words, which it is not lawful for a man to utter.
5 Of such a one I will boast; yet of myself I will not boast, except in my infirmities.

Paul was speaking of himself. He was caught up into Paradise and heard inexpressible words. Is it any wonder that God used him in such a powerful way?

Another rapture of believers is prophesied. We will study more thoroughly the topic "two witnesses" who die during the tribulation and are raised again at the end of the tribulation. Listen to the account of their ministry.

Revelation 11:3-12 (NKJ)
3 "And I will give power to my two witnesses, and they will prophesy one thousand two hundred and sixty days, clothed in sackcloth."
4 These are the two olive trees and the two lampstands standing before the God of the earth.
5 And if anyone wants to harm them, fire proceeds from their mouth and devours their enemies. And if anyone wants to harm them, he must be killed in this manner.
6 These have power to shut heaven, so that no rain falls in the days of their prophecy; and they have power over waters to turn them to blood, and to strike the earth with all plagues, as often as they desire.
7 Now when they finish their testimony, the beast that ascends out of the bottomless pit will make war against them, overcome them, and kill them.

8 And their dead bodies will lie in the street of the great city which spiritually is called Sodom and Egypt, where also our Lord was crucified.
9 Then those from the peoples, tribes, tongues, and nations will see their dead bodies three-and-a-half days, and not allow their dead bodies to be put into graves.
10 And those who dwell on the earth will rejoice over them, make merry, and send gifts to one another, because these two prophets tormented those who dwell on the earth.
11 Now after the three-and-a-half days the breath of life from God entered them, and they stood on their feet, and great fear fell on those who saw them.
12 And they heard a loud voice from heaven saying to them, "Come up here." And they ascended to heaven in a cloud, and their enemies saw them.

"They ascended to heaven in a cloud." That is a "rapture" event. The single event that was of most significance to believers is the rapture of our Lord and Savior. Listen to the account of His ascendancy to heaven.

Acts 1:7-11 (NKJ)
7 And He said to them, "It is not for you to know times or seasons which the Father has put in His own authority.
8 "But you shall receive power when the Holy Spirit has come upon you; and you shall be witnesses to Me in Jerusalem, and in all Judea and Samaria, and to the end of the earth."
9 Now when He had spoken these things, while they watched, He was taken up, and a cloud received Him out of their sight.
10 And while they looked steadfastly toward heaven as He went up, behold, two men stood by them in white apparel,
11 who also said, "Men of Galilee, why do you stand gazing up into heaven? This same Jesus, who was taken up from you into heaven, will so come in like manner as you saw Him go into heaven."

When some are taken up into heaven, what about those that are left? Let's focus on "not being left." What must one do to be assured of ascendancy? The choice is a personal one, made independently by each person. Salvation is not a "team" effort. Your record is "yours." Listen to the Scriptures about how personal the choice is and where the responsibility lies.

1 Chronicles 28:9 (NKJ)
9 "As for you, my son Solomon, know the God of your father, and serve Him with a loyal heart and with a willing mind; for the LORD searches all hearts and understands all the intent of the thoughts. If you seek Him, He will be found by you; but if you forsake Him, He will cast you off forever.

2 Chronicles 15:1-2 (NKJ)
1 Now the Spirit of God came upon Azariah the son of Oded.
2 ..."Hear me, Asa, and all Judah and Benjamin. The LORD is with you while you are with Him. If you seek Him, He will be found by you; but if you forsake Him, He will forsake you.

Psalm 73:27-28 (NKJ)
27 For indeed, those who are far from You shall perish; you have destroyed all those who desert You for harlotry.
28 But it is good for me to draw near to God; I have put my trust in the Lord GOD, that I may declare all Your works.

Psalm 145:17-19 (NKJ)
17 The LORD is righteous in all His ways, gracious in all His works.
18 The LORD is near to all who call upon Him, to all who call upon Him in truth.
19 He will fulfill the desire of those who fear Him; he also will hear their cry and save them.

Isaiah 55:6-9 (NKJ)
6 Seek the LORD while He may be found, call upon Him while He is near.
7 Let the wicked forsake his way, and the unrighteous man his thoughts; let him return to the LORD, and He will have mercy on him; and to our God, for He will abundantly pardon.
8 "For My thoughts are not your thoughts, nor are your ways My ways," says the LORD.

9 "For as the heavens are higher than the earth, so are My ways higher than your ways, and My thoughts than your thoughts.

Hosea 6:1 (NKJ)
1 Come, and let us return to the LORD; for He has torn, but He will heal us; He has stricken, but He will bind us up.

There are going to be some very surprised "Christians," I suspect, when the rapture of the Body of Believers, the true Church, occurs. Why? They will be surprised because they have mistakenly relied upon "membership in a local church" and all of the busy activities of the church as a means to salvation. These are very good people, in terms of morals and attitudes, usually, but their comfort is in "ritual" and their personal relationship with the Father, Son and Holy Spirit is either non-existent or impotent.

If it is non-existent, then they simply have mistaken church membership, attendance, participation, tithes and offerings as acts of "merit" which will be rewarded. If it is impotent, then their lives simply do not bear "fruit." They are like the fig tree that takes up space but yields nothing or worse yet they say they are a fig tree and yet, their life yields olives. Listen very carefully to the word of God.

Matthew 7:13-29 (NKJ)
13 "Enter by the narrow gate; for wide is the gate and broad is the way that leads to destruction, and there are many who go in by it."
14 "Because narrow is the gate and difficult is the way which leads to life, and there are few who find it.
15 "Beware of false prophets, who come to you in sheep's clothing, but inwardly they are ravenous wolves.
16 "You will know them by their fruits. Do men gather grapes from thornbushes or figs from thistles?
17 "Even so, every good tree bears good fruit, but a bad tree bears bad fruit.
18 "A good tree cannot bear bad fruit, nor can a bad tree bear good fruit.
19 "Every tree that does not bear good fruit is cut down and thrown into the fire.
20 "Therefore by their fruits you will know them.

21 "Not everyone who says to Me, 'Lord, Lord,' shall enter the kingdom of heaven, but he who does the will of My Father in heaven.
22 "Many will say to Me in that day, 'Lord, Lord, have we not prophesied in Your name, cast out demons in Your name, and done many wonders in Your name?'
23 "And then I will declare to them, 'I never knew you; depart from Me, you who practice lawlessness!'
24 "Therefore whoever hears these sayings of Mine, and does them, I will liken him to a wise man who built his house on the rock:
25 "and the rain descended, the floods came, and the winds blew and beat on that house; and it did not fall, for it was founded on the rock.
26 "Now everyone who hears these sayings of Mine, and does not do them, will be like a foolish man who built his house on the sand:
27 "and the rain descended, the floods came, and the winds blew and beat on that house; and it fell. And great was its fall."
28 And so it was, when Jesus had ended these sayings, that the people were astonished at His teaching,
29 for He taught them as one having authority, and not as the scribes.

The last words you and I want to ever hear are...
"... I never knew you; depart from Me..."

Does your life bear fruit? The one "measuring stick" which I feel confirms that the Holy Spirit dwells in you is described by the apostle Paul in his letter to the Galatians.

Galatians 5:22-25 (NKJ)
22 But the fruit of the Spirit is love, joy, peace, longsuffering, kindness, goodness, faithfulness,
23 gentleness, self-control. Against such there is no law.
24 And those who are Christ's have crucified the flesh with its passions and desires.
25 If we live in the Spirit, let us also walk in the Spirit.

Consider memorizing this list of the "fruits of the Spirit." You will have to remember "love, joy and peace" on your own but try using this mnemonic device for the others. Think, "package figs," but visualize it as, PKG

FGS. Then use the letters PKG FGS to memorize the list of fruits. I.e., Patience, (I know it says longsuffering, but that means patience), Kindness, Goodness, Faithfulness, Gentleness, Self control. PKG FGS.

The reason you should memorize that list is because those are the fruits of the Spirit, the evidence of the Holy Spirit in you. Which of us would like the opposite of those terms to characterize our life? Just start naming the opposite of those words. Love/hate, joy/depression and so on and you will get the point. When does your life become "overcome" by the opposite terms? Are you impatient, unkind, not good, unfaithful, not gentle and lacking in self control? Are you unloving, not joyful and not at peace?

Of course we all suffer from moments of lapse, but it is never God's will that we fail to enjoy the fruits of the Spirit. God calls us to be perfect. Listen to the words of the prophet Samuel.

2 Samuel 22:31-33 (NKJ)
31 As for God, His way is perfect; the word of the LORD is proven; he is a shield to all who trust in Him.
32 "For who is God, except the LORD? And who is a rock, except our God?
33 God is my strength and power, and He makes my way perfect.

Does God make your way perfect? I doubt you or I think our way is perfect. But, when you are sensing that you are completely within His will, don't you feel His presence, His perfection in you? We can take no credit for that feeling, for it is His Spirit in us that rescues us from the impulses of the flesh. We are in the flesh until we die or until we are raptured. The battle between our flesh, which will perish, and our spirit which will endure forever continues, moment by moment as long as we remain in this "testing ground" called earth.

The test is but for a moment because three score and ten years is as nothing, it is as a vapor, in terms of eternity. Yet this "vapor" is all we have to work with. It seems to us to be a big deal. We can't, in this body, get a grip on the eternal existence that we can only visualize.

God has placed His truth deep in our hearts. You know He exists, that He created everything that was made, including you and me and even though we can not reduce it to a level of understanding that will leave us without questions, we can believe. Our faith will sustain us and His grace and mercy will save us.

Perfection will elude us as long as we are in the flesh. The closest thing to perfection available is His Spirit, His perfection, in us. We die to "self" that we might live in the Spirit. His Spirit witnesses to our spirit. We crucify the flesh as it were, that the spirit within us might live, with abundance. Listen to the words that God gave to King David for our benefit.

Psalm 19:7-14 (NKJ)
7 The law of the LORD is perfect, converting the soul; the testimony of the LORD is sure, making wise the simple;
8 The statutes of the LORD are right, rejoicing the heart; the commandment of the LORD is pure, enlightening the eyes;
9 The fear of the LORD is clean, enduring forever; the judgments of the LORD are true and righteous altogether.
10 More to be desired are they than gold, yea, than much fine gold; sweeter also than honey and the honeycomb.
11 Moreover by them Your servant is warned, and in keeping them there is great reward.
12 Who can understand his errors? Cleanse me from secret faults.
13 Keep back Your servant also from presumptuous sins; let them not have dominion over me. Then I shall be blameless, and I shall be innocent of great transgression.
14 Let the words of my mouth and the meditation of my heart be acceptable in Your sight, O LORD, my strength and my Redeemer.

The Word of God is an astounding treasure of love, strength and wisdom. This Psalm and hundreds of others are...

"... a lamp to my feet and a light to my path" (119:105)

If you feel you are walking in darkness, unguided by God, it is because you have not opened your heart to Him. God wants to place His Spirit in you and to have your spirit be "as one" with Him. This marriage, becoming as one, is not forced upon you.

God has extended His hand, repeatedly, but He will not enter into a relationship with an infidel, sinners like you and me. Since we can not atone for our sin, nor can the sacrifice of bulls and goats atone for our sin, the Messiah, Jesus the Christ, is the only means of salvation. Only He can present us to the Father, blameless. Your faith in the fact of Jesus' life, death and resurrection is the "enabling factor" that allows God's grace to be present in you. If what I just said is true, you had better get to know Jesus, the perfect Lamb of God, very quickly. There is no other means to salvation because there is only one Son of God, only One who has the power to cleanse you and only One who will judge you. The God you and I love and worship has sent Him to us.

I realize that when I say "God" in the context of His Spirit in you, I mean the Trinity, the Father, the Son and the Holy Spirit. In Chapter 39, "The Holy Spirit" is more fully considered. It is His Spirit in you that lifts you into the presence of the Father. But, your flesh must die, daily, for your spirit and His Spirit to function as One. Listen to these wonderful verses.

Galatians 2:20-21 (NKJ)
20 "I have been crucified with Christ; it is no longer I who live, but Christ lives in me; and the life which I now live in the flesh I live by faith in the Son of God, who loved me and gave Himself for me.
21 "I do not set aside the grace of God; for if righteousness comes through the law, then Christ died in vain."

First, memorize verse 20, then as a Jew understand verse 21. Do you feel you have achieved righteousness as a result of your obedience to the Law? Has the Law not become the straight edge by which you are measured? Is your sin still with you or has it been "covered" by sacrifice? You are God's chosen people. It is to you to whom He revealed Himself and it is upon your history, your prophets that we stand. Did the Messiah die in vain? No, many will follow Him but the choice is yours.

These questions are intended to provoke, yes, but they are asked in love and out of a sense of desperation. How can I, a Gentile, grafted into the branch not seek your eternal salvation? If your prophets are my guides and if their prophecy is true, the One to whom they point, with such precision has come. If the Jewish nation has delayed in acknowledging His mission of mercy, His love for God's chosen people, then it is only because God willed that it be so, allowing the Gentiles to enter into His presence.

In this chapter, we are concerned with the rapture of the Body of Believers, the one true Church. It will either include you, as a believer, or it will not. If it does not, signs like the rebuilding of the Temple are going to become increasingly important to you. Doesn't prophecy fulfilled motivate you? Isn't it a wonderful fact that God sent His Word to His prophets and we can now witness all of the times in which prophecy was fulfilled. It is as though we could peek behind the curtain of uncertainty and see what was going on backstage. We have been invited into the presence of the Creator, the orchestrator of the history of man on earth. He has revealed Himself to us.

Listen to how Jesus explains the intimacy that God intends for His children.

John 15:1-26 (NKJ)
1 "I am the true vine, and My Father is the vinedresser.
2 "Every branch in Me that does not bear fruit He takes away; and every branch that bears fruit He prunes, that it may bear more fruit.
3 "You are already clean because of the word which I have spoken to you.
4 "Abide in Me, and I in you. As the branch cannot bear fruit of itself, unless it abides in the vine, neither can you, unless you abide in Me.
5 "I am the vine, you are the branches. He who abides in Me, and I in him, bears much fruit; for without Me you can do nothing.
6 "If anyone does not abide in Me, he is cast out as a branch and is withered; and they gather them and throw them into the fire, and they are burned.
7 "If you abide in Me, and My words abide in you, you will ask what you desire, and it shall be done for you.
8 "By this My Father is glorified, that you bear much fruit; so you will be My disciples.

9 "As the Father loved Me, I also have loved you; abide in My love.

10 "If you keep My commandments, you will abide in My love, just as I have kept My Father's commandments and abide in His love.

11 "These things I have spoken to you, that My joy may remain in you, and that your joy may be full.

12 "This is My commandment, that you love one another as I have loved you.

13 "Greater love has no one than this, than to lay down one's life for his friends.

14 "You are My friends if you do whatever I command you.

15 "No longer do I call you servants, for a servant does not know what his master is doing; but I have called you friends, for all things that I heard from My Father I have made known to you.

16 "You did not choose Me, but I chose you and appointed you that you should go and bear fruit, and that your fruit should remain, that whatever you ask the Father in My name He may give you.

17 "These things I command you, that you love one another.

18 "If the world hates you, you know that it hated Me before it hated you.

19 "If you were of the world, the world would love its own. Yet because you are not of the world, but I chose you out of the world, therefore the world hates you.

20 "Remember the word that I said to you, 'A servant is not greater than his master.' If they persecuted Me, they will also persecute you. If they kept My word, they will keep yours also.

21 "But all these things they will do to you for My name's sake, because they do not know Him who sent Me.

22 "If I had not come and spoken to them, they would have no sin, but now they have no excuse for their sin.

23 "He who hates Me hates My Father also.

24 "If I had not done among them the works which no one else did, they would have no sin; but now they have seen and also hated both Me and My Father.

25 "But this happened that the word might be fulfilled which is written in their law, 'They hated Me without a cause.'

26 "But when the Helper comes, whom I shall send to you from the Father, the Spirit of truth who proceeds from the Father, He will testify of Me.

Jesus tells us many wonderful truths here, but notice that we are called "friends," no longer servants, but friends. And now, our Messiah says that He will send the Helper, the Holy Spirit in you, who proceeds from the Father. The Trinity is summarized in verse 26.

Notice that Jesus says that if they persecuted Him, they will persecute His followers. Following Jesus, with dedication and enthusiasm will not be "easy." It will be glorious and exciting but many that say they love you, in your state of unforgiven sinfulness, will hate you because of your faith in Jesus. Your faith will offend. The scriptures assure you of that. You will, in that faith, send off signals of your rebirth that are unmistakable. You will change. You will exchange your righteousness for His. Your friends and family will see your joy. Listen.

2 Corinthians 2:14-17 (NKJ)
14 Now thanks be to God who always leads us in triumph in Christ, and through us diffuses the fragrance of His knowledge in every place.
15 For we are to God the fragrance of Christ among those who are being saved and among those who are perishing.
16 To the one we are the aroma of death leading to death, and to the other the aroma of life leading to life. And who is sufficient for these things?
17 For we are not, as so many, peddling the word of God; but as of sincerity, but as from God, we speak in the sight of God in Christ.

You will be the aroma of life to some, the aroma of death to others. Why? It is because you will be changed, forever. Your flesh, even while you live, will die. The Spirit within you will live, lifting you from the heaviness of the flesh. The battle for your soul will continue for a while, but Satan can never defeat the Holy Spirit in you. In time, you will become more and more attune to the presence and power of the Holy Spirit in you. Listen.

Romans 8:22-28 (NKJ)
22 For we know that the whole creation groans and labors with birth pangs together until now.
23 Not only that, but we also who have the firstfruits of the Spirit, even we ourselves groan within ourselves, eagerly waiting for the adoption, the redemption of our body.

24 For we were saved in this hope, but hope that is seen is not hope; for why does one still hope for what he sees?
25 But if we hope for what we do not see, we eagerly wait for it with perseverance.
26 Likewise the Spirit also helps in our weaknesses. For we do not know what we should pray for as we ought, but the Spirit Himself makes intercession for us with groanings which cannot be uttered.
27 Now He who searches the hearts knows what the mind of the Spirit is, because He makes intercession for the saints according to the will of God.
28 And we know that all things work together for good to those who love God, to those who are the called according to His purpose.

Do you not see what happens when you commit your soul to the Father and accept the empowerment of the Holy Spirit? The Spirit Himself makes intercession for you, with groanings, which cannot be uttered. He makes intercession for you, according to the will of God. Do you now feel that is true, in your present condition? Notice verse 23. We have the "first fruits" of the Spirit. Jesus, the Christ is the first fruit of the Spirit of God. It is Jesus who is the "only begotten Son of God." It is He who broke the barrier of death and showed us His resurrected Self. It is He who paid the price for our sins. It is His mind "in us" that we seek. Listen.

1 Corinthians 2:12-16 (NKJ)
12 Now we have received, not the spirit of the world, but the Spirit who is from God, that we might know the things that have been freely given to us by God.
13 These things we also speak, not in words which man's wisdom teaches but which the Holy Spirit teaches, comparing spiritual things with spiritual.
14 But the natural man does not receive the things of the Spirit of God, for they are foolishness to him; nor can he know them, because they are spiritually discerned.
15 But he who is spiritual judges all things, yet he himself is rightly judged by no one.
16 For "who has known the mind of the Lord that he may instruct Him?" But we have the mind of Christ.

I am completely unworthy as a spokesperson to you. Fortunately, it does not matter. God can use anyone to accomplish His will, even a Gentile sinner. He has given me access to the "mind of Christ." My constant prayer in this endeavor is to not miss His will and to know that I am His "good and faithful servant," serving, not leading. It is He who leads. It is our magnificent pleasure to be His servant. We stand in the court of the King at His invitation, and in the worthiness of the Messiah, not our own. It is in His power, His wisdom, in which we stand, knowing that we are as nothing, apart from Him. Listen.

John 16:13-15 (NKJ)
13 "However, when He, the Spirit of truth, has come, He will guide you into all truth; for He will not speak on His own authority, but whatever He hears He will speak; and He will tell you things to come.
14 "He will glorify Me, for He will take of what is Mine and declare it to you.
15 "All things that the Father has are Mine. Therefore I said that He will take of Mine and declare it to you.

I will make one final point about your decision to either join the "Body of Believers" or not. The decision is yours, not anyone else's. You stand completely alone before your Judge. You will not be able to blame anyone for your decisions. You stand alone, completely alone, before God, even this moment. You will be held accountable. Listen to these scriptures.

Psalm 62:12 (NKJ)
12 Also to You, O Lord, belongs mercy; for You render to each one according to his work.

Proverbs 24:10-12 (NKJ)
10 If you faint in the day of adversity, your strength is small.
11 Deliver those who are drawn toward death, and hold back those stumbling to the slaughter.
12 If you say, "Surely we did not know this," does not He who weighs the hearts consider it? He who keeps your soul, does He not know it? And will He not render to each man according to his deeds?

Zechariah 13:9 (NKJ)
9 ...They will call on My name, and I will answer them. I will say, 'This is My people'; and each one will say, 'The LORD is my God.'"

Matthew 16:27 (NKJ)
27 "For the Son of Man will come in the glory of His Father with His angels, and then He will reward each according to his works.

Romans 2:5-11 (NKJ)
5 But in accordance with your hardness and your impenitent heart you are treasuring up for yourself wrath in the day of wrath and revelation of the righteous judgment of God,
6 who "will render to each one according to his deeds":
7 eternal life to those who by patient continuance in doing good seek for glory, honor, and immortality;
8 but to those who are self-seeking and do not obey the truth, but obey unrighteousness– indignation and wrath,
9 tribulation and anguish, on every soul of man who does evil, of the Jew first and also of the Greek;
10 but glory, honor, and peace to everyone who works what is good, to the Jew first and also to the Greek.
11 For there is no partiality with God.

Romans 12:3-5 (NKJ)
3 For I say, through the grace given to me, to everyone who is among you, not to think of himself more highly than he ought to think, but to think soberly, as God has dealt to each one a measure of faith.
4 For as we have many members in one body, but all the members do not have the same function,
5 so we, being many, are one body in Christ, and individually members of one another.

1 Corinthians 3:13 (NKJ)
13 each one's work will become clear; for the Day will declare it, because it will be revealed by fire; and the fire will test each one's work, of what sort it is.

1 Corinthians 4:5 (NKJ)
5 Therefore judge nothing before the time, until the Lord comes, who will both bring to light the hidden things of darkness and reveal the counsels of the hearts. Then each one's praise will come from God.

1 Corinthians 7:17 (NKJ)
17 But as God has distributed to each one, as the Lord has called each one, so let him walk...

1 Corinthians 12:7 (NKJ)
7 ... the manifestation of the Spirit is given to each one for the profit of all:

2 Corinthians 5:10 (NKJ)
10 For we must all appear before the judgment seat of Christ, that each one may receive the things done in the body, according to what he has done, whether good or bad.

Galatians 6:4-5 (NKJ)
4 But let each one examine his own work, and then he will have rejoicing in himself alone, and not in another.
5 For each one shall bear his own load.

Ephesians 4:7 (NKJ)
7 ...to each one of us grace was given according to the measure of Christ's gift.

Revelation 20:13 (NKJ)
13 The sea gave up the dead who were in it, and Death and Hades delivered up the dead who were in them. And they were judged, each one according to his works.

If you suspect that you may feel "lonely" in making this decision, you are correct. If you want to commune with God, to confess your sins, to beg for forgiveness, to pour out your heart to Him, you will find that He awaits. Not necessarily in a synagogue or church, but perhaps by the sea or on a mountain or in the privacy of your back yard. Jesus taught many important truths, but perhaps the one I am going to offer here, is what you need to hear. Listen.

Matthew 7:7-8 (NKJ)
7 "Ask, and it will be given to you; seek, and you will find; knock, and it will be opened to you.
8 "For everyone who asks receives, and he who seeks finds, and to him who knocks it will be opened.

Revelation 3:15-21 (NKJ)
15 "I know your works, that you are neither cold nor hot. I could wish you were cold or hot.
16 "So then, because you are lukewarm, and neither cold nor hot, I will vomit you out of My mouth.
17 "Because you say, 'I am rich, have become wealthy, and have need of nothing'– and do not know that you are wretched, miserable, poor, blind, and naked–
18 "I counsel you to buy from Me gold refined in the fire, that you may be rich; and white garments, that you may be clothed, that the shame of your nakedness may not be revealed; and anoint your eyes with eye salve, that you may see.
19 "As many as I love, I rebuke and chasten. Therefore be zealous and repent.
20 "Behold, I stand at the door and knock. If anyone hears My voice and opens the door, I will come in to him and dine with him, and he with Me.
21 "To him who overcomes I will grant to sit with Me on My throne, as I also overcame and sat down with My Father on His throne.

If the rapture occurs while you are still alive, it will be an unmistakable sign to you, one more prophecy fulfilled. If you are "left behind," do not accept The Mark of the Beast. That decision will shape your eternal future. The situation will be calamitous. You may feel that you will be up to handling that trial. You will only do so in the strength and grace of God and I pray that is the case.

CHAPTER 12

DEFINING THE BODY OF BELIEVERS

Jewish readers will need to work their way through a lot of references to what Christians call the first coming of the Messiah, in order to grasp the full meaning of prophecy directed specifically to the Jews. If you have never done so, for whatever reason, this may be a good time.

Those "who believe" is a reference to those who believe that Jesus Christ is the Messiah, the Son of God, that He was crucified and buried and rose on the third day, and that He is now at the right hand of the Father. The body of believers consists only of those who, by the grace of God, have experienced salvation by faith in the atoning sacrifice made by Jesus, faith that has brought them to repentance. The Word makes clear what it is that God wants you to know about the church and its Foundation.

Ephesians 1:22-23 (NKJ)
22 And He put all things
23 which is His body, the fullness of Him who fills all in all.

Ephesians 3:8-10 (NKJ)
8 To me, who am less than the least of all the saints, this grace was given, that I should
9 and to make all see what is the fellowship of the mystery, which from the beginning of the ages has been hidden in God who created all things through Jesus Christ;

10 to the intent that now the manifold wisdom of God might be made known by the church to the principalities and powers in the heavenly places,

Ephesians 5:23 (NKJ)
23 For the husband is head of the wife, as also Christ is head of the church; and He is the Savior of the body.

Ephesians 5:25-27 (NKJ)
25 ...Christ also loved
26 that He might sanctify and cleanse her with the washing of water by the word,
27 that He might present her to Himself a glorious church, not having spot or wrinkle or any such thing, but that she should be holy and without blemish.

"Believers" is perhaps too broad a word, as we identify the church because the Bible says:

James 2:19 (NKJ)
19 "You believe that there is one God. You do well. Even the demons believe– and tremble"!

Jesus adds meaning to what the word believe means.

Luke 8:1-18 (NKJ)
1 Now it came to pass, afterward, that He went through every city and village, preaching and bringing the glad tidings of the kingdom of God. And the twelve were with Him,
2 and certain women who had been healed of evil spirits and infirmities– Mary called Magdalene, out of whom had come seven demons,
3 and Joanna the wife of Chuza, Herod's steward, and Susanna, and many others who provided for Him from their substance.
4 And when a great multitude had gathered, and they had come to Him from every city, He spoke by a parable:
5 "A sower went out to sow his seed. And as he sowed, some fell by the wayside; and it was trampled down, and the birds of the air devoured it.

6 "Some fell on rock; and as soon as it sprang up, it withered away because it lacked moisture.

7 "And some fell among thorns, and the thorns sprang up with it and choked it.

8 "But others fell on good ground, sprang up, and yielded a crop a hundredfold." When He had said these things He cried, "He who has ears to hear, let him hear!"

9 Then His disciples asked Him, saying, "What does this parable mean?"

10 And He said, "To you it has been given to know the mysteries of the kingdom of God, but to the rest it is given in parables, that 'Seeing they may not see, and hearing they may not understand.'

11 "Now the parable is this: The seed is the word of God.

12 "Those by the wayside are the ones who hear; then the devil comes and takes away the word out of their hearts, lest they should believe and be saved.

13 "But the ones on the rock are those who, when they hear, receive the word with joy; and these have no root, who believe for a while and in time of temptation fall away.

14 "And the ones that fell among thorns are those who, when they have heard, go out and are choked with cares, riches, and pleasures of life, and bring no fruit to maturity.

15 "But the ones that fell on the good ground are those who, having heard the word with a noble and good heart, keep it and bear fruit with patience.

16 "No one, when he has lit a lamp, covers it with a vessel or puts it under a bed, but sets it on a lampstand, that those who enter may see the light.

17 "For nothing is secret that will not be revealed, nor anything hidden that will not be known and come to light.

18 "Therefore take heed how you hear. For whoever has, to him more will be given; and whoever does not have, even what he seems to have will be taken from him."

The message is clear. A true believer is one whose witness and life has "staying power." They do not, as Jesus said, have shallow roots nor do they reside in sin. Their lives bear fruit and they declare the secret that has been revealed to them. As they do so, not only will their opportunities to witness, bear fruit, but God will bless them more abundantly than those who do not serve Him. Those who believe that God's blessings are only "material" fail to understand that the material blessings are temporal. Material things, including our flesh, will perish. The true blessing of God is an eternal life, but right now we are blessed by being in His will and by enjoying the fruits of the Holy Spirit. What God gives us more of is love, joy, peace, patience, kindness, goodness, faithfulness, gentleness and self control (Galatians 5:22, 23) and these gifts will distinguish us from those who hate, are depressed and angry. The Scriptures say:

1 John 4:7-11 (NKJ)
7 Beloved, let us love one another, for love is of God; and everyone who loves is born of God and knows God.
8 He who does not love does not know God, for God is love.
9 In this the love of God was manifested toward us, that God has sent His only begotten Son into the world, that we might live through Him.
10 In this is love, not that we loved God, but that He loved us and sent His Son to be the propitiation for our sins.
11 Beloved, if God so loved us, we also ought to love one another.

If you, as a Jew, understand the issues surrounding the rapture of the church (the body of believers), the events prophesied will be as a beacon to your path. Whether the rapture occurs before, during or after the "great tribulation," the scriptures indicate that it will occur. When it does, your choices will become increasingly complex and yet very clear. You will see the rest of the signs unfold. Pray for courage and discernment.

Paul presents a good summary of Jesus as the Head of the church. He said:

Colossians 1:18 (NKJ)
18 And He is the head of the body, the church, who is the beginning, the firstborn from the dead, that in all things He may have the preeminence.

Colossians 1:24 (NKJ)
24 I now rejoice in my sufferings for you, and fill up in my flesh what is lacking in the afflictions of Christ, for the sake of His body, which is the church,

First, in verse 18 and again in verse 24, Paul refers to the "body" as being "the church." When you think about the "body of believers" being caught up in the clouds," in the "rapture" (this is defined in the chapter 11, (The Rapture), you are referring to the church.

Therefore, there is only "one" church. In heaven there will not be denominations, each independently seeking to serve God, but one single "body of believers," the church. I suspect that denominationalism, with its "We are right, you are wrong" mentality greatly grieves God. God calls you to a personal relationship with Him and has provided an Enabler, a Redeemer who can present you blameless to the Father. Then and only then will you be in the body of believers, the one and only true church.

CHAPTER 13

THE TWO WITNESSES—DROUGHT AND FIERY JUDGMENT

One of the most incredible occurrences during the 7-year period of the tribulation will be triggered by the destruction of the temple at the end of the first 3½ years. At that moment, two "witnesses" will arrive. This fact is presented in the Revelation of Jesus Christ to His servant, John. Listen to these words.

Revelation 11:1-14 (NKJ)
1 Then I was given a reed like a measuring rod. And the angel stood, saying, "Rise and measure the temple of God, the altar, and those who worship there.
2 "But leave out the court which is outside the temple, and do not measure it, for it has been given to the Gentiles. And they will tread the holy city underfoot for forty-two months.
3 "And I will give power to my two witnesses, and they will prophesy one thousand two hundred and sixty days, clothed in sackcloth."
4 These are the two olive trees and the two lampstands standing before the God of the earth.
5 And if anyone wants to harm them, fire proceeds from their mouth and devours their enemies. And if anyone wants to harm them, he must be killed in this manner.
6 These have power to shut heaven, so that no rain falls in the days of their prophecy; and they have power over waters to turn them to blood, and to strike the earth with all plagues, as often as they desire.

7 Now when they finish their testimony, the beast that ascends out of the bottomless pit will make war against them, overcome them, and kill them.
8 And their dead bodies will lie in the street of the great city which spiritually is called Sodom and Egypt, where also our Lord was crucified.
9 Then those from the peoples, tribes, tongues, and nations will see their dead bodies three-and-a-half days, and not allow their dead bodies to be put into graves.
10 And those who dwell on the earth will rejoice over them, make merry, and send gifts to one another, because these two prophets tormented those who dwell on the earth.
11 Now after the three-and-a-half days the breath of life from God entered them, and they stood on their feet, and great fear fell on those who saw them.
12 And they heard a loud voice from heaven saying to them, "Come up here." And they ascended to heaven in a cloud, and their enemies saw them.
13 In the same hour there was a great earthquake, and a tenth of the city fell. In the earthquake seven thousand men were killed, and the rest were afraid and gave glory to the God of heaven.
14 The second woe is past. Behold, the third woe is coming quickly.

First, understand that the arrival of the two witnesses will coincide with the trampling of the holy city, Jerusalem, for forty-two months. If we reference the prophecy of Daniel we will see that the one who was making war against the saints (Daniel 7:21) is the antichrist. He will persecute the saints of the Most High and intend to change the course of history. He will prevail for 3½ years but not without resistance from God's two witnesses.

Read again what it said above:

Revelation 11:5-6 (NKJ)
5 And if anyone wants to harm them, fire proceeds from their mouth and devours their enemies. And if anyone wants to harm them, he must be killed in this manner.
6 These have power to shut heaven, so that no rain falls in the days of their prophecy; and they have power over waters to turn them to blood, and to strike the earth with all plagues, as often as they desire.

These two will have power. They will be able to destroy their enemies with fire. Listen to an example of that power when King Ahaziah asked Elijah if an injury he incurred in a fall was going to cause him to die.

2 Kings 1:2-17 (NKJ)
2 Now Ahaziah fell through the lattice of his upper room in Samaria, and was injured; so he sent messengers and said to them, "Go, inquire of Baal-Zebub, the god of Ekron, whether I shall recover from this injury."
3 But the angel of the LORD said to Elijah the Tishbite, "Arise, go up to meet the messengers of the king of Samaria, and say to them, 'Is it because there is no God in Israel that you are going to inquire of Baal-Zebub, the god of Ekron?'
4 "Now therefore, thus says the LORD: 'You shall not come down from the bed to which you have gone up, but you shall surely die.'" So Elijah departed.
5 And when the messengers returned to him, he said to them, "Why have you come back?"
6 So they said to him, "A man came up to meet us, and said to us, 'Go, return to the king who sent you, and say to him, "Thus says the LORD: 'Is it because there is no God in Israel that you are sending to inquire of Baal-Zebub, the god of Ekron? Therefore you shall not come down from the bed to which you have gone up, but you shall surely die.'"'"
7 Then he said to them, "What kind of man was it who came up to meet you and told you these words?"
8 So they answered him, "A hairy man wearing a leather belt around his waist." And he said, "It is Elijah the Tishbite."
9 Then the king sent to him a captain of fifty with his fifty men. So he went up to him; and there he was, sitting on the top of a hill. And he spoke to him: "Man of God, the king has said, 'Come down!'"
10 So Elijah answered and said to the captain of fifty, "If I am a man of God, then let fire come down from heaven and consume you and your fifty men." And fire came down from heaven and consumed him and his fifty.
11 Then he sent to him another captain of fifty with his fifty men. And he answered and said to him: "Man of God, thus has the king said, 'Come down quickly!'"

12 So Elijah answered and said to them, "If I am a man of God, let fire come down from heaven and consume you and your fifty men." And the fire of God came down from heaven and consumed him and his fifty.

13 Again, he sent a third captain of fifty with his fifty men. And the third captain of fifty went up, and came and fell on his knees before Elijah, and pleaded with him, and said to him: "Man of God, please let my life and the life of these fifty servants of yours be precious in your sight.

14 "Look, fire has come down from heaven and burned up the first two captains of fifties with their fifties. But let my life now be precious in your sight."

15 And the angel of the LORD said to Elijah, "Go down with him; do not be afraid of him." So he arose and went down with him to the king.

16 Then he said to him, "Thus says the LORD: 'Because you have sent messengers to inquire of Baal-Zebub, the god of Ekron, is it because there is no God in Israel to inquire of His word? Therefore you shall not come down from the bed to which you have gone up, but you shall surely die.'"

17 So Ahaziah died according to the word of the LORD which Elijah had spoken.

Here Elijah says that, "If I am a man of God, then let fire come down from heaven and consume you and your fifty men." And fire came down from heaven and consumed him and his fifty.

Elijah demonstrated God's power. The two witnesses will have this same power. They will be able to destroy an enemy simply by calling on God's power to do so. This will not exactly make these two popular. Their mission and their power will gain international attention, to say the least.

Let's review again the second thing these two do that will cause the entire world to suffer (except those who God miraculously leads to water).

Revelation 11:6 (NKJ)
6 These have power to shut heaven, so that no rain falls in the days of their prophecy; and they have power over waters to turn them to blood, and to strike the earth with all plagues, as often as they desire.

The "days of their prophecy" are 42 months (Rev. 11:2). No rain will fall from the time that the 3rd Temple is destroyed by the antichrist. Again, the world will suffer because of the power of the two witnesses to withhold the rain. This is not the first time in Israel's history that the rain was withheld. Listen:

1 Kings 17:1 (NKJ)
1 And Elijah the Tishbite, of the inhabitants of Gilead, said to Ahab, "As the LORD God of Israel lives, before whom I stand, there shall not be dew nor rain these years, except at my word."

Luke 4:25 (NKJ)
25 "But I tell you truly, many widows were in Israel in the days of Elijah, when the heaven was shut up three years and six months, and there was a great famine throughout all the land;

In these next verses, Jeremiah tells Israel why the latter rain will be withheld.

Jeremiah 3:1-3 (NKJ)
1 "They say, 'If a man divorces his wife, and she goes from him and becomes another man's, may he return to her again?' Would not that land be greatly polluted? But you have played the harlot with many lovers; yet return to Me," says the LORD.
2 "Lift up your eyes to the desolate heights and see: where have you not lain with men? By the road you have sat for them like an Arabian in the wilderness; and you have polluted the land with your harlotries and your wickedness.
3 Therefore the showers have been withheld, and there has been no latter rain. You have had a harlot's forehead; you refuse to be ashamed.

Does it surprise you at all, that the world, under the authority and leadership of the antichrist will be angry with these two? They have the power to kill anyone who defies them and they withhold the rain. Finally, as we read in Rev. 11:7, they are killed by the beast (Satan). What do you think happens when these two who have made the enemies of God suffer, then die? The world throws a party celebrating their death! Listen:

Revelation 11:10 (NKJ)
10 And those who dwell on the earth will rejoice over them, make merry, and send gifts to one another, because these two prophets tormented those who dwell on the earth.

But the party is premature. Listen:

Revelation 11:8-9, 11 (NKJ)
8 And their dead bodies will lie in the street of the great city which spiritually is called Sodom and Egypt, where also our Lord was crucified.
9 Then those from the peoples, tribes, tongues, and nations will see their dead bodies three-and-a-half days, and not allow their dead bodies to be put into graves.
11 Now after the three-and-a-half days the breath of life from God entered them, and they stood on their feet, and great fear fell on those who saw them.

Can you imagine this scene? The world has been celebrating, for 3 ½ days, the death of these two who have tormented them and then they stand up and are alive. From that moment on, God's wrath is poured out upon His enemies. The great time of tribulation will be concluded with an earthquake that will destroy many and finally be brought to an end by the battle of Armageddon, a battle fought by God against His enemies.

To place these events in perspective, listen to how Daniel describes the rise of the antichrist and his fate.

Daniel 7:25-28 (NKJ)
25 He shall speak pompous words against the Most High, shall persecute the saints of the Most High, and shall intend to change times and law. Then the saints shall be given into his hand for a time and times and half a time.
26 'But the court shall be seated, and they shall take away his dominion, to consume and destroy it forever.
27 Then the kingdom and dominion, and the greatness of the kingdoms under the whole heaven, shall be given to the people, the saints of the

Most High. His kingdom is an everlasting kingdom, and all dominions shall serve and obey Him.'

28 "This is the end of the account. As for me, Daniel, my thoughts greatly troubled me, and my countenance changed; but I kept the matter in my heart."

Daniel 8:23-27 (NKJ)
23 "And in the latter time of their kingdom, when the transgressors have reached their fullness, a king shall arise, having fierce features, who understands sinister schemes.
24 His power shall be mighty, but not by his own power; he shall destroy fearfully, and shall prosper and thrive; he shall destroy the mighty, and also the holy people.
25 "Through his cunning he shall cause deceit to prosper under his rule; and he shall exalt himself in his heart. He shall destroy many in their prosperity. He shall even rise against the Prince of princes; but he shall be broken without human means.
26 "And the vision of the evenings and mornings which was told is true; therefore seal up the vision, for it refers to many days in the future."
27 And I, Daniel, fainted and was sick for days; afterward I arose and went about the king's business. I was astonished by the vision, but no one understood it.

Daniel concludes each of these two accounts with these words:

… "my thoughts greatly troubled me, and my countenance changed; but I kept the matter in my heart."

… "I was astonished by the vision, but no one understood it."

If you are reading the account of the two witnesses as a casual observer you may be missing the point. This will be a time of terrific turmoil and unrest. Your personal position in all of this will be tested. If you are faithful to God and seek to understand what is in store, you will not be surprised at all this. You will be severely tested but during this last 3½ years, preceding the millennium, God has promised to care for His people, those who love Him and are obedient to His Word. This period of time, for many of the faithful, will be much like the Exodus, when God preserved His people in miraculous ways in a barren and hostile land.

Listen to the prophecy of Isaiah. Is this a scenario much like the one described above? Will the land be desolate and will a tenth remain as God's holy seed?

Isaiah 6:9-13 (NKJ)
9 And He said, "Go, and tell this people: 'Keep on hearing, but do not understand; keep on seeing, but do not perceive.'
10 "Make the heart of this people dull, and their ears heavy, and shut their eyes; lest they see with their eyes, and hear with their ears, and understand with their heart, and return and be healed."
11 Then I said, "Lord, how long?" And He answered: "Until the cities are laid waste and without inhabitant, the houses are without a man, the land is utterly desolate,
12 The LORD has removed men far away, and the forsaken places are many in the midst of the land.
13 But yet a tenth will be in it, and will return and be for consuming, as a terebinth tree or as an oak, whose stump remains when it is cut down. So the holy seed shall be its stump."

All of this would seem to point to a significant amount of despair for a very large number of people.

Jeremiah, in the Book of Lamentations offers prophecy that seems to fit three times. Once when Nebuchadnezzar destroyed the Temple, again when the Romans destroyed the rebuilt Temple (whose western wall remains today) and finally here in the end times, after the Temple is rebuilt for a third time.

Lamentations 2:1-8 (NKJ)
1 How the Lord has covered the daughter of Zion with a cloud in His anger! He cast down from heaven to the earth the beauty of Israel, and did not remember His footstool in the day of His anger.
2 The Lord has swallowed up and has not pitied all the dwelling places of Jacob. He has thrown down in His wrath the strongholds of the

daughter of Judah; he has brought them down to the ground; he has profaned the kingdom and its princes.

3 He has cut off in fierce anger every horn of Israel; he has drawn back His right hand from before the enemy. He has blazed against Jacob like a flaming fire devouring all around.

4 Standing like an enemy, He has bent His bow; with His right hand, like an adversary, he has slain all who were pleasing to His eye; on the tent of the daughter of Zion, he has poured out His fury like fire.

5 The Lord was like an enemy. He has swallowed up Israel, he has swallowed up all her palaces; he has destroyed her strongholds, and has increased mourning and lamentation in the daughter of Judah.

6 He has done violence to His tabernacle, as if it were a garden; he has destroyed His place of assembly; the LORD has caused the appointed feasts and Sabbaths to be forgotten in Zion. In His burning indignation He has spurned the king and the priest.

7 The Lord has spurned His altar, he has abandoned His sanctuary; he has given up the walls of her palaces into the hand of the enemy. They have made a noise in the house of the LORD as on the day of a set feast.

8 The LORD has purposed to destroy the wall of the daughter of Zion. He has stretched out a line; he has not withdrawn His hand from destroying; therefore He has caused the rampart and wall to lament; they languished together.

Notice the words in verse 6: He has done violence to His tabernacle. Many mistakenly think that evil people independently "do the violent things" because they are in control. Evil people perform evil acts because God permits them to do so. They do so to their own detriment but God Himself is in control and what they do, they do with His permission or by His design.

God could prevent evil people from drawing their first breath and He certainly is not surprised when they do violence to His tabernacle or His people. Does this mean that what God foreknew (our every thought and action), He preordained? The Scriptures make the following point over and over again. Listen.

Romans 9:20-24 (NKJ)
20 But indeed, O man, who are you to reply against God? Will the thing formed say to him who formed it, "Why have you made me like this?"
21 Does not the potter have power over the clay, from the same lump to make one vessel for honor and another for dishonor?
22 What if God, wanting to show His wrath and to make His power known, endured with much longsuffering the vessels of wrath prepared for destruction,
23 and that He might make known the riches of His glory on the vessels of mercy, which He had prepared beforehand for glory,
24 even us whom He called, not of the Jews only, but also of the Gentiles?

Listen again to Isaiah and understand that your faithful obedience also leads to a wonderful result.

Isaiah 66:5-14 (NKJ)
5 Hear the word of the LORD, you who tremble at His word: "Your brethren who hated you, who cast you out for My name's sake, said, 'Let the LORD be glorified, that we may see your joy.' But they shall be ashamed."
6 The sound of noise from the city! A voice from the temple! The voice of the LORD, who fully repays His enemies!
7 "Before she was in labor, she gave birth; before her pain came, she delivered a male child.
8 Who has heard such a thing? Who has seen such things? Shall the earth be made to give birth in one day?
Or shall a nation be born at once? For as soon as Zion was in labor, she gave birth to her children.
9 Shall I bring to the time of birth, and not cause delivery?" says the LORD. "Shall I who cause delivery shut up the womb?" says your God.
10 "Rejoice with Jerusalem, and be glad with her, all you who love her; rejoice for joy with her, all you who mourn for her;
11 That you may feed and be satisfied with the consolation of her bosom, that you may drink deeply and be delighted with the abundance of her glory."

12 **For thus says the LORD: "Behold, I will extend peace to her like a river, and the glory of the Gentiles like a flowing stream. Then you shall feed; on her sides shall you be carried, and be dandled on her knees.**
13 **As one whom his mother comforts, so I will comfort you; and you shall be comforted in Jerusalem."**
14 **When you see this, your heart shall rejoice, and your bones shall flourish like grass; the hand of the LORD shall be known to His servants, and His indignation to His enemies.**

This kind of encouragement is present throughout the Scriptures. There is the "blessing" and the "curse." Choose which you will have and if you choose the curse, pray for mercy, because judgment awaits those who are disobedient, just as peace, like a river, awaits those who are obedient and faithful and who love God with all their hearts, mind, soul and strength and their neighbor as themselves.

As to who the two witnesses are, their identity is not revealed. Many scholars have debated this topic and there is no need to "nail down" an answer. It matters less "who they are" than "why they are." They have a specific role to fulfill and prophesy tells us what that role is.

I will speculate that the two witnesses are Elijah and Enoch. From the readings above you can see that Elijah already was used by God to destroy the enemy by fire and to withhold the rain. That fact, in itself, means little, since God can impart power to anyone He chooses, including another witness beside Elijah.

In addition, listen to these verses which were written by John, the Apostle, concerning John the Baptist, where people asked John the Baptist, "are you Elijah?" I will offer this quotation in a more full context than is called for, simply because I feel that these words are perhaps the most important words in the New Testament.

John 1:1-34 (NKJ)
1 **In the beginning was the Word, and the Word was with God, and the Word was God.**
2 **He was in the beginning with God.**

3 All things were made through Him, and without Him nothing was made that was made.

4 In Him was life, and the life was the light of men.

5 And the light shines in the darkness, and the darkness did not comprehend it.

6 There was a man sent from God, whose name was John.

7 This man came for a witness, to bear witness of the Light, that all through him might believe.

8 He was not that Light, but was sent to bear witness of that Light.

9 That was the true Light which gives light to every man coming into the world.

10 He was in the world, and the world was made through Him, and the world did not know Him.

11 He came to His own, and His own did not receive Him.

12 But as many as received Him, to them He gave the right to become children of God, to those who believe in His name:

13 who were born, not of blood, nor of the will of the flesh, nor of the will of man, but of God.

14 And the Word became flesh and dwelt among us, and we beheld His glory, the glory as of the only begotten of the Father, full of grace and truth.

15 John bore witness of Him and cried out, saying, "This was He of whom I said, 'He who comes after me is preferred before me, for He was before me.'"

16 And of His fullness we have all received, and grace for grace.

17 For the law was given through Moses, but grace and truth came through Jesus Christ.

18 No one has seen God at any time. The only begotten Son, who is in the bosom of the Father, He has declared Him.

19 Now this is the testimony of John, when the Jews sent priests and Levites from Jerusalem to ask him, "Who are you?"

20 He confessed, and did not deny, but confessed, "I am not the Christ."

21 And they asked him, "What then? Are you Elijah?" He said, "I am not." "Are you the Prophet?" And he answered, "No."

22 Then they said to him, "Who are you, that we may give an answer to those who sent us? What do you say about yourself?"

23 He said: "I am 'The voice of one crying in the wilderness: "Make straight the way of the Lord," 'as the prophet Isaiah said."
24 Now those who were sent were from the Pharisees.
25 And they asked him, saying, "Why then do you baptize if you are not the Christ, nor Elijah, nor the Prophet?"
26 John answered them, saying, "I baptize with water, but there stands One among you whom you do not know.
27 "It is He who, coming after me, is preferred before me, whose sandal strap I am not worthy to loose."
28 These things were done in Bethabara beyond the Jordan, where John was baptizing.
29 The next day John saw Jesus coming toward him, and said, "Behold! The Lamb of God who takes away the sin of the world!
30 "This is He of whom I said, 'After me comes a Man who is preferred before me, for He was before me.'
31 "I did not know Him; but that He should be revealed to Israel, (my emphasis) therefore I came baptizing with water."
32 And John bore witness, saying, "I saw the Spirit descending from heaven like a dove, and He remained upon Him.
33 "I did not know Him, but He who sent me to baptize with water said to me, 'Upon whom you see the Spirit descending, and remaining on Him, this is He who baptizes with the Holy Spirit.'
34 "And I have seen and testified that this is the Son of God."

Here John is the herald, announcing the coming of the Messiah, the Lamb of God who takes away the sin of the world. They ask, "Are you Elijah?" Why? Listen to what Malachi told God's people.

Malachi 4:5 (NKJ)
5 Behold, I will send you Elijah the prophet before the coming of the great and dreadful day of the LORD.

Malachi said Elijah would be the herald announcing the coming of the great and dreadful day of the Lord. The two witnesses do just that. They precede the coming of the Messiah. That coming will be good news to some and bad news to others, but just as John the Baptist announced the first coming, here Elijah announces the second coming.

In addition, when John the Baptist had been thrown into prison (for scolding Herod about marrying his brother's wife), the disciples of Jesus brought a question from John the Baptist. Listen:

Matthew 11:1-15 (NKJ)
1 Now it came to pass, when Jesus finished commanding His twelve disciples, that He departed from there to teach and to preach in their cities.
2 And when John had heard in prison about the works of Christ, he sent two of his disciples
3 and said to Him, "Are You the Coming One, or do we look for another?"
4 Jesus answered and said to them, "Go and tell John the things which you hear and see:
5 "The blind see and the lame walk; the lepers are cleansed and the deaf hear; the dead are raised up and the poor have the gospel preached to them.
6 "And blessed is he who is not offended because of Me."
7 As they departed, Jesus began to say to the multitudes concerning John: "What did you go out into the wilderness to see? A reed shaken by the wind?
8 "But what did you go out to see? A man clothed in soft garments? Indeed, those who wear soft clothing are in kings' houses.
9 "But what did you go out to see? A prophet? Yes, I say to you, and more than a prophet.
10 "For this is he of whom it is written: 'Behold, I send My messenger before Your face, who will prepare Your way before You.'
11 "Assuredly, I say to you, among those born of women there has not risen one greater than John the Baptist; but he who is least in the kingdom of heaven is greater than he.
12 "And from the days of John the Baptist until now the kingdom of heaven suffers violence, and the violent take it by force.
13 "For all the prophets and the law prophesied until John.
14 "And if you are willing to receive it, he is Elijah who is to come.
15 "He who has ears to hear, let him hear!

Jesus tells us, John is Elijah, who is to come. These verses concerning John's identity and role are not easily understood, in my opinion, but if the role of Elijah and John are similar, they are both heralds of the coming of the Messiah.

There is one other reason that is more compelling, in my opinion. The Bible is true, every word of it. There is a verse that says: And as it is appointed for men to die once, but after this the judgment, (Hebrews 9:27) Only two persons do not die in the Biblical record. Those two are Enoch and Elijah. Listen to the description of their departures:

Genesis 5:23-24 (NKJ)
23 So all the days of Enoch were three hundred and sixty-five years.
24 And Enoch walked with God; and he was not, for God took him.

The circumstances of Elijah's departure were more dramatic and it is better, I think, to look at it in a more full context. Listen:

2 Kings 2:1-17 (NKJ)
1 And it came to pass, when the LORD was about to take up Elijah into heaven by a whirlwind, that Elijah went with Elisha from Gilgal.
2 Then Elijah said to Elisha, "Stay here, please, for the LORD has sent me on to Bethel." But Elisha said, "As the LORD lives, and as your soul lives, I will not leave you!" So they went down to Bethel.
3 Now the sons of the prophets who were at Bethel came out to Elisha, and said to him, "Do you know that the LORD will take away your master from over you today?" And he said, "Yes, I know; keep silent!"
4 Then Elijah said to him, "Elisha, stay here, please, for the LORD has sent me on to Jericho." But he said, "As the LORD lives, and as your soul lives, I will not leave you!" So they came to Jericho.
5 Now the sons of the prophets who were at Jericho came to Elisha and said to him, "Do you know that the LORD will take away your master from over you today?" So he answered, "Yes, I know; keep silent!"
6 Then Elijah said to him, "Stay here, please, for the LORD has sent me on to the Jordan." But he said, "As the LORD lives, and as your soul lives, I will not leave you!" So the two of them went on.
7 And fifty men of the sons of the prophets went and stood facing them at a distance, while the two of them stood by the Jordan.

8 Now Elijah took his mantle, rolled it up, and struck the water; and it was divided this way and that, so that the two of them crossed over on dry ground.
9 And so it was, when they had crossed over, that Elijah said to Elisha, "Ask! What may I do for you, before I am taken away from you?" Elisha said, "Please let a double portion of your spirit be upon me."
10 So he said, "You have asked a hard thing. Nevertheless, if you see me when I am taken from you, it shall be so for you; but if not, it shall not be so."
11 Then it happened, as they continued on and talked, that suddenly a chariot of fire appeared with horses of fire, and separated the two of them; and Elijah went up by a whirlwind into heaven.
12 And Elisha saw it, and he cried out, "My father, my father, the chariot of Israel and its horsemen!" So he saw him no more. And he took hold of his own clothes and tore them into two pieces.
13 He also took up the mantle of Elijah that had fallen from him, and went back and stood by the bank of the Jordan.
14 Then he took the mantle of Elijah that had fallen from him, and struck the water, and said, "Where is the LORD God of Elijah?" And when he also had struck the water, it was divided this way and that; and Elisha crossed over.
15 Now when the sons of the prophets who were from Jericho saw him, they said, "The spirit of Elijah rests on Elisha." And they came to meet him, and bowed to the ground before him.
16 Then they said to him, "Look now, there are fifty strong men with your servants. Please let them go and search for your master, lest perhaps the Spirit of the LORD has taken him up and cast him upon some mountain or into some valley." And he said, "You shall not send anyone."
17 But when they urged him till he was ashamed, he said, "Send them!" Therefore they sent fifty men, and they searched for three days but did not find him.

Whether Elijah and Enoch come back as witnesses and do what is recorded above, I do not know, for certain, but it makes a lot of sense to place them in this role so the verse about every man dying once, can be fulfilled. It can be fulfilled in other ways, I am sure, but this is one way that seems to fit.

I believe you get the point. The tribulation period will be one of miraculous events, both good and bad. It appears that few will remain faithful and obedient to God during this period. You may choose to be "different" now or then, but in any event the choice will carry with it either great mercy or eternal judgment. If you are praying for the former, give "legs" to your prayer. Seek a personal relationship with Him now by accepting the redemptive act of His Son and being filled with the Holy Spirit, equipped to do the work of the saints, by His Grace.

You do believe the Messiah is coming. Search the Old Testament for the evidence pointing to His lineage, His birthplace, and the circumstances of His ministry and His death on the cross. If you await One who must precisely fulfill these prophecies, it would indeed be a miracle to have another do so.

CHAPTER 14

PREPARE TO FLEE THE FINAL EXODUS

At the end of 3½ years, when the "abomination of desolation," described by Daniel 9:27, occurs, and Temple sacrifices are discontinued, it will have become clear to those who first thought that "peace and safety" had come upon Israel, that instead, the great tribulation was upon them. Then the words of the Messiah will ring true. Read on.

Matthew 24:15-22 (NKJ)
15 "Therefore when you see the 'abomination of desolation,' spoken of by Daniel the prophet, standing in the holy place" (whoever reads, let him understand),
16 "then let those who are in Judea flee to the mountains.
17 "Let him who is on the housetop not go down to take anything out of his house.
18 "And let him who is in the field not go back to get his clothes.
19 "But woe to those who are pregnant and to those who are nursing babies in those days!
20 "And pray that your flight may not be in winter or on the Sabbath.
21 "For then there will be great tribulation, such as has not been since the beginning of the world until this time, no, nor ever shall be.
22 "And unless those days were shortened, no flesh would be saved; but for the elect's sake those days will be shortened.

The prophet Zechariah made the same point as he described the events leading up to the restoration of the Kingdom.

Zechariah 2:6-8 (NKJ)
6 "Up, up! Flee from the land of the north," says the LORD; "for I have spread you abroad like the four winds of heaven," says the LORD.
7 "Up, Zion! Escape, you who dwell with the daughter of Babylon."
8 For thus says the LORD of hosts: "He sent Me after glory, to the nations which plunder you; for he who touches you touches the apple of His eye.

Jeremiah foresaw the same event and cited the enemy as coming out of the north.

Jeremiah 6:1 (NKJ)
1 "O you children of Benjamin, gather yourselves to flee from the midst of Jerusalem! Blow the trumpet in Tekoa, and set up a signal-fire in Beth Haccerem; for disaster appears out of the north, and great destruction.

This exodus will be triggered by severe persecution and survival will come either by compromise or by fleeing. Families will be split up and what we witness almost daily, somewhere in the world, will become a reality of a different kind.

Jeremiah 10:17-25 (NKJ)
17 Gather up your wares from the land, O inhabitant of the fortress!
18 For thus says the LORD: "Behold, I will throw out at this time the inhabitants of the land, and will distress them, that they may find it so."
19 Woe is me for my hurt! My wound is severe. But I say, "Truly this is an infirmity, and I must bear it."
20 My tent is plundered, and all my cords are broken; my children have gone from me, and they are no more. There is no one to pitch my tent anymore, or set up my curtains.
21 For the shepherds have become dull-hearted, and have not sought the LORD; therefore they shall not prosper, and all their flocks shall be scattered.

22 Behold, the noise of the report has come, and a great commotion out of the north country, to make the cities of Judah desolate, a den of jackals.
23 O LORD, I know the way of man is not in himself; it is not in man who walks to direct his own steps.
24 O LORD, correct me, but with justice; not in Your anger, lest You bring me to nothing.
25 Pour out Your fury on the Gentiles, who do not know You, and on the families who do not call on Your name; for they have eaten up Jacob, devoured him and consumed him, and made his dwelling place desolate.

The tribulation associated with the last 3½ years of the upcoming 7-year period will be a period of suffering as none other. We have seen what it is to be a refugee and a captive. We have seen the evil that man can administer to man. For you to hide successfully and survive will be another miracle that only God is able to provide. Just as God provided for His people in the wilderness, He will again provide, as only He could.

The following statement by Jacob clarifies what we "need" to survive and to effectively serve God.

Genesis 28:20-21 (NKJ)
20 Then Jacob made a vow, saying, "If God will be with me, and keep me in this way that I am going, and give me bread to eat and clothing to put on,
21 "so that I come back to my father's house in peace, then the LORD shall be my God.

Paul taught Timothy the same concept regarding what one really needs. Listen.

1 Timothy 6:6-8 (NKJ)
6 Now godliness with contentment is great gain.
7 For we brought nothing into this world, and it is certain we can carry nothing out.
8 And having food and clothing, with these we shall be content.

If you attempt to flee, rather than to accept the mark of the beast, do you realize what you will "need?" Jacob and Paul just told you. You will need food and clothing. You will pray for shelter but the scriptures do not include shelter as a "need." God may provide somewhat more abundantly than you require in order to survive, but your personal resources will be of no value to you, other than the clothing and small amount of food that you can take with you when you flee the enemy.

I believe Jesus taught us a much broader understanding of basic needs than I have introduced here but notice how perfectly His teaching fits the moment if you are "fleeing the enemy."

Matthew 6:25-34 (NKJ)
25 "Therefore I say to you, do not worry about your life, what you will eat or what you will drink; nor about your body, what you will put on. Is not life more than food and the body more than clothing?
26 "Look at the birds of the air, for they neither sow nor reap nor gather into barns; yet your heavenly Father feeds them. Are you not of more value than they?
27 "Which of you by worrying can add one cubit to his stature?
28 "So why do you worry about clothing? Consider the lilies of the field, how they grow: they neither toil nor spin;
29 "and yet I say to you that even Solomon in all his glory was not arrayed like one of these.
30 "Now if God so clothes the grass of the field, which today is, and tomorrow is thrown into the oven, will He not much more clothe you, O you of little faith?
31 "Therefore do not worry, saying, 'What shall we eat?' or 'What shall we drink?' or 'What shall we wear?'
32 "For after all these things the Gentiles seek. For your heavenly Father knows that you need all these things.
33 "But seek first the kingdom of God and His righteousness, and all these things shall be added to you.
34 "Therefore do not worry about tomorrow, for tomorrow will worry about its own things. Sufficient for the day is its own trouble.

Now let's look at how valuable your earthly assets will be to you as you flee the enemy and the circumstances of one who is busy escaping an enemy that wants to kill you. Listen.

Ezekiel 7:16-19 (NKJ)
16 'Those who survive will escape and be on the mountains like doves of the valleys, all of them mourning, each for his iniquity.
17 Every hand will be feeble, and every knee will be as weak as water.
18 They will also be girded with sackcloth; horror will cover them; shame will be on every face, baldness on all their heads.
19 'They will throw their silver into the streets, and their gold will be like refuse; their silver and their gold will not be able to deliver them in the day of the wrath of the LORD; they will not satisfy their souls, nor fill their stomachs, because it became their stumbling block of iniquity.

In the final analysis, each of us knows that our assets can not redeem our "life." Here Solomon puts it in perspective. Only a repentant heart and the righteousness of Christ in you, will deliver you from death.

Proverbs 11:4 (NKJ)
4 **Riches do not profit in the day of wrath, but righteousness delivers from death.**

In the following set of verses, Isaiah and Zephaniah depict how you and I will feel if we are present during the last half of the 7 years of great tribulation.

Isaiah 2:17-21 (NKJ)
17 **The loftiness of man shall be bowed down, and the haughtiness of men shall be brought low; the LORD alone will be exalted in that day,
18 But the idols He shall utterly abolish.
19 They shall go into the holes of the rocks, and into the caves of the earth, from the terror of the LORD and the glory of His majesty, when He arises to shake the earth mightily.
20 In that day a man will cast away his idols of silver and his idols of gold, which they made, each for himself to worship, to the moles and bats,**

21 **To go into the clefts of the rocks, and into the crags of the rugged rocks, from the terror of the LORD and the glory of His majesty, when He arises to shake the earth mightily.**

Zephaniah 1:15-18 (NKJ)
15 **That day is a day of wrath, a day of trouble and distress, a day of devastation and desolation, a day of darkness and gloominess, a day of clouds and thick darkness,**
16 **A day of trumpet and alarm against the fortified cities and against the high towers.**
17 "I will bring distress upon men, and they shall walk like blind men, because they have sinned against the LORD; their blood shall be poured out like dust, and their flesh like refuse."
18 **Neither their silver nor their gold shall be able to deliver them in the day of the LORD'S wrath; but the whole land shall be devoured by the fire of His jealousy, for He will make speedy riddance of all those who dwell in the land.**

Having the courage to reject the mark on your right hand or on your forehead will, in many cases, lead to an immediate death sentence. Having that courage will set you apart for eternity, provided your courage stems from your faith. You will come to believe that your only hope lies in the mercy and grace of the Father, Son and Holy Spirit. Your resources will be as refuse and as "baggage to be discarded," lest it weighs you down and you perish trying to preserve it.

I believe this following prophecy pertains to the living conditions of those "hiding out" during the great tribulation.

2 Kings 19:29-31 (NKJ)
29 'This shall be a sign to you: you shall eat this year such as grows of itself, and in the second year what springs from the same; also in the third year sow and reap, plant vineyards and eat the fruit of them.
30 And the remnant who have escaped of the house of Judah shall again take root downward, and bear fruit upward.
31 **For out of Jerusalem shall go a remnant, and those who escape from Mount Zion. The zeal of the LORD of hosts will do this.'**

You can believe the prophecy above applies to the last 3½ years of the tribulation period, or not. If it does, you will not, without the mark of the beast, be able to buy and sell. I think it might. You would, if this is the case, be living off the land, at the mercy of the elements but God will provide just as He has before. Listen to Isaiah's propehecy concerning the Messiah's role as you flee. The capitalization of the "Y," in the following verse, signifies Deity, the Messiah.

Isaiah 49:8-10 (NKJ)
8 Thus says the LORD: "In an acceptable time I have heard You, and in the day of salvation I have helped You; I will preserve You and give You as a covenant to the people, to restore the earth, to cause them to inherit the desolate heritages;
9 That You may say to the prisoners, 'Go forth,' to those who are in darkness, 'Show yourselves.' "They shall feed along the roads, and their pastures shall be on all desolate heights.
10 They shall neither hunger nor thirst, neither heat nor sun shall strike them; for He who has mercy on them will lead them, even by the springs of water He will guide them.

Notice that in II Kings, verse 30, it clearly says that only a remnant will escape. I will speculate that those who did not escape either died as martyrs or succumbed to the pressure of accepting the mark of the beast. The primary mission of this book is to tell you that the Messiah awaits now, to redeem you from the severe test before you, that you might be assured of His redemptive, regenerative power, now.

If you go through the tribulation, the "upward fruit" described in verse 30 will manifest itself in your offerings to God of your lives and livelihood. The fruit that you bear will be fruits of righteousness, fruits of the Holy Spirit, because the Messiah will provide.

I am going to estimate that salvation for the remnant will occur during this final 3½ year period and if not during the 3½ years, then certainly immediately after or concurrent with the battle of Armageddon. Why? Aside from the fact that Ezekiel's prophecy says you shall "mourn for your iniquity" as you escape. No one will be in the Kingdom of God, on earth, that does not acknowledge the Lordship and Deity of the Messiah. Listen.

Philippians 2:9-11 (NKJ)
9 Therefore God also has highly exalted Him and given Him the name which is above every name,
10 that at the name of Jesus every knee should bow, of those in heaven, and of those on earth, and of those under the earth,
11 and that every tongue should confess that Jesus Christ is Lord, to the glory of God the Father.

There are three occasions in which these verses state, "every knee shall bow…and every tongue should confess that Jesus Christ is Lord." First, it will occur in New Jerusalem, heaven. Second, it will occur on the earth and third, under the earth. We have no problem understanding why this would be true in heaven. The second though, on earth, means every one on earth will confess. This could either be as millions are dying during the final battle (finally acknowledging God is in control) or more likely it will be in the Kingdom, where the Messiah reigns.

You may be thinking, "If during the Kingdom Age, every person will acknowledge Jesus as Lord and Savior, why, when Satan is unbound at the end of the 1000 years, will there be those who will choose to follow his evil ways? Didn't they 'acknowledge' Jesus as the Christ, the Messiah?" Amazingly, there are people today who acknowledge Jesus as the Christ and who then go right on sinning, right on serving Satan. Acknowledging Him will not save you now nor will it save you then. Listen Israel to your prophets.

Ezekiel 18:30-32 (NKJ)
30 "Therefore I will judge you, O house of Israel, every one according to his ways," says the Lord GOD. "Repent, and turn from all your transgressions, so that iniquity will not be your ruin.
31 "Cast away from you all the transgressions which you have committed, and get yourselves a new heart and a new spirit. For why should you die, O house of Israel?

32 "For I have no pleasure in the death of one who dies," says the Lord GOD. "Therefore turn and live!"

As to those "under the earth," clearly those who are "judged" will recognize the Judge and will bow before Him. This is a calamitous reality, the worst of circumstances. The One sent to redeem you, you now acknowledge and your sorrow at your sin will be forever with you. Say that to yourself, "your sorrow at your sin will be forever with you," and then realize that Jesus Christ came and paid the price for your sin, atoned for all the evil you ever thought or ever committed, that you might stand before the Father, blameless. You will acknowledge the Savior. Why are you waiting?

CHAPTER 15

THE PRINCE OF PEACE OR THE PRINCE—GOOD AND EVIL PERSONIFIED

There are two entities in the Scriptures referred to as "Prince." One spelled with a capital and the other not. In Daniel 9:25 he refers to "Messiah the Prince," and in 9:26 to the "prince who is to come" to destroy the city and the sanctuary. In Isaiah 9:6 the prophet says,

Isaiah 9:6 (KJV)
"For unto us a child is born, unto us a son is given: and the government shall be upon his shoulder: and his name shall be called Wonderful, Counselor, The mighty God, The everlasting Father, The Prince of Peace.

Here Isaiah cites the fact that the Messiah is "born," unto us a Son is given. This Child is our Prince of Peace, The Mighty God, (for who is Jesus Christ but God incarnate), the Counselor (for who is Jesus Christ but the Holy Spirit, sent), and The everlasting Father, (for who is Jesus but the one who will reign eternally, The Father). Consider this. How can the Messiah return as an adult Entity except that He was "born?" Isaiah says He was born. Read that verse again!

We have a very difficult time with the Father, Son and Holy Spirit being "one" owing to our human perspective. But our limitations are not His limitations. We try too hard to make the God of creation fit the expectations of those whom He created. He is the potter and we are the clay and the scriptures say, how can the clay say to the potter, what are you doing?

Ezekiel prophesies directly to the prince. He will be overthrown when He (the Messiah) comes. Listen.

Ezekiel 21:25-27 (NKJ)
25 'Now to you, O profane, wicked prince of Israel, whose day has come, whose iniquity shall end,
26 "thus says the Lord GOD: 'Remove the turban, and take off the crown; nothing shall remain the same. Exalt the humble, and humble the exalted.
27 Overthrown, overthrown, I will make it overthrown! It shall be no longer, until He comes whose right it is, and I will give it to Him.'

The "prince to come," cited by Daniel 9:25, is going to destroy the Temple mid way through the 7 year period. He is the prince of this world. He will compel the nations to worship him and to obey him until the Prince of Peace, our Messiah, comes. The fact that you are a slave and I am a "slave" to one prince or the other Prince is the choice that the scriptures offer. Have you ever thought of yourself as a slave of Satan? Probably not, yet if you accept the mark of the beast, you will be vowing to be a slave of the evil one. That is the reason that the decision to serve Satan is fatal. How else could it be?

Listen to the words of the Messiah concerning freedom and slavery.

John 8:31-36 (NKJ)
31 Then Jesus said to those Jews who believed Him, "If you abide in My word, you are My disciples indeed.
32 "And you shall know the truth, and the truth shall make you free."
33 They answered Him, "We are Abraham's descendants, and have never been in bondage to anyone. How can you say, 'You will be made free'?"
34 Jesus answered them, "Most assuredly, I say to you, whoever commits sin is a slave of sin.

35 **"And a slave does not abide in the house forever, but a son abides forever.**
36 **"Therefore if the Son makes you free, you shall be free indeed.**

Free from what? Free from slavery to sin. Only the Prince of Peace can free you from slavery to the prince of the earth. You are on Satan's turf and this turf and every thing upon it will be destroyed. Freedom from slavery to the prince is freedom from the flesh.

Why would one want "freedom from the flesh?" Because the flesh will perish. As unbecoming as it is to visualize what happens to the body when it dies, you should consider it. The flesh, after going through extensive decay, simply turns to dust. It is only your spirit that will survive. The Prince of Peace is offering you His Spirit that it might redeem your spirit. The prince of the earth is offering you eternal punishment, that which he has been promised as a fallen angel, one who defied God and seeks to prove that man is indeed a slave to evil.

Redemption is about choosing. Repeatedly, the Scriptures say, "Choose, this day, whom you will follow." If your spirit is not communing with and guided by His Spirit, you have chosen to be dominated by the power of the flesh and it is powerful. Listen:

Ephesians 6:12 (NKJ)
12 For we do not wrestle against flesh and blood, but against principalities, against powers, against the rulers of the darkness of this age, against spiritual hosts of wickedness in the heavenly places.

Satan is more "attractive" than most would think. He has power but he does not have more power than the Holy Spirit, in you. You have only one single source of power that can overcome the sins of the flesh. Listen:

1 Corinthians 10:13 (NKJ)
13 No temptation has overtaken you except such as is common to man; but God is faithful, who will not allow you to be tempted beyond what you are able, but with the temptation will also make the way of escape, that you may be able to bear it.

1 Corinthians 6:9-20 (NKJ)
9 Do you not know that the unrighteous will not inherit the kingdom of God? Do not be deceived. Neither fornicators, nor idolaters, nor adulterers, nor homosexuals, nor sodomites,

10 nor thieves, nor covetous, nor drunkards, nor revilers, nor extortioners will inherit the kingdom of God.

11 And such were some of you. But you were washed, but you were sanctified, but you were justified in the name of the Lord Jesus and by the Spirit of our God.

12 All things are lawful for me, but all things are not helpful. All things are lawful for me, but I will not be brought under the power of any.

13 Foods for the stomach and the stomach for foods, but God will destroy both it and them. Now the body is not for sexual immorality but for the Lord, and the Lord for the body.

14 And God both raised up the Lord and will also raise us up by His power.

15 Do you not know that your bodies are members of Christ? Shall I then take the members of Christ and make them members of a harlot? Certainly not!

16 Or do you not know that he who is joined to a harlot is one body with her? For "the two," He says, "shall become one flesh."

17 But he who is joined to the Lord is one spirit with Him.

18 Flee sexual immorality. Every sin that a man does is outside the body, but he who commits sexual immorality sins against his own body.

19 Or do you not know that your body is the temple of the Holy Spirit who is in you, whom you have from God, and you are not your own?

20 For you were bought at a price; therefore glorify God in your body and in your spirit, which are God's.

Yes, you were bought at a price and the One who has paid for you offers you freedom from sin. Temptation will continue. It is common to all men but the difference between those who serve the flesh, Satan, and those who serve the Holy Spirit is that the Holy Spirit can and will overcome sin in your life. If you choose to serve the Prince of Peace, your life will be "different" than those who choose to serve the prince of the earth. Ask yourself if the following list of traits characterize your life, right now.

Galatians 5:22-23 (NKJ)
22 ...the fruit of the Spirit is love, joy, peace, longsuffering, kindness, goodness, faithfulness,
23 gentleness, self-control. Against such there is no law.

Notice the capital "S" in Spirit. It is His Spirit in you that produces these fruits. If your life does not bear this kind of fruit it is because you do not have the Holy Spirit in you. If you do not have the Holy Spirit in you, you are a slave to the prince of this earth. These sentences may sound harsh and they are. We are not toying with a philosophical issue. We are engaged in a battle for your soul and mine. The Messiah came that we might have eternal life, in Him. Empowerment awaits. Impotence against the prince of this earth is the "default" setting in which we find ourselves. Neither you nor I can win this battle through our own accomplishments or efforts.

CHAPTER 16

THE MARK OF THE BEAST— A CHOICE FOR ETERNITY

Revelation 13:16-18 (NKJ)
16 He causes all, both small and great, rich and poor, free and slave, to receive a mark on their right hand or on their foreheads,
17 and that no one may buy or sell except one who has the mark or the name of the beast, or the number of his name.
18 Here is wisdom. Let him who has understanding calculate the number of the beast, for it is the number of a man: His number is 666. (NKJ)

The decision to reject the mark of the beast is an eternal decision. It will take great courage, not of yourself, to declare your faith when faced with the question, "will you accept the mark, or not?" Take note that you will know whether you are taking the mark or the number of his name by understanding that you can not buy or sell without it. You do not have to take the mark or number of his name but listen to what happened to some that did not.

Revelation 20:4 (NKJ)
4 And I saw thrones, and they sat on them, and judgment was committed to them. Then I saw the souls of those who had been beheaded for their witness to Jesus and for the word of God, who had not worshiped the beast or his image, and had not received his mark on their foreheads or on their hands. And they lived and reigned with Christ for a thousand years.

Rather than face certain death, many will flee to the hills and valleys and hide among the rocks to avoid the persecution that is about to occur. Daniel, in his vision, listens to a question regarding the timing of these events. Notice the precision of God's answer.

Daniel 12:4-13 (NKJ)
4 "But you, Daniel, shut up the words, and seal the book until the time of the end; many shall run to and fro, and knowledge shall increase."
5 Then I, Daniel, looked; and there stood two others, one on this riverbank and the other on that riverbank.
6 And one said to the man clothed in linen, who was above the waters of the river, "How long shall the fulfillment of these wonders be?"
7 Then I heard the man clothed in linen, who was above the waters of the river, when he held up his right hand and his left hand to heaven, and swore by Him who lives forever, that it shall be for a time, times, and half a time; and when the power of the holy people has been completely shattered, all these things shall be finished.
8 Although I heard, I did not understand. Then I said, "My lord, what shall be the end of these things?"
9 And he said, "Go your way, Daniel, for the words are closed up and sealed till the time of the end.
10 "Many shall be purified, made white, and refined, but the wicked shall do wickedly; and none of the wicked shall understand, but the wise shall understand.
11 "And from the time that the daily sacrifice is taken away, and the abomination of desolation is set up, there shall be one thousand two hundred and ninety days.
12 "Blessed is he who waits, and comes to the one thousand three hundred and thirty-five days.
13 "But you, go your way till the end; for you shall rest, and will arise to your inheritance at the end of the days."

First, the precision of 1,290 days is stated as the length of time the persecution will last. The persecution will begin when the "daily sacrifice is taken away." Of course, to be taken away, it would have commenced coincident with the rebuilding of the Temple. Thousands of years ago Daniel was told that the Temple would be rebuilt and sacrifices would commence. When it happens it will be yet another prophecy fulfilled before your eyes. What will it take to humble yourself before God, repent and serve Him? More evidence? No, a changed heart, a will to worship Him and acknowledge Him in every way is what it takes.

Notice also that in Daniel's vision he is told to "seal the book until the time of the end; many shall run to and fro, and knowledge shall increase." Has knowledge ever increased at a faster rate? Has the vision of Daniel been sealed to the end? For instance, have you understood this vision before this time?

But, who is the beast?

Revelation 13:3 (NKJ)
3 And I saw one of his heads as if it had been mortally wounded, and his deadly wound was healed. And all the world marveled and followed the beast.

Practically every noted commentator who writes on this verse introduces the fall of Rome and the ascension of the Papacy as representations of the wound that was healed. Their observations may be correct. But perhaps a simple sign we should look for is that the beast will be a leader who has recovered from a mortal wound. The "leader" could be a political entity and not a person, but the Scriptures lead you to feel that it is an individual. Perhaps the "wound" will not be physical. One can speculate in any direction, but the beast will, by some measure, have recovered from a "wound," whether physical, social or political.

If in fact the beast actually has recovered from a physical and mortal wound, I should think his identity would be unquestionable.

Revelation 13:4-5 (NKJ)
4 So they worshiped the dragon who gave authority to the beast; and they worshiped the beast, saying, "Who is like the beast? Who is able to make war with him?"
5 And he was given a mouth speaking great things and blasphemies, and he was given authority to continue for forty-two months.

Here the beast is respected and worshipped. The beast will speak "great things," thus be an orator who is able to sway the masses, but the beast will not honor God. He will lead the nations into "peace and safety" but not as a man of God. Listen.

1 Thessalonians 5:2-3 (NKJ)
2 For you yourselves know perfectly that the day of the Lord so comes as a thief in the night.
3 For when they say, "Peace and safety!" then sudden destruction comes upon them, as labor pains upon a pregnant woman. And they shall not escape.

The time leading up to the "ending of the sacrifices" will be considered good times. The beast will speak great things and peace and safety will be evident. But when the sacrifices are stopped in the Temple, understand, in advance, that the next 42 months are going to be times of extreme persecution. You will have to decide whether to worship the beast and take the mark of the beast or not. Listen.

Revelation 13:6-8 (NKJ)
6 Then he opened his mouth in blasphemy against God, to blaspheme His name, His tabernacle, and those who dwell in heaven.
7 It was granted to him to make war with the saints and to overcome them. And authority was given him over every tribe, tongue, and nation.
8 All who dwell on the earth will worship him, whose names have not been written in the Book of Life of the Lamb slain from the foundation of the world.

This last verse should help you understand that the name of every redeemed soul is already known to God and is written in the Book of Life. Yes, you have volition. You choose and you decide. But God, who knows the Alpha from the Omega, who knows all things, also knows who will choose Him. You whom He knows are the Elect. Your names are already in the Book of Life. God also knows who will reject Him. God knows the beginning from the end. He knows all your decisions, thoughts, and actions. This truth exceeds our understanding but does not exceed our ability to believe it, by faith.

When the beast makes "war with the saints," the saints will not prevail, in these 42 months. Several times I have mentioned the rapture of the Church, that event when believers will be caught up in the clouds. Two sentences make the rapture "before the tribulation," less certain than we believers might hope. First in;

Daniel 12:7 (NKJ)
7 "…when the power of the holy people has been completely shattered".

and again in;

Revelation 13:7 (NKJ)
7 "It was granted to him to make war with the saints and to overcome them".

We find holy people and saints being persecuted during the last 3 1/2 years of the tribulation. I do not care to focus on the debate of pre, mid and post tribulation positions, but I would strongly suggest that "being ready" is far more important than being correct. If you are ready it will not matter which of these scenarios is correct. Whether you believe that the Church will be raptured before the tribulation, in the middle (3½ years) of the tribulation or at the end of the tribulation has no bearing on your personal salvation. Being ready is the primary issue.

Those who are purified by their faith granted by the grace of God, in that time period will be those who have made or who are going to make a commitment to the Lord. They will refuse the mark of the beast, the mark that permits men to buy and sell. This will require great resolve in the face of very strong persecution. Those acquaintances of yours who consort with the beast will become your enemies. You are going to understand what it means to be a "remnant." Read on concerning key prophecy regarding the beast also called the Antichrist and the dragon, Satan.

Revelation 13:9-15 (NKJ)
9 If anyone has an ear, let him hear.

10 He who leads into captivity shall go into captivity; he who kills with the sword must be killed with the sword. Here is the patience and the faith of the saints.
11 Then I saw another beast coming up out of the earth, and he had two horns like a lamb and spoke like a dragon.
12 And he exercises all the authority of the first beast in his presence, and causes the earth and those who dwell in it to worship the first beast, whose deadly wound was healed.
13 He performs great signs, so that he even makes fire come down from heaven on the earth in the sight of men.
14 And he deceives those who dwell on the earth by those signs which he was granted to do in the sight of the beast, telling those who dwell on the earth to make an image to the beast who was wounded by the sword and lived.
15 He was granted power to give breath to the image of the beast, that the image of the beast should both speak and cause as many as would not worship the image of the beast to be killed.

The "other beast" who "spoke like a dragon," exhibits great power and does wondrous things such as commanding fire to come down from heaven. During these times Satan, the one who gave power to the beast, will have great power, to deceive if possible, even the elect. He gives power and "breath" to the beast to kill those who will not accept the mark of the beast on their right hand or foreheads. No mark, no transactions. No mark and your death shall be decreed.

If you must have the mark of the beast to buy or sell and you refuse the mark, how will you survive? Recall that the "Church," the Body of Believers, is promised that they are not "appointed to wrath." At least the "pre tribulation" argument is that the body of believers will be caught up in the clouds with Christ and avoid the wrath of the tribulation. But the question isn't whether they will avoid the wrath of God, but when? Will it be before the tribulation, during or the tribulation period or after? Does the wrath from which men are to be protected specifically refer to the wrath of God and not the wrath of man? Perhaps, but understand that just as Nebuchadnezzar dished out "wrath" to God's people, saints and sinners, so might the Antichrist. No "wrath" is served up by man, absent the consent of the Lord and not all wrath leads to bad results.

Listen to the Word.

Job 1:6-12 (NKJ)
6 Now there was a day when the sons of God came to present themselves before the LORD, and Satan also came among them.
7 And the LORD said to Satan, "From where do you come?" So Satan answered the LORD and said, "From going to and fro on the earth, and from walking back and forth on it."
8 Then the LORD said to Satan, "Have you considered My servant Job, that there is none like him on the earth, a blameless and upright man, one who fears God and shuns evil?"
9 So Satan answered the LORD and said, "Does Job fear God for nothing?
10 "Have You not made a hedge around him, around his household, and around all that he has on every side? You have blessed the work of his hands, and his possessions have increased in the land.
11 "But now, stretch out Your hand and touch all that he has, and he will surely curse You to Your face!"
12 So the LORD said to Satan, "Behold, all that he has is in your power; only do not lay a hand on his person." So Satan went out from the presence of the LORD.

Here God permitted one of His saints to be tested. Job passed the test. He remained faithful even though all that he had was destroyed including his children. But Satan wasn't through in his effort to break Job's faith. Listen.

Job 2:1-6 (NKJ)
1 Again there was a day when the sons of God came to present themselves before the LORD, and Satan came also among them to present himself before the LORD.
2 And the LORD said to Satan, "From where do you come?" So Satan answered the LORD and said, "From going to and fro on the earth, and from walking back and forth on it."

3 Then the LORD said to Satan, "Have you considered My servant Job, that there is none like him on the earth, a blameless and upright man, one who fears God and shuns evil? And still he holds fast to his integrity, although you incited Me against him, to destroy him without cause."
4 So Satan answered the LORD and said, "Skin for skin! Yes, all that a man has he will give for his life.
5 "But stretch out Your hand now, and touch his bone and his flesh, and he will surely curse You to Your face!"
6 And the LORD said to Satan, "Behold, he is in your hand, but spare his life."

You need to read the entire account of Job's experiences to grasp the many truths it presents, but here was the outcome:

Job 42:12 (NKJ)
12 Now the LORD blessed the latter days of Job more than his beginning… (because Job remained faithful.)

The wrath Job experienced was permitted but God foreknew the entire circumstance and used Satan's evil intent to glorify Himself and to demonstrate the faith of Job to the world, forever. You must read the book of Job carefully if you want to grasp the power of Satan, whose power is limited by God, but who nevertheless seeks to destroy your faith and mine.

Job, after being restored, doubly, then went on to die "full of days." His flesh did die and his spirit did live for redemption, to be housed in a body that will be eternal. Listen to the fate of Job and those who love God.

1 Thessalonians 4:13-18 (NKJ)
13 But I do not want you to be ignorant, brethren, concerning those who have fallen asleep, lest you sorrow as others who have no hope.
14 For if we believe that Jesus died and rose again, even so God will bring with Him those who sleep in Jesus.
15 For this we say to you by the word of the Lord, that we who are alive and remain until the coming of the Lord will by no means precede those who are asleep.

16 For the Lord Himself will descend from heaven with a shout, with the voice of an archangel, and with the trumpet of God. And the dead in Christ will rise first.
17 Then we who are alive and remain shall be caught up together with them in the clouds to meet the Lord in the air. And thus we shall always be with the Lord.
18 Therefore comfort one another with these words.

This prophecy covers all those who are "dead in Christ" as well as "alive in Christ," and this is the rapture event. Its exact timing is in question. We are warned many times to be ready, but not to "predict" the time of the rapture.

A careful reader may have wondered aloud, "where did it ever say that Job believed that Jesus Christ was his Redeemer?" It did not say Jesus was the One in whom Job had faith. Job's life, as well as the lives of Noah, Moses, and Abraham all preceded the birth of Christ. One could ask, how were they saved if their Redeemer had not yet been born? The answer is provided in the Word. They had faith and it was accounted to them for righteousness. But what is faith? Listen.

Hebrews 11:1-3 (NKJ)
1 Now faith is the substance of things hoped for, the evidence of things not seen.
2 For by it the elders obtained a good testimony.
3 By faith we understand that the worlds were framed by the word of God, so that the things which are seen were not made of things which are visible. (NKJ)

Hebrews 11:7-10 (NKJ)
7 By faith Noah, being divinely warned of things not yet seen, moved with godly fear, prepared an ark for the saving of his household, by which he condemned the world and became heir of the righteousness which is according to faith.
8 By faith Abraham obeyed when he was called to go out to the place which he would receive as an inheritance. And he went out, not knowing where he was going.

9 By faith he dwelt in the land of promise as in a foreign country, dwelling in tents with Isaac and Jacob, the heirs with him of the same promise;
10 for he waited for the city which has foundations, whose builder and maker is God.

Hebrews 11:32-34 (NKJ)
32 And what more shall I say? For the time would fail me to tell of Gideon and Barak and Samson and Jephthah, also of David and Samuel and the prophets:
33 who through faith subdued kingdoms, worked righteousness, obtained promises, stopped the mouths of lions,
34 quenched the violence of fire, escaped the edge of the sword, out of weakness were made strong, became valiant in battle, turned to flight the armies of the aliens. (NKJ)

Job's faith and the faith of all God's children, before the redeeming sacrifice of Jesus Christ, was accounted to them for righteousness. But let's return to the primary focus of this topic. Was it God's intent that His chosen people, his saints, be appointed to wrath? Listen.

1 Thessalonians 5:9 (NKJ)
9 For God did not appoint us to wrath, but to obtain salvation through our Lord Jesus Christ,

You may have some problems with the imagery of the beast, but most agree that the beasts are Satan and his servant, the Antichrist. The specifics of the identity of the beast should not escape your attention. It is a precise prophecy.

Accepting the mark of the Beast, in order that "one may buy or sell" may take several forms but I believe you know that implanted "chips" already exist as a means of identification. Each implanted chip will have all of your personal data imbedded in a scannable format, and the day will come when all transactions will be based on the data on the chip or some other form of scannable identification. This may seem to be a little far fetched, but technologically, we are already there. Doesn't it get your attention to know that the technology to have this be true is very recent? This prophecy was written thousands of years ago and readers over the centuries must have wondered how these things could be true. These are "end time signs," not to be missed!

Now listen to the fate of those who accept the mark of the beast, as well as the promise to those who do not.

Revelation 14:9-13 (NKJ)
9 ... "If anyone worships the beast and his image, and receives his mark on his forehead or on his hand,
10 "he himself shall also drink of the wine of the wrath of God, which is poured out full strength into the cup of His indignation. He shall be tormented with fire and brimstone in the presence of the holy angels and in the presence of the Lamb.
11 "And the smoke of their torment ascends forever and ever; and they have no rest day or night, who worship the beast and his image, and whoever receives the mark of his name."
12 Here is the patience of the saints; here are those who keep the commandments of God and the faith of Jesus.
13 Then I heard a voice from heaven saying to me, "Write: 'Blessed are the dead who die in the Lord from now on.'" "Yes," says the Spirit, "that they may rest from their labors, and their works follow them."

In these verses you are told that the wrath of God will be poured out "full strength" to those who accept the mark of the beast. But the saints, those, who keep the commandments of God and the faith of Jesus, will be blessed. Your choice is made crystal clear. Do not accept the mark!

The scriptures indicate that the return of the Messiah will occur when the "fullness of the Gentiles has come in." In other words, the period of the great tribulation, the last segment of time prior to the establishment of the Kingdom on earth, will not commence until this occurs.

I heard one commentator say recently that there is not one single event unfulfilled regarding the moment in time in which the Church is to be raptured. Yet there is one. There must be one more soul, at least, to be saved. When the last "believer" has been added to the Church, as a result of their confession of faith, bathed in the Grace of God, then the rapture will occur. God knows who will turn to Him and love Him and His hand is extended still but there will be a time in which time runs out. Are you that soul for whom the door is being help open?

The "blindness of Israel" we spoke of earlier, refers to Israel's lack of recognition of Jesus Christ as their personal Savior and Messiah. The statement refers to Israel but Israel is both a country and a people.

The individual Jews, and there of course are some, who claim Jesus as the Messiah and their personal Savior, have removed themselves from the uncertainty of the events that will occur during the tribulation, a period in which Israel will eventually undergo the worst persecution ever.

I say uncertainty, because some Jews will survive the persecution of the tribulation period with their faith in God, in tact. As to whether you personally have the resolve and inner strength that will be required when you are forced to accept the mark of the beast and to obey the Antichrist or to die, time will tell. Perhaps the primary point of this book is to tell you that there is a way to prepare yourself and to replace the uncertainty of your response to a death sentence with the certainty of your salvation, now. I do not say that to frighten you, but if that is what it takes…

As much as I would like to think that this presentation will "persuade" you, nothing could be further from the truth. The Holy Spirit calls you, not a man. Your faith and belief in the Father, Son and Holy Spirit redeem you, not some external advocate. It is your belief that the Lord exists and loves you and that you are willing to come before him in all humility and with heartfelt contrition that saves you. Even reading the Word daily can not save you. It takes a new heart, one sustainable and available only by the power of the Holy Spirit in you. We who seek to serve sometimes get overly excited about our sense of mission, but it is His mission in you and His message to you that matters.

Go in all humility and contrition to the Word, go in prayer to God, declare your belief and faith in the atoning act of Jesus Christ. Repent; be baptized in the name of the Father, Son and Holy Ghost. Go beyond the limitations of your flesh. Seek to be filled with the Holy Spirit. God knows whether you will respond or not and may He have mercy on those who fail to seek and obey.

Listen to the fate of those who accepted the mark of the beast. I know I have quoted these verses in another topic, but honestly, you will learn something new every day that you read the Scriptures, over and over again. The Word is alive and active. It is dynamic. It witnesses to you more powerfully than any man.

Revelation 16:1-21 (NKJ)
1 Then I heard a loud voice from the temple saying to the seven angels, "Go and pour out the bowls of the wrath of God on the earth."
2 So the first went and poured out his bowl upon the earth, and a foul and loathsome sore came upon the men who had the mark of the beast and those who worshiped his image.
3 Then the second angel poured out his bowl on the sea, and it became blood as of a dead man; and every living creature in the sea died.
4 Then the third angel poured out his bowl on the rivers and springs of water, and they became blood.
5 And I heard the angel of the waters saying: "You are righteous, O Lord, the One who is and who was and who is to be, because You have judged these things.
6 For they have shed the blood of saints and prophets, and You have given them blood to drink. For it is their just due."
7 And I heard another from the altar saying, "Even so, Lord God Almighty, true and righteous are Your judgments."
8 Then the fourth angel poured out his bowl on the sun, and power was given to him to scorch men with fire.
9 And men were scorched with great heat, and they blasphemed the name of God who has power over these plagues; and they did not repent and give Him glory.
10 Then the fifth angel poured out his bowl on the throne of the beast, and his kingdom became full of darkness; and they gnawed their tongues because of the pain.
11 They blasphemed the God of heaven because of their pains and their sores, and did not repent of their deeds.

12 Then the sixth angel poured out his bowl on the great river Euphrates, and its water was dried up, so that the way of the kings from the east might be prepared.
13 And I saw three unclean spirits like frogs coming out of the mouth of the dragon, out of the mouth of the beast, and out of the mouth of the false prophet.
14 For they are spirits of demons, performing signs, which go out to the kings of the earth and of the whole world, to gather them to the battle of that great day of God Almighty.
15 "Behold, I am coming as a thief. Blessed is he who watches, and keeps his garments, lest he walk naked and they see his shame."
16 And they gathered them together to the place called in Hebrew, Armageddon.
17 Then the seventh angel poured out his bowl into the air, and a loud voice came out of the temple of heaven, from the throne, saying, "It is done!"
18 And there were noises and thunderings and lightnings; and there was a great earthquake, such a mighty and great earthquake as had not occurred since men were on the earth.
19 Now the great city was divided into three parts, and the cities of the nations fell. And great Babylon was remembered before God, to give her the cup of the wine of the fierceness of His wrath.
20 Then every island fled away, and the mountains were not found.
21 And great hail from heaven fell upon men, each hailstone about the weight of a talent. Men blasphemed God because of the plague of the hail, since that plague was exceedingly great.

There are those who will recoil from the thought of such awful judgment. Let's agree that the scriptures say that those who refuse the mark of the beast will suffer at the hands of the Antichrist, some unto death. One thing appears certain. If you are here for the Great Tribulation, you are going to be tested as never before. Listen to the circumstance of those who refuse the mark of the beast.

Revelation 15:2-4 (NKJ)
2 And I saw something like a sea of glass mingled with fire, and those who have the victory over the beast, over his image and over his mark

and over the number of his name, standing on the sea of glass, having harps of God.
3 They sing the song of Moses, the servant of God, and the song of the Lamb, saying: "Great and marvelous are Your works, lord God Almighty! Just and true are Your ways, O King of the saints!
4 Who shall not fear You, O Lord, and glorify Your name? For You alone are holy. For all nations shall come and worship before You, for Your judgments have been manifested."

Those who sing the song of Moses and the song of the Lamb will be in a situation where "all nations shall come and worship before You, for Your judgments have been manifested." This, in my opinion, is a Millennium experience and this joy will follow the judgment of the Antichrist and all who have accepted the mark of the Beast.

Consider yourself warned, many times over, if you have read these scriptures before, and choose life, eternal life, now. The scriptures make many references to the "remnant" but check the references provided here which make the following point: The gate is narrow that leads to life and there are few that find it!

Luke 13:23-30 (NKJ)
23 Then one said to Him, "Lord, are there few who are saved?" And He said to them,
24 "Strive to enter through the narrow gate, for many, I say to you, will seek to enter and will not be able.
25 "When once the Master of the house has risen up and shut the door, and you begin to stand outside and knock at the door, saying, 'Lord, Lord, open for us,' and He will answer and say to you, 'I do not know you, where you are from,'
26 "then you will begin to say, 'We ate and drank in Your presence, and You taught in our streets.'
27 "But He will say, 'I tell you I do not know you, where you are from. Depart from Me, all you workers of iniquity.'
28 "There will be weeping and gnashing of teeth, when you see Abraham and Isaac and Jacob and all the prophets in the kingdom of God, and yourselves thrust out.

29 "They will come from the east and the west, from the north and the south, and sit down in the kingdom of God.
30 "And indeed there are last who will be first, and there are first who will be last."

Matthew 7:13-14 (NKJ)
13 "Enter by the narrow gate; for wide is the gate and broad is the way that leads to destruction, and there are many who go in by it.
14 "Because narrow is the gate and difficult is the way which leads to life, and there are few who find it.

Matthew 16:24-26 (NKJ)
24 Then Jesus said to His disciples, "If anyone desires to come after Me, let him deny himself, and take up his cross, and follow Me.
25 "For whoever desires to save his life will lose it, but whoever loses his life for My sake will find it.
26 "For what profit is it to a man if he gains the whole world, and loses his own soul? Or what will a man give in exchange for his soul?

Acts 14:22 (NKJ)
22 ..."We must through many tribulations enter the kingdom of God."

I know that neither you nor I have been able to keep the whole Law and I know that the sacrifices and offerings that we have made are insufficient. There is only one sacrifice that can cleanse us of our sins, only One who can deliver us to the Father, as if we had never sinned. You do not have to go through the tribulation, absent the enabling power of the Holy Spirit, and if you choose to do so it appears few will be faithful unto death.

Choose life, eternal life, now. Go to God's Holy Word as one dying of thirst. He will give you Rivers of Living Water; He will give you His peace now and forever. Relax in His love and His caring Hands. Commit your resources, of every imaginable kind to His service. Know that resources represent an opportunity and a liability and that "to whom much is given, much is required." The only asset that will survive is your soul, your spiritual self. Every other asset will perish. The poet has asked, "How can we cherish that which will perish?" Childish prose, to be sure, but an almost universal error in judgment.

As an aside, if you believe evil spirits exist, how can you not believe the Spirit of God exists? There are even those who "worship" Satan, therefore acknowledging evil spirits. Those who "worship" the stars which God created, or inanimate objects (gods?) that must be transported about and which are made of perishable material, are missing the greatest possible blessing. God loves every person He created, including "worshippers" of false gods. God will forgive, welcome you back and rejoice that a "lost child" has returned home.

Doesn't that kind of parental affection, that depth of forgiveness and mercy, humble you? God will not remain angry at your sin if you stop sinning! Turn to the only God that is Omnipotent, Omnipresent and Omniscient that exists. Turn to the only God that has sent a Messiah; One who is able to erase your sins from the sight and the memory of God; One who, when he was rejected by man, then reached out, again and forever, saying "Forgive them Father, for they do not know what they are doing." That is our God, completely different than any god contrived by man. The reason that accepting the mark of the beast is such a fatal error is that it is an act of allegiance and obedience to a false god.

We could continue in discussing the details concerning the tribulation and all of the scriptures in the Old and New Testament that point to it as a crucial event, but suffice it to say that it is one of the final events before the battle of Armageddon, where the enemies of God will be slain by God. Those who are led to understand that they must choose to resist the beast (by refusing to accept the mark) will find that they either must die or flee to survive.

In the wake of the event September 11, 2001, secure identity cards are now being widely discussed. These cards perform a narrow function compared to the purpose of the mark of the beast. However, the speed with which identity cards are being considered should simply help you understand that it is a small step to implant a data chip, if that is indeed what will be considered, in order to buy and sell. Prophecy fulfilled is at hand!

CHAPTER 17

THE BATTLE OF ARMAGEDDON—THE PRELUDE TO A RESTORED KINGDOM

When the final 3½ year period of the tribulation is completed what is known as the "Grapes of Wrath" will commence. Listen.

Revelation 14:14-20 (NKJ)
14 Then I looked, and behold, a white cloud, and on the cloud sat One like the Son of Man, having on His head a golden crown, and in His hand a sharp sickle.
15 And another angel came out of the temple, crying with a loud voice to Him who sat on the cloud, "Thrust in Your sickle and reap, for the time has come for You to reap, for the harvest of the earth is ripe."
16 So He who sat on the cloud thrust in His sickle on the earth, and the earth was reaped.
17 Then another angel came out of the temple which is in heaven, he also having a sharp sickle.
18 And another angel came out from the altar, who had power over fire, and he cried with a loud cry to him who had the sharp sickle, saying, "Thrust in your sharp sickle and gather the clusters of the vine of the earth, for her grapes are fully ripe."
19 So the angel thrust his sickle into the earth and gathered the vine of the earth, and threw it into the great winepress of the wrath of God.
20 And the winepress was trampled outside the city, and blood came out of the winepress, up to the horses' bridles, for one thousand six hundred furlongs.

Those who accept the mark of the beast, those who serve evil, those who have not found safety in the mountains and valleys, will be destroyed during this period where the wrath of God is poured out as the grapes are gathered into the winepress of God.

What follows are the prophecies of the seven last plagues and the seven bowls of the wrath of God (Read Chapters 15 and 16 of the Book of Revelation for the details). Suffice it so say there will be suffering such as could not be imagined. Those events will wind up with the kings of the earth assembling for a final battle, the battle of Armageddon, where God destroys evil, not for the last time, but for a period of 1000 years.

Revelation 16:11-12 (NKJ)
11 They blasphemed the God of heaven because of their pains and their sores, and did not repent of their deeds.
12 Then the sixth angel poured out his bowl on the great river Euphrates, and its water was dried up, so that the way of the kings from the east might be prepared.

(I believe this miracle mirrors the miracle of the parting of the Red Sea when the warriors of Egypt pursued the fleeing Jews, but in this case, it is the enemies of God having their way to the final battle made easy. They are coming after the Jews again, but now they come to a final battle which God, not the Jews, fights.)

Revelation 16:13-21 (NKJ)
13 And I saw three unclean spirits like frogs coming out of the mouth of the dragon, out of the mouth of the beast, and out of the mouth of the false prophet.
14 For they are spirits of demons, performing signs, which go out to the kings of the earth and of the whole world, to gather them to the battle of that great day of God Almighty.
15 "Behold, I am coming as a thief. Blessed is he who watches, and keeps his garments, lest he walk naked and they see his shame."
16 And they gathered them together to the place called in Hebrew, Armageddon.

17 Then the seventh angel poured out his bowl into the air, and a loud voice came out of the temple of heaven, from the throne, saying, "It is done!"
18 And there were noises and thunderings and lightnings; and there was a great earthquake, such a mighty and great earthquake as had not occurred since men were on the earth.
19 Now the great city was divided into three parts, and the cities of the nations fell. And great Babylon was remembered before God, to give her the cup of the wine of the fierceness of His wrath.
20 Then every island fled away, and the mountains were not found.
21 And great hail from heaven fell upon men, each hailstone about the weight of a talent. Men blasphemed God because of the plague of the hail, since that plague was exceedingly great.

You may either believe verses 18-20 or not, but if you do believe, then you know the powerful manner in which God will "reorganize" the world physically, politically and spiritually. This will not be the same place after the battle of Armageddon. This will be a world preparing itself for the Millennium, the 1000 year reign of Christ, here on earth. Below, in verses 23 and 24 you will see how God's power will be unleashed against all evil. The promise to Israel lies in verse 27. The battle of Armageddon will touch every living soul and its impact will exceed your ability to envision it. Listen:

Jeremiah 4:9-29 (NKJ)
9 "And it shall come to pass in that day," says the LORD, "That the heart of the king shall perish, and the heart of the princes; the priests shall be astonished, and the prophets shall wonder."
10 Then I said, "Ah, Lord GOD! Surely You have greatly deceived this people and Jerusalem, saying, 'You shall have peace,' whereas the sword reaches to the heart."
11 At that time it will be said to this people and to Jerusalem, "A dry wind of the desolate heights blows in the wilderness toward the daughter of My people– not to fan or to cleanse–
12 A wind too strong for these will come for Me; now I will also speak judgment against them."

13 "Behold, he shall come up like clouds, and his chariots like a whirlwind. His horses are swifter than eagles. Woe to us, for we are plundered!"
14 O Jerusalem, wash your heart from wickedness, that you may be saved. How long shall your evil thoughts lodge within you?
15 For a voice declares from Dan and proclaims affliction from Mount Ephraim:
16 "Make mention to the nations, yes, proclaim against Jerusalem, that watchers come from a far country and raise their voice against the cities of Judah.
17 Like keepers of a field they are against her all around, because she has been rebellious against Me," says the LORD.
18 "Your ways and your doings have procured these things for you. This is your wickedness, because it is bitter, because it reaches to your heart."
19 O my soul, my soul! I am pained in my very heart! My heart makes a noise in me; I cannot hold my peace, because you have heard, O my soul, the sound of the trumpet, the alarm of war.
20 Destruction upon destruction is cried, for the whole land is plundered. Suddenly my tents are plundered, and my curtains in a moment.
21 How long will I see the standard, and hear the sound of the trumpet?
22 "For My people are foolish, they have not known Me. They are silly children, and they have no understanding. They are wise to do evil, but to do good they have no knowledge."
23 I beheld the earth, and indeed it was without form, and void; and the heavens, they had no light.
24 I beheld the mountains, and indeed they trembled, and all the hills moved back and forth.
25 I beheld, and indeed there was no man, and all the birds of the heavens had fled.
26 I beheld, and indeed the fruitful land was a wilderness, and all its cities were broken down at the presence of the LORD, by His fierce anger.
27 For thus says the LORD: "The whole land shall be desolate; yet I will not make a full end.
28 For this shall the earth mourn, and the heavens above be black, because I have spoken. I have purposed and will not relent, nor will I turn back from it.

29 The whole city shall flee from the noise of the horsemen and bowmen. They shall go into thickets and climb up on the rocks. Every city shall be forsaken, and not a man shall dwell in it.

I believe that when evil is judged, prior to the Millennium, it will be a far reaching judgment and that the Battle of Armageddon is only one of the visions that will manifest God's power. The entire world will experience God's power and only those who have responded to His love will experience the first resurrection of their dead bodies or the transition from life, to life, if you are still alive.

This horrible destruction will render death to those whose bodies will await the final judgment at the end of the millennium, that time when Jesus Christ separates the sheep from the goats, the sinners from the saints and it will signal the resurrection of believers to reign in the millennium with their Savior and Lord, the Messiah, Jesus Christ.

The final destruction of the earth and of sin will occur at the end of the millennium, right after Satan has been unloosed to tempt whomever he can. The judgment will be either to eternal life or to eternal suffering, according to the Scriptures. New Jerusalem, heaven, will descend and all those who love God will be with Him for eternity. The other topics that describe these events provide the scriptural references.

But let's not get too involved in studying what will happen. Instead, make your peace with your Maker, now. Repent, turn from your sin, be cleansed of all iniquity by the redeeming Blood of Jesus, the only sacrifice that will allow you to stand before the Father, wrapped in the righteousness of your personal Savior. This last sentence is hugely more important than any other sentence in this book. It is not knowing what is going to happen or not happen that will save you. If you want a new heart, a new start, a rebirth, reconciliation, ask and you shall receive. It is not complicated, but it does require a humble and contrite heart, one that recognizes its sinful past and a heart that wants to serve God, in the perfection of the Holy Spirit. We seek not our perfection or our righteousness, but His in us.

CHAPTER 18

HOW DOES ONE DEFINE THE REMNANT?

One of the most difficult portions of scripture for me to comment upon is the point that "all Israel will be saved." Does that mean that the saints of Israel as well as sinners will be saved? Does it mean the family of those who married "outsiders" will be saved? Does it mean only those who obeyed the laws of God and faithfully worshipped Him will be saved? Gratefully, neither you nor I have to make that call.

The scriptures teach two major themes regarding the redemption of the Jews, throughout the Bible. The first point is frightening, in my opinion. Only a remnant will be saved. Listen to one occasion where God's word makes that point.

2 Kings 21:12-15 (NKJ)
12 "therefore thus says the LORD God of Israel: 'Behold, I am bringing such calamity upon Jerusalem and Judah, that whoever hears of it, both his ears will tingle.
13 'And I will stretch over Jerusalem the measuring line of Samaria and the plummet of the house of Ahab; I will wipe Jerusalem as one wipes a dish, wiping it and turning it upside down.
14 'So I will forsake the remnant of My inheritance and deliver them into the hand of their enemies; and they shall become victims of plunder to all their enemies,

15 'because they have done evil in My sight, and have provoked Me to anger since the day their fathers came out of Egypt, even to this day.'"

Then the prophet Ezra scolds Israel. The time was "then" but the sense is "now."

Ezra 9:6-15 (NKJ)
6 And I said, "O my God: I am too ashamed and humiliated to lift up my face to You, my God; for our iniquities have risen higher than our heads, and our guilt has grown up to the heavens.
7 "Since the days of our fathers to this day we have been very guilty, and for our iniquities we, our kings, and our priests have been delivered into the hand of the kings of the lands, to the sword, to captivity, to plunder, and to humiliation, as it is this day.
8 "And now for a little while grace has been shown from the LORD our God, to leave us a remnant to escape, and to give us a peg in His holy place, that our God may enlighten our eyes and give us a measure of revival in our bondage.
9 "For we were slaves. Yet our God did not forsake us in our bondage; but He extended mercy to us in the sight of the kings of Persia, to revive us, to repair the house of our God, to rebuild its ruins, and to give us a wall in Judah and Jerusalem.
10 "And now, O our God, what shall we say after this? For we have forsaken Your commandments,
11 "which You have commanded by Your servants the prophets, saying, 'The land which you are entering to possess is an unclean land, with the uncleanness of the peoples of the lands, with their abominations which have filled it from one end to another with their impurity.
12 'Now therefore, do not give your daughters as wives for their sons, nor take their daughters to your sons; and never seek their peace or prosperity, that you may be strong and eat the good of the land, and leave it as an inheritance to your children forever.'
13 "And after all that has come upon us for our evil deeds and for our great guilt, since You our God have punished us less than our iniquities deserve, and have given us such deliverance as this,
14 "should we again break Your commandments, and join in marriage with the people committing these abominations? Would You not be

angry with us until You had consumed us, so that there would be no remnant or survivor?
15 "O LORD God of Israel, You are righteous, for we are left as a remnant, as it is this day. Here we are before You, in our guilt, though no one can stand before You because of this!"

The Scriptures say, in many places that all Israel will be saved. If you read long enough you also see that only a remnant will be remain faithful. Listen to an "all Israel" account.

Isaiah 45:15-19 (NKJ)
15 Truly You are God, who hide Yourself, O God of Israel, the Savior!
16 They shall be ashamed and also disgraced, all of them; they shall go in confusion together, who are makers of idols.
17 But Israel shall be saved by the LORD with an everlasting salvation; you shall not be ashamed or disgraced forever and ever.
18 For thus says the LORD, who created the heavens, who is God, who formed the earth and made it, who has established it, who did not create it in vain, who formed it to be inhabited: "I am the LORD, and there is no other.
19 I have not spoken in secret, in a dark place of the earth; I did not say to the seed of Jacob, 'Seek Me in vain'; I, the LORD, speak righteousness, I declare things that are right.

Since neither you nor I have to judge who will enter the Kingdom (and under what conditions), it becomes incumbent on us to focus on our own personal relationship with the Father, Son and Holy Spirit. Will you be part of the remnant? Will the Father say to us, "come unto your rest, good and faithful servant?" That becomes the only question that matters.

As a personal aside, I believe that many will be in the Kingdom, but not all will have the same rewards. We don't serve the Lord for our "rewards." We serve Him in response to His love for us and what He has done to reconcile our spirit with His Spirit. I would never suggest that you are able to rely on God's mercy if you deny the Messiah, don't honor God and are not filled with the Holy Spirit. God may be merciful in one or more of those cases but why would you test His mercy? Our Lord wants us to honor Him in every sense of the word, right now, and to not put off responding to His love.

Finally, if some Jews are not "saved," who decides on those who will comprise the remnant? That is not a question you and I should try to answer. Judgment, has been given by God, to the Messiah. Listen.

Isaiah 11:1-12 (NKJ)
1 There shall come forth a Rod from the stem of Jesse, and a Branch shall grow out of his roots.
2 The Spirit of the LORD shall rest upon Him, the Spirit of wisdom and understanding, the Spirit of counsel and might, the Spirit of knowledge and of the fear of the LORD.
3 His delight is in the fear of the LORD, and He shall not judge by the sight of His eyes, nor decide by the hearing of His ears;
4 But with righteousness He shall judge the poor, and decide with equity for the meek of the earth; he shall strike the earth with the rod of His mouth, and with the breath of His lips He shall slay the wicked.
5 Righteousness shall be the belt of His loins, and faithfulness the belt of His waist.
6 "The wolf also shall dwell with the lamb, the leopard shall lie down with the young goat, the calf and the young lion and the fatling together; and a little child shall lead them.
7 The cow and the bear shall graze; their young ones shall lie down together; and the lion shall eat straw like the ox.
8 The nursing child shall play by the cobra's hole, and the weaned child shall put his hand in the viper's den.
9 They shall not hurt nor destroy in all My holy mountain, for the earth shall be full of the knowledge of the LORD as the waters cover the sea.
10 "And in that day there shall be a Root of Jesse, who shall stand as a banner to the people; for the Gentiles shall seek Him, and His resting place shall be glorious."
11 It shall come to pass in that day that the LORD shall set His hand again the second time to recover the remnant of His people who are left, from Assyria and Egypt, from Pathros and Cush, from Elam and Shinar, from Hamath and the islands of the sea.

12 He will set up a banner for the nations, and will assemble the outcasts of Israel, and gather together the dispersed of Judah from the four corners of the earth.

The first 5 verses tell us the basis of the judgment to come. Read them carefully for they teach you the simple truth about judgment. No comment is necessary, but note that the "rod of His mouth" is a reference to the Word of God. Listen to these two quotes.

Revelation 1:16 (NKJ)
16 He had in His right hand seven stars, out of His mouth went a sharp two-edged sword, and His countenance was like the sun shining in its strength.

This reference to the Messiah then leads you to this quotation in Hebrews, one that I believe you should commit to memory.

Hebrews 4:12-13 (NKJ)
12 For the word of God is living and powerful, and sharper than any two-edged sword, piercing even to the division of soul and spirit, and of joints and marrow, and is a discerner of the thoughts and intents of the heart.
13 And there is no creature hidden from His sight, but all things are naked and open to the eyes of Him to whom we must give account.

If you haven't yet figured out how to get to know God, at the most personal level, it is the absence of His Word in your daily life that is handicapping you. Reread these two verses, again and again, until the truth sinks in. This "commentary" is intended to serve a single purpose. Go to the Word of God as a starving soul and He will feed you as only He can.

Regarding Isaiah 11:1-2, above, Christians believe, and the scriptures confirm, that the genealogy of Jesus, on the human level, is traced to Jesse, the father of David and that Jesus is the promised Messiah. Listen to this quote. It is one of hundreds that make the same point, over and over again throughout the scriptures. I beg you not to stop reading.

John 5:19-47 (NKJ)

19 …"Most assuredly, I say to you, the Son can do nothing of Himself, but what He sees the Father do; for whatever He does, the Son also does in like manner.

20 "For the Father loves the Son, and shows Him all things that He Himself does; and He will show Him greater works than these, that you may marvel.

21 "For as the Father raises the dead and gives life to them, even so the Son gives life to whom He will.

22 "For the Father judges no one, but has committed all judgment to the Son,

23 "that all should honor the Son just as they honor the Father. He who does not honor the Son does not honor the Father who sent Him.

24 "Most assuredly, I say to you, he who hears My word and believes in Him who sent Me has everlasting life, and shall not come into judgment, but has passed from death into life.

25 "Most assuredly, I say to you, the hour is coming, and now is, when the dead will hear the voice of the Son of God; and those who hear will live.

26 "For as the Father has life in Himself, so He has granted the Son to have life in Himself,

27 "and has given Him authority to execute judgment also, because He is the Son of Man.

28 "Do not marvel at this; for the hour is coming in which all who are in the graves will hear His voice

29 "and come forth– those who have done good, to the resurrection of life, and those who have done evil, to the resurrection of condemnation.

30 "I can of Myself do nothing. As I hear, I judge; and My judgment is righteous, because I do not seek My own will but the will of the Father who sent Me.

31 "If I bear witness of Myself, My witness is not true.

32 "There is another who bears witness of Me, and I know that the witness which He witnesses of Me is true.

33 "You have sent to John, and he has borne witness to the truth.

34 "Yet I do not receive testimony from man, but I say these things that you may be saved.

35 "He was the burning and shining lamp, and you were willing for a time to rejoice in his light.
36 "But I have a greater witness than John's; for the works which the Father has given Me to finish– the very works that I do– bear witness of Me, that the Father has sent Me.
37 "And the Father Himself, who sent Me, has testified of Me. You have neither heard His voice at any time, nor seen His form.
38 "But you do not have His word abiding in you, because whom He sent, Him you do not believe.
39 "You search the Scriptures, for in them you think you have eternal life; and these are they which testify of Me.
40 "But you are not willing to come to Me that you may have life.
41 "I do not receive honor from men.
42 "But I know you, that you do not have the love of God in you.
43 "I have come in My Father's name, and you do not receive Me; if another comes in his own name, him you will receive.
44 "How can you believe, who receive honor from one another, and do not seek the honor that comes from the only God?
45 "Do not think that I shall accuse you to the Father; there is one who accuses you– Moses, in whom you trust.
46 "For if you believed Moses, you would believe Me; for he wrote about Me.
47 "But if you do not believe his writings, how will you believe My words?"

These are the words of Jesus Christ, the One who was sent by the Father to be our Savior and to be the Lord of our life, the One who sent the Holy Spirit to fill us with the peace, wisdom and love of God. This business of who is part of the remnant and who is not can be set aside right now. You need not wonder any longer. Acknowledge the promised Messiah and accept the certainty that He offers, now. Every verse is important, but read verses 24-27 again.

CHAPTER 19

THE RESTORATION AND CLEANSING OF THE PROMISED LAND

Following the battle of Armageddon, the Promised Land will be littered with the bodies and weapons of the enemies of God, so much so that a traveler could not make his way. The birds and beasts will feed upon the carcasses and the bones will be everywhere. The Jews, restored to the kingdom, will employ search and burial parties who will spend 7 months burying the bones and cleansing the land. Indeed all the people of Israel will be burying the enemy.

The Jews will not cut down trees for a 7-year period after the battle. They will use the remnants of the weapons of war as fuel. The words given to Ezekiel do not say that forests will be decimated as the enemies of God are destroyed, but it is implied. Listen as God describes the fate of His enemies.

Ezekiel 39:4-17 (NKJ)
4 "You shall fall upon the mountains of Israel, you and all your troops and the peoples who are with you; I will give you to birds of prey of every sort and to the beasts of the field to be devoured.
5 "You shall fall on the open field; for I have spoken," says the Lord GOD.
6 "And I will send fire on Magog and on those who live in security in the coastlands. Then they shall know that I am the LORD.

7 "So I will make My holy name known in the midst of My people Israel, and I will not let them profane My holy name anymore. Then the nations shall know that I am the LORD, the Holy One in Israel.
8 "Surely it is coming, and it shall be done," says the Lord GOD. "This is the day of which I have spoken.
9 "Then those who dwell in the cities of Israel will go out and set on fire and burn the weapons, both the shields and bucklers, the bows and arrows, the javelins and spears; and they will make fires with them for seven years.
10 "They will not take wood from the field nor cut down any from the forests, because they will make fires with the weapons; and they will plunder those who plundered them, and pillage those who pillaged them," says the Lord GOD.
11 "It will come to pass in that day that I will give Gog a burial place there in Israel, the valley of those who pass by east of the sea; and it will obstruct travelers, because there they will bury Gog and all his multitude. Therefore they will call it the Valley of Hamon Gog.
12 "For seven months the house of Israel will be burying them, in order to cleanse the land.
13 "Indeed all the people of the land will be burying them, and they will gain renown for it on the day that I am glorified," says the Lord GOD.
14 "They will set apart men regularly employed, with the help of a search party, to pass through the land and bury those bodies remaining on the ground, in order to cleanse it. At the end of seven months they will make a search.
15 "The search party will pass through the land; and whenever anyone sees a man's bone, he shall set up a marker by it, till the buriers have buried it in the Valley of Hamon Gog.
16 "The name of the city will also be Hamonah. Thus they shall cleanse the land.'"
17 "And as for you, son of man, thus says the Lord GOD, 'Speak to every sort of bird and to every beast of the field: "Assemble yourselves and come; gather together from all sides to My sacrificial meal which I am sacrificing for you, a great sacrificial meal on the mountains of Israel, that you may eat flesh and drink blood.

This last verse is very complex. I will speculate on its meaning and pray that I am not in error. The sacrificial meal is God's sacrifice of the sinful enemy for you, Israel. When the crucifixion of Jesus Christ occurred, The Son of God took upon Himself the sins of the world. He entered into the center of the earth, and suffered for us. Listen.

Ephesians 4:9-10 (NKJ)
9 (Now this, "He ascended"– what does it mean but that He also first descended into the lower parts of the earth?
10 He who descended is also the One who ascended far above all the heavens, that He might fill all things.)

Remember that sin must be paid for and Jesus paid for our sin. When Christians celebrate communion they often repeat some of these verses.

1 Corinthians 11:23-29 (NKJ)
23 For I received from the Lord that which I also delivered to you: that the Lord Jesus on the same night in which He was betrayed took bread;
24 and when He had given thanks, He broke it and said, "Take, eat; this is My body which is broken for you; do this in remembrance of Me."
25 In the same manner He also took the cup after supper, saying, "This cup is the new covenant in My blood. This do, as often as you drink it, in remembrance of Me."
26 For as often as you eat this bread and drink this cup, you proclaim the Lord's death till He comes.
27 Therefore whoever eats this bread or drinks this cup of the Lord in an unworthy manner will be guilty of the body and blood of the Lord.
28 But let a man examine himself, and so let him eat of the bread and drink of the cup.
29 For he who eats and drinks in an unworthy manner eats and drinks judgment to himself, not discerning the Lord's body.

In another verse Jesus said,

John 6:53-58 (NKJ)
53 Then Jesus said to them, "Most assuredly, I say to you, unless you eat the flesh of the Son of Man and drink His blood, you have no life in you.

54 "Whoever eats My flesh and drinks My blood has eternal life, and I will raise him up at the last day.
55 "For My flesh is food indeed, and My blood is drink indeed.
56 "He who eats My flesh and drinks My blood abides in Me, and I in him.
57 "As the living Father sent Me, and I live because of the Father, so he who feeds on Me will live because of Me.
58 "This is the bread which came down from heaven– not as your fathers ate the manna, and are dead. He who eats this bread will live forever."

These verses, even today, create great controversy with the Body of Believers. The entire notion that there is no forgiveness of sin without the shedding of blood is as hard for us to handle now as it was then. At one point, just after Jesus said the words above, the scriptures say...

John 6:60-66 (NKJ)
60 Therefore many of His disciples, when they heard this, said, "This is a hard saying; who can understand it?"
61 When Jesus knew in Himself that His disciples complained about this, He said to them, "Does this offend you?
62 "What then if you should see the Son of Man ascend where He was before?
63 "It is the Spirit who gives life; the flesh profits nothing. The words that I speak to you are spirit, and they are life.
64 "But there are some of you who do not believe." For Jesus knew from the beginning who they were who did not believe, and who would betray Him.
65 And He said, "Therefore I have said to you that no one can come to Me unless it has been granted to him by My Father."
66 From that time many of His disciples went back and walked with Him no more.

Jesus said, It is the Spirit who gives life; the flesh profits nothing. We tend to focus on the "flesh," our human existence, as "important." Getting past that "fatal error" is a matter of eternal consequence. We need to see that "sacrificing the flesh" is a means of destroying that which is temporal so that the spiritual can be "born."

When we celebrate communion we are not only acknowledging the sacrifice of Jesus for our sins, but we are drinking of the cup of His Blood and His Body, that He who is Spirit may live in our hearts. The "offense" that the followers had was, at least in part, their failure to understand that the shed Blood of Jesus and His broken Body, were a sacrifice of what is temporal so that which is eternal can reign.

Yes, our bodies die but they are temporal and "drinking and eating" of the Body of Jesus, is an act of remembrance of the triumph His death provided, over death itself. He is Spirit. We who follow Him are willing to "crucify our flesh" as it were, in order to be "born of the Spirit."

Those who arise from their graves to participate physically with Jesus Christ in the Millennium are those to whom the Gospel was preached while in their graves. Those who arise to participate with Jesus in the millennium as spiritual entities are those who received and acted upon the invitation of the New Covenant, that is they declared their faith, by grace, in the One who could forgive their iniquity. Listen to the Lord explaining the terms of the New Covenant.

Jeremiah 31:31-34 (NKJ)
31 "Behold, the days are coming, says the LORD, when I will make a new covenant with the house of Israel and with the house of Judah–
32 "not according to the covenant that I made with their fathers in the day that I took them by the hand to lead them out of the land of Egypt, My covenant which they broke, though I was a husband to them, says the LORD.
33 "But this is the covenant that I will make with the house of Israel after those days, says the LORD: I will put My law in their minds, and write it on their hearts; and I will be their God, and they shall be My people.
34 "No more shall every man teach his neighbor, and every man his brother, saying, 'Know the LORD,' for they all shall know Me, from the least of them to the greatest of them, says the LORD. For I will forgive their iniquity, and their sin I will remember no more."

Many souls had died before Jesus came and declared that a New Covenant was replacing the Old Covenant, the event foretold by Jeremiah. We who have existed since the death and resurrection of Jesus are under the New Covenant. Those who died before Jesus gave us the New Covenant were under the Old Covenant. There are three quotations that help us understand the fate of those under the Old Covenant. First, listen to the words of Jesus, the Christ, who will judge all men.

John 5:25-29 (NKJ)
25 "Most assuredly, I say to you, the hour is coming, and now is, when the dead will hear the voice of the Son of God; and those who hear will live.
26 "For as the Father has life in Himself, so He has granted the Son to have life in Himself,
27 "and has given Him authority to execute judgment also, because He is the Son of Man.
28 "Do not marvel at this; for the hour is coming in which all who are in the graves will hear His voice
29 "and come forth– those who have done good, to the resurrection of life, and those who have done evil, to the resurrection of condemnation.

Since we know that "doing good" is not a means to salvation, Jesus was referring to those who were in the grave, as He spoke, that is, those who had died under the Old Covenant. Those who were obedient to the laws of the Old Covenant will be called forth to the resurrection of life and those who did evil, to the resurrection of condemnation. Peter offers further insight:

1 Peter 3:17-20 (NKJ)
17 For it is better, if it is the will of God, to suffer for doing good than for doing evil.
18 For Christ also suffered once for sins, the just for the unjust, that He might bring us to God, being put to death in the flesh but made alive by the Spirit,
19 by whom also He went and preached to the spirits in prison,

20 who formerly were disobedient, when once the Divine longsuffering waited in the days of Noah, while the ark was being prepared, in which a few, that is, eight souls, were saved through water.

1 Peter 4:1-8 (NKJ)
1 Therefore, since Christ suffered for us in the flesh, arm yourselves also with the same mind, for he who has suffered in the flesh has ceased from sin,
2 that he no longer should live the rest of his time in the flesh for the lusts of men, but for the will of God.
3 For we have spent enough of our past lifetime in doing the will of the Gentiles– when we walked in lewdness, lusts, drunkenness, revelries, drinking parties, and abominable idolatries.
4 In regard to these, they think it strange that you do not run with them in the same flood of dissipation, speaking evil of you.
5 They will give an account to Him who is ready to judge the living and the dead.
6 For this reason the gospel was preached also to those who are dead, that they might be judged according to men in the flesh, but live according to God in the spirit.
7 But the end of all things is at hand; therefore be serious and watchful in your prayers.
8 And above all things have fervent love for one another, for "love will cover a multitude of sins."

The teachings the Scriptures offer about those who have died are very difficult, given our perspective. We who have not died yet can not fully understand the condition of the spirit of man whose physical body has perished. In general, it seems clear that all will be raised from the dead for judgment and we know that involves two groups. One who died under the Old Covenant and one who died under the New Covenant. Those who died under the Old Covenant and who were obedient, as judged by Jesus, will be resurrected and will yet declare their faith in the Messiah. Their sin must be removed from them for them to enter into the presence of the Father.

I will speculate that those who were obedient will populate the earth during the Millennium, living without temptation (Satan is bound) and they will yet acknowledge Jesus as their Redeemer. Failing to do so, they will fall victim to the judgment of Jesus after having been deceived by Satan at the end of the millennium when Satan is loosed for a season to capture whomever he can.

Now, those Jews who survive the tribulation and are alive on the day of the battle of Armageddon, are not, I don't think, persons who have acknowledged Jesus as their Redeemer, the one who atoned for their sins. Therefore when God says,

"Assemble yourselves and come; gather together from all sides to My sacrificial meal which I am sacrificing for you, a great sacrificial meal on the mountains of Israel, that you may eat flesh and drink blood."

He said this to the birds and the beasts, not to Israel. Israel can not be redeemed without the shedding of blood for the remission of sins and only the unblemished Lamb of God can ultimately atone for sins. It appears that Israel will enter the Millennium without having partaken of the Blood and Body of Jesus. They will spend 1000 years in perfect obedience to the Law, with the prince, King David and the Sons of Zadok, God's sanctified priests, continuing to obey the commandments, including sin offerings and offerings of righteousness.

Why sin offerings, given the presence of Jesus, who has made the one and only sacrifice that can redeem any soul? Because, and I speculate, Israel needs a period of purification, unfettered by Satan, in which they are completely obedient. The Spirit of God will be present. Joy and celebration will be present but those who were obedient to the Law and who were resurrected to participate in the millennium will be present as well. Not only in Israel, but in the other parts of the world, since only those pureblooded Jews of the seed of Abraham will be able to enter the Temple. When Satan is loosed at the end of the 1000 years he will not have victory over God's chosen people, who have refused the mark of the beast, but he will summon the enemies of God to one final battle, the battle preceding the Great White Throne Judgment. Why caps? Because this moment will be the defining moment in the human history of man.

It will be the moment in which the sheep are separated from the goats, the moment in which those, whose names are written in the "Book of Life," will be gathered together to New Jerusalem which will descend from the heavens. We who acknowledge our Savior and appropriate a personal relationship with our Redeemer will depart this earth to that eternal, perfect place, a place of unimaginable beauty and peace. The earth that we leave behind will be destroyed and every enemy of God will be cast into the lake of fire, eternally condemned to separation and suffering. They shall be in the position of the rich man, who looked to Lazarus and said,

Luke 16:24 (NKJ)
24 "Then he cried and said, 'Father Abraham, have mercy on me, and send Lazarus that he may dip the tip of his finger in water and cool my tongue; for I am tormented in this flame.'

These views are most difficult for me, and anyone else who "loves his neighbor as himself," to express. I consider the events of the Millennium a great mystery, in part, and particularly the continuing sacrifice, given the words in Revelation 20. I will speculate that the Saints who return "with Jesus Christ" will be in spiritual bodies, as will Christ during the Millennium.

Revelation 20:1-8 (NKJ)
1 Then I saw an angel coming down from heaven, having the key to the bottomless pit and a great chain in his hand.
2 He laid hold of the dragon, that serpent of old, who is the Devil and Satan, and bound him for a thousand years;
3 and he cast him into the bottomless pit, and shut him up, and set a seal on him, so that he should deceive the nations no more till the thousand years were finished. But after these things he must be released for a little while.
4 And I saw thrones, and they sat on them, and judgment was committed to them. Then I saw the souls of those who had been beheaded for their witness to Jesus and for the word of God, who had not worshiped the

beast or his image, and had not received his mark on their foreheads or on their hands. And they lived and reigned with Christ for a thousand years.
5 But the rest of the dead did not live again until the thousand years were finished. This is the first resurrection.
6 Blessed and holy is he who has part in the first resurrection. Over such the second death has no power, but they shall be priests of God and of Christ, and shall reign with Him a thousand years.
7 Now when the thousand years have expired, Satan will be released from his prison
8 and will go out to deceive the nations which are in the four corners of the earth, Gog and Magog, to gather them together to battle, whose number is as the sand of the sea.

Perhaps the words in verse 4 are the key. Those who will reign with Jesus Christ, during this 1000-year period, will "judge." How could they be in a "judging" role? Again, perhaps it is because they are in a spiritual body, not a physical body, a body like that of the Messiah, after the crucifixion, resurrection and ascension, when he appeared to many. Their "judgment" may well be that of oversight of those participating in the Millennium, not as The Judge, Jesus, but as one who is present, much in the same way that angels are present today.

1 Corinthians 6:2-3 (NKJ)
2 Do you not know that the saints will judge the world? And if the world will be judged by you, are you unworthy to judge the smallest matters?
3 Do you not know that we shall judge angels? How much more, things that pertain to this life?

The Saints who return with Christ will not ever fall from grace. How do we know? First, the Scriptures say: Over such the second death has no power, but they shall be priests of God and of Christ, and shall reign with Him a thousand years. Then Daniel tells us:

Daniel 7:18 (NKJ)
18 'But the saints of the Most High shall receive the kingdom, and possess the kingdom forever, even forever and ever.'

Forever means forever in the kingdom and in eternity.

Since Satan is bound during these 1000 years, will Israel finally be able to fulfill the requirement that they are "obedient to the Law" and will their faith be accounted to them as righteousness? I believe the answer may be yes and no. Yes, they will be restored as a Holy Nation and will glorify God and will acknowledge Jesus Christ as the promised Messiah who has established God's kingdom here on earth. No, the sacrifices prescribed during the millennium will not be sufficient for salvation. They will still be required to born again, to die to the flesh and to be resurrected in a spiritual body into an eternal Jerusalem. They will join with every believer and confess that Jesus Christ is the only means to eternal life.

Forgive me Father for offering such a presumptive scenario. I do so, but not with an air of certainty and not to encourage any reader to look forward to being a physical entity in the millennium, having survived the Tribulation. I do so in order to encourage them to believe now, in the Messiah that has come and will come again, and to choose eternal life now, and to reign with Christ in the Millennium as a Spirit filled entity.

You do not need to go through the tribulation or to place yourself in the position of a physical entity requiring atonement. The price has been paid and no further sacrifice of any kind will ever redeem you. O' God, move now in the heart of the reader that feels they can be redeemed by obedience alone. The Old Covenant has passed.

If you want to think more about what it may be to be like to be a spiritual entity in the millennium, listen. These events occurred right after the resurrection of Jesus Christ.

Luke 24:13-53 (NKJ)
13 Now behold, two of them were traveling that same day to a village called Emmaus, which was about seven miles from Jerusalem.
14 And they talked together of all these things which had happened.
15 So it was, while they conversed and reasoned, that Jesus Himself drew near and went with them.
16 But their eyes were restrained, so that they did not know Him.

17 And He said to them, "What kind of conversation is this that you have with one another as you walk and are sad?"

18 Then the one whose name was Cleopas answered and said to Him, "Are You the only stranger in Jerusalem, and have You not known the things which happened there in these days?"

19 And He said to them, "What things?" So they said to Him, "The things concerning Jesus of Nazareth, who was a Prophet mighty in deed and word before God and all the people,

20 "and how the chief priests and our rulers delivered Him to be condemned to death, and crucified Him.

21 "But we were hoping that it was He who was going to redeem Israel. Indeed, besides all this, today is the third day since these things happened.

22 "Yes, and certain women of our company, who arrived at the tomb early, astonished us.

23 "When they did not find His body, they came saying that they had also seen a vision of angels who said He was alive.

24 "And certain of those who were with us went to the tomb and found it just as the women had said; but Him they did not see."

25 Then He said to them, "O foolish ones, and slow of heart to believe in all that the prophets have spoken!

26 "Ought not the Christ to have suffered these things and to enter into His glory?"

27 And beginning at Moses and all the Prophets, He expounded to them in all the Scriptures the things concerning Himself.

28 Then they drew near to the village where they were going, and He indicated that He would have gone farther.

29 But they constrained Him, saying, "Abide with us, for it is toward evening, and the day is far spent." And He went in to stay with them.

30 Now it came to pass, as He sat at the table with them, that He took bread, blessed and broke it, and gave it to them.

31 Then their eyes were opened and they knew Him; and He vanished from their sight.

32 And they said to one another, "Did not our heart burn within us while He talked with us on the road, and while He opened the Scriptures to us?"

33 So they rose up that very hour and returned to Jerusalem, and found the eleven and those who were with them gathered together,

34 saying, "The Lord is risen indeed, and has appeared to Simon!"

35 And they told about the things that had happened on the road, and how He was known to them in the breaking of bread.

36 Now as they said these things, Jesus Himself stood in the midst of them, and said to them, "Peace to you."

37 But they were terrified and frightened, and supposed they had seen a spirit.

38 And He said to them, "Why are you troubled? And why do doubts arise in your hearts?

39 "Behold My hands and My feet, that it is I Myself. Handle Me and see, for a spirit does not have flesh and bones as you see I have."

40 When He had said this, He showed them His hands and His feet.

41 But while they still did not believe for joy, and marveled, He said to them, "Have you any food here?"

42 So they gave Him a piece of a broiled fish and some honeycomb.

43 And He took it and ate in their presence.

44 Then He said to them, "These are the words which I spoke to you while I was still with you, that all things must be fulfilled which were written in the Law of Moses and the Prophets and the Psalms concerning Me."

45 And He opened their understanding, that they might comprehend the Scriptures.

46 Then He said to them, "Thus it is written, and thus it was necessary for the Christ to suffer and to rise from the dead the third day,

47 "and that repentance and remission of sins should be preached in His name to all nations, beginning at Jerusalem.

48 "And you are witnesses of these things.

49 "Behold, I send the Promise of My Father upon you; but tarry in the city of Jerusalem until you are endued with power from on high."

50 And He led them out as far as Bethany, and He lifted up His hands and blessed them.

51 Now it came to pass, while He blessed them, that He was parted from them and carried up into heaven.

52 And they worshiped Him, and returned to Jerusalem with great joy,

53 and were continually in the temple praising and blessing God. Amen.

I realize that quotation covers a lot more territory than a description of a Spiritual body, but I trust you find the record both encouraging and enlightening.

I pray this topic has not distracted you from the simplicity of the Gospel. Speculation of the sort I have indulged in is intellectually stimulating, to some, but of no consequence at all as you make a decision to accept Jesus Christ as your personal Savior. To overly focus on that which is obscure is to major in minor topics. Satan would love to have us argue over such matters. We often hear the expression "don't even go there" from the mouths of those who are fearful of the dissension that follows a difficult subject. There are many issues to which we should respond as follows:

1 Corinthians 13:12 (NKJ)
12 For now we see in a mirror, dimly, but then face to face. Now I know in part, but then I shall know just as I also am known.

The verse above is followed by admonitions that should characterize the relationships of those who love God, first from Paul and then John.

1 Corinthians 13:13 (NKJ)
13 And now abide faith, hope, love, these three; but the greatest of these is love.

1 John 4:16-21 (NKJ)
16 And we have known and believed the love that God has for us. God is love, and he who abides in love abides in God, and God in him.
17 Love has been perfected among us in this: that we may have boldness in the day of judgment; because as He is, so are we in this world.
18 There is no fear in love; but perfect love casts out fear, because fear involves torment. But he who fears has not been made perfect in love.
19 We love Him because He first loved us.
20 If someone says, "I love God," and hates his brother, he is a liar; for he who does not love his brother whom he has seen, how can he love God whom he has not seen?

21 And this commandment we have from Him: that he who loves God must love his brother also.

Ask the Father to reveal to you what you need to know and to manifest Himself more fully to you, day by day. The land of Israel will be restored and cleansed and so can the heart of every child of God be restored and cleansed.

CHAPTER 20

SATAN BOUND FOR 1000 YEARS

The "jailing" of Satan is described in these words.

Revelation 20:1-3 (NKJ)
1 Then I saw an angel coming down from heaven, having the key to the bottomless pit and a great chain in his hand.
2 He laid hold of the dragon, that serpent of old, who is the Devil and Satan, and bound him for a thousand years;
3 and he cast him into the bottomless pit, and shut him up, and set a seal on him, so that he should deceive the nations no more till the thousand years were finished. But after these things he must be released for a little while.

When Satan is released, at the end of the 1000 years, there will be one final battle, between evil and good. Evil will be destroyed forever and all those that have been judged evil will be cast into the lake of fire, forever separated from God, eternally.

True peace will occur, during the Millennium, because the restored Jewish nation will finally be reconciled with their Creator and Savior, the Messiah, the Prince of Peace. The evil influence of Satan and the temptations of the flesh will be bound. The healing of the nation shall take place, in one day. That healing will be made possible because the Messiah, the Redeemer, the Intercessor, will have been made manifest to Israel and prophecy will be both understood and fulfilled.

Isaiah 53:1-12 (NKJ)

1 Who has believed our report? And to whom has the arm of the LORD been revealed?

2 For He shall grow up before Him as a tender plant, and as a root out of dry ground. He has no form or comeliness; and when we see Him, there is no beauty that we should desire Him.

3 He is despised and rejected by men, a Man of sorrows and acquainted with grief. And we hid, as it were, our faces from Him; He was despised, and we did not esteem Him.

4 Surely He has borne our griefs and carried our sorrows; yet we esteemed Him stricken, smitten by God, and afflicted.

5 But He was wounded for our transgressions, He was bruised for our iniquities; the chastisement for our peace was upon Him, and by His stripes we are healed.

6 All we like sheep have gone astray; we have turned, every one, to his own way; and the LORD has laid on Him the iniquity of us all.

7 He was oppressed and He was afflicted, yet He opened not His mouth; He was led as a lamb to the slaughter, and as a sheep before its shearers is silent, so He opened not His mouth.

8 He was taken from prison and from judgment, and who will declare His generation? For He was cut off from the land of the living; for the transgressions of My people He was stricken.

9 And they made His grave with the wicked– but with the rich at His death, because He had done no violence, nor was any deceit in His mouth.

10 Yet it pleased the LORD to bruise Him; He has put Him to grief. When You make His soul an offering for sin, He shall see His seed, He shall prolong His days, and the pleasure of the LORD shall prosper in His hand.

11 He shall see the labor of His soul, and be satisfied. By His knowledge My righteous Servant shall justify many, for He shall bear their iniquities.

12 Therefore I will divide Him a portion with the great, and He shall divide the spoil with the strong, because He poured out His soul unto death, and He was numbered with the transgressors, and He bore the sin of many, and made intercession for the transgressors.

Read verses 10-12 very carefully. It pleased the LORD because God knew that this was the only sacrifice that could heal His people. The love that God has for His chosen people could not have been expressed in a more complete way.

Consider this. If your son had to die, in order to cover the sins of all mankind, and in doing so, became the redeemer of all those of faith, saved by the Grace of God, would that be pleasing to you? It pleased God to bruise our Messiah, His Son, because in doing so, all of His children now have a Redeemer, a Mediator, a Counselor, One who can bring God's children into His perfect Presence.

Now, at the end of the age, God has told us what a marvelous miracle He will provide. One of the primary reasons that there will be a peaceful, wonderful millennium is that Satan is bound. The great deceiver, the tempter, the accuser, is bound. The other is that the nation of Israel will receive the New Covenant. Christ will reign in the hearts of Israel's people!

Then, following the 1000 years of peace, evil will be eternally and finally judged. New Jerusalem will descend from the heavens and a new heaven and a new earth will begin, without end, and all whose names are written in the Book of Life will be there. Satan, and all of the enemies of God, will have been removed, forever.

New Jerusalem, our eternal heaven, will never see darkness, there will be no temple there and no more sea. There will be a "pure" language, we will all have a new name and we will reign eternally with the Father and the Son. Your status there will depend upon what you did with the amount of Light God gave you here. We will all joyfully "serve," but it appears that we will serve in ways that differ from one another. Jesus will be called by a new name. We will be neither young nor old nor male and female. This will be a perfect, eternal place, without sin. Worship and joy will prevail.

CHAPTER 21

THE REBUILDING OF THE TEMPLES—#3 AND #4

Perhaps the most visible confirmation of prophecy being fulfilled will be the rebuilding of the temple for the 3rd time, in Jerusalem, at the outset of the tribulation period. We have in another section explained how the prophecies of Daniel and Ezekiel make the rebuilding of the temple an event that initiates the 7-year period of tribulation. If you are a "pre-tribulation" believer, you believe the "body of believers" will not be here when Temple number three is rebuilt.

There is no need, in a book written primarily to the Jews, to amplify the pre-tribulation, mid-tribulation and post-tribulation arguments. Suffice it to say that intelligent people disagree on whether the Church, that group of believers filled with the Holy Spirit, will go through any portion of the 7 year period of tribulation described by Daniel.

I would say that if the "pre-tribulation" view is correct, the reader of this letter should realize that Christians, at least those who are, in the judgment of Jesus, true believers, will not be here. They will have been "caught up in the clouds." If the rapture of believers occurs before the rebuilding of the Temple, and you find yourself still here, then you are going to have no choice but to go through the tribulation. You will endure both the joy of the Temple being restored and the tragedy of it being defiled and desecrated. You will, during these last 3½ years of tribulation, have your opportunity to declare your faith in God or to capitulate and worship the Antichrist.

The 3rd Temple will be built in Jerusalem, soon. Listen to this quotation by the leader of the Temple Mount Faithful movement. "My call to all the enemies of Israel is to obey the Word of G-d and to accept His end-time plans for Israel. The redemption of Israel leads to their own redemption. The march of the G-d and people of Israel to accomplish redemption is irreversible. The climax of this march, the rebuilding of the Temple on Mt. Moriah, will come very soon."

Again, prophecy is very clear. The third Temple will be rebuilt. It will be destroyed 3½ years later by the Antichrist, the one who earlier struck the compromises it took to get it rebuilt. The 4th Temple will be built after the Battle of Armageddon. It will be the millennium Temple. It will endure for 1000 years. There will not be another Temple in New Jerusalem, heaven.

Listen to what Haggai says about the rebuilding of the 4th Temple. This must be a prophecy regarding the 4th Temple because Haggai says it will be a place of peace and it will come after the nations have been "shaken." Notice then, after the shaking, they shall come to the Desire of All Nations. Those capital letters refer to our Lord. The Lord, after the purging of sinners, is the Desire of All Nations.

Haggai 2:6-9 (NKJ)
6 "For thus says the LORD of hosts: "Once more (it is a little while) I will shake heaven and earth, the sea and dry land;
7 'and I will shake all nations, and they shall come to the Desire of All Nations, and I will fill this temple with glory,' says the LORD of hosts.
8 'The silver is Mine, and the gold is Mine,' says the LORD of hosts.
9 'The glory of this latter temple shall be greater than the former,' says the LORD of hosts. 'And in this place I will give peace,' says the LORD of hosts."

Scripture places Israel, at the end of the great tribulation, in a privileged position, a position to which all history seems to point. I can not, in this brief presentation, do any more than generalize about history, but bear with me and consider the possibilities.

It is common knowledge, at least in Jerusalem, that preparations for the rebuilding the 3rd Temple and the re-institution of sacrifice are being made. Listen to this quotation from a newsletter of the Temple Mount Faithful Movement:

"The Movement Will Continue with the Preparations for the Temple: Our center has received more items for the worship in the Third Temple—vessels, priestly garments, incense, the silver half-shekel, a model of the golden altar of incense and other items. Soon we shall have two silver trumpets that the priest will use in the Third Temple. We also have the twelve stones of the breastplate of the high priest. These preparations are continuing."

"Construction of the Seven-Branched Menorah: Our wonderful friends continue to donate gold and jewelry for this purpose. Each piece of donated gold brings its construction closer."

These preparations are a necessary condition in order to apply Daniel's subsequent prophecy to the current situation.

Daniel 12:7-13 (NKJ)
7 Then I heard the man clothed in linen, who was above the waters of the river, when he held up his right hand and his left hand to heaven, and swore by Him who lives forever, that it shall be for a time, times, and half a time; and when the power of the holy people has been completely shattered, all these things shall be finished.
8 Although I heard, I did not understand. Then I said, "My lord, what shall be the end of these things?"
9 And he said, "Go your way, Daniel, for the words are closed up and sealed till the time of the end.
10 "Many shall be purified, made white, and refined, but the wicked shall do wickedly; and none of the wicked shall understand, but the wise shall understand.
11 "And from the time that the daily sacrifice is taken away, and the abomination of desolation is set up, there shall be one thousand two hundred and ninety days.

12 "Blessed is he who waits, and comes to the one thousand three hundred and thirty-five days.
13 "But you, go your way till the end; for you shall rest, and will arise to your inheritance at the end of the days."

Here Daniel is told that during the last period, many will be purified, made white and refined and that others will do wickedly. He is also told that daily sacrifice will be taken away. To be taken away, sacrifices would have had to commence. Doesn't this astonish you? Can you envision animal sacrifices in the Temple? You will have to read most of this book for a better understanding of why God instituted the ritual of sacrifice in the beginning and how it all pointed to the "final sacrifice" of God's only Son for the atonement of our personal sins. One can not enter into God's presence, as a sinner. We know that all have sinned and fallen short of the Glory of God. Animal sacrifices, as a means to redemption, were not sufficient in history nor will they be in the future.

Listen as God spoke through the Psalmist regarding sacrifice.

Psalm 50:8-23 (NKJ)
8 I will not rebuke you for your sacrifices or your burnt offerings, which are continually before Me.
9 I will not take a bull from your house, nor goats out of your folds.
10 For every beast of the forest is Mine, and the cattle on a thousand hills.
11 I know all the birds of the mountains, and the wild beasts of the field are Mine.
12 "If I were hungry, I would not tell you; for the world is Mine, and all its fullness.
13 Will I eat the flesh of bulls, or drink the blood of goats?
14 Offer to God thanksgiving, and pay your vows to the Most High.
15 Call upon Me in the day of trouble; I will deliver you, and you shall glorify Me."
16 But to the wicked God says: "What right have you to declare My statutes, or take My covenant in your mouth,
17 Seeing you hate instruction and cast My words behind you?

18 When you saw a thief, you consented with him, and have been a partaker with adulterers.
19 You give your mouth to evil, and your tongue frames deceit.
20 You sit and speak against your brother; you slander your own mother's son.
21 These things you have done, and I kept silent; you thought that I was altogether like you; but I will rebuke you, and set them in order before your eyes.
22 "Now consider this, you who forget God, lest I tear you in pieces, and there be none to deliver:
23 Whoever offers praise glorifies Me; and to him who orders his conduct aright I will show the salvation of God."

Psalm 51:1-19 (NKJ)
1 Have mercy upon me, O God, according to Your lovingkindness; according to the multitude of Your tender mercies, blot out my transgressions.
2 Wash me thoroughly from my iniquity, and cleanse me from my sin.
3 For I acknowledge my transgressions, and my sin is always before me.
4 Against You, You only, have I sinned, and done this evil in Your sight– that You may be found just when You speak, and blameless when You judge.
5 Behold, I was brought forth in iniquity, and in sin my mother conceived me.
6 Behold, You desire truth in the inward parts, and in the hidden part You will make me to know wisdom.
7 Purge me with hyssop, and I shall be clean; wash me, and I shall be whiter than snow.
8 Make me to hear joy and gladness, that the bones You have broken may rejoice.
9 Hide Your face from my sins, and blot out all my iniquities.
10 Create in me a clean heart, O God, and renew a steadfast spirit within me.
11 Do not cast me away from Your presence, and do not take Your Holy Spirit from me.

12 Restore to me the joy of Your salvation, and uphold me by Your generous Spirit.
13 Then I will teach transgressors Your ways, and sinners shall be converted to You.
14 Deliver me from bloodshed, O God, the God of my salvation, and my tongue shall sing aloud of Your righteousness.
15 O Lord, open my lips, and my mouth shall show forth Your praise.
16 For You do not desire sacrifice, or else I would give it; you do not delight in burnt offering.
17 The sacrifices of God are a broken spirit, a broken and a contrite heart– these, O God, You will not despise.
18 Do good in Your good pleasure to Zion; build the walls of Jerusalem.
19 Then You shall be pleased with the sacrifices of righteousness, with burnt offering and whole burnt offering; then they shall offer bulls on Your altar.

Sacrifices will resume, but properly understood, they need to be preceded by a broken spirit, a broken and contrite heart, then they shall be sacrifices of righteousness. You need to first be able to say, "Hide Your face from my sins, and blot out all my iniquities. Create in me a clean heart, O God, and renew a steadfast spirit within me. Do not cast me away from Your presence, and do not take Your Holy Spirit from me."

But, if in your opinion the Messiah has not come, what do you intend to do to atone for your sin? God has spoken through the psalmist who says (You, Lord) do not desire sacrifice, or else I would give it; you do not delight in burnt offering? What does God delight in? Your salvation, your redemption, your cleansing and your declaration of faith, all available by His Grace, and because of His love for you, personally.

Again, corporate worship is good and desirable, but your salvation is a personal issue, not a corporate issue. You stand alone, before God. You can either choose to do so in "your righteousness" or in the Righteousness of Jesus Christ, the Messiah. You can not redeem yourself by acts of kindness or by sacrificing animals. Only the Messiah can present you blameless before the Father.

These sacrifices will cease 1,290 days (3½) after they start. Then the Antichrist will require the world to worship him.

Daniel 11:36-39 (NKJ)
36 "Then the king shall do according to his own will: he shall exalt and magnify himself above every god, shall speak blasphemies against the God of gods, and shall prosper till the wrath has been accomplished; for what has been determined shall be done.
37 "He shall regard neither the God of his fathers nor the desire of women, nor regard any god; for he shall exalt himself above them all.
38 "But in their place he shall honor a god of fortresses; and a god which his fathers did not know he shall honor with gold and silver, with precious stones and pleasant things.
39 "Thus he shall act against the strongest fortresses with a foreign god, which he shall acknowledge, and advance its glory; and he shall cause them to rule over many, and divide the land for gain.

The words you just read are very explicit. They define the character and mission of the one who will blaspheme God, honor a false god, oppress God's people and prosper in the process. He will regard neither the God of his fathers nor the desire of women and exalt himself above all. You should have no problem identifying this person.

These prophecies reach their fulfillment just before the beginning of the Kingdom Age, that 1000 year period referred to by John in Revelation 20:1-8. The Kingdom Age is the period of time right after the end of the great tribulation described in Daniel. If you believe that Daniel's most precise prophecy is accurate, then you probably agree that the last half of the 7-year tribulation will end up being the worst time of persecution that the Jews have ever faced.

The Kingdom Age will be the fulfillment of a great many prophecies in which God finally redeems His chosen people. Let's consider the events leading up to the period of great tribulation. I believe that "consensus" exists among those who study the Bible, regarding the following events:

There will be a scattering, then gathering of Israel. There will be a rapture of believers at some point in time. There will be declarations of peace and safety in Israel. There will be a new treaty that includes the resolution of the problem regarding the precise location of the foundation for the 3rd Temple. The Temple will be rebuilt for the 3rd time. The reinstitution of sacrifices in the new Temple will commence.

Still, the recognition of such events or times except as God visits your heart and confirms it with you personally, may not "register" with you. You will have to invest great time and energy in studying the Holy Scriptures themselves, in order to more fully understand all that God wants to reveal to you. This brief time "in the flesh" represents a test for you. If you fail this very short test, called life, your spirit will spend an eternity separated from God and all those souls He has redeemed or will yet redeem.

Yet, this brief time is the only time we have been allotted. Upon the fulcrum of this short test, your eternal existence rests. Thank God you need only "finish well." Our lives have been and are imperfect, but even now God extends His Hand of redemption. The door is open but as it was with the Ark, the door did close. The Scriptures say, "redeem the time." Seek rebirth now. Be a new creature in Christ in the days or hours that remain.

Do you want to know how much time that God spends thinking about you? Focus on this Psalm, particularly verse 5.

Psalm 40:1-13 (NKJ)
1 I waited patiently for the LORD; and He inclined to me, and heard my cry.
2 He also brought me up out of a horrible pit, out of the miry clay, and set my feet upon a rock, and established my steps.
3 He has put a new song in my mouth– praise to our God; many will see it and fear, and will trust in the LORD.
4 Blessed is that man who makes the LORD his trust, and does not respect the proud, nor such as turn aside to lies.
5 Many, O LORD my God, are Your wonderful works which You have done; and Your thoughts toward us cannot be recounted to You in order; if I would declare and speak of them, they are more than can be numbered.

6 Sacrifice and offering You did not desire; my ears You have opened; burnt offering and sin offering You did not require.
7 Then I said, "Behold, I come; in the scroll of the book it is written of me.
8 I delight to do Your will, O my God, and Your law is within my heart."
9 I have proclaimed the good news of righteousness in the great assembly; indeed, I do not restrain my lips, O LORD, You Yourself know.
10 I have not hidden Your righteousness within my heart; I have declared Your faithfulness and Your salvation; I have not concealed Your lovingkindness and Your truth from the great assembly.
11 Do not withhold Your tender mercies from me, O LORD; let Your lovingkindness and Your truth continually preserve me.
12 For innumerable evils have surrounded me; my iniquities have overtaken me, so that I am not able to look up; they are more than the hairs of my head; therefore my heart fails me.
13 Be pleased, O LORD, to deliver me; O LORD, make haste to help me!

God's thoughts toward you are more than can be numbered. Let that sink in! Our Omniscient, Omnipresent, Omnipotent Father loves you constantly, seeks to commune with you and thinks about you in ways you can not comprehend. Listen to these words.

Psalm 139:17-18 (NKJ)
17 How precious also are Your thoughts to me, O God! How great is the sum of them!
18 If I should count them, they would be more in number than the sand; when I awake, I am still with You.

Ezekiel, in chapters 40-46, tells of the vision God gave him, while in exile. Ezekiel's vision was of the restored Kingdom, the precise dimensions of the Temple, rules regarding who would serve whom, the role of the prince (King David), the boundaries of the tribes, the Holy Festivals, rules regarding sacrificial offerings and the commencement of healing waters flowing east and west from the temple, with the eastward flow, "curing the waters of the Dead Sea."

This vision, given the unfulfilled prophecies that lie within it, has to be of the Kingdom to be established after the battle of Armageddon. Listen.

Ezekiel 40:2-7 (NKJ)
2 In the visions of God He took me into the land of Israel and set me on a very high mountain; on it toward the south was something like the structure of a city.
3 He took me there, and behold, there was a man whose appearance was like the appearance of bronze. He had a line of flax and a measuring rod in his hand, and he stood in the gateway.
4 And the man said to me, "Son of man, look with your eyes and hear with your ears, and fix your mind on everything I show you; for you were brought here so that I might show them to you. Declare to the house of Israel everything you see."
5 Now there was a wall all around the outside of the temple. In the man's hand was a measuring rod six cubits long, each being a cubit and a handbreadth; and he measured the width of the wall structure, one rod; and the height, one rod.
6 Then he went to the gateway which faced east; and he went up its stairs and measured the threshold of the gateway, which was one rod wide, and the other threshold was one rod wide.
7 Each gate chamber was one rod long and one rod wide; between the gate chambers was a space of five cubits; and the threshold of the gateway by the vestibule of the inside gate was one rod.

God told Ezekiel there "was," and then went on to describe "what was," in great detail, with precise measurements. This prophecy implies that the Temple will be provided, not built, or it at least does not say who would build it. It may be too much a reach for you, but consider this. This temple will not be built with human hands. Listen.

Zechariah 6:12 (NKJ)
12 "Then speak to him, saying, 'Thus says the LORD of hosts, saying: "Behold, the Man whose name is the BRANCH! From His place He shall branch out, and He shall build the temple of the LORD;

Mark 14:58 (NKJ)

58 "We heard Him say, 'I will destroy this temple that is made with hands, and within three days I will build another made without hands.'"

Now we agree, I am sure, that the Temple is the dwelling place of God, but there is in a sense, a "fixed" Temple and a "mobile" Temple. Listen.

1 Corinthians 3:16-17 (NKJ)

16 **Do you not know that you are the temple of God and that the Spirit of God dwells in you?**
17 **If anyone defiles the temple of God, God will destroy him. For the temple of God is holy, which temple you are.**

Now, moving back to Ezekiel, his vision includes the "chambers for the singers."

Ezekiel 40:44 (NKJ)

44 **"Outside the inner gate were the chambers for the singers…"**

We will make a small digression by pointing out that our God is a God of joy and celebration, One who has told us to expect joy to be a "condition" of our eternal existence. Listen to what Moses had to say about the absence of joy and gladness.

Deuteronomy 28:47-48 (NKJ)

47 "Because you did not serve the LORD your God with joy and gladness of heart, for the abundance of everything,
48 "therefore you shall serve your enemies, whom the LORD will send against you, in hunger, in thirst, in nakedness, and in need of everything; and He will put a yoke of iron on your neck until He has destroyed you.

Here we find Samuel and Zadok, the priest who anointed Solomon, witnessing a celebration that sounds extremely joyful.

1 Kings 1:39-40 (NKJ)

39 **Then Zadok the priest took a horn of oil from the tabernacle and anointed Solomon. And they blew the horn, and all the people said, "Long live King Solomon!"**

40 And all the people went up after him; and the people played the flutes and rejoiced with great joy, so that the earth seemed to split with their sound.

When David returned the ark, great joy overflowed.

1 Chronicles 13:7-8 (NKJ)
7 So they carried the ark of God on a new cart from the house of Abinadab, and Uzza and Ahio drove the cart.
8 Then David and all Israel played music before God with all their might, with singing, on harps, on stringed instruments, on tambourines, on cymbals, and with trumpets.

As the Ark came to rest David added new instructions.

1 Chronicles 15:16 (NKJ)
16 Then David spoke to the leaders of the Levites to appoint their brethren to be the singers accompanied by instruments of music, stringed instruments, harps, and cymbals, by raising the voice with resounding joy.

The second time the Temple was rebuilt, after the captivity in Babylon, Ezra tells of us how it effected the people.

Ezra 3:10-13 (NKJ)
10 When the builders laid the foundation of the temple of the LORD, the priests stood in their apparel with trumpets, and the Levites, the sons of Asaph, with cymbals, to praise the LORD, according to the ordinance of David king of Israel.
11 And they sang responsively, praising and giving thanks to the LORD: "For He is good, for His mercy endures forever toward Israel." Then all the people shouted with a great shout, when they praised the LORD, because the foundation of the house of the LORD was laid.
12 But many of the priests and Levites and heads of the fathers' houses, old men who had seen the first temple, wept with a loud voice when the foundation of this temple was laid before their eyes. Yet many shouted aloud for joy,

13 so that the people could not discern the noise of the shout of joy from the noise of the weeping of the people, for the people shouted with a loud shout, and the sound was heard afar off.

When the 4th temple is rebuilt, as prophesied by Ezekiel, he tells you who the priests are. They are the Sons of Zadok, the same priest who anointed Solomon when the first Temple was built.

Ezekiel 40:45-46 (NKJ)
45 Then he said to me, "This chamber which faces south is for the priests who have charge of the temple.
46 "The chamber which faces north is for the priests who have charge of the altar; these are the sons of Zadok, from the sons of Levi, who come near the LORD to minister to Him."

Doesn't it amaze you how God's plan comes together? Centuries and centuries change nothing. The scriptures say:

Psalm 90:4-6 (NKJ)
4 For a thousand years in Your sight are like yesterday when it is past, and like a watch in the night.
5 You carry them away like a flood; they are like a sleep. In the morning they are like grass which grows up:
6 In the morning it flourishes and grows up; in the evening it is cut down and withers.

Even today we hear of water emerging from the area of the foundation of the original Temple. The reason it is significant is based on Ezekiel's vision and prophecy, as well as Joel and Zechariah.

Joel 3:18 (NKJ)
18 And it will come to pass in that day that the mountains shall drip with new wine, the hills shall flow with milk, and all the brooks of Judah shall be flooded with water; a fountain shall flow from the house of the LORD and water the Valley of Acacias.

Zechariah 14:8 (NKJ)
8 And in that day it shall be that living waters shall flow from Jerusalem, half of them toward the eastern sea and half of them toward the western sea; in both summer and winter it shall occur.

The waters will "heal" the sea (Dead Sea) and fish will return. The trees will be for food, and their leaves for medicine.

Ezekiel 47:1-12 (NKJ)
1 Then he brought me back to the door of the temple; and there was water, flowing from under the threshold of the temple toward the east, for the front of the temple faced east; the water was flowing from under the right side of the temple, south of the altar.
2 He brought me out by way of the north gate, and led me around on the outside to the outer gateway that faces east; and there was water, running out on the right side.
3 And when the man went out to the east with the line in his hand, he measured one thousand cubits, and he brought me through the waters; the water came up to my ankles.
4 Again he measured one thousand and brought me through the waters; the water came up to my knees. Again he measured one thousand and brought me through; the water came up to my waist.
5 Again he measured one thousand, and it was a river that I could not cross; for the water was too deep, water in which one must swim, a river that could not be crossed.
6 He said to me, "Son of man, have you seen this?" Then he brought me and returned me to the bank of the river.
7 When I returned, there, along the bank of the river, were very many trees on one side and the other.
8 Then he said to me: "This water flows toward the eastern region, goes down into the valley, and enters the sea. When it reaches the sea, its waters are healed.
9 "And it shall be that every living thing that moves, wherever the rivers go, will live. There will be a very great multitude of fish, because these waters go there; for they will be healed, and everything will live wherever the river goes.

10 "It shall be that fishermen will stand by it from En Gedi to En Eglaim; they will be places for spreading their nets. Their fish will be of the same kinds as the fish of the Great Sea, exceedingly many.

11 "But its swamps and marshes will not be healed; they will be given over to salt.

12 "Along the bank of the river, on this side and that, will grow all kinds of trees used for food; their leaves will not wither, and their fruit will not fail. They will bear fruit every month, because their water flows from the sanctuary. Their fruit will be for food, and their leaves for medicine."

These prophecies will be fulfilled. Listen to God's word. Read it as one thirsting. This verse must continually be before you. The Word is the Bread of Life.

Hebrews 4:12 (NKJ)
12 For the word of God is living and powerful, and sharper than any two-edged sword, piercing even to the division of soul and spirit, and of joints and marrow, and is a discerner of the thoughts and intents of the heart.

CHAPTER 22

THE KINGDOM RESTORED

Once Satan has been bound and the enemies of God have been destroyed at the battle of Armageddon, the Kingdom Age will commence and there will be 1000 years of true peace. Satan will be bound for 1000 years.

Zechariah 3:1-10 (NKJ)
1 Then he showed me Joshua the high priest standing before the Angel of the LORD, and Satan standing at his right hand to oppose him.
2 And the LORD said to Satan, "The LORD rebuke you, Satan! The LORD who has chosen Jerusalem rebuke you! Is this not a brand plucked from the fire?"
3 Now Joshua was clothed with filthy garments, and was standing before the Angel.
4 Then He answered and spoke to those who stood before Him, saying, "Take away the filthy garments from him." And to him He said, "See, I have removed your iniquity from you, and I will clothe you with rich robes."
5 And I said, "Let them put a clean turban on his head." So they put a clean turban on his head, and they put the clothes on him. And the Angel of the LORD stood by.
6 Then the Angel of the LORD admonished Joshua, saying,
7 "Thus says the LORD of hosts: 'If you will walk in My ways, and if you will keep My command, then you shall also judge My house, and likewise have charge of My courts; I will give you places to walk among these who stand here.

8 'Hear, O Joshua, the high priest, you and your companions who sit before you, for they are a wondrous sign; for behold, I am bringing forth My Servant the BRANCH.
9 For behold, the stone that I have laid before Joshua: upon the stone are seven eyes. Behold, I will engrave its inscription,' says the LORD of hosts, 'And I will remove the iniquity of that land in one day.
10 In that day,' says the LORD of hosts, 'Everyone will invite his neighbor under his vine and under his fig tree.'"

Notice that the iniquity of the land will be removed in one day. Joshua, the high priest and his companions will be a wondrous sign. Behold, God is bringing forth His Servant, the BRANCH. I believe this will be the day in which the Messiah returns to reign with the saints, on earth, for 1000 years. Listen to how God describes His restored Kingdom.

Isaiah 51:3 (NKJ)
3 For the LORD will comfort Zion, he will comfort all her waste places; he will make her wilderness like Eden, and her desert like the garden of the LORD; joy and gladness will be found in it, thanksgiving and the voice of melody.

Eden in the beginning and Eden in the end. Jerusalem will be as the garden of the Lord. But realize that the next sentence written by Ezekiel tells you that the restoration will follow the destruction. Jerusalem will be made desolate first, as a result of the Battle of Armageddon.

Ezekiel 36:33-38 (NKJ)
33 'Thus says the Lord GOD: "On the day that I cleanse you from all your iniquities, I will also enable you to dwell in the cities, and the ruins shall be rebuilt.
34 "The desolate land shall be tilled instead of lying desolate in the sight of all who pass by.
35 "So they will say, 'This land that was desolate has become like the garden of Eden; and the wasted, desolate, and ruined cities are now fortified and inhabited.'

36 "Then the nations which are left all around you shall know that I, the LORD, have rebuilt the ruined places and planted what was desolate. I, the LORD, have spoken it, and I will do it."
37 'Thus says the Lord GOD: "I will also let the house of Israel inquire of Me to do this for them: I will increase their men like a flock.
38 "Like a flock offered as holy sacrifices, like the flock at Jerusalem on its feast days, so shall the ruined cities be filled with flocks of men. Then they shall know that I am the LORD."

Israel will be restored. Following the great destruction of the Battle of Armageddon, the wasted, desolate and ruined cities will be restored, like Eden. And don't fail to notice, "On the day that I cleanse you from all your iniquities," as being the enabling event. Your sins will be forgiven by the only One who can truly cleanse you. The chosen people shall be redeemed! Jerusalem will be restored and the Kingdom will be established.

CHAPTER 23

THESE BONES ARE GOING TO "WALK AROUND" AGAIN—DAVID AS KING

What I am about to share with you is a prophecy that some biblical scholars simply do not believe. I have no reason not to believe it, to the very last word. God gave these words to Ezekiel and I find them confirmed over and over. This prophecy uses some language as to the identity of the remnant, in general, but if you know the Scriptures, you know that God's chosen people, and all of His Saints, are going to reign with Christ for 1000 years. Listen carefully.

Ezekiel 37:1-25 (NKJ)
The hand of the LORD came upon me and brought me out in the Spirit of the LORD, and set me down in the midst of the valley; and it was full of bones.
2 Then He caused me to pass by them all around, and behold, there were very many in the open valley; and indeed they were very dry.
3 And He said to me, "Son of man, can these bones live?" So I answered, "O Lord GOD, You know."
4 Again He said to me, "Prophesy to these bones, and say to them, 'O dry bones, hear the word of the LORD!
5 'Thus says the Lord GOD to these bones: "Surely I will cause breath to enter into you, and you shall live.

6 "I will put sinews on you and bring flesh upon you, cover you with skin and put breath in you; and you shall live. Then you shall know that I am the LORD."'"

7 So I prophesied as I was commanded; and as I prophesied, there was a noise, and suddenly a rattling; and the bones came together, bone to bone.

8 Indeed, as I looked, the sinews and the flesh came upon them, and the skin covered them over; but there was no breath in them.

9 Then He said to me, "Prophesy to the breath, prophesy, son of man, and say to the breath, 'Thus says the Lord GOD: "Come from the four winds, O breath, and breathe on these slain, that they may live."'"

10 So I prophesied as He commanded me, and breath came into them, and they lived, and stood upon their feet, an exceedingly great army.

11 Then He said to me, "Son of man, these bones are the whole house of Israel. They indeed say, 'Our bones are dry, our hope is lost, and we ourselves are cut off!'

12 "Therefore prophesy and say to them, 'Thus says the Lord GOD: "Behold, O My people, I will open your graves and cause you to come up from your graves, and bring you into the land of Israel.

13 "Then you shall know that I am the LORD, when I have opened your graves, O My people, and brought you up from your graves.

14 "I will put My Spirit in you, and you shall live, and I will place you in your own land. Then you shall know that I, the LORD, have spoken it and performed it," says the LORD.'"

15 Again the word of the LORD came to me, saying,

16 "As for you, son of man, take a stick for yourself and write on it: 'For Judah and for the children of Israel, his companions.' Then take another stick and write on it, 'For Joseph, the stick of Ephraim, and for all the house of Israel, his companions.'

17 "Then join them one to another for yourself into one stick, and they will become one in your hand.

18 "And when the children of your people speak to you, saying, 'Will you not show us what you mean by these?'–

19 "say to them, 'Thus says the Lord GOD: "Surely I will take the stick of Joseph, which is in the hand of Ephraim, and the tribes of Israel, his

companions; and I will join them with it, with the stick of Judah, and make them one stick, and they will be one in My hand."'
20 "And the sticks on which you write will be in your hand before their eyes.
21 "Then say to them, 'Thus says the Lord GOD: "Surely I will take the children of Israel from among the nations, wherever they have gone, and will gather them from every side and bring them into their own land;
22 "and I will make them one nation in the land, on the mountains of Israel; and one king shall be king over them all; they shall no longer be two nations, nor shall they ever be divided into two kingdoms again.
23 "They shall not defile themselves anymore with their idols, nor with their detestable things, nor with any of their transgressions; but I will deliver them from all their dwelling places in which they have sinned, and will cleanse them. Then they shall be My people, and I will be their God.
24 "David My servant shall be king over them, and they shall all have one shepherd; they shall also walk in My judgments and observe My statutes, and do them.
25 "Then they shall dwell in the land that I have given to Jacob My servant, where your fathers dwelt; and they shall dwell there, they, their children, and their children's children, forever; and My servant David shall be their prince forever.

Some of you may have heard a song whose words included the phrase, "These bones these bones are going to walk around", " knee bone connected to the hip bone" and so on. The song is about a prophecy that describes what will happen when the Father restores Jerusalem for the Millennium and inhabits it with those Jews who have died and been resurrected, including King David.

The most difficult question for myself is "Which Jews will be resurrected to serve in the Millennium?" It would be wonderful if the answer was "every Jew", and it may be. But what is a Jew. Listen.

Romans 2:28-29 (NKJ)
28 For he is not a Jew who is one outwardly, nor is circumcision that which is outward in the flesh;

29 but he is a Jew who is one inwardly; and circumcision is that of the heart, in the Spirit, not in the letter; whose praise is not from men but from God.

Earlier I said that neither you nor I have to make the call as to who is a true Jew or who will be in the Kingdom. We are dealing with the province of God when we discuss the "judgment of men". God makes it very clear that sin separates us from Him. God hates sin and disobedience. My concern is that since we all have sinned and since we all have been disobedient, what does God require of us in order to enter into His Holy Presence?

The Bible says that every knee will bow and every tongue will confess that Jesus Christ is Lord. We can choose to make that confession now or later. If a person says, "later", it does not mean you will not confess that Jesus Christ is Lord, it means you have chosen to postpone the decision. You will, at some point, bow your knee before Jesus. If you do so as a person who has never placed their faith in Jesus, you will be doing so on the Day of Judgment.

Are you now among the faithful and obedient, using the Law as your yardstick? Do you really want to be judged on your obedience to the Law? If the answer is yes, then you should pray that mercy triumphs over justice and that the love of God for His children completely exceeds reason, from a human point of view.

Are your sins still with you? The Messiah, the Redeemer, is the only One who could ever atone for your sins and mine, and He did. At every junction, His redemptive powers are our only path to salvation. Our works will be as nothing; our personal efforts are completely futile.

Salvation does not depend on "which sin" one has committed, for all sin separates man from God. Salvation is about repentance and redemption, confessing your sins and having your sins forgiven. Salvation begins with you understanding that there is "flesh" and a soul and spirit. The flesh will die; the spirit will exist forever. Salvation is about your spending eternity "with God" and not in eternal separation, thus eternal suffering.

Many devout Jews love and worship God. Many adhere to the Law, as best they can. Many pray unceasingly for the power and presence of God in their lives. Many read the Scriptures daily. In fact, some have decided that the Messiah did come and is about to return and their faith in that belief has brought them out of the darkness Isaiah described. Listen again to the words of Isaiah.

Isaiah 6:10 (NKJ)
10 "Make the heart of this people dull, and their ears heavy, and shut their eyes; lest they see with their eyes, and hear with their ears, and understand with their heart, and return and be healed."

The choice to "return and be healed" remains before you. It is not a popular choice among Jews. But it never was a popular choice. The name of Jesus has been a point of offense to many, to this day. If you claim Jesus Christ as the Messiah, your personal Redeemer, you will be persecuted. But even among the Gentiles, such persecution is common. The scriptures speak very clearly to what one might expect if you respond to the invitation of the Gospel. First, you are assured that eternal life is yours and second you are told to expect persecution up to the time of Christ's return. But persecution for your faith is not a bad thing. Listen.

2 Timothy 3:12 (NKJ)
12 Yes, and all who desire to live godly in Christ Jesus will suffer persecution.

Matthew 5:10-12 (NKJ)
10 "…Blessed are those who are persecuted for righteousness' sake, for theirs is the kingdom of heaven.
11 "Blessed are you when they revile and persecute you, and say
12 "Rejoice and be exceedingly glad, for great is your reward in heaven, for so they persecuted the prophets who were before you."

CHAPTER 24

THE LAME – THE DEAF AND THOSE WHO ARE "LAST" WILL EMERGE AS "FIRST"

Micah 4:6-7 (NKJ)
6 "In that day," says the LORD, "I will assemble the lame, I will gather the outcast and those whom I have afflicted;
7 I will make the lame a remnant, and the outcast a strong nation; so the LORD will reign over them in Mount Zion from now on, even forever.

Are you afflicted, lame, or an outcast? God is telling us He is in control of those He has afflicted. Doesn't it sound wrong to say "He has afflicted?" We must rely on the fact that He is the potter and we are the clay and the Potter knows what He is doing. Our afflictions are but for the moment, if you place the span of our human lives in the perspective of eternity.

Some have been afflicted from birth, others only recently, but in every case these verses are true.

Matthew 10:29-31 (NKJ)
29 "Are not two sparrows sold for a copper coin? And not one of them falls to the ground apart from your Father's will.
30 "But the very hairs of your head are all numbered.
31 "Do not fear therefore; you are of more value than many sparrows.

Why else would Jesus have given us these words except to have us understand that God loves us, is watching over us and is totally aware of every tiny event in our lives? The fact that some are fleet of foot and others lame in this lifetime seems very unfair. But to write those words is to challenge the prerogatives of God and God alone. God knows the beginning from the end and makes the following promise.

Romans 8:28-35 (NKJ)
28 …we know that all things work together for good to those who love God, to those who are the called according to His purpose.
29 **For whom He foreknew, He also predestined to be conformed to the image of His Son, that He might be the firstborn among many brethren.**
30 **Moreover whom He predestined, these He also called; whom He called, these He also justified; and whom He justified, these He also glorified.**
31 **What then shall we say to these things? If God is for us, who can be against us?**
32 **He who did not spare His own Son, but delivered Him up for us all, how shall He not with Him also freely give us all things?**
33 **Who shall bring a charge against God's elect? It is God who justifies.**
34 **Who is he who condemns? It is Christ who died, and furthermore is also risen, who is even at the right hand of God, who also makes intercession for us.**
35 **Who shall separate us from the love of Christ? Shall tribulation, or distress, or persecution, or famine, or nakedness, or peril, or sword?**

This last verse is the most telling. In spite of the temptations and trials of life, there is nothing you experience here on earth that can separate you from the love of God. God knows your heart, He knows your needs and He knows who it is that will serve Him and glorify Him in this life. Our very tiny life span, mathematically smaller than we can visualize, is but a moment and our lives but a vapor. Listen to how King David and James, the son of Joseph and Mary express this truth.

Psalm 39:4-5 (NKJ)
4 **"LORD, make me to know my end, and what is the measure of my days, that I may know how frail I am.**

5 Indeed, You have made my days as handbreadths, and my age is as nothing before You; certainly every man at his best state is but vapor.

James 4:13-15 (NKJ)
13 Come now, you who say, "Today or tomorrow we will go to such and such a city, spend a year there, buy and sell, and make a profit";
14 whereas you do not know what will happen tomorrow. For what is your life? It is even a vapor that appears for a little time and then vanishes away.
15 Instead you ought to say, "If the Lord wills, we shall live and do this or that."

Notice this last verse. How often have you heard people attach "Lord willing" to a statement. It is not an idle comment. What we vow to do, if the vow is made in our own strength, we must do. How often have we said, "Lord if you will only bless me in this certain way, I will serve you with all my heart." Such prayers are often about our health. We know better than to "bargain" with the Lord over trivial, transitory needs but our health is another matter. Vows made to the Lord represent a serious obligation. Listen.

Deuteronomy 23:21-23 (NKJ)
21 "When you make a vow to the LORD your God, you shall not delay to pay it; for the LORD your God will surely require it of you, and it would be sin to you.
22 "But if you abstain from vowing, it shall not be sin to you.
23 "That which has gone from your lips you shall keep and perform, for you voluntarily vowed to the LORD your God what you have promised with your mouth.

Ecclesiastes 5:4-5 (NKJ)
4 When you make a vow to God, do not delay to pay it; for He has no pleasure in fools. Pay what you have vowed–
5 Better not to vow than to vow and not pay.

James states this fact in another way, focusing both on our need to endure our temporary circumstance with patience and on our requirement not to make promises which we intend to fulfill in and of our own strength. Listen.

James 5:10-12 (NKJ)
10 My brethren, take the prophets, who spoke in the name of the Lord, as an example of suffering and patience.
11 Indeed we count them blessed who endure. You have heard of the perseverance of Job and seen the end intended by the Lord– that the Lord is very compassionate and merciful.
12 But above all, my brethren, do not swear, either by heaven or by earth or with any other oath. But let your "Yes," be "Yes," and your "No," "No," lest you fall into judgment.

It is what we do with whatever assets that God has given us during this life that determines our eternal relationship with Him. One could argue that it seems unfair that some are "blessed" more than others. Not all "blessings" are of eternal value. Some of the blessings of life weigh us down. They encumber us and the cares and worries of "this" world, become our entire agenda. We are so busy "managing our assets" that we lose sight of why God has chosen to bless us. Our blessings, our assets, become, in a sense, our liabilities. Listen to the words of Jesus.

Luke 12:48 (NKJ)
48 ...For everyone to whom much is given, from him much will be required; and to whom much has been committed, of him they will ask the more.

We who have been blessed with physical and mental health, who have prospered and who have been blessed beyond our perceived "entitlement," are equipped to run the race and to run it well. To the extent that we forget the source of our strength and the source of our blessings, we ignore God and claim the victory for ourselves. If that is the case, then you can understand the meaning of the following verse.

Mark 10:24-25 (NKJ)
24 ..."Children, how hard it is for those who trust in riches to enter the kingdom of God!

25 "It is easier for a camel to go through the eye of a needle than for a rich man to enter the kingdom of God."

None of this is to say, "I guess it is a good thing to be afflicted, lame or outcast, since very little, in comparison, is expected of me." That is hardly the case. History is full of examples of so called "handicapped" persons functioning at extremely high levels of effectiveness, hopefully, to the glory of God.

But let's move this discussion to what I believe is the point of the matter. The Lord said, "I will make the lame a remnant, and the outcast a strong nation; so the LORD will reign over them in Mount Zion from now on, even forever."

To whom is He referring? I will speculate that He is referring to the "unaccountable," those persons so disabled that they have been unable to serve God in the capacity that He and they would have preferred, and now their opportunity is going to be gloriously different in the Kingdom Age than it was during their life here. Listen.

Isaiah 35:1-10 (NKJ)
1 The wilderness and the wasteland shall be glad for them, and the desert shall rejoice and blossom as the rose;
2 It shall blossom abundantly and rejoice, even with joy and singing. The glory of Lebanon shall be given to it, the excellence of Carmel and Sharon. They shall see the glory of the LORD, the excellency of our God.
3 Strengthen the weak hands, and make firm the feeble knees.
4 Say to those who are fearful-hearted, "Be strong, do not fear! Behold, your God will come with vengeance, with the recompense of God; he will come and save you."
5 Then the eyes of the blind shall be opened, and the ears of the deaf shall be unstopped.
6 Then the lame shall leap like a deer, and the tongue of the dumb sing. For waters shall burst forth in the wilderness, and streams in the desert.

7 The parched ground shall become a pool, and the thirsty land springs of water; in the habitation of jackals, where each lay, there shall be grass with reeds and rushes.
8 A highway shall be there, and a road, and it shall be called the Highway of Holiness. The unclean shall not pass over it, but it shall be for others. Whoever walks the road, although a fool, shall not go astray.
9 No lion shall be there, nor shall any ravenous beast go up on it; it shall not be found there. But the redeemed shall walk there,
10 And the ransomed of the LORD shall return, and come to Zion with singing, with everlasting joy on their heads. They shall obtain joy and gladness, and sorrow and sighing shall flee away.

Matthew 20:16 (NKJ)
16 "So the last will be first, and the first last. For many are called, but few chosen."

These are wonderful promises. They are to the poor of the world who are rich in faith. Those who are the rich of the world but poor in faith will experience the very opposite reward. The blessings of this life will become their curse and will serve as a testimony against them, if they fail to understand that not one thing they possess here, is truly theirs, and not one thing on this earth will survive the judgment of God. "Every" thing belongs to God.

Colossians 1:16-17 (NKJ)
16 For by Him all things were created that are in heaven and that are on earth, visible and invisible, whether thrones or dominions or principalities or powers. All things were created through Him and for Him.
17 And He is before all things, and in Him all things consist.

James 2:5 (NKJ)
5 Listen, my beloved brethren: Has God not chosen the poor of this world to be rich in faith and heirs of the kingdom which He promised to those who love Him?

In the Millennium, the Kingdom Age, Jerusalem will flourish and those nations that are left on earth will come to Jerusalem to worship the Lord and to observe the Jewish Festivals. Listen.

Zechariah 8:20-23 (NKJ)
20 "Thus says the LORD of hosts: 'Peoples shall yet come, inhabitants of many cities;
21 The inhabitants of one city shall go to another, saying, "Let us continue to go and pray before the LORD, and seek the LORD of hosts. I myself will go also."
22 Yes, many peoples and strong nations shall come to seek the LORD of hosts in Jerusalem, and to pray before the LORD.'
23 "Thus says the LORD of hosts: 'In those days ten men from every language of the nations shall grasp the sleeve of a Jewish man, saying, "Let us go with you, for we have heard that God is with you."

I do not see clearly, who the inhabitants of the "other strong nations" will be during the millennium, but I believe at least one group will be those who have been "last" during their life, those who were oppressed, due to no fault of their own. These may well be "first" in the millennium I believe they may actually become the leaders of the other nations and that the burden of their lives will be lifted from them.

There is another side to this scenario, if it is true. No one will ever enter the Kingdom of Heaven, that eternal state of existence, unless they are wrapped in the "cloak of righteousness," not of their own, but of the Messiah, the savior, Jesus Christ.

Micah 7:9 (NKJ)
9 I will bear the indignation of the LORD, because I have sinned against Him, until He pleads my case and executes justice for me. He will bring me forth to the light; I will see His righteousness.

Isaiah 45:23-25 (NKJ)
23 I have sworn by Myself; the word has gone out of My mouth in righteousness, and shall not return, that to Me every knee shall bow, every tongue shall take an oath.

24 He shall say, 'Surely in the LORD I have righteousness and strength. To Him men shall come, and all shall be ashamed who are incensed against Him.
25 In the LORD all the descendants of Israel shall be justified, and shall glory.'"

1 Corinthians 1:29-31 (NKJ)
29 ... no flesh should glory in His presence.
30 But of Him you are in Christ Jesus, who became for us wisdom from God– and righteousness and sanctification and redemption–
31 that, as it is written, "He who glories, let him glory in the Lord."

Our glory, no matter what our physical condition or our status, is in the Lord and it is He who shall justify us and present us to the Father. We seek His righteousness.

Recall that when Satan is loosed at the end of the 1000 years, it will be to "tempt" those who have experienced a wonderful period of blessings to somehow think that the Jews and the God "of the Jews" is their enemy. Many will fall and one final battle, fought by God against the enemies of the Nation of Israel, will ensue. This is the battle immediately preceding the Great White Throne judgment, where saints and sinners are separated, forever. (And what is a saint except one wrapped in the righteousness of Christ) Those who were "last" and have become "first," may well allow pride and "control" to distort their judgment, just as it has distorted the judgment of so many today.

Recall as well, that during the Millennium, these heads of nations and their people will be required to attend the Feast of Tabernacles, annually in Jerusalem, or in failing to attend, their land will receive no rain and their crops will fail. Listen to that verse.

Zechariah 14:17 (NKJ)
17 And it shall be that whichever of the families of the earth do not come up to Jerusalem to worship the King, the LORD of hosts, on them there will be no rain.

Animosity and jealousy could easily develop and according to prophecy, it will develop. That is why Satan will be loosed. No one will get into heaven by "default" or by simply being "in attendance," nor will anyone get in "out of pity."

We will be in heaven together because of God's Grace and our faith in a risen Redeemer who has atoned for our sins and presents us to the Father wrapped in His righteousness, not ours. It takes a personal relationship with the Father, the Son and the Holy Spirit to overcome evil. and its influence, whether you are handicapped or not. The flesh will plague you, even in times of great blessings, and tempt you to sin, but the flesh, which may be very weak in this world, is perishing. You will have a new, perfect body in heaven. These are wonderful verses. Listen.

Romans 8:18 (NKJ)
18 For I consider that the sufferings of this present time are not worthy to be compared with the glory which shall be revealed in us.

Isaiah 25:8-9 (NKJ)
8 He will swallow up death forever, and the Lord GOD will wipe away tears from all faces; the rebuke of His people he will take away from all the earth; for the LORD has spoken.
9 And it will be said in that day: "Behold, this is our God; we have waited for Him, and He will save us. This is the LORD; we have waited for Him; we will be glad and rejoice in His salvation."

Isaiah 61:1-3 (NKJ)
1 "The Spirit of the Lord GOD is upon Me, because the LORD has anointed Me to preach good tidings to the poor; he has sent Me to heal the brokenhearted, to proclaim liberty to the captives, and the opening of the prison to those who are bound;
2 To proclaim the acceptable year of the LORD, and the day of vengeance of our God; to comfort all who mourn,
3 To console those who mourn in Zion, to give them beauty for ashes, the oil of joy for mourning, the garment of praise for the spirit of heaviness; that they may be called trees of righteousness, the planting of the LORD, that He may be glorified."

1 Corinthians 15:54-55 (NKJ)
54 So when this corruptible has put on incorruption, and this mortal has put on immortality, then shall be brought to pass the saying that is written: "Death is swallowed up in victory."
55 "O Death, where is your sting? O Hades, where is your victory?"

Revelation 7:16-17 (NKJ)
16 "They shall neither hunger anymore nor thirst anymore; the sun shall not strike them, nor any heat;
17 "for the Lamb who is in the midst of the throne will shepherd them and lead them to living fountains of waters. And God will wipe away every tear from their eyes."

Revelation 21:1-7 (NKJ)
1 Now I saw a new heaven and a new earth, for the first heaven and the first earth had passed away. Also there was no more sea.
2 Then I, John, saw the holy city, New Jerusalem, coming down out of heaven from God, prepared as a bride adorned for her husband.
3 And I heard a loud voice from heaven saying, "Behold, the tabernacle of God is with men, and He will dwell with them, and they shall be His people. God Himself will be with them and be their God.
4 "And God will wipe away every tear from their eyes; there shall be no more death, nor sorrow, nor crying. There shall be no more pain, for the former things have passed away."
5 Then He who sat on the throne said, "Behold, I make all things new." And He said to me, "Write, for these words are true and faithful."
6 And He said to me, "It is done! I am the Alpha and the Omega, the Beginning and the End. I will give of the fountain of the water of life freely to him who thirsts.
7 "He who overcomes shall inherit all things, and I will be his God and he shall be My son.

Two final, telling, references. Listen.

Zephaniah 3:19 (NKJ)
19 Behold, at that time I will deal with all who afflict you; I will save the lame, and gather those who were driven out; I will appoint them for praise and fame in every land where they were put to shame.

Hebrews 12:11-13 (NKJ)
11 Now no chastening seems to be joyful for the present, but painful; nevertheless, afterward it yields the peaceable fruit of righteousness to those who have been trained by it.
12 Therefore strengthen the hands which hang down, and the feeble knees,
13 and make straight paths for your feet, so that what is lame may not be dislocated, but rather be healed.

It seems too easy for we who are physically and mentally healthy to say these words of consolation and wisdom to the afflicted. We really do not understand what it is like to be in the situation of one who experiences such pain. You and I have known some wonderful examples of people who were "handicapped" and whose lives have produced astounding results, hopefully to the glory of God.

Finally, listen to Words of consolation and hope sent by God:

2 Corinthians 4:16-18 (NKJ)
16 ...we do not lose heart. Even though our outward man is perishing, yet the inward man is being renewed day by day.
17 For our light affliction, which is but for a moment, is working for us a far more exceeding and eternal weight of glory,
18 while we do not look at the things which are seen, but at the things which are not seen. For the things which are seen are temporary, but the things which are not seen are eternal.

Praise God for His Holy Word, His love and the strength that He gives freely to us.

CHAPTER 25

THE ENEMY IS DEFEATED— THE MESSIAH ESTABLISHES "NEW JERUSALEM"

The circumstances of heaven escape our understanding. The scriptures make it clear it is a place of joy, worship and contentment, better than anything we can imagine. Satan will never again be an evil force in the hearts of God's children.

1 Corinthians 2:9 (NKJ)
9 But as it is written: "Eye has not seen, nor ear heard, nor have entered into the heart of man the things which God has prepared for those who love Him."

If you believe God exists and that His prophecies, fulfilled and unfulfilled are true, and that the revelations of His scriptures are true, then what greater priority exists than to seek His face and to enter into His presence?

Psalm 27:4 (NKJ)
4 One thing I have desired of the LORD, that will I seek: that I may dwell in the house of the LORD all the days of my life, to behold the beauty of the LORD, and to inquire in His temple.

1 Kings 8:30, 34, 36 (NKJ)
30 ...Hear in heaven Your dwelling place; and when You hear, forgive.

34 ..."hear in heaven, and forgive the sin of Your people Israel, and bring them back to the land which You gave to their fathers.
36 ..."hear in heaven, and forgive the sin of Your servants

I suggest again that you will be without excuse if you have not sought His presence in your life. You know too much to claim ignorance as a defense. Those, whose names are not "blotted" out, are those who "overcome." Sometimes we feel we can "wait and see." No, the initiative is ours and Satan, manifested in our flesh, is an enemy to be overcome. As it says in the Bible, the spirit is willing, but the flesh is weak. Either choose to "enable the Spirit" or be overcome by the flesh. Listen.

Revelation 3:5 (NKJ)
5 "He who overcomes shall be clothed in white garments, and I will not blot out his name from the Book of Life; but I will confess his name before My Father and before His angels.

Revelation 3:7-13 (NKJ)
7 "And to the angel of the church in Philadelphia write, 'These things says He who is holy, He who is true, "He who has the key of David, He who opens and no one shuts, and shuts and no one opens":
8 "I know your works. See, I have set before you an open door, and no one can shut it; for you have a little strength, have kept My word, and have not denied My name.
9 "Indeed I will make those of the synagogue of Satan, who say they are Jews and are not, but lie– indeed I will make them come and worship before your feet, and to know that I have loved you.
10 "Because you have kept My command to persevere, I also will keep you from the hour of trial which shall come upon the whole world, to test those who dwell on the earth.
11 "Behold, I am coming quickly! Hold fast what you have, that no one may take your crown.
12 "He who overcomes, I will make him a pillar in the temple of My God, and he shall go out no more. And I will write on him the name of My God and the name of the city of My God, the New Jerusalem, which comes down out of heaven from My God. And I will write on him My new name.

13 "He who has an ear, let him hear what the Spirit says to the churches."

Here, Jesus is telling you that your name is in the Book of Life and that He will not blot it out if you have "overcome." Then He defines "overcome" by saying it includes those who have "kept my word and not denied My name." Then Jesus says a harsh sentence. He says, "Indeed I will make those of the synagogue of Satan, who say they are Jews and are not, but lie– indeed I will make them come and worship before your feet, and to know that I have loved you.

This last sentence could be considered one of hope, in that a Jew that has not kept God's word and who has denied the Messiah, is present in the millennium, even though as one who appears subservient, but that is not what the Messiah prefers. In verse 10 He states that:

"Because you have kept My command to persevere, I also will keep you from the hour of trial which shall come upon the whole world, to test those who dwell on the earth". Jesus does not want you to endure the "hour of trial." He wants you to obey and to persevere, so He can keep you from the trial.

Then notice that He refers to the trial as a "test." If you kneel to a false god, if you accept the mark of the beast, you will have failed the test. But He doesn't want you to endure the test, He wants to keep you from it!

I know we await the coming or the return of the same Messiah. It isn't that a Jew can't be saved who denies Christ, because throughout history there are those who have denied Christ and then repented. They changed their mind. If we worship the same precise Messiah, The Christ, now and then, we will both have seen Him as the Lamb of God, the only One who could redeem us from our sin. We are going to come to the same point. But if prophecy is true, the tribulation may be too much for you to endure, and certainly Jesus Christ, the Judge, does not want you to endure it.

We see the word "overcome" as a depiction of the act of repenting. In a sense, the will to overcome is derived from the inner conflict between your flesh and your spirit. The more "out of sync" you feel, that is, the greater the gap between what you want to be and what you are, the more you are experiencing both God's love and His chastisement. Parents understand this perfectly. We rebuke, if done God's way, out of love. It is love first, then discipline.

Revelation 3:19-21 (NKJ)
19 "As many as I love, I rebuke and chasten. Therefore be zealous and repent.
20 "Behold, I stand at the door and knock. If anyone hears My voice and opens the door, I will come in to him and dine with him, and he with Me.
21 "To him who overcomes I will grant to sit with Me on My throne, as I also overcame and sat down with My Father on His throne.

God's elect will, in heaven, be in the presence of the 144,000 young Jewish male virgins representing the 12 tribes of Israel who have been beheaded for refusing the mark of the beast; but before heaven is the millennium, here on earth. He who overcomes will reign with Christ during the millennium Those who do so are referred to as priests to God. The "scroll," able to be opened only by the Lamb, tells of the events of the end times. Listen.

Revelation 5:9-10 (NKJ)
9 And they sang a new song, saying: "You are worthy to take the scroll, and to open its seals; for You were slain, and have redeemed us to God by Your blood out of every tribe and tongue and people and nation,
10 And have made us kings and priests to our God; and we shall reign on the earth."

Read those two verses very carefully. Jesus Christ is worthy to open the seals of the scroll, because He was slain and redeemed us to God, by His blood. Then we who, by God's grace, love and obey, are made kings and priests to our God on earth, during the millennium I know the verse says "on the earth" and does not say "the millennium," but the reign of Christ with His saints on earth is during the millennium, only. It precedes the great white throne judgment where the sheep are separated from the goats, to enter into God's presence in New Jerusalem. Listen.

Revelation 20:4-6 (NKJ)
4 And I saw thrones, and they sat on them, and judgment was committed to them. Then I saw the souls of those who had been beheaded for their witness to Jesus and for the word of God, who had not worshiped the beast or his image, and had not received his mark on their foreheads or on their hands. And they lived and reigned with Christ for a thousand years.
5 But the rest of the dead did not live again until the thousand years were finished. This is the first resurrection.
6 Blessed and holy is he who has part in the first resurrection. Over such the second death has no power, but they shall be priests of God and of Christ, and shall reign with Him a thousand years.

Those who overcome reign with Christ as kings and priests. Here we see that the "rest of the dead" did not live again until the 1000 years were finished. They were not part of the "first resurrection." For those who are part of the first resurrection, the "second death" has no power over them.

What is the second death? The first death is our physical death, the second death is our spiritual death, but the second death has no power over those who are part of the first resurrection. You choose to be born twice, once physically and once spiritually or to die twice, once physically and once spiritually. Those who "die twice" will do so on judgment day, when their souls are sentenced to an eternal place whose full characteristics are known only to God, but we know it is not a place to which you want to go.

We know that at the end of the millennium, Satan is released and he deceives many again, but not the blessed and holy priests reigning with Christ, nor God's children. Satan will cause the enemies of God to rally against Jerusalem in an effort to destroy God's people. God will fight the battle and the enemy will be destroyed, finally and forever. Satan will be cast into the lake of fire with the beast and the false prophet and they will be tormented night and day, forever.

Then comes the judgment. The dead will be resurrected and all will stand before God in the great white throne judgment. Who is not included among the "dead?" It will be those blessed and holy priests who have been reigning with Christ during the Millennium Now that means every soul will appear before God to be judged. There are "two books" present at judgment. One is the Book of Life. Anyone whose name is in the Lamb's Book of Life will enter into New Jerusalem. Listen.

Revelation 21:1-11 (NKJ)
1 Now I saw a new heaven and a new earth, for the first heaven and the first earth had passed away. Also there was no more sea.
2 Then I, John, saw the holy city, New Jerusalem, coming down out of heaven from God, prepared as a bride adorned for her husband.
3 And I heard a loud voice from heaven saying, "Behold, the tabernacle of God is with men, and He will dwell with them, and they shall be His people. God Himself will be with them and be their God.
4 "And God will wipe away every tear from their eyes; there shall be no more death, nor sorrow, nor crying. There shall be no more pain, for the former things have passed away."
5 Then He who sat on the throne said, "Behold, I make all things new." And He said to me, "Write, for these words are true and faithful."
6 And He said to me, "It is done! I am the Alpha and the Omega, the Beginning and the End. I will give of the fountain of the water of life freely to him who thirsts.
7 "He who overcomes shall inherit all things, and I will be his God and he shall be My son.
8 "But the cowardly, unbelieving, abominable, murderers, sexually immoral, sorcerers, idolaters, and all liars shall have their part in the lake which burns with fire and brimstone, which is the second death."
9 Then one of the seven angels who had the seven bowls filled with the seven last plagues came to me and talked with me, saying, "Come, I will show you the bride, the Lamb's wife."
10 And he carried me away in the Spirit to a great and high mountain, and showed me the great city, the holy Jerusalem, descending out of heaven from God,
11 having the glory of God. Her light was like a most precious stone, like a jasper stone, clear as crystal.

Skipping down a few verses,

Revelation 21:22-27 (NKJ)
22 But I saw no temple in it, for the Lord God Almighty and the Lamb are its temple.
23 The city had no need of the sun or of the moon to shine in it, for the glory of God illuminated it. The Lamb is its light.
24 And the nations of those who are saved shall walk in its light, and the kings of the earth bring their glory and honor into it.
25 Its gates shall not be shut at all by day (there shall be no night there).
26 And they shall bring the glory and the honor of the nations into it.
27 But there shall by no means enter it anything that defiles, or causes an abomination or a lie, but only those who are written in the Lamb's Book of Life.

Do you see that only those names that are written in the Lamb's Book of Life will live eternally? Who is the Lamb? The Lamb is the promised Messiah. Listen.

John 1:29-36 (NKJ)
29 The next day John saw Jesus coming toward him, and said, "Behold! The Lamb of God who takes away the sin of the world!
30 "This is He of whom I said, 'After me comes a Man who is preferred before me, for He was before me.'
31 "I did not know Him; but that He should be revealed to Israel, therefore I came baptizing with water."
32 And John bore witness, saying, "I saw the Spirit descending from heaven like a dove, and He remained upon Him.
33 "I did not know Him, but He who sent me to baptize with water said to me, 'Upon whom you see the Spirit descending, and remaining on Him, this is He who baptizes with the Holy Spirit.'
34 "And I have seen and testified that this is the Son of God."
35 Again, the next day, John stood with two of his disciples.
36 And looking at Jesus as He walked, he said, "Behold the Lamb of God!"

CHAPTER 26

WHY WOULD GOD BE ANGRY WITH HIS PEOPLE?

I would rather that the reader fills in the answer to this question, because in pointing out the reasons, it sounds like I am offering criticism of the Jews. Of course the Gentiles face the same judgment as the Jews. Whether the Jews have had more "light" (thus they should have less darkness) is a question you must consider. God's Word has told us, repeatedly, what it is that makes Him angry. The specific incidents that caused God to spell out the reason for His anger simply serve to point us to the nature of the underlying sin.

I believe it is safe to say that the 10 commandments (Exodus 20:1-17) cover all forms of the kind of obedience and righteousness that God expects from us. We have reviewed this in another topic, but it bears some repeating that there are two over-arching commandments. The Messiah quotes them. Listen.

Matthew 22:37-40 (NKJ)
37 **Jesus said to him," 'You shall love the Lord your God with all your heart, with all your soul, and with all your mind.**
38 **"This is the first and great commandment.**
39 **"And the second is like it: 'You shall love your neighbor as yourself.'**
40 **"On these two commandments hang all the Law and the Prophets."**

Some of my Jewish friends have said, Jesus is not the Messiah. They say that the Torah is that to which they are dedicated. But listen to what Jesus said about the Law.

Matthew 5:17-19 (NKJ)
17 "Do not think that I came to destroy the Law or the Prophets. I did not come to destroy but to fulfill.
18 "For assuredly, I say to you, till heaven and earth pass away, one jot or one tittle will by no means pass from the law till all is fulfilled.
19 "Whoever therefore breaks one of the least of these commandments, and teaches men so, shall be called least in the kingdom of heaven; but whoever does and teaches them, he shall be called great in the kingdom of heaven.

Regarding the utilitarian purpose of the Law in our daily lives, listen to the words of Moses.

Exodus 20:20 (NKJ)
20 And Moses said to the people, "Do not fear; for God has come to test you, and that His fear may be before you, so that you may not sin."

People debate over which laws are the most important. Aside from the fact that Jesus tried to end that debate by giving you a simple, complete summary of the Law by saying "You shall love the Lord your God with all your heart, with all your soul, and with all your mind.' " and "You shall love your neighbor as yourself.," you are taught by Moses that the Law is a "test," so that you might not sin. Please grasp the view that if there were no law, there would be no straight edge by which to measure your sin. Listen.

Romans 4:15 (NKJ)
15 …where there is no law there is no transgression.

What is sin except the transgression of the Law? Is there a single reader of these words who has never sinned? Of course not and that is why sacrifice, offerings and atonement exist. We seek to be forgiven so we humbly come before God with our efforts to be cleansed. But these efforts of sacrifice simply do not endure. They fail to keep us from sin and we go on in a cycle of sin-sacrifice-offering for our whole lives.

Isn't it clear that a more perfect way was provided when God sent His only Son as a final sacrifice, a final offering to cleanse us of our sins and to provide us with perfect, final atonement. The "cycle" of sin and sacrifice is ended. Jesus Christ is now our Redeemer. He paid the price for our sins and we can stand in the presence of the Father, not in our righteousness, but in the righteousness of God's only begotten Son.

When we acknowledge the Messiah, we receive the gift of the Holy Spirit. That is the power that truly allows the sinner, you and me, to escape from the power of the flesh. It is our flesh that must "die" and it is our spirit that must live. They contend constantly and you are serving one or the other, all of the time. Being "in the Spirit" is to be Christ like, to be saintly in a way that you and I could never be, aside from Him in us.

Does this sound too religious? Hopefully you will understand that it is not "religious" at all, in the ritual sense of the word, but it is simply a "relationship" with the Father, Son and Holy Ghost. It is a moment by moment relationship that you carry into every transactional event, every thought and every decision.

Now, if one prefers to try to stand before the Father in your own righteousness, instead of His Son, you are going to find your righteousness insufficient, and the anger that God feels about your sin is well documented. You are His Chosen Children, His Special People to whom He has entrusted His Holy Word. The prophets spoke clearly of the events to unfold and they were your prophets.

In short, when we are disobedient, it angers God. When Miriam and Aaron built the golden calf and the people worshipped before it, recall how it angered God. Read the account of that event with care. There are many lessons in this chapter.

Exodus 32:1-35 (NKJ)

1 Now when the people saw that Moses delayed coming down from the mountain, the people gathered together to Aaron, and said to him, "Come, make us gods that shall go before us; for as for this Moses, the man who brought us up out of the land of Egypt, we do not know what has become of him."

2 And Aaron said to them, "Break off the golden earrings which are in the ears of your wives, your sons, and your daughters, and bring them to me."

3 So all the people broke off the golden earrings which were in their ears, and brought them to Aaron.

4 And he received the gold from their hand, and he fashioned it with an engraving tool, and made a molded calf. Then they said, "This is your god, O Israel, that brought you out of the land of Egypt!"

5 So when Aaron saw it, he built an altar before it. And Aaron made a proclamation and said, "Tomorrow is a feast to the LORD."

6 Then they rose early on the next day, offered burnt offerings, and brought peace offerings; and the people sat down to eat and drink, and rose up to play.

7 And the LORD said to Moses, "Go, get down! For your people whom you brought out of the land of Egypt have corrupted themselves.

8 "They have turned aside quickly out of the way which I commanded them. They have made themselves a molded calf, and worshiped it and sacrificed to it, and said, 'This is your god, O Israel, that brought you out of the land of Egypt!'"

9 And the LORD said to Moses, "I have seen this people, and indeed it is a stiff-necked people!

10 "Now therefore, let Me alone, that My wrath may burn hot against them and I may consume them. And I will make of you a great nation."

11 Then Moses pleaded with the LORD his God, and said: "LORD, why does Your wrath burn hot against Your people whom You have brought out of the land of Egypt with great power and with a mighty hand?

12 "Why should the Egyptians speak, and say, 'He brought them out to harm them, to kill them in the mountains, and to consume them from the face of the earth'? Turn from Your fierce wrath, and relent from this harm to Your people.

13 "Remember Abraham, Isaac, and Israel, Your servants, to whom You swore by Your own self, and said to them, 'I will multiply your descendants as the stars of heaven; and all this land that I have spoken of I give to your descendants, and they shall inherit it forever.'"

14 So the LORD relented from the harm which He said He would do to His people.

15 And Moses turned and went down from the mountain, and the two tablets of the Testimony were in his hand. The tablets were written on both sides; on the one side and on the other they were written.

16 Now the tablets were the work of God, and the writing was the writing of God engraved on the tablets.

17 And when Joshua heard the noise of the people as they shouted, he said to Moses, "There is a noise of war in the camp."

18 But he said: "It is not the noise of the shout of victory, nor the noise of the cry of defeat, but the sound of singing I hear."

19 So it was, as soon as he came near the camp, that he saw the calf and the dancing. So Moses' anger became hot, and he cast the tablets out of his hands and broke them at the foot of the mountain.

20 Then he took the calf which they had made, burned it in the fire, and ground it to powder; and he scattered it on the water and made the children of Israel drink it.

21 And Moses said to Aaron, "What did this people do to you that you have brought so great a sin upon them?"

22 So Aaron said, "Do not let the anger of my lord become hot. You know the people, that they are set on evil.

23 "For they said to me, 'Make us gods that shall go before us; as for this Moses, the man who brought us out of the land of Egypt, we do not know what has become of him.'

24 "And I said to them, 'Whoever has any gold, let them break it off.' So they gave it to me, and I cast it into the fire, and this calf came out."

25 Now when Moses saw that the people were unrestrained (for Aaron had not restrained them, to their shame among their enemies),

26 then Moses stood in the entrance of the camp, and said, "Whoever is on the LORD'S side, come to me." And all the sons of Levi gathered themselves together to him.

27 And he said to them, "Thus says the LORD God of Israel: 'Let every man put his sword on his side, and go in and out from entrance to entrance throughout the camp, and let every man kill his brother, every man his companion, and every man his neighbor.'"
28 So the sons of Levi did according to the word of Moses. And about three thousand men of the people fell that day.
29 Then Moses said, "Consecrate yourselves today to the LORD, that He may bestow on you a blessing this day, for every man has opposed his son and his brother."
30 Now it came to pass on the next day that Moses said to the people, "You have committed a great sin. So now I will go up to the LORD; perhaps I can make atonement for your sin."
31 Then Moses returned to the LORD and said, "Oh, these people have committed a great sin, and have made for themselves a god of gold!
32 "Yet now, if You will forgive their sin– but if not, I pray, blot me out of Your book which You have written."
33 And the LORD said to Moses, "Whoever has sinned against Me, I will blot him out of My book.
34 "Now therefore, go, lead the people to the place of which I have spoken to you. Behold, My Angel shall go before you. Nevertheless, in the day when I visit for punishment, I will visit punishment upon them for their sin."
35 So the LORD plagued the people because of what they did with the calf which Aaron made.

Notice the effort of Moses to personally atone for the sin of the people. He said,

"Yet now, if You will forgive their sin- but if not, I pray, blot me out of Your book which You have written." God's response was to hold the people who sinned accountable, not Moses. In addition, notice that Moses' name is in the book. What book? Listen to what the Lord said

Revelation 3:5 (NKJ)
5 "He who overcomes shall be clothed in white garments, and I will not blot out his name from the Book of Life; but I will confess his name before My Father and before His angels."

Israel the Chosen or the Enemy?

When only Joshua and Caleb voted to go into the Promised Land, recall how God reacted, angrily, saying only those under twenty years of age, except for Joshua and Caleb would enter the promised land. Listen to the record of that pivotal incident.

Numbers 14:22-24 (NKJ)
22 "because all these men who have seen My glory and the signs which I did in Egypt and in the wilderness, and have put Me to the test now these ten times, and have not heeded My voice,
23 "they certainly shall not see the land of which I swore to their fathers, nor shall any of those who rejected Me see it.
24 "But My servant Caleb, because he has a different spirit in him and has followed Me fully, I will bring into the land where he went, and his descendants shall inherit it.

Numbers 14:29-38 (NKJ)
29 'The carcasses of you who have complained against Me shall fall in this wilderness, all of you who were numbered, according to your entire number, from twenty years old and above.
30 'Except for Caleb the son of Jephunneh and Joshua the son of Nun, you shall by no means enter the land which I swore I would make you dwell in.
31 'But your little ones, whom you said would be victims, I will bring in, and they shall know the land which you have despised.
32 'But as for you, your carcasses shall fall in this wilderness.
33 'And your sons shall be shepherds in the wilderness forty years, and bear the brunt of your infidelity, until your carcasses are consumed in the wilderness.
34 'According to the number of the days in which you spied out the land, forty days, for each day you shall bear your guilt one year, namely forty years, and you shall know My rejection.
35 'I the LORD have spoken this; I will surely do so to all this evil congregation who are gathered together against Me. In this wilderness they shall be consumed, and there they shall die.'"
36 And the men whom Moses sent to spy out the land, who returned and made all the congregation complain against him by bringing a bad report of the land,

37 those very men who brought the evil report about the land, died by the plague before the LORD.
38 But Joshua the son of Nun and Caleb the son of Jephunneh remained alive, of the men who went to spy out the land.

Some might say that such retribution is unwarranted. For example, each day of the time they spent spying turned into one year of punishment. I would suggest that we, in our flesh, completely fail in our estimate of what God expects. When God demands obedience, He means it. We tend to value "this life" so much that we lose perspective on the brevity of life, compared to eternity, and we then attach great significance to the events of this life. In a sense, the events are of great significance, but not as an end unto themselves, but as a means to determine our place in eternity.

Will our disobedience lead to eternal punishment, eternal banishment from the presence of the Father? Only God knows, but one thing is certain. Our sins are ever before us, large and small, and we plead for mercy, not judgment. On what basis do you expect your sins to be forgiven? Certainly we would agree it is not on the basis of personal merit. I think you would agree that the sacrifice of bulls and goats will not do it. What will make us acceptable in the sight of the Lord? Only one thing and that is our confession of faith in the redeeming act of the Messiah.

Even Moses, whom God held accountable for a sin of disobedience, did not enter into the Promised Land. Listen to the incident that caused God to be angry with Moses.

Numbers 20:2-12 (NKJ)
2 Now there was no water for the congregation; so they gathered together against Moses and Aaron.
3 And the people contended with Moses and spoke, saying: "If only we had died when our brethren died before the LORD!
4 "Why have you brought up the assembly of the LORD into this wilderness, that we and our animals should die here?
5 "And why have you made us come up out of Egypt, to bring us to this evil place? It is not a place of grain or figs or vines or pomegranates; nor is there any water to drink."

6 So Moses and Aaron went from the presence of the assembly to the door of the tabernacle of meeting, and they fell on their faces. And the glory of the LORD appeared to them.
7 Then the LORD spoke to Moses, saying,
8 "Take the rod; you and your brother Aaron gather the congregation together. Speak to the rock before their eyes, and it will yield its water; thus you shall bring water for them out of the rock, and give drink to the congregation and their animals."
9 So Moses took the rod from before the LORD as He commanded him.
10 And Moses and Aaron gathered the congregation together before the rock; and he said to them, "Hear now, you rebels! Must we bring water for you out of this rock?"
11 Then Moses lifted his hand and struck the rock twice with his rod; and water came out abundantly, and the congregation and their animals drank.
12 Then the LORD spoke to Moses and Aaron, "Because you did not believe Me, to hallow Me in the eyes of the children of Israel, therefore you shall not bring this assembly into the land which I have given them."

Do any of you think that Moses was perfect? No and neither did Moses. God forgive me for speaking about a saint in this way, but if Moses needed forgiveness, doesn't that magnify our sense of insufficiency? His life was one of being a faithful servant, imperfect, but certainly knowing that God was with him, guiding and directing him, loving him, forgiving him and assuring him of his place in eternity. Moses knew the Messiah was coming. Listen to the testimony of those who walked with the Messiah in Jerusalem.

Matthew 17:1-8 (NKJ)
1 ... Jesus took Peter, James, and John his brother, led them up on a high mountain by themselves;
2 and He was transfigured before them. His face shone like the sun, and His clothes became as white as the light.
3 And behold, Moses and Elijah appeared to them, talking with Him.
4 Then Peter answered and said to Jesus, "Lord, it is good for us to be here; if You wish, let us make here three tabernacles: one for You, one for Moses, and one for Elijah."

5 While he was still speaking, behold, a bright cloud overshadowed them; and suddenly a voice came out of the cloud, saying, "This is My beloved Son, in whom I am well pleased. Hear Him!"
6 And when the disciples heard it, they fell on their faces and were greatly afraid.
7 But Jesus came and touched them and said, "Arise, and do not be afraid."
8 When they had lifted up their eyes, they saw no one but Jesus only.

Why did God show us that Moses lives? I believe He chose to do so in a scene witnessed by men and in the presence of the Messiah, to both validate his relationship with Jesus, His Redeemer, and to show us that the sin of Moses had temporal but not eternal consequence. Our sin does not separate us from God when we stand in the presence and power of our Redeemer, our Messiah.

Let's reconsider one of the most prolific sins of modern history. We all know that the first 4 commandments are summarized by saying, love God with all of your heart, mind, soul and strength. Given that expectation, doesn't it strike you as bizarre that our society, even those who claim they love God, use His Holy name both vainly and profanely and with a total lack of respect. Do people have any idea how terrible the sin of blasphemy is? Listen.

Exodus 20:7 (NKJ)
7 "You shall not take the name of the LORD your God in vain, for the LORD will not hold him guiltless who takes His name in vain.

Ezekiel 39:7 (NKJ)
7 "So I will make My holy name known in the midst of My people Israel, and I will not let them profane My holy name anymore. Then the nations shall know that I am the LORD, the Holy One in Israel."

Can you think of any sin more prevalent in society today than the constant use of the name of our Holy God in phrases that have nothing to do with our recognition of His Deity? Even the children use His name in vain, imitating the adults. Every exclamation, whether of joy or sorrow, seems to begin and end with G-D, but the person using God's name in vain appears to be clueless as to the offense.

When confronted over their vain use of the Lord's name, most are shocked that someone would think that they meant to offend the Lord. Their hearts have been hardened and the Holiness of His presence and Holy Name no longer stir them to a sense of His majesty and power. It is almost impossible to watch television without hearing the Lord's name as an exclamation. If you clicked away from a television show every time it occurred you would find it difficult to watch most of what is produced.

Do you use the Lord's name in vain? If so, you must stop now and beg His forgiveness. To continue in this sin is mindless disobedience. It is my sense that God takes great offense at profanity and in particular in cases where those who claim to love Him use His name with the most unholy of intentions. The scriptures make it clear that our words count heavily.

Matthew 12:36-37 (NKJ)
36 "But I say to you that for every idle word men may speak, they will give account of it in the day of judgment.
37 "For by your words you will be justified, and by your words you will be condemned."

Why would God be angry? You fill in the answer, in terms of your personal relationship with Him and then resolve to do something about the problem. Eternity is forever and the mistakes of this short life will govern the outcome. Try to make the changes in your own strength and you will fail. It is the power of the Holy Spirit in you that enables you to become a loving child of God, accepting His mercy and grace.

The Holy Spirit will not come upon you "in your unforgiven state." Redemption awaits those who repent, whose heart is humble and contrite, and there is only one Redeemer, only One who can present you spotless. You need not be an object of God's anger. Instead, seek Him and respond to His love, now.

CHAPTER 27

HOW COULD A LOVING GOD ALLOW HIS CHILDREN TO DIE?

This question has always plagued mankind. It seems incongruous that a loving father would ever permit his child to perish, much less a Holy Father, His child. The primary fact to take into consideration when anyone dies, who is "in Christ" and especially a child, is that they must leave a temporary "testing ground" in order to enter into a permanent state of peace and joy. They in effect, "go to their reward." They give up the transient for the permanent. They leave temptation behind. They inherit eternal life. They are comforted in a way that we who are still bound to this physical earth can not understand.

One could go on and on in contrasting heaven with earth, but our understanding of heaven is far too dim for us to do so with any accuracy. Certainty, yes, but grasping the "feel" of being in heaven will require us to be there, before we can fully understand. Let's just agree that the person that is there would not have us mourn for them. It is proper and expected that we would mourn, on this side, for one who has left us behind. But it is we who are left behind. We live with uncertainty.

What is certainty? I think we would agree that it is something you can prove, something that is not up for debate. Is the "reality" of God a certainty? Listen.

Habakkuk 2:1-4 (NKJ)
1 I will stand my watch and set myself on the rampart, and watch to see what He will say to me, and what I will answer when I am corrected.
2 Then the LORD answered me and said: "Write the vision and make it plain on tablets, that he may run who reads it.
3 For the vision is yet for an appointed time; but at the end it will speak, and it will not lie. Though it tarries, wait for it; because it will surely come, it will not tarry.
4 "Behold the proud, his soul is not upright in him; but the just shall live by his faith."

When Habakkuk wrote this prophecy, God told him, the vision is yet for an appointed time, but at the end it will speak and it will not lie. Though it tarries, wait for it. Then, Habakkuk's visions are of various sins and as is true throughout the scriptures, pride is a signal of a soul that is not upright. What then is the signal of an upright soul? It is one who lives by faith. And what is faith but hope.

Noah's faith in God saved him and his family when God declared that Noah had found grace in the eyes of the Lord.

Genesis 6:5-8 (NKJ)
5 Then the LORD saw that the wickedness of man was great in the earth, and that every intent of the thoughts of his heart was only evil continually.
6 And the LORD was sorry that He had made man on the earth, and He was grieved in His heart.
7 So the LORD said, "I will destroy man whom I have created from the face of the earth, both man and beast, creeping thing and birds of the air, for I am sorry that I have made them."
8 But Noah found grace in the eyes of the LORD.

Then Abraham exhibited the "faith" that was counted unto him as righteousness. Listen to God's promise to Abraham.

Genesis 12:1-3 (NKJ)
1 Now the LORD had said to Abram: "Get out of your country, from your family and from your father's house, to a land that I will show you.
2 I will make you a great nation; I will bless you and make your name great; and you shall be a blessing.
3 I will bless those who bless you, and I will curse him who curses you; and in you all the families of the earth shall be blessed."

What is faith? What is the Presence "behind the veil" that drives a believer to obedience?

Hebrews 11:1 (NKJ)
1 Now faith is the substance of things hoped for, the evidence of things not seen.

Hebrews 6:19 (NKJ)
19 This hope we have as an anchor of the soul, both sure and steadfast, and which enters the Presence behind the veil...

Faith, an anchor of the soul, is that which enters the Presence "behind the veil." Notice that the "P" is capitalized. Our hope centers on God. Faith is the "substance" of things hoped for, the evidence of things not seen. These words are so clear in their meaning. Listen as Paul further explains how faith, the hope within us, is our link to the Holy Spirit, our Counselor, our personal guiding Light.

Romans 8:24-31 (NKJ)
24 For we were saved in this hope, but hope that is seen is not hope; for why does one still hope for what he sees?
25 But if we hope for what we do not see, we eagerly wait for it with perseverance.
26 Likewise the Spirit also helps in our weaknesses. For we do not know what we should pray for as we ought, but the Spirit Himself makes intercession for us with groanings which cannot be uttered.
27 Now He who searches the hearts knows what the mind of the Spirit is, because He makes intercession for the saints according to the will of God.

28 And we know that all things work together for good to those who love God, to those who are the called according to His purpose.
29 For whom He foreknew, He also predestined to be conformed to the image of His Son, that He might be the firstborn among many brethren.
30 Moreover whom He predestined, these He also called; whom He called, these He also justified; and whom He justified, these He also glorified.
31 What then shall we say to these things? If God is for us, who can be against us?

Paul introduces the word "predestination." It is not my intent to thoroughly treat that subject here, but you might consider a couple of key issues. God knows the Alpha from the Omega, the beginning from the end. That means God stands outside the human dimensions of time and space. We are here, given the restrictions of time and space, making choices and making decisions. We feel our decisions are not "ordained" because we exercise volition. As we exercise volition, "our will," we create a record. But God "saw" the record and "sees" the record before you decide. Yet, you are given choices. What you choose to do is foreknown to God and your thoughts this moment not only are known, but they were known before you thought them.

Listen as God speaks through Ezekiel and explains how righteousness and sin are choices that create results. Not results that surprise God, but results that are just and fair.

Ezekiel 18:20-32 (NKJ)
20 "The soul who sins shall die. The son shall not bear the guilt of the father, nor the father bear the guilt of the son. The righteousness of the righteous shall be upon himself, and the wickedness of the wicked shall be upon himself.
21 "But if a wicked man turns from all his sins which he has committed, keeps all My statutes, and does what is lawful and right, he shall surely live; he shall not die.
22 "None of the transgressions which he has committed shall be remembered against him; because of the righteousness which he has done, he shall live.

23 "Do I have any pleasure at all that the wicked should die?" says the Lord GOD, "and not that he should turn from his ways and live?

24 "But when a righteous man turns away from his righteousness and commits iniquity, and does according to all the abominations that the wicked man does, shall he live? All the righteousness which he has done shall not be remembered; because of the unfaithfulness of which he is guilty and the sin which he has committed, because of them he shall die.

25 "Yet you say, 'The way of the Lord is not fair.' Hear now, O house of Israel, is it not My way which is fair, and your ways which are not fair?

26 "When a righteous man turns away from his righteousness, commits iniquity, and dies in it, it is because of the iniquity which he has done that he dies.

27 "Again, when a wicked man turns away from the wickedness which he committed, and does what is lawful and right, he preserves himself alive.

28 "Because he considers and turns away from all the transgressions which he committed, he shall surely live; he shall not die.

29 "Yet the house of Israel says, 'The way of the Lord is not fair.' O house of Israel, is it not My ways which are fair, and your ways which are not fair?

30 "Therefore I will judge you, O house of Israel, every one according to his ways," says the Lord GOD. "Repent, and turn from all your transgressions, so that iniquity will not be your ruin.

31 "Cast away from you all the transgressions which you have committed, and get yourselves a new heart and a new spirit. For why should you die, O house of Israel?

32 "For I have no pleasure in the death of one who dies," says the Lord GOD. "Therefore turn and live!"

Remember that when God spoke through Ezekiel, the Messiah had not yet been sent. Obedience to the Law was what God expected of His people. Repentance was linked to an Israelite getting a new heart and a new spirit, just as it is now, but now the Great Enabler, the Holy Spirit, the Messiah in you has been sent. If Israel was to repent, turn from their transgressions and get a new heart, God says they would not die. Then God clarifies, as a Father to His child, "I have no pleasure in the death of one who dies. Turn and live."

These verses also make it very clear that "finishing well" is what God expects. I am sure it would please the Father if we had never sinned and that we both started well and finished well, but that can never be the case. Read verses 27 and 28 above, again. We must "finish well." Then consider verse 24. Clearly, moving into God's presence and accepting His Grace and then turning your back on Him is a very serious error. This important topic is discussed more carefully in the topic, The Unpardonable Sin.

The fact that God knows what you are going to do does not relieve you from choosing. God knows who will respond to His love and His call. Those whom He "knew," He predestined, even before you were formed in the womb. You have either responded to His call or not. It is God's stated will that you answer His call and live. But what kind of human existence is this, if we have no volition? Would you rather your child be forced to love you or choose to love you?

In the Letter to the Romans, Paul teaches a point about God's omnipotence, His "control," while responding to a question concerning man's volition. Listen.

Romans 9:15-33 (NKJ)
15 For He says to Moses, "I will have mercy on whomever I will have mercy, and I will have compassion on whomever I will have compassion."
16 So then it is not of him who wills, nor of him who runs, but of God who shows mercy.
17 For the Scripture says to Pharaoh, "For this very purpose I have raised you up, that I may show My power in you, and that My name may be declared in all the earth."
18 Therefore He has mercy on whom He wills, and whom He wills He hardens.
19 You will say to me then, "Why does He still find fault? For who has resisted His will?"
20 But indeed, O man, who are you to reply against God? Will the thing formed say to him who formed it, "Why have you made me like this?"

21 Does not the potter have power over the clay, from the same lump to make one vessel for honor and another for dishonor?
22 What if God, wanting to show His wrath and to make His power known, endured with much longsuffering the vessels of wrath prepared for destruction,
23 and that He might make known the riches of His glory on the vessels of mercy, which He had prepared beforehand for glory,
24 even us whom He called, not of the Jews only, but also of the Gentiles?
25 As He says also in Hosea: "I will call them My people, who were not My people, and her beloved, who was not beloved."
26 "And it shall come to pass in the place where it was said to them, 'You are not My people,' there they shall be called sons of the living God."
27 Isaiah also cries out concerning Israel: "Though the number of the children of Israel be as the sand of the sea, the remnant will be saved.
28 For He will finish the work and cut it short in righteousness, because the Lord will make a short work upon the earth."
29 And as Isaiah said before: "Unless the Lord of Sabaoth had left us a seed, we would have become like Sodom, and we would have been made like Gomorrah."
30 What shall we say then? That Gentiles, who did not pursue righteousness, have attained to righteousness, even the righteousness of faith;
31 but Israel, pursuing the law of righteousness, has not attained to the law of righteousness.
32 Why? Because they did not seek it by faith, but as it were, by the works of the law. For they stumbled at that stumbling stone.
33 As it is written: "Behold, I lay in Zion a stumbling stone and rock of offense, and whoever believes on Him will not be put to shame."

Here we see that God's choice to extend "mercy" to those who love Him, is in effect, a promised action on His part to those who He knew from the beginning, would love Him. Not only does our love of God not surprise Him but also our love of God does not "earn" us anything. It is His mercy, derived from our faith in a Messiah that redeems, that saves us. The stumbling stone referred to in verse 31 is the Messiah who allows any of God's children to "attain righteousness," not of themselves, but that of a risen Messiah. Re-read verses 31 and 32. You can not attain righteousness by works of the Law.

Now listen to the following teaching. In essence you will find that wisdom, accomplishments and pride in your "sense of control" are anchors, not launching pads. Christ in you is the launching pad! What is required is simple faith in the One who is able to redeem you, to empower you and to preserve your soul and spirit for eternity.

1 Corinthians 1:17-31 (NKJ)
17 For Christ did not send me to baptize, but to preach the gospel, not with wisdom of words, lest the cross of Christ should be made of no effect.
18 For the message of the cross is foolishness to those who are perishing, but to us who are being saved it is the power of God.
19 For it is written: "I will destroy the wisdom of the wise, and bring to nothing the understanding of the prudent."
20 Where is the wise? Where is the scribe? Where is the disputer of this age? Has not God made foolish the wisdom of this world?
21 For since, in the wisdom of God, the world through wisdom did not know God, it pleased God through the foolishness of the message preached to save those who believe.
22 For Jews request a sign, and Greeks seek after wisdom;
23 but we preach Christ crucified, to the Jews a stumbling block and to the Greeks foolishness,
24 but to those who are called, both Jews and Greeks, Christ the power of God and the wisdom of God.
25 Because the foolishness of God is wiser than men, and the weakness of God is stronger than men.
26 For you see your calling, brethren, that not many wise according to the flesh, not many mighty, not many noble, are called.
27 But God has chosen the foolish things of the world to put to shame the wise, and God has chosen the weak things of the world to put to shame the things which are mighty;
28 and the base things of the world and the things which are despised God has chosen, and the things which are not, to bring to nothing the things that are,

29 that no flesh should glory in His presence.
30 But of Him you are in Christ Jesus, who became for us wisdom from God— and righteousness and sanctification and redemption—
31 that, as it is written, "He who glories, let him glory in the Lord."

Get this point. No flesh shall "glory" in His presence. Read verse 31 again. If you are "righteous," it is "in the Lord." If you are without continuing sin, it is because you are "in the Lord." If you are forgiven, it is because you are "in the Lord." Our lives either glorify Him or not. Some have asked, "Why were we created?" I believe the right answer is to glorify God. In how many ways does your daily existence glorify God? Can your flesh glorify God? No, your flesh and mine represents a side of our existence that will perish. Our body is the Temple of the Holy Spirit and we should take care of it but don't spend a lifetime trying to preserve the flesh (exercise, beauty treatments, diets), while ignoring His Spirit in you.

You might want to respond to that point as some did when Paul taught the concept of life being transitory. Listen.

2 Corinthians 4:16-18 (NKJ)
16 Even though our outward man is perishing, yet the inward man is being renewed day by day.
17 For our light affliction, which is but for a moment, is working for us a far more exceeding and eternal weight of glory,
18 while we do not look at the things which are seen, but at the things which are not seen. For the things which are seen are temporary, but the things which are not seen are eternal.

The following quotation is of pivotal significance to anyone who is seeking to be saved by faith. Listen.

Galatians 3:22-29 (NKJ)
22 ...the Scripture has confined all under sin, that the promise by faith in Jesus Christ might be given to those who believe.
23 But before faith came, we were kept under guard by the law, kept for the faith which would afterward be revealed.

24 Therefore the law was our tutor to bring us to Christ, that we might be justified by faith.
25 But after faith has come, we are no longer under a tutor.
26 For you are all sons of God through faith in Christ Jesus.
27 For as many of you as were baptized into Christ have put on Christ.
28 There is neither Jew nor Greek, there is neither slave nor free, there is neither male nor female; for you are all one in Christ Jesus.
29 And if you are Christ's, then you are Abraham's seed, and heirs according to the promise.

You must not miss this point. Faith in Jesus Christ, the Messiah, who was present with God in the beginning, who did come and will come again, is your only hope for salvation. If the scriptures permitted any slack in this regard, one might hope that their allegiance to the Law, their prayers and their good deeds, would save them. There is no slack because if there was, the Messiah suffered for nothing and your sins are still with you. No atonement, by the only One who can present you blameless before the Holy Father, no salvation.

Such language must make my sincere Jewish friends, who dearly love God and who seek to obey the Torah, shrink from such assertions. I pray earnestly that this is not the case. Jesus came as the sinless Lamb of God, to save you and your faith in Him will bring you to a renewal, a rebirth reserved for those whose hearts have been changed, forever. Listen.

2 Corinthians 5:17 (NKJ)
17 Therefore, if anyone is in Christ, he is a new creation; old things have passed away; behold, all things have become new.

To be "born again" is how one becomes a "new creation." The invitation is to you who would exchange a heart of flesh for one in which the Spirit of God resides. Our flesh is at war with our spirit and the Holy Spirit wants to release you from that tug of war. Jesus came to forgive us and to cleanse us of all unrighteousness. It is His righteousness in us that we seek.

One might ask, why did you go into that topic when the header says "How Could a Loving God Allow His Children to Die?" First, it is because you and I are going to die and we are His children. Can you see that it is not the will of God that your flesh goes to the grave, unredeemed? He sent His Son to die for your sin and mine. Yet, do you not believe that volition remains yours? You make choices, including the choice to live eternally or to die eternally. How else could it be? What kind of a father wants his child to love him by edict? The compassion of Jesus shines through time and again.

The shortest verse in the Bible is, "Jesus wept." What was the occasion? It was when the sisters of Lazarus were crying and mourning at the death of their brother, a man that Jesus loved. We properly mourn at the death of our loved ones, just as Jesus mourned. On this occasion he mourned because the sisters of Lazarus were so distressed over their loss. Since Jesus knew He was going to raise Lazarus from the dead, was He mourning for any other reason other than out of compassion? No, the mourning of His children touches His heart over their sense of loss. He knows the trauma of separation by death. It was He who spent 3 days, separate from the Father, suffering for our sins. His disciples properly mourned at the death of Jesus, but just as the sisters of Lazarus rejoiced as their brother was brought back to life, so we rejoice because our Savior rose from the dead.

First, let's be certain that we understand that God does not let any person's spirit "die," who is "unaccountable." That includes one who is a youngster too young to grasp the meaning of God's existence or one who is so oppressed by his or her physical and mental condition that they too are unaccountable. God's love of the children is made perfectly clear. Listen.

Mark 10:13-16 (NKJ)
13 ...they brought young children to Him, that He might touch them; but the disciples rebuked those who brought them.
14 But when Jesus saw it, He was greatly displeased and said to them, "Let the little children come to Me, and do not forbid them; for of such is the kingdom of God.
15 "Assuredly, I say to you, whoever does not receive the kingdom of God as a little child will by no means enter it."
16 And He took them up in His arms, put His hands on them, and blessed them.

I am so glad that Jesus said this next verse, not only because it reinforces my understanding of His protective hand upon His children here on earth, but if Jesus protects them here, how much more will he embrace them for eternity. Our joy in Christ is tempered by our knowledge of our unworthiness. A child's joy in Christ is unbridled, open and pure, undefiled by the flesh.

The next time you look at an infant, especially, know that the innocence of that baby is the kind of innocence you possess before the Father for one solitary reason. You are presented "blameless" because Jesus Christ has borne your sins and mine. How else could we "receive the kingdom of God as a little child?"

Matthew 18:10 (NKJ)
10 "Take heed that you do not despise one of these little ones, for I say to you that in heaven their angels always see the face of My Father who is in heaven.

As to those who abuse children one way or another, a very special form of retribution from Jesus Christ awaits them. Listen.

Luke 17:1-2 (NKJ)
1 Then He said to the disciples, "It is impossible that no offenses should come, but woe to him through whom they do come!
2 "It would be better for him if a millstone were hung around his neck, and he were thrown into the sea, than that he should offend one of these little ones.

The faith of a child is a wonderful thing to observe. They trust you to love and protect them. Their trust in you often raises your level of "dependability" to levels higher than your normal level. That is, parents and others will go to great lengths to protect and nurture a child, where they sometimes are wary of adults and their motives, probably for good reason. God would have us be pure, holy and dependent on Him, in the same way a child depends on those who care for him. Our trust in Him can be as that of a child trusting his father.

One of the more interesting things to notice as you read the letters of John, written when he was very old, is his use of the term children. Listen.

1 John 2:1-2 (NKJ)
1 My little children, these things I write to you, so that you may not sin. And if anyone sins, we have an Advocate with the Father, Jesus Christ the righteous.
2 And He Himself is the propitiation for our sins, and not for ours only but also for the whole world.

1 John 3:2-3 (NKJ)
2 Beloved, now we are children of God; and it has not yet been revealed what we shall be, but we know that when He is revealed, we shall be like Him, for we shall see Him as He is.
3 And everyone who has this hope in Him purifies himself, just as He is pure.

As to the fact that God constantly refers to all of us as His children, listen to a glimpse of "age" as it relates to eternity.

Isaiah 65:17-20 (NKJ)
17 "For behold, I create new heavens and a new earth; and the former shall not be remembered or come to mind.
18 But be glad and rejoice forever in what I create; for behold, I create Jerusalem as a rejoicing, and her people a joy.
19 I will rejoice in Jerusalem, and joy in My people; the voice of weeping shall no longer be heard in her, nor the voice of crying.
20 "No more shall an infant from there live but a few days, nor an old man who has not fulfilled his days; for the child shall die one hundred years old, but the sinner being one hundred years old shall be accursed.

Infants and old men here, shall be neither, there. How else could it be? Would God have old men be old for an eternity or children remain infants forever? Even though we can not grasp the full understanding that we would like to grasp, these kind of "revelations" are throughout God's Word.

Back to the primary point. You and I and the infants, and the others, who are unaccountable, will all be judged based on what we knew, when we knew it and what we did with that knowledge. What are you doing with the knowledge of His presence? Listen.

Luke 12:47-48 (NKJ)
47 "And that servant who knew his master's will, and did not prepare himself or do according to his will, shall be beaten with many stripes.
48 "But he who did not know, yet committed things deserving of stripes, shall be beaten with few. For everyone to whom much is given, from him much will be required; and to whom much has been committed, of him they will ask the more.

A friend of mine asked, "Would I have been better off if I did not understand all of this?" Perhaps, but God knew you would read this and God knows how much Light is within you. What you do with that Light is up to you. You just read that "to whom much has been committed, of him they will ask the more." I capitalize Light because of the following verse, a theme amplified many times in the Bible.

Romans 1:18-22 (NKJ)
18 For the wrath of God is revealed from heaven against all ungodliness and unrighteousness of men, who suppress the truth in unrighteousness,
19 because what may be known of God is manifest in them, for God has shown it to them.
20 For since the creation of the world His invisible attributes are clearly seen, being understood by the things that are made, even His eternal power and Godhead, so that they are without excuse,
21 because, although they knew God, they did not glorify Him as God, nor were thankful, but became futile in their thoughts, and their foolish hearts were darkened.se, they became fools,

I love the way Moses expressed it. Listen.

Deuteronomy 30:9-14 (NKJ)
9 "The LORD your God will make you abound in all the work of your hand, in the fruit of your body, in the increase of your livestock, and in

the produce of your land for good. For the LORD will again rejoice over you for good as He rejoiced over your fathers,

10 "if you obey the voice of the LORD your God, to keep His commandments and His statutes which are written in this Book of the Law, and if you turn to the LORD your God with all your heart and with all your soul.

11 "For this commandment which I command you today, it is not too mysterious for you, nor is it far off.

12 "It is not in heaven, that you should say, 'Who will ascend into heaven for us and bring it to us, that we may hear it and do it?'

13 "Nor is it beyond the sea, that you should say, 'Who will go over the sea for us and bring it to us, that we may hear it and do it?'

14 "But the word is very near you, in your mouth and in your heart, that you may do it.

Where is the truth, where is the wisdom of God? Moses just told you! Read verse 14 and rejoice. There is a single verse in James that says something you must not miss. Listen.

James 1:21 (NKJ)
21 Therefore lay aside all filthiness and overflow of wickedness, and receive with meekness the implanted word, which is able to save your souls.

Receive the "implanted" word. Don't you see how much God loves you. His presence is not a mystery nor is His love dispensed with "partiality." He has revealed His Spirit to your spirit. To the Jew, there is a very special promise. Listen.

Hebrews 8:10-11 (NKJ)
10 "For this is the covenant that I will make with the house of Israel after those days, says the Lord: I will put My laws in their mind and write them on their hearts; and I will be their God, and they shall be My people.
11 "None of them shall teach his neighbor, and none his brother, saying, 'Know the Lord,' for all shall know Me, from the least of them to the greatest of them.

The New Covenant is upon you. Deliverance is at hand! You do not need to be taught. God says: "I will put My laws in their mind and write them on their hearts; and I will be their God, and they shall be My people." The "New Covenant" is a great gift. It replaces the Old Covenant. Be certain that the Scriptures, which teach that fact, are perfectly clear to you. It is the basis of an entirely new relationship with the Father. What a glorious promise He has given us. Now think with me about the following parable.

Luke 13:6-9 (NKJ)
6 He also spoke this parable: "A certain man had a fig tree planted in his vineyard, and he came seeking fruit on it and found none.
7 "Then he said to the keeper of his vineyard, 'Look, for three years I have come seeking fruit on this fig tree and find none. Cut it down; why does it use up the ground?'
8 "But he answered and said to him, 'Sir, let it alone this year also, until I dig around it and fertilize it.
9 'And if it bears fruit, well. But if not, after that you can cut it down.'"

Have you ever thought of yourself as a person taking up space, consuming the resources around you but not bearing fruit? Think on the matter a bit and the meaning of the parable will become very clear. You are one of God's resources. You have fruit bearing capability. The kind of fruit referred to here endures and does not perish.

Luke 21:1-4 (NKJ)
1 And He looked up and saw the rich putting their gifts into the treasury,
2 and He saw also a certain poor widow putting in two mites.
3 So He said, "Truly I say to you that this poor widow has put in more than all;
4 "for all these out of their abundance have put in offerings for God, but she out of her poverty put in all the livelihood that she had."

The Messiah, who will judge all men, judges the heart. He knows our thoughts and our actions as though the thoughts were actions and we will be judged by both. But this topic is about "How could a loving God allow His children to die." The child will be judged by his or her degree of accountability, just as will the retarded, the mentally ill and the oppressed.

The widow gave two mites and it was counted unto her as greater than the gifts of those who gave from their abundance.

God knows what we do with the amount of life and Light we have been given. The "unaccountable" are His and your personal degree of accountability is known to you, right now, and is known to God. Do something with what He has given you. Be a vessel in His Hand. Bear fruit!

CHAPTER 28

THE NEW COVENANT

The New Covenant will be granted to a nation whose Old Covenant, The Law, had served to illuminate their need for a perfect and final sacrifice for sin. The New Covenant, a gift made possible only by the shed blood of the sinless Lamb of God, once and forever becomes the strength of Israel, as it has been the strength of all believers to this date. Jewish believers and Gentile believers become as one the moment they believe in and serve their risen Savior. Listen to this wonderful prophecy and promise.

Jeremiah 31:31-34 (NKJ)
31 "Behold, the days are coming, says the LORD, when I will make a new covenant with the house of Israel and with the house of Judah–
32 "not according to the covenant that I made with their fathers in the day that I took them by the hand to lead them out of the land of Egypt, My covenant which they broke, though I was a husband to them, says the LORD.
33 "But this is the covenant that I will make with the house of Israel after those days, says the LORD: I will put My law in their minds, and write it on their hearts; and I will be their God, and they shall be My people.
34 "No more shall every man teach his neighbor, and every man his brother, saying, 'Know the LORD,' for they all shall know Me, from the least of them to the greatest of them, says the LORD. For I will forgive their iniquity, and their sin I will remember no more."

Those Jews who participate in the Millennium will have received a new heart, not one of stone, but one of flesh. The law will no longer judge Israel. Listen to the prophet Ezekiel.

Ezekiel 36:23-28 (NKJ)
23 "And I will sanctify My great name, which has been profaned among the nations, which you have profaned in their midst; and the nations shall know that I am the LORD," says the Lord GOD, "when I am hallowed in you before their eyes.
24 "For I will take you from among the nations, gather you out of all countries, and bring you into your own land.
25 "Then I will sprinkle clean water on you, and you shall be clean; I will cleanse you from all your filthiness and from all your idols.
26 "I will give you a new heart and put a new spirit within you; I will take the heart of stone out of your flesh and give you a heart of flesh.
27 "I will put My Spirit within you and cause you to walk in My statutes, and you will keep My judgments and do them.
28 "Then you shall dwell in the land that I gave to your fathers; you shall be My people, and I will be your God.

Notice that the heart of stone will be removed. To be removed, it must have been present. This is the heart that needs healing, now or then, but it needs healing. As it says, "after those days" there will be a New Covenant. Listen to the words of the New Covenant again. But this is the covenant that I will make with the house of Israel after those days, says the LORD: I will put My law in their minds, and write it on their hearts; and I will be their God, and they shall be My people. After what days? Listen to this wonderful prophecy.

Jeremiah 31:1-14 (NKJ)
1 "At the same time," says the LORD, "I will be the God of all the families of Israel, and they shall be My people."
2 Thus says the LORD: "The people who survived the sword found grace in the wilderness– Israel, when I went to give him rest."
3 The LORD has appeared of old to me, saying: "Yes, I have loved you with an everlasting love; therefore with lovingkindness I have drawn you.

4 Again I will build you, and you shall be rebuilt, O virgin of Israel! You shall again be adorned with your tambourines, and shall go forth in the dances of those who rejoice.
5 You shall yet plant vines on the mountains of Samaria; the planters shall plant and eat them as ordinary food.
6 For there shall be a day when the watchmen will cry on Mount Ephraim, 'Arise, and let us go up to Zion, to the LORD our God.'"
7 For thus says the LORD: "Sing with gladness for Jacob, and shout among the chief of the nations; proclaim, give praise, and say, 'O LORD, save Your people, the remnant of Israel!'
8 Behold, I will bring them from the north country, and gather them from the ends of the earth, among them the blind and the lame, the woman with child and the one who labors with child, together; a great throng shall return there.
9 They shall come with weeping, and with supplications I will lead them. I will cause them to walk by the rivers of waters, in a straight way in which they shall not stumble; for I am a Father to Israel, and Ephraim is My firstborn.
10 "Hear the word of the LORD, O nations, and declare it in the isles afar off, and say, 'He who scattered Israel will gather him, and keep him as a shepherd does his flock.'
11 For the LORD has redeemed Jacob, and ransomed him from the hand of one stronger than he.
12 Therefore they shall come and sing in the height of Zion, streaming to the goodness of the LORD– for wheat and new wine and oil, for the young of the flock and the herd; their souls shall be like a well-watered garden, and they shall sorrow no more at all.
13 "Then shall the virgin rejoice in the dance, and the young men and the old, together; for I will turn their mourning to joy, will comfort them, and make them rejoice rather than sorrow.
14 I will satiate the soul of the priests with abundance, and My people shall be satisfied with My goodness, says the LORD."

Notice verse 7. It declares these promises are to the "remnant of Israel." Are you part of the remnant? The writer of Hebrews teaches, some 600 years after Jeremiah's prophecy, about the New Covenant. This is a long quotation, out of context, but assuming the reader does not have a Bible at hand, here it is. Again, reading the entire Word, in context, is a far richer experience.

Hebrews 8:8-13 (NKJ)

8…"Behold, the days are coming, says the Lord, when I will make a new covenant with the house of Israel and with the house of Judah–

9 "not according to the covenant that I made with their fathers in the day when I took them by the hand to lead them out of the land of Egypt; because they did not continue in My covenant, and I disregarded them, says the Lord.

10 "For this is the covenant that I will make with the house of Israel after those days, says the Lord: I will put My laws in their mind and write them on their hearts; and I will be their God, and they shall be My people.

11 "None of them shall teach his neighbor, and none his brother, saying, 'Know the Lord,' for all shall know Me, from the least of them to the greatest of them.

12 "For I will be merciful to their unrighteousness, and their sins and their lawless deeds I will remember no more."

13 In that He says, "A new covenant," He has made the first obsolete. Now what is becoming obsolete and growing old is ready to vanish away.

Hebrews 9:1-28 (NKJ)

1 Then indeed, even the first covenant had ordinances of divine service and the earthly sanctuary.

2 For a tabernacle was prepared: the first part, in which was the lampstand, the table, and the showbread, which is called the sanctuary;

3 and behind the second veil, the part of the tabernacle which is called the Holiest of All,

4 which had the golden censer and the ark of the covenant overlaid on all sides with gold, in which were the golden pot that had the manna, Aaron's rod that budded, and the tablets of the covenant;

5 and above it were the cherubim of glory overshadowing the mercy seat. Of these things we cannot now speak in detail.

6 Now when these things had been thus prepared, the priests always went into the first part of the tabernacle, performing the services.

7 But into the second part the high priest went alone once a year, not without blood, which he offered for himself and for the people's sins committed in ignorance;
8 the Holy Spirit indicating this, that the way into the Holiest of All was not yet made manifest while the first tabernacle was still standing.
9 It was symbolic for the present time in which both gifts and sacrifices are offered which cannot make him who performed the service perfect in regard to the conscience–
10 concerned only with foods and drinks, various washings, and fleshly ordinances imposed until the time of reformation.
11 But Christ came as High Priest of the good things to come, with the greater and more perfect tabernacle not made with hands, that is, not of this creation.
12 Not with the blood of goats and calves, but with His own blood He entered the Most Holy Place once for all, having obtained eternal redemption.
13 For if the blood of bulls and goats and the ashes of a heifer, sprinkling the unclean, sanctifies for the purifying of the flesh,
14 how much more shall the blood of Christ, who through the eternal Spirit offered Himself without spot to God, cleanse your conscience from dead works to serve the living God?
15 And for this reason He is the Mediator of the new covenant, by means of death, for the redemption of the transgressions under the first covenant, that those who are called may receive the promise of the eternal inheritance.
16 For where there is a testament, there must also of necessity be the death of the testator.
17 For a testament is in force after men are dead, since it has no power at all while the testator lives.
18 Therefore not even the first covenant was dedicated without blood.
19 For when Moses had spoken every precept to all the people according to the law, he took the blood of calves and goats, with water, scarlet wool, and hyssop, and sprinkled both the book itself and all the people,
20 saying, "This is the blood of the covenant which God has commanded you."

21 Then likewise he sprinkled with blood both the tabernacle and all the vessels of the ministry.
22 And according to the law almost all things are purified with blood, and without shedding of blood there is no remission.
23 Therefore it was necessary that the copies of the things in the heavens should be purified with these, but the heavenly things themselves with better sacrifices than these.
24 For Christ has not entered the holy places made with hands, which are copies of the true, but into heaven itself, now to appear in the presence of God for us;
25 not that He should offer Himself often, as the high priest enters the Most Holy Place every year with blood of another–
26 He then would have had to suffer often since the foundation of the world; but now, once at the end of the ages, He has appeared to put away sin by the sacrifice of Himself.
27 And as it is appointed for men to die once, but after this the judgment,
28 so Christ was offered once to bear the sins of many. To those who eagerly wait for Him He will appear a second time, apart from sin, for salvation.

Hebrews 10:1-18 (NKJ)
1 For the law, having a shadow of the good things to come, and not the very image of the things, can never with these same sacrifices, which they offer continually year by year, make those who approach perfect.
2 For then would they not have ceased to be offered? For the worshipers, once purified, would have had no more consciousness of sins.
3 But in those sacrifices there is a reminder of sins every year.
4 For it is not possible that the blood of bulls and goats could take away sins.
5 Therefore, when He came into the world, He said: "Sacrifice and offering You did not desire, but a body You have prepared for Me.
6 In burnt offerings and sacrifices for sin you had no pleasure.
7 Then I said, 'Behold, I have come– in the volume of the book it is written of Me– to do Your will, O God.'"

8 Previously saying, "Sacrifice and offering, burnt offerings, and offerings for sin You did not desire, nor had pleasure in them" (which are offered according to the law),
9 then He said, "Behold, I have come to do Your will, O God." He takes away the first that He may establish the second.
10 By that will we have been sanctified through the offering of the body of Jesus Christ once for all.
11 And every priest stands ministering daily and offering repeatedly the same sacrifices, which can never take away sins.
12 But this Man, after He had offered one sacrifice for sins forever, sat down at the right hand of God,
13 from that time waiting till His enemies are made His footstool.
14 For by one offering He has perfected forever those who are being sanctified.
15 But the Holy Spirit also witnesses to us; for after He had said before,
16 "This is the covenant that I will make with them after those days, says the Lord: I will put My laws into their hearts, and in their minds I will write them,"
17 then He adds, "Their sins and their lawless deeds I will remember no more."
18 Now where there is remission of these, there is no longer an offering for sin.

This is a critical point. The sacrifice of animals and other first fruits was never sufficient, for all of the reasons you have just been told. The sacrifice Jesus made for my sins and yours is sufficient. Therefore, there is no longer an "offering for sin." But there will be offerings of first fruits, as an act of obedience, an offering in righteousness as earlier quoted from Malachi 3:3-4. This is the reason that sacrifice will continue in the Millennium, not for the remission of sins, but as "an offering in righteousness."

Re-read these following verses from above, and as you do, note that is says the blood of animals "purifies the flesh." It is the blood of Jesus that purifies the spirit. It is our spirit that need redemption, not our flesh. Listen.

Hebrews 9:13-14 (NKJ)
13 For if the blood of bulls and goats and the ashes of a heifer, sprinkling the unclean, sanctifies for the purifying of the flesh,
14 how much more shall the blood of Christ, who through the eternal Spirit offered Himself without spot to God, cleanse your conscience from dead works to serve the living God?

Continuing in Hebrews, it then says:

Hebrews 10:19-31 (NKJ)
19 Therefore, brethren, having boldness to enter the Holiest by the blood of Jesus,
20 by a new and living way which He consecrated for us, through the veil, that is, His flesh,
21 and having a High Priest over the house of God,
22 let us draw near with a true heart in full assurance of faith, having our hearts sprinkled from an evil conscience and our bodies washed with pure water.
23 Let us hold fast the confession of our hope without wavering, for He who promised is faithful.
24 And let us consider one another in order to stir up love and good works,
25 not forsaking the assembling of ourselves together, as is the manner of some, but exhorting one another, and so much the more as you see the Day approaching.
26 For if we sin willfully after we have received the knowledge of the truth, there no longer remains a sacrifice for sins,
27 but a certain fearful expectation of judgment, and fiery indignation which will devour the adversaries.
28 Anyone who has rejected Moses' law dies without mercy on the testimony of two or three witnesses.
29 Of how much worse punishment, do you suppose, will he be thought worthy who has trampled the Son of God underfoot, counted the blood of the covenant by which he was sanctified a common thing, and insulted the Spirit of grace?
30 For we know Him who said, "Vengeance is Mine; I will repay," says the Lord. And again, "The Lord will judge His people."

31 It is a fearful thing to fall into the hands of the living God.

I would re-read verses 26-31 very carefully. This is not a point often made in our liberal world. We tend, though we say we love God, to continue sinning, willfully, or at least in what appears to be a reckless way. I am digressing from the point at hand, but just in case you decide to join the body of believers, learn the words of Jesus well.

Matthew 7:13-23 (NKJ)
13 "Enter by the narrow gate; for wide is the gate and broad is the way that leads to destruction, and there are many who go in by it.
14 "Because narrow is the gate and difficult is the way which leads to life, and there are few who find it.
15 "Beware of false prophets, who come to you in sheep's clothing, but inwardly they are ravenous wolves.
16 "You will know them by their fruits. Do men gather grapes from thornbushes or figs from thistles?
17 "Even so, every good tree bears good fruit, but a bad tree bears bad fruit.
18 "A good tree cannot bear bad fruit, nor can a bad tree bear good fruit.
19 "Every tree that does not bear good fruit is cut down and thrown into the fire.
20 "Therefore by their fruits you will know them.
21 "Not everyone who says to Me, 'Lord, Lord,' shall enter the kingdom of heaven, but he who does the will of My Father in heaven.
22 "Many will say to Me in that day, 'Lord, Lord, have we not prophesied in Your name, cast out demons in Your name, and done many wonders in Your name?'
23 "And then I will declare to them, 'I never knew you; depart from Me, you who practice lawlessness!'

Matthew 12:33-37 (NKJ)
33 "Either make the tree good and its fruit good, or else make the tree bad and its fruit bad; for a tree is known by its fruit.
34 "Brood of vipers! How can you, being evil, speak good things? For out of the abundance of the heart the mouth speaks.

35 "A good man out of the good treasure of his heart brings forth good things, and an evil man out of the evil treasure brings forth evil things.
36 "But I say to you that for every idle word men may speak, they will give account of it in the day of judgment.
37 "For by your words you will be justified, and by your words you will be condemned."

Then James, the half brother of Jesus teaches this same concept.

James 3:1-18 (NKJ)
1 My brethren, let not many of you become teachers, knowing that we shall receive a stricter judgment.
2 For we all stumble in many things. If anyone does not stumble in word, he is a perfect man, able also to bridle the whole body.
3 Indeed, we put bits in horses' mouths that they may obey us, and we turn their whole body.
4 Look also at ships: although they are so large and are driven by fierce winds, they are turned by a very small rudder wherever the pilot desires.
5 Even so the tongue is a little member and boasts great things. See how great a forest a little fire kindles!
6 And the tongue is a fire, a world of iniquity. The tongue is so set among our members that it defiles the whole body, and sets on fire the course of nature; and it is set on fire by hell.
7 For every kind of beast and bird, of reptile and creature of the sea, is tamed and has been tamed by mankind.
8 But no man can tame the tongue. It is an unruly evil, full of deadly poison.
9 With it we bless our God and Father, and with it we curse men, who have been made in the similitude of God.
10 Out of the same mouth proceed blessing and cursing. My brethren, these things ought not to be so.
11 Does a spring send forth fresh water and bitter from the same opening?
12 Can a fig tree, my brethren, bear olives, or a grapevine bear figs? Thus no spring can yield both salt water and fresh.
13 Who is wise and understanding among you? Let him show by good conduct that his works are done in the meekness of wisdom.

14 But if you have bitter envy and self-seeking in your hearts, do not boast and lie against the truth.
15 This wisdom does not descend from above, but is earthly, sensual, demonic.
16 For where envy and self-seeking exist, confusion and every evil thing are there.
17 But the wisdom that is from above is first pure, then peaceable, gentle, willing to yield, full of mercy and good fruits, without partiality and without hypocrisy.
18 Now the fruit of righteousness is sown in peace by those who make peace.

This digression, though unplanned, is very, very important. If you are God's witness "in the law," you are obligated to obey the law. When people see your acts of faith and obedience, they should see them as being consistent with the whole law. This, of course, is impossible. No one is perfect, Satan's power is real, and temptation is everywhere. Adam sinned and set the cycle of sin in motion. We are born therefore, with a "default" setting of being in the flesh, not the Spirit. Being without sin is impossible.

Followers of Jesus Christ are those who have surrendered. They have admitted their weakness in the flesh and have come to a point in which the sin in their life makes them feel totally unworthy to stand in God's Holy presence. They want "the righteousness of God" in their lives. They know right from wrong, yet they have continued to sin.

Once a person realizes that God is who He said He was and has accepted the fact that Jesus is who He said He was and that He would take all of their sin upon Himself, be crucified, and suffer for them in a way not fully understood by any who have not yet entered into Sheol, then, with a humble and contrite heart they can be forgiven, cleansed and receive the gift of the Holy Spirit, Christ in them.

I won't, at this juncture, quote all the verses or make all the arguments that make those statements very clear, but go to the Epilogue, "Got Eternity?", if you want to focus on this particular issue.

Here we are dealing with verses 9-12 above. Do not miss the fact that your life is an open book before God. Every word you say, every thought you possess creates a record and your record and mine is imperfect. But, if you want to stand before God in eternity, you must be cleansed, purified and made ready.

As a Jew there appear to be two choices. Either obey the law, perfectly, continuing to offer sacrifice for your continuing sins or accept the acts of Jesus Christ, the promised Messiah, who was, is and will be again, as being a sacrifice made for you personally. If you choose the latter, the contest determining your fate is over. Your place in eternity is assured. If you choose the former, pray that you will be among the remnant that will inherit the Kingdom. Only God knows who those persons are. The scriptures clearly teach that if you remain faithful, even to death, during the tribulation and if you do not accept the mark of the beast that you will be an heir in the Kingdom and will reign with Christ.

As to those who are among the remnant that will be regenerated in the Millennium, listen to the Prophet Ezekiel describe your return, if you die before the tribulation or if you live through it doing the will of God.

Ezekiel 36:8-15 (NKJ)
8 "But you, O mountains of Israel, you shall shoot forth your branches and yield your fruit to My people Israel, for they are about to come.
9 "For indeed I am for you, and I will turn to you, and you shall be tilled and sown.
10 "I will multiply men upon you, all the house of Israel, all of it; and the cities shall be inhabited and the ruins rebuilt.
11 "I will multiply upon you man and beast; and they shall increase and bear young; I will make you inhabited as in former times, and do better for you than at your beginnings. Then you shall know that I am the LORD.
12 "Yes, I will cause men to walk on you, My people Israel; they shall take possession of you, and you shall be their inheritance; no more shall you bereave them of their children."
13 'Thus says the Lord GOD: "Because they say to you, 'You devour men and bereave your nation of children,'

14 "therefore you shall devour men no more, nor bereave your nation anymore," says the Lord GOD.
15 "Nor will I let you hear the taunts of the nations anymore, nor bear the reproach of the peoples anymore, nor shall you cause your nation to stumble anymore," says the Lord GOD.'"

In the following verses, Jeremiah makes the same point. The restoration of Israel will be glorious. Understand that at the end of the great tribulation, the Promised Land will be in very bad shape and all those who have taken the mark of the beast will be destroyed. It is in this moment that the resurrection of the saints will occur and those saints will join with the Messiah and King David in establishing the Kingdom, along with the survivors of the great tribulation.

Jeremiah 33:7-18 (NKJ)
7 'And I will cause the captives of Judah and the captives of Israel to return, and will rebuild those places as at the first.
8 'I will cleanse them from all their iniquity by which they have sinned against Me, and I will pardon all their iniquities by which they have sinned and by which they have transgressed against Me.
9 'Then it shall be to Me a name of joy, a praise, and an honor before all nations of the earth, who shall hear all the good that I do to them; they shall fear and tremble for all the goodness and all the prosperity that I provide for it.'
10 "Thus says the LORD: 'Again there shall be heard in this place– of which you say, "It is desolate, without man and without beast"– in the cities of Judah, in the streets of Jerusalem that are desolate, without man and without inhabitant and without beast,
11 'the voice of joy and the voice of gladness, the voice of the bridegroom and the voice of the bride, the voice of those who will say: "Praise the LORD of hosts, for the LORD is good, for His mercy endures forever"– and of those who will bring the sacrifice of praise into the house of the LORD. For I will cause the captives of the land to return as at the first,' says the LORD.
12 "Thus says the LORD of hosts: 'In this place which is desolate, without man and without beast, and in all its cities, there shall again be a dwelling place of shepherds causing their flocks to lie down.

13 'In the cities of the mountains, in the cities of the lowland, in the cities of the South, in the land of Benjamin, in the places around Jerusalem, and in the cities of Judah, the flocks shall again pass under the hands of him who counts them,' says the LORD.

14 'Behold, the days are coming,' says the LORD, 'that I will perform that good thing which I have promised to the house of Israel and to the house of Judah:

15 'In those days and at that time I will cause to grow up to David a Branch of righteousness; he shall execute judgment and righteousness in the earth.

16 In those days Judah will be saved, and Jerusalem will dwell safely. And this is the name by which she will be called: THE LORD OUR RIGHTEOUSNESS.'

17 "For thus says the LORD: 'David shall never lack a man to sit on the throne of the house of Israel;

18 'nor shall the priests, the Levites, lack a man to offer burnt offerings before Me, to kindle grain offerings, and to sacrifice continually.'"

The New Covenant will become a reality for you or it already is. I pray that you enter into His peace and rest now, with a new heart or in postponing it, you enter into His presence later, after enduring tribulation beyond anything you have ever seen. Obviously, this is written in the hope that salvation and repentance come to you now and that you live the remainder of your life in the Lord's righteousness, with His Spirit in you, sustaining you moment by moment.

CHAPTER 29

OMNIPOTENCE— OMNISCIENCE—OMNIPRESENCE

We have a very limited ability to understand the mind of God. Words like omniscience, omnipresence and omnipotence are easily defined but completely outside of our experience and in the case of many people, stumbling blocks. What we can't grasp, we often deny. But listen to what God's Word says about God.

Job 26:5-14 (NKJ)
5 "The dead tremble, those under the waters and those inhabiting them.
6 Sheol is naked before Him, and Destruction has no covering.
7 He stretches out the north over empty space; he hangs the earth on nothing.
8 He binds up the water in His thick clouds, yet the clouds are not broken under it.
9 He covers the face of His throne, and spreads His cloud over it.
10 He drew a circular horizon on the face of the waters, at the boundary of light and darkness.
11 The pillars of heaven tremble, and are astonished at His rebuke.
12 He stirs up the sea with His power, and by His understanding He breaks up the storm.
13 By His Spirit He adorned the heavens; his hand pierced the fleeing serpent.
14 Indeed these are the mere edges of His ways, and how small a whisper we hear of Him! But the thunder of His power who can understand?"

Indeed, what Job says about our God are the "mere edges of His ways." Read on.

Isaiah 55:8-11 (NKJ)
8 "For My thoughts are not your thoughts, nor are your ways My ways," says the LORD.
9 "For as the heavens are higher than the earth, so are My ways higher than your ways, and My thoughts than your thoughts.
10 "For as the rain comes down, and the snow from heaven, and do not return there, but water the earth, and make it bring forth and bud, that it may give seed to the sower and bread to the eater,
11 So shall My word be that goes forth from My mouth; it shall not return to Me void, but it shall accomplish what I please, and it shall prosper in the thing for which I sent it.

Do you sense what God is teaching you? We can't get our mind around the breadth of God's reality. "…so are My ways higher than your ways, and My thoughts than your thoughts." When we try to reduce the ways of God to man's understanding, we mistakenly "limit God," something we should not do.

God's Omniscience is well defined throughout the Holy Scriptures, but focus on the wonderful truth of the following verses:

Psalm 139:1-10 (NKJ)
1 O LORD, You have searched me and known me.
2 You know my sitting down and my rising up; you understand my thought afar off.
3 You comprehend my path and my lying down, and are acquainted with all my ways.
4 For there is not a word on my tongue, but behold, O LORD, You know it altogether.
5 You have hedged me behind and before, and laid Your hand upon me.
6 Such knowledge is too wonderful for me; it is high, I cannot attain it.
7 Where can I go from Your Spirit? Or where can I flee from Your presence?

8 If I ascend into heaven, You are there; if I make my bed in hell, behold, You are there.
9 If I take the wings of the morning, and dwell in the uttermost parts of the sea,
10 Even there Your hand shall lead me, and Your right hand shall hold me.

Do you fully understand that God is Omnipresent? Your every thought is before Him, constantly.

Jeremiah 23:23-24 (NKJ)
23 "Am I a God near at hand," says the LORD, "And not a God afar off?
24 Can anyone hide himself in secret places, so I shall not see him?" says the LORD; "Do I not fill heaven and earth?" says the LORD.

In the following verses, it says, God will dwell with you if you have a humble and contrite heart. God's Omnipresence is the foundation of your personal reality, either to your comfort or to your pain. Over and over again, personal pride is held up as the stumbling block and humility and contrition as the path to righteousness. One path leads to eternal life, the other to eternal judgment. God is present. Listen:

Isaiah 57:15-21 (NKJ)
15 For thus says the High and Lofty One who inhabits eternity, whose name is Holy: "I dwell in the high and holy place, with him who has a contrite and humble spirit, to revive the spirit of the humble, and to revive the heart of the contrite ones.
16 For I will not contend forever, nor will I always be angry; for the spirit would fail before Me, and the souls which I have made.
17 For the iniquity of his covetousness I was angry and struck him; I hid and was angry, and he went on backsliding in the way of his heart.
18 I have seen his ways, and will heal him; I will also lead him, and restore comforts to him and to his mourners.
19 "I create the fruit of the lips: peace, peace to him who is far off and to him who is near," says the LORD, "And I will heal him."
20 But the wicked are like the troubled sea, when it cannot rest, whose waters cast up mire and dirt.

21 "There is no peace," says my God, "for the wicked."

Now focus on:

Isaiah 55:11 (NKJ)
11 So shall My word be that goes forth from My mouth; it shall not return to Me void, but it shall accomplish what I please, and it shall prosper in the thing for which I sent it.

God's word went forth from His mouth and it shall not return void. The Bible is God's word. If you fail in believing that, you fail to have any ability to discern His message. Seek His Word as one dying of thirst, for in fact, at some point His Word will be taken from you. If you have stored His Word in your heart you will have followed one of His admonitions and will be able to draw upon that strength, forever.

Listen:

Psalm 119:11 (NKJ)
11 Your word I have hidden in my heart, that I might not sin against You!

The Bible says that His word shall prosper "in the thing for which I sent it." In other words, He knows this minute if you are a "chosen vessel," because He knows if you have chosen to believe. If you believe then His word will enlighten you. If not, you will consider it foolishness.

1 Corinthians 2:13-14 (NKJ)
13 These things we also speak, not in words which man's wisdom teaches but which the Holy Spirit teaches, comparing spiritual things with spiritual.
14 But the natural man does not receive the things of the Spirit of God, for they are foolishness to him; nor can he know them, because they are spiritually discerned.

To "receive the things of the Spirit of God" is to have Him and His Word dwell in you. That is Omnipresence in its most personal sense. How can you have His Word dwell in you if you do not read it? Again, go to the Word!

Listen to this parable and see if the truth of it is immediately is clear to you.

Matthew 13:31-32 (NKJ)
31 Another parable He put forth to them, saying: "The kingdom of heaven is like a mustard seed, which a man took and sowed in his field, 32 "which indeed is the least of all the seeds; but when it is grown it is greater than the herbs and becomes a tree, so that the birds of the air come and nest in its branches."

I would not suggest that the meaning is singular, because interpretation of prophecy and parables is not a personal matter, but a matter between you and the Holy Spirit. But I would say that absent the Holy Spirit this parable and many like it makes little difference in the thinking of the reader.

Allow me to offer you one possible understanding. The magnificence of heaven can not be grasped this side of experiencing it. My understanding, and I believe yours, is so minuscule as to be "as tiny as a mustard seed." What heaven is really like makes any definition we might attach to it, completely insufficient. It is greater than we can envision.

So are the words, Omniscient, Omnipresent and Omnipotent. They exceed our experience and even though we can define them, our Lord is greater than our conceptual images and prognostications. We simply believe and in doing so, use words like "awesome" in an attempt to attribute magnificence beyond description.

Romans 11:33-36 (NKJ)
33 Oh, the depth of the riches both of the wisdom and knowledge of God! How unsearchable are His judgments and His ways past finding out!
34 "For who has known the mind of the Lord? Or who has become His counselor?"
35 "Or who has first given to Him and it shall be repaid to him?"
36 For of Him and through Him and to Him are all things, to whom be glory forever. Amen.

Then, in an effort to properly position ourselves in relation to our Lord and Savior, we beg for mercy, while maintaining our faith in Jesus, our only means of salvation. Even though my sins are as separate from me as the east is from the west, I know I deserve judgment and so does King David in the following verses. The fact that God loves me and you, even though our sins were as scarlet when He called us, is a miracle that man can not understand.

Psalm 51:1-19 (NKJ)
1 Have mercy upon me, O God, according to Your lovingkindness; according to the multitude of Your tender mercies, blot out my transgressions.
2 Wash me thoroughly from my iniquity, and cleanse me from my sin.
3 For I acknowledge my transgressions, and my sin is always before me.
4 Against You, You only, have I sinned, and done this evil in Your sight– that You may be found just when You speak, and blameless when You judge.
5 Behold, I was brought forth in iniquity, and in sin my mother conceived me.
6 Behold, You desire truth in the inward parts, and in the hidden part You will make me to know wisdom.
7 Purge me with hyssop, and I shall be clean; wash me, and I shall be whiter than snow.
8 Make me to hear joy and gladness, that the bones You have broken may rejoice.
9 Hide Your face from my sins, and blot out all my iniquities.
10 Create in me a clean heart, O God, and renew a steadfast spirit within me.
11 Do not cast me away from Your presence, and do not take Your Holy Spirit from me.
12 Restore to me the joy of Your salvation, and uphold me by Your generous Spirit.
13 Then I will teach transgressors Your ways, and sinners shall be converted to You.
14 Deliver me from bloodshed, O God, the God of my salvation, and my tongue shall sing aloud of Your righteousness.

15 O Lord, open my lips, and my mouth shall show forth Your praise.
16 For You do not desire sacrifice, or else I would give it; you do not delight in burnt offering.
17 The sacrifices of God are a broken spirit, a broken and a contrite heart– these, O God, You will not despise.
18 Do good in Your good pleasure to Zion; build the walls of Jerusalem.
19 Then You shall be pleased with the sacrifices of righteousness, with burnt offering and whole burnt offering; then they shall offer bulls on Your altar.

There is no other god, but The God of the universe, the One who says through His prophet;

Proverbs 30:4-5 (NKJ)
4 Who has ascended into heaven, or descended? Who has gathered the wind in His fists? Who has bound the waters in a garment? Who has established all the ends of the earth? What is His name, and what is His Son's name, if you know?
5 Every word of God is pure; he is a shield to those who put their trust in Him.
Listen to God's question and answer it. "and what is His Son's name, if you know?

CHAPTER 30

FAILING TO REVERE HIS WORD AN OPPORTUNITY LOST – A CRITICAL ERROR

If you have not read Psalm 119 lately, you should do so repeatedly. This Psalm gives you a full understanding of the importance of the Word of God. Listen to these excerpts which focus on the Word.

Psalm 119:9-28 (NKJ)
9 How can a young man cleanse his way? By taking heed according to Your word.
10 With my whole heart I have sought You; Oh, let me not wander from Your commandments!
11 Your word I have hidden in my heart, that I might not sin against You!
12 Blessed are You, O LORD! Teach me Your statutes!
13 With my lips I have declared all the judgments of Your mouth.
14 I have rejoiced in the way of Your testimonies, as much as in all riches.
15 I will meditate on Your precepts, and contemplate Your ways.
16 I will delight myself in Your statutes; I will not forget Your word.
17 Deal bountifully with Your servant, that I may live and keep Your word.
18 Open my eyes, that I may see wondrous things from Your law.
19 I am a stranger in the earth; do not hide Your commandments from me.
20 My soul breaks with longing for Your judgments at all times.

21 You rebuke the proud– the cursed, who stray from Your commandments.

22 Remove from me reproach and contempt, for I have kept Your testimonies.

23 Princes also sit and speak against me, but Your servant meditates on Your statutes.

24 Your testimonies also are my delight and my counselors.

25 My soul clings to the dust; revive me according to Your word.

26 I have declared my ways, and You answered me; teach me Your statutes.

27 Make me understand the way of Your precepts; so shall I meditate on Your wondrous works.

28 My soul melts from heaviness; strengthen me according to Your word.

Psalm 119:40-50

40 Behold, I long for Your precepts; revive me in Your righteousness.

41 Let Your mercies come also to me, O LORD– your salvation according to Your word.

42 So shall I have an answer for him who reproaches me, for I trust in Your word.

43 And take not the word of truth utterly out of my mouth, for I have hoped in Your ordinances.

44 So shall I keep Your law continually, forever and ever.

45 And I will walk at liberty, for I seek Your precepts.

46 I will speak of Your testimonies also before kings, and will not be ashamed.

47 And I will delight myself in Your commandments, which I love.

48 My hands also I will lift up to Your commandments, which I love, and I will meditate on Your statutes.

49 Remember the word to Your servant, upon which You have caused me to hope.

50 This is my comfort in my affliction, for Your word has given me life.

Psalm 119:63-68 (NKJ)

63 I am a companion of all who fear You, and of those who keep Your precepts.

64 The earth, O LORD, is full of Your mercy; teach me Your statutes.
65 You have dealt well with Your servant, O LORD, according to Your word.
66 Teach me good judgment and knowledge, for I believe Your commandments.
67 Before I was afflicted I went astray, but now I keep Your word.
68 You are good, and do good; teach me Your statutes.

Psalm 119:81-82 (NKJ)
81 My soul faints for Your salvation, but I hope in Your word.
82 My eyes fail from searching Your word, saying, "When will You comfort me?"

Psalm 119:88-89 (NKJ)
88 Revive me according to Your lovingkindness, so that I may keep the testimony of Your mouth.
89 Forever, O LORD, your word is settled in heaven.

When the Scriptures tell you what you just read, for you to ignore them is a great offense. A banquet of love, peace and wisdom has been served to you by God and not to partake seems very wrong. I believe that the following verse is the single most powerful verse in the New Testament regarding the Word.

Hebrews 4:12 (NKJ)
12 … the word of God is living and powerful, and sharper than any two-edged sword, piercing even to the division of soul and spirit, and of joints and marrow, and is a discerner of the thoughts and intents of the heart.

The scriptures teach that the day will come when the Word will be unavailable.

Amos 8:11-12 (NKJ)
11 "Behold, the days are coming," says the Lord GOD, "That I will send a famine on the land, not a famine of bread, nor a thirst for water, but of hearing the words of the LORD.

12 They shall wander from sea to sea, and from north to east; they shall run to and fro, seeking the word of the LORD, but shall not find it.

We shall see later that this prophecy will be fulfilled when the Beast declares himself as the one to be worshipped, not God. You who accept his mark, 666, probably in the form of an imbedded chip in your right hand, will be denied access to the Holy Word of God. Possessing the Word will be a crime. If you do not store the word of God in your heart, I have no idea how you are going to cope with what is about to happen. Yes, the Spirit of God will be present but your access to His specific written words will be denied. Do you treasure the Word now? Do you, in all humility revere His Word and understand His warnings as well as His promises?

Isaiah 66:2 (NKJ)
2 For all those things My hand has made, and all those things exist," says the LORD. "But on this one will I look: on him who is poor and of a contrite spirit, and who trembles at My word.

Lord willing, the words of Jeremiah will become your personal circumstance. Here he was being persecuted for teaching the Word and this was his response.

Jeremiah 20:9 (NKJ)
9 Then I said, "I will not make mention of Him, nor speak anymore in His name." But His word was in my heart like a burning fire shut up in my bones; I was weary of holding it back, and I could not.

Listen to the first verse from the book of Malachi.

Malachi 1:1 (NKJ)
1 The burden of the word of the LORD to Israel by Malachi.

Do you get the sense that God's faithful prophets knew that speaking God's Word to the people was not going to gain "praise from men." Why might that be? I would suggest that the Word is a two-edged sword. On the one side, it is truth, God's Holy truth and on the other, judgment, God's Holy wrath. The message is clear. Either be encouraged and enlightened by His Word or be judged by it. To not revere it, is a mistake and the clock is running. You can not today, make up for the time lost yesterday, when you chose to ignore His Word. The prophets of God were not "popular" nor was their message of repentance.

If you have read your Scriptures, you know many prophecies have been fulfilled. Whether we are rapidly approaching the end times, only God knows. In any case, there is a Kingdom Age scenario that I find is seldom discussed among my Jewish friends. What seems about to happen is both glorious and frightening. I do not claim to be an "Oracle of God." This book is intended to direct you to the Holy Scriptures where you can move from the "milk" of the word to the "meat" of the word. This book is a mere taste of the tremendous treasure of God's Word.

CHAPTER 31

LIFE – ONE TWO-SIDED PAGE

We have a difficult time thinking of this life as being "brief." We value the days of our lives greatly and pray for peace, abundance and blessings. But consider this. Eternity is time without measure. It has no end. If you could envision this life as a "single page" of paper and then envision billions and billions of pages, without an ending number, then you might sense how little can be written on the single page called "life." Yet the scriptures tell us that what we "write," the "record" that we create, on this single page, determines our eternal circumstance. If so, the countless numbers of pages in eternity are yet to be experienced. If you are reading this, your life is not over and the record you are developing is still "in progress."

If you now possess eternal life, your name is in the Book of Life. If, in the end, it turns out that you have sentenced your soul to banishment from the presence of God, your name is in "other books." Understand, that if your record is now being recorded in "other books," it is a record that can be expunged, wiped away, forgotten and cleansed by the Grace of God as a result of the atoning sacrifice of the Messiah, the One that God promised would come. The record in the "other books" is not indelibly written. That record can be made invisible.

Consider this very important concept. The page of "this life" is a two-sided page. On one side is the part that precedes your moment of salvation, that moment in which you confess your sins, repent and turn to your Savior whose atoning sacrifice provides for your redemption. You are not held accountable for the side of the page that precedes salvation. Your sins are forgiven. Listen to this very important truth.

Psalm 103:8-12 (NKJ)
8 The LORD is merciful and gracious, slow to anger, and abounding in mercy.
9 He will not always strive with us, nor will He keep His anger forever.
10 He has not dealt with us according to our sins, nor punished us according to our iniquities.
11 For as the heavens are high above the earth, so great is His mercy toward those who fear Him;
12 As far as the east is from the west, so far has He removed our transgressions from us.

The reverse side of the single page, the eternal salvation side, is only available to those whose sins have been forgiven and removed. Again, the record on side one, the record established before salvation, which can be expunged and forgotten, will never be remembered against you again. Please grasp this fact. When you repent and are forgiven, your sins have been washed by the blood of the Lamb, Jesus Christ, the Messiah. I will give you many references that explain that sentence, in detail, but here we are focusing on the fact that it would be more than useful to understand the following point. Prior to your acceptance of the plan of salvation, provided by God, when He sent His only begotten Son to provide for the remission of your sins, prior to that moment, you are creating a record on one side of the single page of life.

When you repent and are reborn, when you have that stony heart of flesh replaced by the Spirit of God, in you, you begin to create a record on the flip side of page one. You are assured of your place in eternity. You will not experience the wrath of God, Satan will have no more absolute, unobstructed power over you, due to the presence of the power of the Holy Spirit in you, and you will be "born again." You will have crossed over and you will never be a slave to the flesh again. You will have chosen eternal life.

As to what you do with the flip side of the single page of life, that is, everything you do after you choose to respond to God's love, the record does remain. Every thought, every thing that you do with the remainder of your life is recorded. You will be establishing a "permanent record." Listen.

Isaiah 30:8 (NKJ)
8 Now go, write it before them on a tablet, and note it on a scroll, that it may be for time to come, forever and ever:

What is written is recorded for a time to come, forever and ever. Every thought you have is known to God and His thoughts toward you exceed number. Listen.

Psalm 139:1-18 (NKJ)
1 O LORD, You have searched me and known me.
2 You know my sitting down and my rising up; you understand my thought afar off.
3 You comprehend my path and my lying down, and are acquainted with all my ways.
4 For there is not a word on my tongue, but behold, O LORD, You know it altogether.
5 You have hedged me behind and before, and laid Your hand upon me.
6 Such knowledge is too wonderful for me; it is high, I cannot attain it.
7 Where can I go from Your Spirit? Or where can I flee from Your presence?
8 If I ascend into heaven, You are there; if I make my bed in hell, behold, You are there.
9 If I take the wings of the morning, and dwell in the uttermost parts of the sea,
10 Even there Your hand shall lead me, and Your right hand shall hold me.
11 If I say, "Surely the darkness shall fall on me," even the night shall be light about me;
12 Indeed, the darkness shall not hide from You, but the night shines as the day; the darkness and the light are both alike to You.
13 For You formed my inward parts; you covered me in my mother's womb.
14 I will praise You, for I am fearfully and wonderfully made; marvelous are Your works, and that my soul knows very well.

15 My frame was not hidden from You, when I was made in secret, and skillfully wrought in the lowest parts of the earth.
16 Your eyes saw my substance, being yet unformed. And in Your book they all were written, the days fashioned for me, when as yet there were none of them.
17 How precious also are Your thoughts to me, O God! How great is the sum of them!
18 If I should count them, they would be more in number than the sand; when I awake, I am still with You.

Job, when he was being tested by Satan, did not know that his words would be permanently recorded and read by men for centuries. Here he states a prayer that God fulfilled. Your words and mine are inscribed as well.

Job 19:23-27 (NKJ)
23 "Oh, that my words were written! Oh, that they were inscribed in a book!
24 That they were engraved on a rock with an iron pen and lead, forever!
25 For I know that my Redeemer lives, and He shall stand at last on the earth;
26 And after my skin is destroyed, this I know, that in my flesh I shall see God,
27 Whom I shall see for myself, and my eyes shall behold, and not another. How my heart yearns within me!

We know that the Lord, the Messiah has been given the power to separate the saints from the sinners, the sheep from goats. Did you know that once you are among the Lord's flock that God Himself will judge between the fat and the lean sheep (Ezekiel 34:20)?

Ezekiel 34:11-22 (NKJ)
11 'For thus says the Lord GOD: "Indeed I Myself will search for My sheep and seek them out.
12 "As a shepherd seeks out his flock on the day he is among his scattered sheep, so will I seek out My sheep and deliver them from all the places where they were scattered on a cloudy and dark day.

13 "And I will bring them out from the peoples and gather them from the countries, and will bring them to their own land; I will feed them on the mountains of Israel, in the valleys and in all the inhabited places of the country.

14 "I will feed them in good pasture, and their fold shall be on the high mountains of Israel. There they shall lie down in a good fold and feed in rich pasture on the mountains of Israel.

15 "I will feed My flock, and I will make them lie down," says the Lord GOD.

16 "I will seek what was lost and bring back what was driven away, bind up the broken and strengthen what was sick; but I will destroy the fat and the strong, and feed them in judgment."

17 'And as for you, O My flock, thus says the Lord GOD: "Behold, I shall judge between sheep and sheep, between rams and goats.

18 "Is it too little for you to have eaten up the good pasture, that you must tread down with your feet the residue of your pasture— and to have drunk of the clear waters, that you must foul the residue with your feet?

19 "And as for My flock, they eat what you have trampled with your feet, and they drink what you have fouled with your feet."

20 'Therefore thus says the Lord GOD to them: "Behold, I Myself will judge between the fat and the lean sheep.

21 "Because you have pushed with side and shoulder, butted all the weak ones with your horns, and scattered them abroad,

22 "therefore I will save My flock, and they shall no longer be a prey; and I will judge between sheep and sheep.

The point you may want to consider is that judgment between the sheep, the fat and the lean, will occur. It appears that there are different levels of rewards, even within the Kingdom. As you live life, after your salvation is assured, you are creating a record. That record is important and will determine your status in the Kingdom and in eternity, as ordained by God.

The primary challenge, and the choice is yours, is to become one of the sheep, one of the followers of the Lamb of God, the Messiah. That done, your sins are forgiven and you are starting a new life with a new heart. Thereafter, every thought and action count, forever. We Christians, who misbehave, by God's standards, are doing so at our own peril.

CHAPTER 32

GOD HAS REVEALED HIMSELF TO EVERY MAN

Jeremiah 31:33-34 (NKJ)
33 "But this is the covenant that I will make with the house of Israel after those days, says the LORD: I will put My law in their minds, and write it on their hearts; and I will be their God, and they shall be My people. 34 "No more shall every man teach his neighbor, and every man his brother, saying, 'Know the LORD,' for they all shall know Me, from the least of them to the greatest of them, says the LORD. For I will forgive their iniquity, and their sin I will remember no more."

These two verses present one of the most significant universal truths of the Scriptures. God has chosen to make a New Covenant with Israel and with the Gentiles, those grafted to the family of His chosen people. God has revealed Himself to every man and woman. You either know Him or you know of Him. The word "know" is used in the same sense as "a man knew a woman:" that is, it depicts intimacy in a way that differentiates itself from "being an acquaintance" in a very significant way. Therefore, in another topic we have discussed the unforgivable sin as that sin which manifests itself as adultery, the single reason offered by the Scriptures as a rationale for divorce. To "know" God and then to blaspheme the Holy Spirit (to seek a relationship with the god of the flesh and to turn your back on your first love) is a sin of unparalleled magnitude, just as adultery is the most heinous sin one can commit against his or her chosen one.

You know you are obeying His laws or you know you are not. What we call a "conscience" is in fact revealed truth. God has placed His law in your mind and written it upon your heart. You will be without excuse if you say you did not know these facts to be true. I think people have it slightly wrong when they speak of the "God shaped vacuum" that needs to be filled for man to be "complete." There is no vacuum "to be filled." It has been filled and you, if you are not intimate with God, are turning away from the Light that is within you.

A good friend who had committed adultery and who had chosen to leave his wife and family to marry the woman, said to me "You are the last person I wanted to have to tell about what I have chosen to do" or words to that effect. My witness to this person had been so persistent that I suppose that he thought, I would regard his sin as being worse than others might regard it. He may have been right but understand this. Your true friend is Jesus Christ, the truth in you and your offense is against God. If you think it is hard to tell a friend of your adultery how hard will it be to stand before God and explain it away?

Now, let's examine the Scriptures for more detail. Paul, a converted Jew, says that the gospel has been preached to every creature.

Colossians 1:21-23 (NKJ)
21 And you, who once were alienated and enemies in your mind by wicked works, yet now He has reconciled
22 in the body of His flesh through death, to present you holy, and blameless, and above reproach in His sight–
23 if indeed you continue in the faith, grounded and steadfast, and are not moved away from the hope of the gospel which you heard, which was preached to every creature under heaven, of which I, Paul, became a minister.

Romans 2:14-16 (NKJ)
14 ...(for when Gentiles, who do not have the law, by nature do the things in the law, these, although not having the law, are a law to themselves,

15 who show the work of the law written in their hearts, their conscience also bearing witness, and between themselves their thoughts accusing or else excusing them)
16 in the day when God will judge the secrets of men by Jesus Christ, according to my gospel.

Paul states that the hope of the gospel "was" preached to every creature under heaven and that the law is written in their hearts. This proclamation is of great importance. It essentially means that you and every creature everywhere has been "preached" the gospel. Paul made the same point earlier but here he also adds a "consequence." Those who ignore the truth "in them" and the truth evident in creation are without excuse. It says, they will experience the wrath of God. Listen…

Romans 1:18-21 (NKJ)
18 For the wrath of God is revealed from heaven against all ungodliness and unrighteousness of men, who suppress the truth in unrighteousness,
19 because what may be known of God is manifest in them, for God has shown it to them.
20 For since the creation of the world His invisible attributes are clearly seen, being understood by the things that are made, even His eternal power and Godhead, so that they are without excuse,
21 because, although they knew God, they did not glorify Him as God, nor were thankful, but became futile in their thoughts, and their foolish hearts were darkened.

Doesn't the truth revealed here simply scream at you? Do you want to experience the wrath of God? Read verse 21 again and again and if it applies to you, do something! Has Satan so deceived you that your heart is darkened? You do not have to yield to the weakness of the flesh and suffer eternal separation from God and all those you have ever known. Choice, it is always about choice.

Here the half brother of Jesus (same mother) declares the word has been "implanted."

James 1:21 (NKJ)
21 Therefore lay aside all filthiness and overflow of wickedness, and receive with meekness the implanted word, which is able to save your souls.

The writer of Hebrews then quotes Jeremiah, reminding Israel that the Messiah has provided them with a New Covenant, one not based upon the Law, but upon grace and mercy and the implanted word. I realize we quoted Jeremiah earlier but I want you to see that the New Testament and the Old Testament are to be studied in tandem. They cast light on each other. Listen again to this Old Testament and New Testament fundamental truth.

Hebrews 8:10-11 (NKJ)
10 "For this is the covenant that I will make with the house of Israel after those days, says the Lord: I will put My laws in their mind and write them on their hearts; and I will be their God, and they shall be My people.
11 "None of them shall teach his neighbor, and none his brother, saying, 'Know the Lord,' for all shall know Me, from the least of them to the greatest of them.

This restates what James said. Every Jew and Gentile has heard the gospel.

I am sure you agree that no one you have ever met has obeyed the whole law. Therefore, everyone has been disobedient. Our disobedience needs to be forgiven if we are to enter into God's presence and His "rest." Jesus is the means by which we enter into God's rest. His sacrifice covered our sins. We know that there is no remission of sins without the shedding of blood (Hebrews 9:22). We can not "earn" salvation. It is a gift, given by the grace of God. If one wants the "gift," one must simply believe that the promised Messiah died in their place, separating their sin from them.

Belief will lead to obedience, not because we are "more worthy," but because God will empower us, through the presence of the Holy Spirit, to love and to obey. We will, by the power of the Holy Spirit, a great and pivotal gift of God, be able to lay aside the burden of the "flesh" and appropriate the righteousness of Jesus Christ, our Redeemer. We become "born again." We shed the burden of the flesh and put on the empowerment of the Holy Spirit. That is why the Messiah came. He came to redeem us from the grasp of sin. We no longer have to "serve sin" but instead can "serve God."

Your sins are forgiven, you are presented blameless before the Father and what did you have to do? Simply believe and enter into His rest. The battle between good and evil, at least in terms of your life, can be finished. The victory, if you attain it, belongs to the Messiah, Jesus Christ, and you simply partake, being strengthened moment by moment by the Holy Spirit in you. Sanctification will come as obedience replaces sin. The Lord "sanctifies" and you, as you trust in Him, will become one of those who "are being sanctified," meaning you will enabled, by the power of the Holy Spirit in you, to be more and more like Jesus, your sinless Redeemer and Advocate.

Hebrews 2:11 (NKJ)
11 For both He who sanctifies and those who are being sanctified are all of one, for which reason He is not ashamed to call them brethren,

When you hear those who love the Lord refer to each other as "brother and sister," know that it is the Lord who calls you brethren, as well.

You will not be able to resist evil, in and of yourself. The power of sin far exceeds your personal ability to resist. Temptation will come to you like a flood, daily. Whether you sin in your heart or by deed, the result is the same. Sin disconnects you from God but the righteousness of Jesus, not only reconnects you, but the sins that you have committed and will commit are separated as far as the east is from the west, never to be remembered against you again. Interestingly, God used the words "east from the west" rather than "north from the south." If one heads north you will eventually be heading south but if you head east, you will never be heading west. A separation to infinity; that is how far your sins will be separated from you.

Do you think then, that we can confess our faith in Jesus Christ and go on sinning? Yes, of course we can, and our test of the boundaries of God's mercy will be dealt with in time. It sort of feels wrong to say that our level of obedience leads to different rewards, given the fact that it is the Holy

Spirit within us that facilitates our service to Him, but that is what the Scriptures teach. Listen to what the writer of Hebrews had to say to what I will refer to as juvenile followers of the Lord.

Hebrews 5:12-14 (NKJ)
12 For though by this time you ought to be teachers, you need someone to teach you again the first principles of the oracles of God; and you have come to need milk and not solid food.
13 For everyone who partakes only of milk is unskilled in the word of righteousness, for he is a babe.
14 But solid food belongs to those who are of full age, that is, those who by reason of use have their senses exercised to discern both good and evil.

The words, by reason of use, should help you understand that "babes" remain babes if they do not exercise their senses and partake of the Word of Righteousness.

You are not the only person that wrestles with the question of your flesh warring against the Holy Spirit, the truth that is written on your heart. Listen to the teachings of Paul.

Romans 6:21-23 (NKJ)
21 What fruit did you have then in the things of which you are now ashamed? For the end of those things is death.
22 But now having been set free from sin, and having become slaves of God, you have your fruit to holiness, and the end, everlasting life.
23 For the wages of sin is death, but the gift of God is eternal life in Christ Jesus our Lord.

Romans 7:15-25 (NKJ)
15 For what I am doing, I do not understand. For what I will to do, that I do not practice; but what I hate, that I do.
16 If, then, I do what I will not to do, I agree with the law that it is good.
17 But now, it is no longer I who do it, but sin that dwells in me.
18 For I know that in me (that is, in my flesh) nothing good dwells; for to will is present with me, but how to perform what is good I do not find.

19 For the good that I will to do, I do not do; but the evil I will not to do, that I practice.
20 Now if I do what I will not to do, it is no longer I who do it, but sin that dwells in me.
21 I find then a law, that evil is present with me, the one who wills to do good.
22 For I delight in the law of God according to the inward man.
23 But I see another law in my members, warring against the law of my mind, and bringing me into captivity to the law of sin which is in my members.
24 O wretched man that I am! Who will deliver me from this body of death?
25 I thank God– through Jesus Christ our Lord! So then, with the mind I myself serve the law of God, but with the flesh the law of sin.

There are two key concepts regarding our continuing struggle with sin that are taught in Scripture. First, since Jesus went to the cross and bore your sins and mine, would you, after cleansing and forgiveness, sin again, expecting Jesus to return to the cross, again and again? The scriptures make "knowing Him" and then falling away, in a conscious, declared manner, a very risky proposition. God can and will forgive us for a multitude of sins but if we sin intentionally, after redemption, we have a serious problem. Listen.

Hebrews 6:4-6 (NKJ)
4 For it is impossible for those who were once enlightened, and have tasted the heavenly gift, and have become partakers of the Holy Spirit,
5 and have tasted the good word of God and the powers of the age to come,
6 if they fall away, to renew them again to repentance, since they crucify again for themselves the Son of God, and put Him to an open shame.

Second, since we remain "in the flesh" though bathed in the Holy Spirit, temptation will still be before us constantly. Listen.

1 Corinthians 10:13 (NKJ)
13 No temptation has overtaken you except such as is common to man; but God is faithful, who will not allow you to be tempted beyond what you are able, but with the temptation will also make the way of escape, that you may be able to bear it.

That is a verse you should memorize. You can sum all this up in two words. Repent and obey. But listen to what the scriptures say about the reward God has in store for the heart of a repentant soul.

Romans 8:38-39 (NKJ)
38 For I am persuaded that neither death nor life, nor angels nor principalities nor powers, nor things present nor things to come,
39 nor height nor depth, nor any other created thing, shall be able to separate us from the love of God which is in Christ Jesus our Lord.

When you read the verse above, "What fruit did you have then in the things of which you are now ashamed? For the end of those things is death" (Romans 6:21 NKJ), did that verse not strike a responsive chord with you? First you know how miserable sin has made you feel and second, the end of those things is death. Reread Romans 8:38-39 until the truth sinks in. God has not only revealed Himself to you but nothing, except for your "informed" withdrawal, can separate you from His love.

CHAPTER 33

THE UNPARDONABLE SIN

You will sin, while establishing your "new record," the one that ensures that your name will not be "blotted out" of the Book of Life. We have discussed the Book of Life before, but it bears repeating because your understanding of it has a lot to do with some very fundamental truths. The idea of "blotting out" only makes sense if there is something written that needs to be removed. Your name is in the Book of Life and only Jesus will determine if it is blotted out. Let's look at a number of references that will help you understand the issue.

First, your iniquity can remove your name from the book of the living. Listen.

Psalm 69:27-28 (NKJ)
27 Add iniquity to their iniquity, and let them not come into Your righteousness.
28 Let them be blotted out of the book of the living, and not be written with the righteous.

When you are "delivered" it will be because your name is found written in the book.

Daniel 12:1 (NKJ)
1 "At that time Michael shall stand up, the great prince who stands watch over the sons of your people; and there shall be a time of trouble, such as never was since there was a nation, even to that time. And at that

time your people shall be delivered, every one who is found written in the book.

Rejoice if your name is written in heaven.

Luke 10:20 (NKJ)
20 "Nevertheless do not rejoice in this, that the spirits are subject to you, but rather rejoice because your names are written in heaven."

Philippians 4:3 (NKJ)
3 And I urge you also, true companion, help these women who labored with me in the gospel, with Clement also, and the rest of my fellow workers, whose names are in the Book of Life.

Revelation 3:5 (NKJ)
5 "He who overcomes shall be clothed in white garments, and I will not blot out his name from the Book of Life; but I will confess his name before My Father and before His angels.

Listen to one definition of those whose names are not in the Lamb's Book of Life:

Revelation 21:27 (NKJ)
27 But there shall by no means enter it anything that defiles, or causes an abomination or a lie, but only those who are written in the Lamb's Book of Life.

But since all have sinned, who is it to whom sin is not imputed? Sin is not imputed to those who believe in a risen Messiah.

John 3:14-18 (NKJ)
14 "And as Moses lifted up the serpent in the wilderness, even so must the Son of Man be lifted up,
15 "that whoever believes in Him should not perish but have eternal life.
16 "For God so loved the world that He gave His only begotten Son, that whoever believes in Him should not perish but have everlasting life.

17 "For God did not send His Son into the world to condemn the world, but that the world through Him might be saved.
18 "He who believes in Him is not condemned; but he who does not believe is condemned already, because he has not believed in the name of the only begotten Son of God.

Your sin will not be unto eternal death, unless you commit the "unpardonable sin." That sin, a sin of immense proportions, is one of blasphemy of the Holy Spirit, once you have "known" Him.

Hebrews 6:4-6 (NKJ)
4 For it is impossible for those who were once enlightened, and have tasted the heavenly gift, and have become partakers of the Holy Spirit,
5 and have tasted the good word of God and the powers of the age to come,
6 if they fall away, to renew them again to repentance, since they crucify again for themselves the Son of God, and put Him to an open shame.

Hebrews 10:26-27 (NKJ)
26 For if we sin willfully after we have received the knowledge of the truth, there no longer remains a sacrifice for sins,
27 but a certain fearful expectation of judgment, and fiery indignation which will devour the adversaries.

The word "know," as used twice in these verses, refers to the same kind of intimacy as between a husband and a wife. In fact, the Bible makes it clear that those who repent and obey, those who love the Father, Son and Holy Ghost, with all their heart, mind, soul and strength and who love their neighbor as themselves, are as the "bride" of Christ, the Messiah. Listen to the way the bride is characterized in Scripture.

Isaiah 61:10 (NKJ)
10 I will greatly rejoice in the LORD, my soul shall be joyful in my God; for He has clothed me with the garments of salvation, he has covered me with the robe of righteousness, as a bridegroom decks himself with ornaments, and as a bride adorns herself with her jewels.

Isaiah 62:5 (NKJ)
5 For as a young man marries a virgin, so shall your sons marry you; and as the bridegroom rejoices over the bride, so shall your God rejoice over you.

As much as adultery ruins human relationships, thank God it is not an unforgivable sin. It does not have to ruin a marriage but it usually does so. There is a form of adultery, "blasphemy of the Holy Spirit," that does have eternal consequence. If you turn to other gods instead of the Truth in you, after having known the Truth, I believe you are in serious trouble and you had better repent in a hurry. Our God is a jealous God.

Exodus 34:14 (NKJ)
14 'for you shall worship no other god, for the LORD, whose name is Jealous, is a jealous God.

It is because of the fact that we are as the bride of Christ that blasphemy is as adultery, a sin of immense proportions between a man and his wife, the only sin upon which "divorce" can be scripturally based.

There may be some that feel, "I wish I had never read about the unforgivable sin. If I am going to be judged having confessed that I know the Light is in me, I would just as soon have had no knowledge of the Light. You will only think such thoughts while in the flesh. Your flesh, Satan in you I am sorry to say (and everyone not born of the Spirit) is at war with your spirit. Satan would have you understand nothing at all of God's love. But whether you acknowledge that the Light is in you or not, you will, on judgment Day, see our Redeemer, face to face. You will confess that he is Lord and you will not even consider denying it.

For reasons known only to God, Jesus Christ has defeated the power of sin over you. He has provided you with the power of the Holy Spirit, the Helper. You could never commit the unpardonable sin if you persevere, by the power and presence of the Holy Spirit in you, in your personal war with Satan and his intent to defeat you. Your fidelity is anchored in the presence of your personal Savior in your life. Absent your complete dependence on the power of the Holy Spirit in you, you are as a leaf in the wind, tossed about by circumstance.

If you do not understand and believe that fact, then the following verse will not empower you to fight the fight, a battle which will never cease as long as we are in this flesh.

Galatians 2:20 (NKJ)
20 "I have been crucified with Christ; it is no longer I who live, but Christ lives in me; and the life which I now live in the flesh I live by faith in the Son of God, who loved me and gave Himself for me."

Listen to God's word, carefully.

John 14:16-17 (NKJ)
16 "And I will pray the Father, and He will give you another Helper, that He may abide with you forever–
17 "the Spirit of truth, whom the world cannot receive, because it neither sees Him nor knows Him; but you know Him, for He dwells with you and will be in you.

Some people have argued that there is no "unpardonable sin." I would be prone to agree with them from a human perspective. But, again, the Word says what it says and I think we should take it very seriously. That does not mean that the Father will not show mercy to many of us who do not deserve it. I believe that it does mean that obedience is more than just a suggestion. Those who would be disobedient, willingly, and then say that they are counting on God to be merciful, are testing our Lord in a way that the Scriptures do not support. Get born again, get cleansed and empowered, and remain faithful forever! Then the debate of whether there is an unpardonable sin will not be of consequence to you.

CHAPTER 34

SANCTIFICATION—A RESULT OF GOD'S GRACE

Sanctification is a lifelong process of maturation in Christ and though it may be pursued diligently, it is never fully attained, in this life. Let me share with you one area of your life in which "sanctification" is able to lift you, immediately from a powerful sin. Adultery, sexual immorality and pornography are huge problems in our world. Temptation abounds, as perhaps never before. But it is not only the act of adultery or sexual sin that convicts you; it is the "contemplation" of adultery or sexual sin that convicts you, as well. Listen.

Matthew 5:27-28 (NKJ)
27 "You have heard that it was said to those of old, 'You shall not commit adultery.'
28 "But I say to you that whoever looks at a woman to lust for her has already committed adultery with her in his heart.

Our aim is to be sanctified by the presence and power of the Holy Spirit. We seek to have the mind of Messiah in us, to behave in a saintly fashion towards others, and to be able to say, "I live, yet not I, but Christ lives in me."

From the moment that you accept Jesus Christ as your personal Savior, you are saved from eternal suffering and eternal death. There is no other way to "join." You can not by "membership, family affiliations, good works, merit badges, plaques honoring your contributions and services" achieve your salvation. These "works" and "affirmations by man," are as nothing in the eyes of God.

If salvation could be achieved, Jesus Christ went to the cross for nothing. Those words must be indelibly impressed upon our hearts for one very big reason. Pride is the "not so silent" killer. Pride in "serving," pride in "being used," pride in "leading people to Jesus," is just as insidious a sin as any other sin, perhaps even more so. Pride is at the very seat of sin. Our need for "control" and "affirmation from others" drives us to a self-centeredness, which distances us from seeking to serve the will of God. It is our will, not His that we often seek to fulfill.

Salvation is a gift from God, given by grace, not something we could ever merit. It is a gift, freely given, because He loves you and He loves me. He wants us, through faith in the fact of the cross, through the gift of the Holy Spirit, to enter into His eternal peace, starting now. God wants your heart, your servant's heart toward Him, now. Yes "works" are of consequence, but only as evidence of our love, not as a means to gain personal merit. Our strength is in Him, not ourselves. It is His Heart in you that makes your works, His works.

As you pursue a personal relationship with the Messiah, the Lord, you will come to find, if you haven't already, that it is exactly that; a pursuit. You do not, this side of eternity, realize complete victory. You are living in a pigpen, so to speak, in which Satan is referred to as the "ruler." The contamination is all around you. Listen to Solomon.

Ecclesiastes 9:10-12 (NKJ)
10 Whatever your hand finds to do, do it with your might; for there is no work or device or knowledge or wisdom in the grave where you are going.
11 I returned and saw under the sun that– the race is not to the swift, nor the battle to the strong, nor bread to the wise, nor riches to men of understanding, nor favor to men of skill; but time and chance happen to them all.

12 For man also does not know his time: like fish taken in a cruel net, like birds caught in a snare, so the sons of men are snared in an evil time, when it falls suddenly upon them.

We are snared in an evil time. Would you not agree that is true? You can surround yourself with the power of the Holy Spirit in the midst of this chaos and know the peace and power of the Holy Spirit, but you are greatly mistaken if you believe this earth is capable of perfection, peace and eternal safety. There is only one haven and that is heaven. We seek to be there, yet we run the race set before us. Listen to the way Paul puts it.

Hebrews 12:1-2 (NKJ)
1 Therefore we also, since we are surrounded by so great a cloud of witnesses, let us lay aside every weight, and the sin which so easily ensnares us, and let us run with endurance the race that is set before us, 2 looking unto Jesus, the author and finisher of our faith, who for the joy that was set before Him endured the cross, despising the shame, and has sat down at the right hand of the throne of God.

Jesus did for us what no other person could have done. He came from the presence of the Father, to fulfill the will of the Father. Absent the resolve of the Father to rescue His children from the sin which engulfs them, sin would remain an unresolved circumstance and would prevent our being in His Holy Presence. The race, as it were, had to be run. Jesus did not look forward to the punishment but He did look forward to the end result. Listen again to Paul.

1 Corinthians 9:24-27 (NKJ)
24 Do you not know that those who run in a race all run, but one receives the prize? Run in such a way that you may obtain it.
25 And everyone who competes for the prize is temperate in all things. Now they do it to obtain a perishable crown, but we for an imperishable crown.
26 Therefore I run thus: not with uncertainty. Thus I fight: not as one who beats the air.
27 But I discipline my body and bring it into subjection, lest, when I have preached to others, I myself should become disqualified.

Sanctification is a process, a lifelong process. Run the race that God set before you, fortified in your heart, with the knowledge that you are seeking to fulfill His will for your life, not your will. Do not despair if your relationship with Him is more "quiet" than "showy." We are all called to serve and we each have been equipped differently. You are one of God's resources. Listen to the Apostle Paul's message to you.

Romans 12:1-21 (NKJ)
1 I beseech you therefore, brethren, by the mercies of God, that you present your bodies a living sacrifice, holy, acceptable to God, which is your reasonable service.
2 And do not be conformed to this world, but be transformed by the renewing of your mind, that you may prove what is that good and acceptable and perfect will of God.
3 For I say, through the grace given to me, to everyone who is among you, not to think of himself more highly than he ought to think, but to think soberly, as God has dealt to each one a measure of faith.
4 For as we have many members in one body, but all the members do not have the same function,
5 so we, being many, are one body in Christ, and individually members of one another.
6 Having then gifts differing according to the grace that is given to us, let us use them: if prophecy, let us prophesy in proportion to our faith;
7 or ministry, let us use it in our ministering; he who teaches, in teaching;
8 he who exhorts, in exhortation; he who gives, with liberality; he who leads, with diligence; he who shows mercy, with cheerfulness.
9 Let love be without hypocrisy. Abhor what is evil. Cling to what is good.
10 Be kindly affectionate to one another with brotherly love, in honor giving preference to one another;
11 not lagging in diligence, fervent in spirit, serving the Lord;
12 rejoicing in hope, patient in tribulation, continuing steadfastly in prayer;
13 distributing to the needs of the saints, given to hospitality.
14 Bless those who persecute you; bless and do not curse.
15 Rejoice with those who rejoice, and weep with those who weep.

16 Be of the same mind toward one another. Do not set your mind on high things, but associate with the humble. Do not be wise in your own opinion.
17 Repay no one evil for evil. Have regard for good things in the sight of all men.
18 If it is possible, as much as depends on you, live peaceably with all men.
19 Beloved, do not avenge yourselves, but rather give place to wrath; for it is written, "Vengeance is Mine, I will repay," says the Lord.
20 Therefore "If your enemy is hungry, feed him; if he is thirsty, give him a drink; for in so doing you will heap coals of fire on his head."
21 Do not be overcome by evil, but overcome evil with good.

Ask God what He wants you to do with the intellectual, economic and physical resources He has given you. Seek to "bear fruit." In the process of seeking Him lies total uncertainty, in terms of how God may use you, but total certainty that He has expectations of you that far more exciting and of eternal value than any role in life in which He is absent.

You may be thinking, "Of what use can I be? I am not a writer or a preacher or even able physically to serve God in some special way." Each of us needs to learn the lesson of what Jesus taught in these next verses.

Luke 21:1-4 (NKJ)
1 And He looked up and saw the rich putting their gifts into the treasury,
2 and He saw also a certain poor widow putting in two mites.
3 So He said, "Truly I say to you that this poor widow has put in more than all;
4 "for all these out of their abundance have put in offerings for God, but she out of her poverty put in all the livelihood that she had."

This lesson does not just pertain to economic wealth, although it is clear that giving more than others matters not. What matters is answered by the question, "What did you do with the resources I gave you?" If you feel you have meager resources, of any kind, do not get comfortable with the idea that God expects meager effort. What each of us must do is appeal to God for His will to be fulfilled in our lives. Sanctification is the lifelong process of seeking His presence and seeking to serve Him and to glorify Him. What are you doing with the resources He has given you? This is a question you must answer because surely it is going to be asked. Listen to the wisdom of the Word:

2 Corinthians 8:12 (NKJ)
12 For if there is first a willing mind, it is accepted according to what one has, and not according to what he does not have.

That verse, as well as the entire Bible, is typical of the wisdom that God wants you to seek. You must resolve to be taught His Word, through the Word, now! I have quoted this verse before, but if sanctification is your hope, the Word is your only reliable resource.

Hebrews 4:12 (NKJ)
12 For the word of God is living and powerful, and sharper than any two-edged sword, piercing even to the division of soul and spirit, and of joints and marrow, and is a discerner of the thoughts and intents of the heart.

Sanctification involves obedience to God's laws and precepts. One could hardly move toward sanctification as you move away from obedience. If you are making a decision to obey God in all things, it will require you to rethink some of your habits. The world's disdain, for example, of keeping the Sabbath holy, has moved us in a direction God never intended and in a direction for which I suspect we shall all be judged. Listen to what the Lord said to Moses.

Exodus 31:12-17 (NKJ)
12 And the LORD spoke to Moses, saying,
13 "Speak also to the children of Israel, saying: 'Surely My Sabbaths you shall keep, for it is a sign between Me and you throughout your generations, that you may know that I am the LORD who sanctifies you. 14 'You shall keep the Sabbath, therefore, for it is holy to you. Everyone who profanes it shall surely be put to death; for whoever does any work on it, that person shall be cut off from among his people.

15 'Work shall be done for six days, but the seventh is the Sabbath of rest, holy to the LORD. Whoever does any work on the Sabbath day, he shall surely be put to death.
16 'Therefore the children of Israel shall keep the Sabbath, to observe the Sabbath throughout their generations as a perpetual covenant.
17 'It is a sign between Me and the children of Israel forever; for in six days the LORD made the heavens and the earth, and on the seventh day He rested and was refreshed.'"

I realize that this teaching has become very unpopular, especially among the Gentiles. It is often classified as "legalism" and discarded as a "works" based righteousness. The result has been that the Sabbath has become no different than any other day of the week for many people. I am not suggesting that the "Blue Laws" (closing all stores on Sunday) are the law of the land, but you do not need a law of men to honor the Law of God.

The Sabbath should be a day in which we honor the Lord. It should be a day of "righteousness and thanksgiving," a day for families to join together in worship. I believe that Satan rejoices at the mockery that the world has made of the Sabbath just as he rejoices when the Lord's name in taken in vain, repeatedly.

Sanctification is a personal matter. You decide whether or not you should honor the Lord's day differently than you do now (which day of the week you choose to rest in Him matters not, in my opinion). But this is the heart of the matter, isn't it? You, communing with His Holy Word, you listening to God, you asking for His guidance, you seeking His wisdom, you seeking His powers of discernment in you. Sanctification is about your personal growth as you get to know God. It will take time but don't make childish excuses for clinging to sin if you sense that it is indeed, sin. Listen.

James 4:17 (NKJ)
17 Therefore, to him who knows to do good and does not do it, to him it is sin.

Is there something more important to you than developing a close personal relationship with the Lord? Whatever it is, it is classified as an "idol" because you look more to "it" than to God. I pray that you will place communion with the Father, Son and Holy Spirit above all other endeavors. You are going to be judged based on the Light in you. Let that Light become a beacon that you move toward without wavering. Sanctification awaits those who seek to be saints, not in and of their own power, but by the will of God.

I will not be able to quote this next point accurately because I lack the reference at hand, but the author knows I honor his efforts as I support the point. You can have one of two kinds of relationship to God's Light, His powers of discernment, and His guidance. Compare the first kind of "relationship" to a banquet table of wonderful food, perfectly prepared and bountifully available.

Compare the second to a table full of food that has been eaten by others, spit out and also readily available for consumption. When you read what I and other men and women have to say, you are feasting on "waste" as it were, compared to the perfect diet. God's Holy Word is where you need to go for guidance. It is perfectly and abundantly served by One who has revealed Himself, willingly, to those who would look to Him.

I have made this point in other topics but it bears repeating. The day will come when the Word that you may have largely ignored will no longer be available. Listen.

Amos 8:11-13 (NKJ)
11 "Behold, the days are coming," says the Lord GOD, "That I will send a famine on the land, not a famine of bread, nor a thirst for water, but of hearing the words of the LORD.
12 They shall wander from sea to sea, and from north to east; they shall run to and fro, seeking the word of the LORD, but shall not find it.
13 "In that day the fair virgins and strong young men shall faint from thirst.

The thirst, from which you will someday faint, is a thirst for hearing the words of the Lord. I don't know if you grasp this truth, but as you stand in a place where opportunity to listen to God abounds and you fail to partake, you will someday be very sorry. When you step into His

presence, you may very well hear the words, "Depart from me for I never knew you."

How do you get to know our Lord? What steps are you taking? You could not be the "enemy" or you would not be reading this! If you seek sanctification, join with David who said:

Psalm 19:7-14 (NKJ)
7 The law of the LORD is perfect, converting the soul; the testimony of the LORD is sure, making wise the simple;
8 The statutes of the LORD are right, rejoicing the heart; the commandment of the LORD is pure, enlightening the eyes;
9 The fear of the LORD is clean, enduring forever; the judgments of the LORD are true and righteous altogether.
10 More to be desired are they than gold, yea, than much fine gold; sweeter also than honey and the honeycomb.
11 Moreover by them Your servant is warned, and in keeping them there is great reward.
12 Who can understand his errors? Cleanse me from secret faults.
13 Keep back Your servant also from presumptuous sins; let them not have dominion over me. Then I shall be blameless, and I shall be innocent of great transgression.
14 Let the words of my mouth and the meditation of my heart be acceptable in Your sight, O LORD, my strength and my Redeemer.

CHAPTER 35

I'VE BEEN A SINNER MY ENTIRE LIFE—SALVATION IS TOO LATE FOR ME

One of the most compelling parables, told by Jesus, in the entire New Testament, is about His view of your having been a sinner for many years, perhaps too many to appear to be "redeemable." Again, every man is a sinner; every man needs forgiveness, so no one is picking on you personally. This writer and every reader of these words is a sinner in need of forgiveness and the number of years that you have been an unredeemed sinner is of no consequence! Listen.

Matthew 20:1-16 (NKJ)
1 "For the kingdom of heaven is like a landowner who went out early in the morning to hire laborers for his vineyard.
2 "Now when he had agreed with the laborers for a denarius a day, he sent them into his vineyard.
3 "And he went out about the third hour and saw others standing idle in the marketplace,
4 "and said to them, 'You also go into the vineyard, and whatever is right I will give you.' So they went.
5 "Again he went out about the sixth and the ninth hour, and did likewise.
6 "And about the eleventh hour he went out and found others standing idle, and said to them, 'Why have you been standing here idle all day?'

7 "They said to him, 'Because no one hired us.' He said to them, 'You also go into the vineyard, and whatever is right you will receive.'
8 "So when evening had come, the owner of the vineyard said to his steward, 'Call the laborers and give them their wages, beginning with the last to the first.'
9 "And when those came who were hired about the eleventh hour, they each received a denarius.
10 "But when the first came, they supposed that they would receive more; and they likewise received each a denarius.
11 "And when they had received it, they complained against the landowner,
12 "saying, 'These last men have worked only one hour, and you made them equal to us who have borne the burden and the heat of the day.'
13 "But he answered one of them and said, 'Friend, I am doing you no wrong. Did you not agree with me for a denarius?
14 'Take what is yours and go your way. I wish to give to this last man the same as to you.
15 'Is it not lawful for me to do what I wish with my own things? Or is your eye evil because I am good?'
16 "So the last will be first, and the first last. For many are called, but few chosen."

It does not matter how long you serve the Lord. It does not matter that you came to the vineyard to serve Him very late in life. From a human perspective, we can not understand this scenario, at all. We fail to see the breadth and depth of God's mercy and patience. The fact that His hand is outstretched to you, if you have not yet been cleansed and made ready for the "marriage," is in itself, a miracle of God. God wants to redeem you as His child, wrapped in the perfection of the Lamb of God, just as you, if you are an earthly father, want your child to be in eternity with the Father.

By the way, trying to get your act together in order to be "acceptable" to God, is an idea based upon a huge misunderstanding. If you think that you can "work" your way into acceptability and God will like you better without all of the baggage of sin you are carrying, you are wrong. Wrong to think you can defeat sin by yourself and wrong to think God only cares for the "righteous." Listen.

Luke 15:7 (NKJ)
7 "I say to you that likewise there will be more joy in heaven over one sinner who repents than over ninety-nine just persons who need no repentance.

Those who think they "need no repentance" are those who think of themselves as "just" persons. There is only One who is Just, One who is good and that One is our Lord and Savior, Our God.

CHAPTER 36

MY SINS ARE SUCH THAT GOD WOULD NEVER ALLOW ME TO ENTER INTO HIS PRESENCE

We have read how "it is never too late" to receive the gift of Salvation. Let's address the other disabling condition that plagues the souls of men. I am unworthy. My sin is of immense proportion. I have sinned beyond measure, sometimes secretly and sometimes openly. I am stained beyond repair. It is as if my heart was tattooed with evil, so indelibly inscribed that the stains can not be removed. The feeling that you have this moment, if you are as that person described here, is perhaps Satan's greatest device in preventing your salvation.

One of the reasons I love to read about King David is that God's Word presents David exactly as he was. A man, whose heart sought God, but whose flesh was weak. David's sins are well chronicled as well as his servant's heart. David is clearly God's man, chosen before the beginning of time to be a righteous leader and servant. But isn't it useful, for we who have sinned, to know that King David, a man after God's Heart, sinned also? David's position in the Kingdom of God is assured and God's love and mercy made it so, not David's perfect record.

What joy it must have brought to God's Heart that David's heart sought God. The stories of David's love and mercy toward God's anointed and towards those whose loyalty to David and to God's will, abound. Thank God we are able to see both sides. The flesh, in which David's sin resided and the spirit, in which God's Spirit resided. The Spirit led David because David sought God with all of his strength. God greatly blessed David, even though he was a sinner. Why? God's mercy triumphs over judgment by the Law. The Law is much too straight an edge by which to be judged. David truly loved God, but God first loved David. David responded to God's love.

Psalm 32:1-11 (NKJ)
1 Blessed is he whose transgression is forgiven, whose sin is covered.
2 Blessed is the man to whom the LORD does not impute iniquity, and in whose spirit there is no deceit.
3 When I kept silent, my bones grew old through my groaning all the day long.
4 For day and night Your hand was heavy upon me; my vitality was turned into the drought of summer. Selah
5 I acknowledged my sin to You, and my iniquity I have not hidden. I said, "I will confess my transgressions to the LORD," and You forgave the iniquity of my sin. Selah
6 For this cause everyone who is godly shall pray to You in a time when You may be found; surely in a flood of great waters they shall not come near him.
7 You are my hiding place; you shall preserve me from trouble; you shall surround me with songs of deliverance. Selah
8 I will instruct you and teach you in the way you should go; I will guide you with My eye.
9 Do not be like the horse or like the mule, which have no understanding, which must be harnessed with bit and bridle, else they will not come near you.
10 Many sorrows shall be to the wicked; but he who trusts in the LORD, mercy shall surround him.
11 Be glad in the LORD and rejoice, you righteous; and shout for joy, all you upright in heart!

David knew the Messiah, the unblemished Lamb of God, was coming to redeem his soul and to establish the Kingdom. So did the woman who talked to Jesus at Jacob's well. Listen.

John 4:25 (NKJ)
25 The woman said to Him, "I know that Messiah is coming" (who is called Christ). "When He comes, He will tell us all things."

How did she know the Messiah is coming? The only time in the Old Testament that the word "Messiah" is used, although He is referred to in other ways, is in Daniel's prophecy. Listen

Daniel 9:25-26 (NKJ)
25 "Know therefore and understand, that from the going forth of the command to restore and build Jerusalem until Messiah the Prince, there shall be seven weeks and sixty-two weeks; the street shall be built again, and the wall, even in troublesome times.
26 "And after the sixty-two weeks Messiah shall be cut off, but not for Himself; and the people of the prince who is to come shall destroy the city and the sanctuary...

Listen to the Psalm David wrote in which he knew "atonement" would be provided. Since David had participated in many sacrifices before, to what atonement did he refer?

Psalm 65:2-3 (NKJ)
2 O You who hear prayer, to You all flesh will come.
3 Iniquities prevail against me; as for our transgressions, you will provide atonement for them.

It is Satan who wants you to believe that your soul is beyond redemption, that no atonement is available to you. It is Satan who wants you to believe that you are destined to die, anyway, and that death is not all that bad. You may have had a "good life," accomplished a lot of things and so on, but listen. Death is only pleasant if your "spirit" was to die, not live on. If death was a sort of "permanent silence," one might say, that is an improvement.

There is only one force on the earth that is more powerful than the power of Satan. That Force is the Father, Son and Holy Spirit. If you, in your own strength believe that you can reverse the power of sin in your life, you under estimate the power of the flesh and the power of Satan. This prince of the power of the air, the evil spirit who now works in the sons of disobedience is not anything like the cartoon character portrayed with a red cape, horns and a spear. This is a powerful spirit, one that neither you nor I can combat. If you do not think Satan is the ruler of this world, look around. Are those you observe from up close and from afar serving God?

How powerful is Satan? Listen to the truth about Satan's power. This is the one with whom you do battle, every day.

Ephesians 6:11-17 (NKJ)
11 Put on the whole armor of God, that you may be able to stand against the wiles of the devil.
12 For we do not wrestle against flesh and blood, but against principalities, against powers, against the rulers of the darkness of this age, against spiritual hosts of wickedness in the heavenly places.
13 Therefore take up the whole armor of God, that you may be able to withstand in the evil day, and having done all, to stand.
14 Stand therefore, having girded your waist with truth, having put on the breastplate of righteousness,
15 and having shod your feet with the preparation of the gospel of peace;
16 above all, taking the shield of faith with which you will be able to quench all the fiery darts of the wicked one.
17 And take the helmet of salvation, and the sword of the Spirit, which is the word of God;

1 Peter 5:8-9 (NKJ)
8 Be sober, be vigilant; because your adversary the devil walks about like a roaring lion, seeking whom he may devour.
9 Resist him, steadfast in the faith, knowing that the same sufferings are experienced by your brotherhood in the world.

The devil is your adversary, the one with whom you do battle. Your flesh seeks to serve him by sinning. Let's not bother to categorize your sins and mine but let's simply acknowledge that our flesh "defaults" to sin unless the Holy Spirit communes with your spirit and mine to rescue us from temptation. We have more than "a tendency" to sin. It is much more like a compulsion. Remember sin is sin, no matter how subtle or invisible to others, it appears. Pride, lust and all sorts of more obvious sins abound in the life of every person and the only victory is to wrap ones self in the Righteousness of Christ and be filled with the Holy Spirit. The Lord will fight the battle with Satan, not you and not me. If we say we are without sin or beyond sin, we simply delude ourselves and unwittingly, at times, serve Satan by asserting that we have the personal power not to sin.

The battle, again, is not ours. Listen.

Revelation 12:9-11 (NKJ)
9 So the great dragon was cast out, that serpent of old, called the Devil and Satan, who deceives the whole world; he was cast to the earth, and his angels were cast out with him.
10 Then I heard a loud voice saying in heaven, "Now salvation, and strength, and the kingdom of our God, and the power of His Christ have come, for the accuser of our brethren, who accused them before our God day and night, has been cast down.
11 "And they overcame him by the blood of the Lamb and by the word of their testimony, and they did not love their lives to the death.

Does it surprise you to hear Satan characterized as the deceiver and accuser of the whole world? He is also the "ruler of this world?" Listen.

John 12:31 (NKJ)
31 "Now is the judgment of this world; now the ruler of this world will be cast out.

John 14:30 (NKJ)
30 "I will no longer talk much with you, for the ruler of this world is coming, and he has nothing in Me.

John 16:7-8 (NKJ)
7 "Nevertheless I tell you the truth. It is to your advantage that I go away; for if I do not go away, the Helper will not come to you; but if I depart, I will send Him to you.
8 "And when He has come, He will convict the world of sin, and of righteousness, and of judgment:

John 16:11 (NKJ)
11 "of judgment, because the ruler of this world is judged.

Jesus, the Messiah, has defeated the power of death. The Messiah rules, but only where you have His power within you. Satan, on his best day, can not overcome the power of the Holy Spirit. In the following verses, the "evil one" is referred to as a prince. Let's put his identity in context as you learn how to overcome the prince. Listen.

Ephesians 2:1-9 (NKJ)
1 And you He made alive, who were dead in trespasses and sins,
2 in which you once walked according to the course of this world, according to the prince of the power of the air, the spirit who now works in the sons of disobedience,
3 among whom also we all once conducted ourselves in the lusts of our flesh, fulfilling the desires of the flesh and of the mind, and were by nature children of wrath, just as the others.
4 But God, who is rich in mercy, because of His great love with which He loved us,
5 even when we were dead in trespasses, made us alive together with Christ (by grace you have been saved),
6 and raised us up together, and made us sit together in the heavenly places in Christ Jesus,
7 that in the ages to come He might show the exceeding riches of His grace in His kindness toward us in Christ Jesus.
8 For by grace you have been saved through faith, and that not of yourselves; it is the gift of God,
9 not of works, lest anyone should boast.

No, Satan does not "own" you because of the depth of your sin. Your sin needs to cease and you need permanent relief from being its captive and slave but understand this. You are the reason the Messiah came. You are the one whom God created in His image. God loves every person that He created and it is His will that none perish, including you.

If you had no sin, if you were righteous in your own strength, none of this would make sense. God's plan for the eternal redemption of your soul pivots on the redeeming power of the blood of Jesus, being shed to cover your sins and mine. Once you grasp that fact, a new heart, a new perspective, a new form of empowerment, is yours.

Psalm 62:11-12 (NKJ)
11 God has spoken once, twice I have heard this: that power belongs to God.
12 Also to You, O Lord, belongs mercy; for You render to each one according to his work.

Psalm 63:1-8 (NKJ)
1 O God, You are my God; early will I seek You; my soul thirsts for You; my flesh longs for You in a dry and thirsty land where there is no water.
2 So I have looked for You in the sanctuary, to see Your power and Your glory.
3 Because Your lovingkindness is better than life, my lips shall praise You.
4 Thus I will bless You while I live; I will lift up my hands in Your name.
5 My soul shall be satisfied as with marrow and fatness, and my mouth shall praise You with joyful lips.
6 When I remember You on my bed, I meditate on You in the night watches.
7 Because You have been my help, therefore in the shadow of Your wings I will rejoice.
8 My soul follows close behind You; your right hand upholds me.

No, your sins are not such that the shed blood of Jesus Christ cannot redeem you. If you are not forgiven and not cleansed, you simply have not acknowledged your Redeemer, the One who atoned for your sins and mine or you have not been enveloped by His Spirit. You can "resolve" to sin no more, but in and of your own strength you will fail. We delude ourselves if we think that our flesh can overcome Satan. We need the constancy of the Holy Spirit in our lives. Not just when we go to synagogue or church, not just when we are reading the Word or praying, but constantly. The enemy is simply more powerful that we fully understand.

Life is not about this physical experience. It is a testing ground of very short duration in which you either serve your Creator, our Lord, or you serve yourself and the inclinations of your flesh. This reality is so pivotal that God sent a form of Himself, His only begotten Son, Jesus to tell us of His love and to redeem us from our sin. The Father, the Son and the Holy Spirit are One and if you can't accept that fact, then your sins are still with you because the Redeemer, at least in the case of an unbeliever, may as well have not come.

What would be worse, in my opinion, is to acknowledge that the Messiah came and to not appropriate His Spirit. This is not an intellectual exercise. We are talking about a "new heart," a new will to serve Him with the hours or days you have left. Our lives can not be about seeking our interests. What we must seek is His will for our life. What does the Lord want you to do with the days of your life? The answer is clear enough. Serve Him, respond to His love and be directed by His Spirit. Worship Him and glorify Him. Turn and live!

Ezekiel 18:31-32 (NKJ)
31 "Cast away from you all the transgressions which you have committed, and get yourselves a new heart and a new spirit. For why should you die, O house of Israel?
32 "For I have no pleasure in the death of one who dies," says the Lord GOD. "Therefore turn and live!"

CHAPTER 37

THE GRACE OF GOD— OUR ONLY HOPE

The first mention of the word grace in the Bible is as follows.

Genesis 6:7-8 (NKJ)
7 So the LORD said, "I will destroy man whom I have created from the face of the earth, both man and beast, creeping thing and birds of the air, for I am sorry that I have made them."
8 But Noah found grace in the eyes of the LORD.

Of course, this was the period of time in which God "started over" with the genealogy of man.

Genesis 9:18-19 (NKJ)
18 Now the sons of Noah who went out of the ark were Shem, Ham, and Japheth. And Ham was the father of Canaan.
19 These three were the sons of Noah, and from these the whole earth was populated.

We are all descendants of Shem, Ham, or Japheth, the three son's of Noah, but it was Noah who is said to have found grace in the eyes of the LORD. The second mention of grace in the Bible involved Moses.

Exodus 33:12 (NKJ)
12 Then Moses said to the LORD, "See, You say to me, 'Bring up this people.' But You have not let me know whom You will send with me.

Yet You have said, 'I know you by name, and you have also found grace in My sight.'

Then Moses asked for the Lord's help and God made a covenant with Moses, which exists to this day.

Exodus 34:9-10 (NKJ)
9 Then he said, "If now I have found grace in Your sight, O Lord, let my Lord, I pray, go among us, even though we are a stiff-necked people; and pardon our iniquity and our sin, and take us as Your inheritance."
10 And He said: "Behold, I make a covenant. Before all your people I will do marvels such as have not been done in all the earth, nor in any nation; and all the people among whom you are shall see the work of the LORD. For it is an awesome thing that I will do with you.

Now listen to the specific and unique grace God has bestowed upon Israel.

Deuteronomy 4:32-38 (NKJ)
32 "For ask now concerning the days that are past, which were before you, since the day that God created man on the earth, and ask from one end of heaven to the other, whether any great thing like this has happened, or anything like it has been heard.
33 "Did any people ever hear the voice of God speaking out of the midst of the fire, as you have heard, and live?
34 "Or did God ever try to go and take for Himself a nation from the midst of another nation, by trials, by signs, by wonders, by war, by a mighty hand and an outstretched arm, and by great terrors, according to all that the LORD your God did for you in Egypt before your eyes?
35 "To you it was shown, that you might know that the LORD Himself is God; there is none other besides Him.
36 "Out of heaven He let you hear His voice, that He might instruct you; on earth He showed you His great fire, and you heard His words out of the midst of the fire.
37 "And because He loved your fathers, therefore He chose their descendants after them; and He brought you out of Egypt with His Presence, with His mighty power,

38 "driving out from before you nations greater and mightier than you, to bring you in, to give you their land as an inheritance, as it is this day.

As an aside, given what has happened and will yet happen in Jerusalem, this last sentence should give pause to those who think that the promises of God regarding the resurrection of God's people and the restoration of Jerusalem are outrageous expectations. We limit God. Awesome is a word that barely approximates what we will feel when God fulfills His prophecies. Listen to Samuel.

2 Samuel 7:22-24 (NKJ)
22 "Therefore You are great, O Lord GOD. For there is none like You, nor is there any God besides You, according to all that we have heard with our ears.
23 "And who is like Your people, like Israel, the one nation on the earth whom God went to redeem for Himself as a people, to make for Himself a name– and to do for Yourself great and awesome deeds for Your land– before Your people whom You redeemed for Yourself from Egypt, the nations, and their gods?
24 "For You have made Your people Israel Your very own people forever; and You, LORD, have become their God.

Now read of God's Grace to the house of David.

Zechariah 12:10 (NKJ)
10 "And I will pour on the house of David and on the inhabitants of Jerusalem the Spirit of grace and supplication; then they will look on Me whom they have pierced; they will mourn for Him as one mourns for his only son, and grieve for Him as one grieves for a firstborn.

When grace is extended to the house of David, it says, "then they will look upon Me whom they have pierced," placing the fullness of "grace" in the context of a redeemer, the Messiah.

The first mention of grace in the New Testament refers to Jesus, the Child, then to Jesus the Man.

Luke 2:40 (NKJ)
40 And the Child grew and became strong in spirit, filled with wisdom; and the grace of God was upon Him.

John 1:14-17 (NKJ)
14 And the Word became flesh and dwelt among us, and we beheld His glory, the glory as of the only begotten of the Father, full of grace and truth.
15 John bore witness of Him and cried out, saying, "This was He of whom I said, 'He who comes after me is preferred before me, for He was before me.'"
16 And of His fullness we have all received, and grace for grace.
17 For the law was given through Moses, but grace and truth came through Jesus Christ.

Do not think that this last verse somehow sets aside the law or your respect of it. The law (referring specifically to the 10 commandments given to Moses) asked you to do good and specific things and "grace" does not change that expectation. The difference is that you are saved by grace and grace only and the grace of God, in whom you place your faith, is a gift. Paul makes this point for us. Listen.

Romans 3:23-31 (NKJ)
23 for all have sinned and fall short of the glory of God,
24 being justified freely by His grace through the redemption that is in Christ Jesus,
25 whom God set forth as a propitiation by His blood, through faith, to demonstrate His righteousness, because in His forbearance God had passed over the sins that were previously committed,
26 to demonstrate at the present time His righteousness, that He might be just and the justifier of the one who has faith in Jesus.
27 Where is boasting then? It is excluded. By what law? Of works? No, but by the law of faith.
28 Therefore we conclude that a man is justified by faith apart from the deeds of the law.
29 Or is He the God of the Jews only? Is He not also the God of the Gentiles? Yes, of the Gentiles also,

30 since there is one God who will justify the circumcised by faith and the uncircumcised through faith.
31 Do we then make void the law through faith? Certainly not! On the contrary, we establish the law.

There are many "Torah observant" Jews. They respect and love the Law yet they adhere to it by faith and know, absent the grace of God, that keeping the Law will not redeem them. It is redemption first and then obedience. Obedience is good, but not unto salvation. Redemption makes your obedience fruitful to God, and the Holy Spirit in you is what enables you to obey, not the will of your flesh. I offer the following verses with some anxiety, not because they are not appropriate or true, but because they may offend. If the Gospel offends, and Scriptures tell us it will, it is because the listener is rejecting the atoning life of the Messiah, Jesus Christ. This book, written specifically to Israel, is intended to bring into focus your choices and the consequences of those choices. Listen to some fairly direct teachings from the Scriptures.

Hebrews 10:28-31 (NKJ)
28 Anyone who has rejected Moses' law dies without mercy on the testimony of two or three witnesses.
29 Of how much worse punishment, do you suppose, will he be thought worthy who has trampled the Son of God underfoot, counted the blood of the covenant by which he was sanctified a common thing, and insulted the Spirit of grace?
30 For we know Him who said, "Vengeance is Mine; I will repay," says the Lord. And again, "The Lord will judge His people."
31 It is a fearful thing to fall into the hands of the living God.

Hebrews 12:14-29 (NKJ)
14 Pursue peace with all people, and holiness, without which no one will see the Lord:
15 looking diligently lest anyone fall short of the grace of God; lest any root of bitterness springing up cause trouble, and by this many become defiled;
16 lest there be any fornicator or profane person like Esau, who for one morsel of food sold his birthright.

17 For you know that afterward, when he wanted to inherit the blessing, he was rejected, for he found no place for repentance, though he sought it diligently with tears.
18 For you have not come to the mountain that may be touched and that burned with fire, and to blackness and darkness and tempest,
19 and the sound of a trumpet and the voice of words, so that those who heard it begged that the word should not be spoken to them anymore.
20 (For they could not endure what was commanded: "And if so much as a beast touches the mountain, it shall be stoned or shot with an arrow."
21 And so terrifying was the sight that Moses said, "I am exceedingly afraid and trembling.")
22 But you have come to Mount Zion and to the city of the living God, the heavenly Jerusalem, to an innumerable company of angels,
23 to the general assembly and church of the firstborn who are registered in heaven, to God the Judge of all, to the spirits of just men made perfect,
24 to Jesus the Mediator of the new covenant, and to the blood of sprinkling that speaks better things than that of Abel.
25 See that you do not refuse Him who speaks. For if they did not escape who refused Him who spoke on earth, much more shall we not escape if we turn away from Him who speaks from heaven,
26 whose voice then shook the earth; but now He has promised, saying, "Yet once more I shake not only the earth, but also heaven."
27 Now this, "Yet once more," indicates the removal of those things that are being shaken, as of things that are made, that the things which cannot be shaken may remain.
28 Therefore, since we are receiving a kingdom which cannot be shaken, let us have grace, by which we may serve God acceptably with reverence and godly fear.
29 For our God is a consuming fire.

The grace of God is our only hope. Grace is not something we can earn. It is an "empowerment," an enabling force that permits us to escape from serving the flesh.

Listen to Paul, the one Jew who God miraculously turned from hating Jesus and His followers to what was and is perhaps the key role in bringing the gospel to the Gentiles. God chose not only the Jews as His people, but chose Paul, a Jew, as a primary oracle to bring the Gentiles under the canopy of God's love. This love was extended primarily to the Jews, until the birth of the Messiah. Listen to Paul.

Ephesians 2:1-10 (NKJ)
1 And you He made alive, who were dead in trespasses and sins,
2 in which you once walked according to the course of this world, according to the prince of the power of the air, the spirit who now works in the sons of disobedience,
3 among whom also we all once conducted ourselves in the lusts of our flesh, fulfilling the desires of the flesh and of the mind, and were by nature children of wrath, just as the others.
4 But God, who is rich in mercy, because of His great love with which He loved us,
5 even when we were dead in trespasses, made us alive together with Christ (by grace you have been saved),
6 and raised us up together, and made us sit together in the heavenly places in Christ Jesus,
7 that in the ages to come He might show the exceeding riches of His grace in His kindness toward us in Christ Jesus.
8 For by grace you have been saved through faith, and that not of yourselves; it is the gift of God,
9 not of works, lest anyone should boast.
10 For we are His workmanship, created in Christ Jesus for good works, which God prepared beforehand that we should walk in them.

Paul just taught you so many basic truths that I want to say again, go to the Holy Bible. Read first hand and discover all that God wants you to know. The Word of God is a treasure only surpassed by the redeeming presence of Jesus and the power of the Holy Spirit in your heart. I probably should not even say that given this next quote from John.

1 John 5:7 (NKJ)
7 For there are three that bear witness in heaven: the Father, the Word, and the Holy Spirit; and these three are one.

Once your love for God is such that you love Him with all your heart, mind, soul and strength, you will not want to distance yourself from listening to God. The manifestation of your love may appear to be "works," as you diligently seek Him, but no, it is by grace that you are saved. Let me quote for you the last verse in the Bible.

Revelation 22:21 (NKJ)
21 The grace of our Lord Jesus Christ be with you all. Amen.

This sentence places all of the emphasis on Jesus. Why? One reason, in my opinion, is that if you don't understand that sin requires sacrifice in order for cleansing and forgiveness, then you fail to understand what God commanded Moses. I believe it is safe to assume that every Jew understands the ritual of sacrifice for the atonement of sin. It is the foundation of their daily renewal. But, sacrifices to cover sin are over. Jesus paid the price and now, your offerings are in "righteousness," His righteousness, not yours and not mine. We "work" but not for salvation. We obey and serve Him because we love Him.

CHAPTER 38

THE FIRSTBORN

The practice of an "offering," of the first fruits began with Cain and Abel. Cain offered a gift of products from the land and Abel offered a gift of the "first born" of his flock. Notice that Abel's "acceptable" offer was of the "first born" of his flock.

Listen to God's word about His "first born."

Exodus 4:22 (NKJ)
22 "Then you shall say to Pharaoh, 'Thus says the LORD: "Israel is My son, My firstborn.

The second mention of the significance of the firstborn concerns the event leading to the Passover.

Exodus 11:4-7 (NKJ)
4 Then Moses said, "Thus says the LORD: 'About midnight I will go out into the midst of Egypt;
5 'and all the firstborn in the land of Egypt shall die, from the firstborn of Pharaoh who sits on his throne, even to the firstborn of the female servant who is behind the handmill, and all the firstborn of the animals.
6 'Then there shall be a great cry throughout all the land of Egypt, such as was not like it before, nor shall be like it again.
7 'But against none of the children of Israel shall a dog move its tongue, against man or beast, that you may know that the LORD does make a difference between the Egyptians and Israel.'

Exodus 12:12-34 (NKJ)

12 'For I will pass through the land of Egypt on that night, and will strike all the firstborn in the land of Egypt, both man and beast; and against all the gods of Egypt I will execute judgment: I am the LORD.

13 'Now the blood shall be a sign for you on the houses where you are. And when I see the blood, I will pass over you; and the plague shall not be on you to destroy you when I strike the land of Egypt.

14 'So this day shall be to you a memorial; and you shall keep it as a feast to the LORD throughout your generations. You shall keep it as a feast by an everlasting ordinance.

15 'Seven days you shall eat unleavened bread. On the first day you shall remove leaven from your houses. For whoever eats leavened bread from the first day until the seventh day, that person shall be cut off from Israel.

16 'On the first day there shall be a holy convocation, and on the seventh day there shall be a holy convocation for you. No manner of work shall be done on them; but that which everyone must eat– that only may be prepared by you.

17 'So you shall observe the Feast of Unleavened Bread, for on this same day I will have brought your armies out of the land of Egypt. Therefore you shall observe this day throughout your generations as an everlasting ordinance.

18 'In the first month, on the fourteenth day of the month at evening, you shall eat unleavened bread, until the twenty-first day of the month at evening.

19 'For seven days no leaven shall be found in your houses, since whoever eats what is leavened, that same person shall be cut off from the congregation of Israel, whether he is a stranger or a native of the land.

20 'You shall eat nothing leavened; in all your dwellings you shall eat unleavened bread.'"

21 Then Moses called for all the elders of Israel and said to them, "Pick out and take lambs for yourselves according to your families, and kill the Passover lamb.

22 "And you shall take a bunch of hyssop, dip it in the blood that is in the basin, and strike the lintel and the two doorposts with the blood that is

in the basin. And none of you shall go out of the door of his house until morning.

23 "For the LORD will pass through to strike the Egyptians; and when He sees the blood on the lintel and on the two doorposts, the LORD will pass over the door and not allow the destroyer to come into your houses to strike you.

24 "And you shall observe this thing as an ordinance for you and your sons forever.

25 "It will come to pass when you come to the land which the LORD will give you, just as He promised, that you shall keep this service.

26 "And it shall be, when your children say to you, 'What do you mean by this service?'

27 "that you shall say, 'It is the Passover sacrifice of the LORD, who passed over the houses of the children of Israel in Egypt when He struck the Egyptians and delivered our households.' " So the people bowed their heads and worshiped.

28 Then the children of Israel went away and did so; just as the LORD had commanded Moses and Aaron, so they did.

29 And it came to pass at midnight that the LORD struck all the firstborn in the land of Egypt, from the firstborn of Pharaoh who sat on his throne to the firstborn of the captive who was in the dungeon, and all the firstborn of livestock.

30 So Pharaoh rose in the night, he, all his servants, and all the Egyptians; and there was a great cry in Egypt, for there was not a house where there was not one dead.

31 Then he called for Moses and Aaron by night, and said, "Rise, go out from among my people, both you and the children of Israel. And go, serve the LORD as you have said.

32 "Also take your flocks and your herds, as you have said, and be gone; and bless me also."

33 And the Egyptians urged the people, that they might send them out of the land in haste. For they said, "We shall all be dead."

34 So the people took their dough before it was leavened, having their kneading bowls bound up in their clothes on their shoulders.

Note verse 27. This is the Passover sacrifice, in which the firstborn of the enemy is destroyed and the firstborn of God's people, preserved. Now see what God said to Moses about all of the firstborn of Israel.

Exodus 13:1-2 (NKJ)
1 Then the LORD spoke to Moses, saying,
2 "Consecrate to Me all the firstborn, whatever opens the womb among the children of Israel, both of man and beast; it is Mine."

Then God establishes the law regarding sacrifice of the firstborn males.

Exodus 13:11-15 (NKJ)
11 "And it shall be, when the LORD brings you into the land of the Canaanites, as He swore to you and your fathers, and gives it to you,
12 "that you shall set apart to the LORD all that open the womb, that is, every firstborn that comes from an animal which you have; the males shall be the LORD'S.
13 "But every firstborn of a donkey you shall redeem with a lamb; and if you will not redeem it, then you shall break its neck. And all the firstborn of man among your sons you shall redeem.
14 "So it shall be, when your son asks you in time to come, saying, 'What is this?' that you shall say to him, 'By strength of hand the LORD brought us out of Egypt, out of the house of bondage.
15 'And it came to pass, when Pharaoh was stubborn about letting us go, that the LORD killed all the firstborn in the land of Egypt, both the firstborn of man and the firstborn of beast. Therefore I sacrifice to the LORD all males that open the womb, but all the firstborn of my sons I redeem.'

Notice verse 13. The donkey, a stubborn animal, shall be redeemed with a lamb. You can attribute any meaning to that you wish but know that if the lamb had not been sacrificed then the stubborn donkey would have had its neck broken. May the reader be given light to understand that point. The first mention of the Messiah being the Lamb of God, is in the Gospel of John. Listen.

John 1:29-36 (NKJ)
29 The next day John saw Jesus coming toward him, and said, "Behold! The Lamb of God who takes away the sin of the world!
30 "This is He of whom I said, 'After me comes a Man who is preferred before me, for He was before me.'
31 "I did not know Him; but that He should be revealed to Israel, therefore I came baptizing with water."
32 And John bore witness, saying, "I saw the Spirit descending from heaven like a dove, and He remained upon Him.
33 "I did not know Him, but He who sent me to baptize with water said to me, 'Upon whom you see the Spirit descending, and remaining on Him, this is He who baptizes with the Holy Spirit.'
34 "And I have seen and testified that this is the Son of God."
35 Again, the next day, John stood with two of his disciples.
36 And looking at Jesus as He walked, he said, "Behold the Lamb of God!"

Then, we find Jesus referred to as the "firstborn," the Lamb of God.

Matthew 1:24-25 (NKJ)
24 Then Joseph, being aroused from sleep, did as the angel of the Lord commanded him and took to him his wife,
25 and did not know her till she had brought forth her first born Son. And He called His name Jesus.

Colossians 1:1-25 (NKJ)
1 Paul, an apostle of Jesus Christ by the will of God, and Timothy our brother,
2 To the saints and faithful brethren in Christ who are in Colosse: Grace to you and peace from God our Father and the Lord Jesus Christ.
3 We give thanks to the God and Father of our Lord Jesus Christ, praying always for you,
4 since we heard of your faith in Christ Jesus and of your love for all the saints;
5 because of the hope which is laid up for you in heaven, of which you heard before in the word of the truth of the gospel,

6 which has come to you, as it has also in all the world, and is bringing forth fruit, as it is also among you since the day you heard and knew the grace of God in truth;

7 as you also learned from Epaphras, our dear fellow servant, who is a faithful minister of Christ on your behalf,

8 who also declared to us your love in the Spirit.

9 For this reason we also, since the day we heard it, do not cease to pray for you, and to ask that you may be filled with the knowledge of His will in all wisdom and spiritual understanding;

10 that you may have a walk worthy of the Lord, fully pleasing Him, being fruitful in every good work and increasing in the knowledge of God;

11 strengthened with all might, according to His glorious power, for all patience and longsuffering with joy;

12 giving thanks to the Father who has qualified us to be partakers of the inheritance of the saints in the light.

13 He has delivered us from the power of darkness and conveyed us into the kingdom of the Son of His love,

14 in whom we have redemption through His blood, the forgiveness of sins.

15 He is the image of the invisible God, the firstborn over all creation.

16 For by Him all things were created that are in heaven and that are on earth, visible and invisible, whether thrones or dominions or principalities or powers. All things were created through Him and for Him.

17 And He is before all things, and in Him all things consist.

18 And He is the head of the body, the church, who is the beginning, the firstborn from the dead, that in all things He may have the preeminence.

19 For it pleased the Father that in Him all the fullness should dwell,

20 and by Him to reconcile all things to Himself, by Him, whether things on earth or things in heaven, having made peace through the blood of His cross.

21 And you, who once were alienated and enemies in your mind by wicked works, yet now He has reconciled

22 in the body of His flesh through death, to present you holy, and blameless, and above reproach in His sight–

23 if indeed you continue in the faith, grounded and steadfast, and are not moved away from the hope of the gospel which you heard, which was preached to every creature under heaven, of which I, Paul, became a minister.
24 I now rejoice in my sufferings for you, and fill up in my flesh what is lacking in the afflictions of Christ, for the sake of His body, which is the church,
25 of which I became a minister.

Israel knows better than anyone that God commanded that the firstborn animal be sacrificed and the firstborn son, redeemed. Our redeemer paid the price. His flesh was crucified and now our "flesh" (Satan's domain in us) needs to be crucified. Listen to Paul's teaching.

Galatians 2:20-21 (NKJ)
20 "I have been crucified with Christ; it is no longer I who live, but Christ lives in me; and the life which I now live in the flesh I live by faith in the Son of God, who loved me and gave Himself for me.
21 "I do not set aside the grace of God; for if righteousness comes through the law, then Christ died in vain."

Galatians 5:24-25 (NKJ)
24 And those who are Christ's have crucified the flesh with its passions and desires.
25 If we live in the Spirit, let us also walk in the Spirit.

Romans 6:3-14 (NKJ)
3 ... do you not know that as many of us as were baptized into Christ Jesus were baptized into His death?
4 Therefore we were buried with Him through baptism into death, that just as Christ was raised from the dead by the glory of the Father, even so we also should walk in newness of life.
5 For if we have been united together in the likeness of His death, certainly we also shall be in the likeness of His resurrection,
6 knowing this, that our old man was crucified with Him, that the body of sin might be done away with, that we should no longer be slaves of sin.
7 For he who has died has been freed from sin.

8 Now if we died with Christ, we believe that we shall also live with Him,
9 knowing that Christ, having been raised from the dead, dies no more. Death no longer has dominion over Him.
10 For the death that He died, He died to sin once for all; but the life that He lives, He lives to God.
11 Likewise you also, reckon yourselves to be dead indeed to sin, but alive to God in Christ Jesus our Lord.
12 Therefore do not let sin reign in your mortal body, that you should obey it in its lusts.
13 And do not present your members as instruments of unrighteousness to sin, but present yourselves to God as being alive from the dead, and your members as instruments of righteousness to God.
14 For sin shall not have dominion over you, for you are not under law but under grace.

Our flesh will not live on. Ours souls, our spirit will live on, in one domain or another. Read these verses carefully and pray for discernment.

Romans 8:1-18 (NKJ)
1 There is therefore now no condemnation to those who are in Christ Jesus, who do not walk according to the flesh, but according to the Spirit.
2 For the law of the Spirit of life in Christ Jesus has made me free from the law of sin and death.
3 For what the law could not do in that it was weak through the flesh, God did by sending His own Son in the likeness of sinful flesh, on account of sin: He condemned sin in the flesh,
4 that the righteous requirement of the law might be fulfilled in us who do not walk according to the flesh but according to the Spirit.
5 For those who live according to the flesh set their minds on the things of the flesh, but those who live according to the Spirit, the things of the Spirit.
6 For to be carnally minded is death, but to be spiritually minded is life and peace.
7 Because the carnal mind is enmity against God; for it is not subject to the law of God, nor indeed can be.
8 So then, those who are in the flesh cannot please God.

9 But you are not in the flesh but in the Spirit, if indeed the Spirit of God dwells in you. Now if anyone does not have the Spirit of Christ, he is not His.
10 And if Christ is in you, the body is dead because of sin, but the Spirit is life because of righteousness.
11 But if the Spirit of Him who raised Jesus from the dead dwells in you, He who raised Christ from the dead will also give life to your mortal bodies through His Spirit who dwells in you.
12 Therefore, brethren, we are debtors– not to the flesh, to live according to the flesh.
13 For if you live according to the flesh you will die; but if by the Spirit you put to death the deeds of the body, you will live.
14 For as many as are led by the Spirit of God, these are sons of God.
15 For you did not receive the spirit of bondage again to fear, but you received the Spirit of adoption by whom we cry out, "Abba, Father."
16 The Spirit Himself bears witness with our spirit that we are children of God,
17 and if children, then heirs– heirs of God and joint heirs with Christ, if indeed we suffer with Him, that we may also be glorified together.
18 For I consider that the sufferings of this present time are not worthy to be compared with the glory which shall be revealed in us.

Jesus Christ is saying to you and I, "I have redeemed you, your spirit need not die." It is circumcision of the heart, not the flesh that will save you. Listen.

Colossians 2:11-15 (NKJ)
11 In Him you were also circumcised with the circumcision made without hands, by putting off the body of the sins of the flesh, by the circumcision of Christ,
12 buried with Him in baptism, in which you also were raised with Him through faith in the working of God, who raised Him from the dead.
13 And you, being dead in your trespasses and the uncircumcision of your flesh, He has made alive together with Him, having forgiven you all trespasses,

14 having wiped out the handwriting of requirements that was against us, which was contrary to us. And He has taken it out of the way, having nailed it to the cross.
15 Having disarmed principalities and powers, He made a public spectacle of them, triumphing over them in it.

The Old Testament identifies the Redeemer as One that lives, the Holy One of Israel.

Job 19:25 (NKJ)
25 For I know that my Redeemer lives, and He shall stand at last on the earth;

Psalm 19:14 (NKJ)
14 Let the words of my mouth and the meditation of my heart be acceptable in Your sight, O LORD, my strength and my Redeemer.

Isaiah 47:4 (NKJ)
4 As for our Redeemer, the LORD of hosts is His name, the Holy One of Israel.

Do you yet await the arrival of the Holy One of Israel? Will He be born of a virgin, in the town of Bethlehem, be crucified and rise from the dead as your prophets declare? Yes those prophecies must be fulfilled and if you are waiting for One to meet those requirements, you need wait no longer. Listen to the words of the Messiah, recorded for you.

Revelation 3:19-21 (NKJ)
19 "As many as I love, I rebuke and chasten. Therefore be zealous and repent.
20 "Behold, I stand at the door and knock. If anyone hears My voice and opens the door, I will come in to him and dine with him, and he with Me.
21 "To him who overcomes I will grant to sit with Me on My throne, as I also overcame and sat down with My Father on His throne.

CHAPTER 39

THE HOLY SPIRIT

What is life? How can you choose life? When the scriptures speak of life and death, life is described as both physical and transitory and as eternal and spiritual. There is no question about the transitory, physical part. We are born, we live and we die. But if that was all there was to it, then those who say, "Eat, drink and be merry, for tomorrow we die" would have a good point.

There is not a single "seeker of pleasure," who does not have a spirit within him that casts light on his self centered existence. That light within you is both your hope and your judge. God knows you intimately. Read and understand this next verse and then read the Psalm following it and you will know, if you carefully consider it, that God is "considering" you right now. His thoughts toward you exceed number. This point needs to be made over and over until you understand because it will lead you to understand that God initiates, you respond. It is His Holy Spirit seeking to commune with your spirit. If you feel Him calling and you fail to respond, you are spurning His affection and love. Your inaction is action.

Psalm 40:5 (NKJ)
5 Many, O LORD my God, are Your wonderful works which You have done; and Your thoughts toward us cannot be recounted to You in order; if I would declare and speak of them, they are more than can be numbered.

Psalm 139:1-18 (NKJ)
1 O LORD, You have searched me and known me.
2 You know my sitting down and my rising up; you understand my thought afar off.
3 You comprehend my path and my lying down, and are acquainted with all my ways.
4 For there is not a word on my tongue, but behold, O LORD, You know it altogether.
5 You have hedged me behind and before, and laid Your hand upon me.
6 Such knowledge is too wonderful for me; it is high, I cannot attain it.
7 Where can I go from Your Spirit? Or where can I flee from Your presence?
8 If I ascend into heaven, You are there; if I make my bed in hell, behold, You are there.
9 If I take the wings of the morning, and dwell in the uttermost parts of the sea,
10 Even there Your hand shall lead me, and Your right hand shall hold me.
11 If I say, "Surely the darkness shall fall on me," even the night shall be light about me;
12 Indeed, the darkness shall not hide from You, but the night shines as the day; the darkness and the light are both alike to You.
13 For You formed my inward parts; you covered me in my mother's womb.
14 I will praise You, for I am fearfully and wonderfully made; marvelous are Your works, and that my soul knows very well.
15 My frame was not hidden from You, when I was made in secret, and skillfully wrought in the lowest parts of the earth.
16 Your eyes saw my substance, being yet unformed. And in Your book they all were written, the days fashioned for me, when as yet there were none of them.
17 How precious also are Your thoughts to me, O God! How great is the sum of them!
18 If I should count them, they would be more in number than the sand; when I awake, I am still with You.

Death is described as both physical and permanent and life as spiritual and eternal. One actually chooses, for eternity, the realm in which you want to exist. Volition is a wonderful gift. But, "To whom much is given, much is required." Those who have the option to choose have a much greater obligation than those that have no option. Our autonomy is both a gift and a liability.

When the prophet Ezekiel spoke of the final gathering of Israel, he described the condition of the heart and the spirit. I believe that this is a promise to the faithful remnant of God's chosen people, bestowed at the onset of the Millennium. Listen.

Ezekiel 36:26-27 (NKJ)
26 "I will give you a new heart and put a new spirit within you; I will take the heart of stone out of your flesh and give you a heart of flesh.
27 "I will put My Spirit within you and cause you to walk in My statutes, and you will keep My judgments and do them.

Perhaps the greatest "mystery" to one, who seeks the approval of God, pertains to man's inability to see himself as an infinite spiritual being. We know we have a body that is certain to die. We can not visualize ourselves as a spiritual entity, one who, "like God," will live eternally. In my opinion, the solution to the mystery hinges on our need to grasp an understanding of the Holy Spirit. First understand that your spirit is the lamp of the Lord and it is God, who is Spirit, that communicates with your spirit. Listen.

Proverbs 20:27 (NKJ)
27 The spirit of a man is the lamp of the LORD, searching all the inner depths of his heart.

1 Corinthians 2:9-16 (NKJ)
9 ...as it is written: "Eye has not seen, nor ear heard, nor have entered into the heart of man the things which God has prepared for those who love Him."
10 But God has revealed them to us through His Spirit. For the Spirit searches all things, yes, the deep things of God.

11 For what man knows the things of a man except the spirit of the man which is in him? Even so no one knows the things of God except the Spirit of God.
12 Now we have received, not the spirit of the world, but the Spirit who is from God, that we might know the things that have been freely given to us by God.
13 These things we also speak, not in words which man's wisdom teaches but which the Holy Spirit teaches, comparing spiritual things with spiritual.
14 But the natural man does not receive the things of the Spirit of God, for they are foolishness to him; nor can he know them, because they are spiritually discerned.
15 But he who is spiritual judges all things, yet he himself is rightly judged by no one.
16 For "who has known the mind of the Lord that he may instruct Him?" But we have the mind of Christ.

1 Corinthians 3:16 (NKJ)
16 Do you not know that you are the temple of God and that the Spirit of God dwells in you?

Now if those last two verses don't wake you up to the reality of God's "reach" into your soul and His willingness and ability to make you His temple, then you don't stand a chance against Satan. It is Christ in you, the power of the Spirit of God in you, which differentiates you from those who believe that this is only a physical world.

If this is only a physical world then you should feel comfortable with evolution, survival of the fittest, even a lifestyle that is focused on your personal achievements. The triumphs and losses are yours. You are in control. If you choose to be charitable, that may make you feel good. In doing so you are elevating your sense of caring and your sense of compassion for those who are less fortunate. But understand this. You will receive all of the credit and all of the blame. You will be trying to add holiness (yours) and to avoid unrighteousness, but you are on your own. And as Solomon said, you are all headed to the same fate, the grave.

One certainty exists in this scenario. You are acting as your own god. You have vowed that this is a physical world without a spiritual dimension, here for your pleasure (and incredibly you think it "evolved" into this magnificent, orderly universe). Life then would be viewed as becoming all you can be, in and of yourself. Your priorities will lead you to compete, using rules that are "situational" and values that are in transition. You will have no anchor to your soul because you do not acknowledge that you have a soul.

But where does all of this kind of thinking lead? Look around you and read the newspapers. Wearying you with commentary about sin is not my mission. My mission is to point you to the Word and to the reality of the Power of the Spirit of God. He has spoken to us about what would be, what is and what is yet to be. Only by the power of the Holy Spirit in you can you understand His mystery, revealed.

Note in the verses above the use of the word Spirit and spirit. When Spirit is capitalized in the Bible it means the Spirit of God or the Holy Spirit. When it refers to an evil spirit, it is a lower case "s" and when it refers to our human spirit it is a lower case "s." Yes, the Holy Spirit communicates with your spirit and it is a mystery, in part. Do not think for one minute that this is simply a physical world or that you are simply flesh and bones, awaiting your demise.

Jesus told a parable. After doing so, the following exchange occurred.

Mark 4:9-11 (NKJ)
9 And He said to them, "He who has ears to hear, let him hear!"
10 But when He was alone, those around Him with the twelve asked Him about the parable.
11 And He said to them, "To you it has been given to know the mystery of the kingdom of God; but to those who are outside, all things come in parables,

Paul further defines the mystery, "solved."

1 Corinthians 2:7-8 (NKJ)
7 But we speak the wisdom of God in a mystery, the hidden wisdom which God ordained before the ages for our glory,
8 which none of the rulers of this age knew; for had they known, they would not have crucified the Lord of glory.

Just as the destruction of the 1st, 2nd, and 3rd temples has been prophesied, so was the crucifixion of the Messiah, Jesus Christ. God knew who would "know" Jesus and who would not. Some Jews did know Him, and some did not. Those who did had the mystery of the Holy Spirit, "Sent," revealed to them.

One who did not recognize Jesus as the Messiah was the apostle Paul. He was a Pharisee and notorious persecutor of the early followers of Jesus Christ. Paul was the author of verse 8 above. He is not exempting himself from blame. He was among the most active of those who denied that Jesus was the Messiah. But Paul did not remain blind spiritually. He is the best example I know of to show God's chosen people, the "Way."

One of the most prominent of Jews, a Jewish ruler named Nicodemus, came to Jesus "by night" and asked him an indirect question. Listen.

John 3:1-8 (NKJ)
1 There was a man of the Pharisees named Nicodemus, a ruler of the Jews.
2 This man came to Jesus by night and said to Him, "Rabbi, we know that You are a teacher come from God; for no one can do these signs that You do unless God is with him."
3 Jesus answered and said to him, "Most assuredly, I say to you, unless one is born again, he cannot see the kingdom of God."
4 Nicodemus said to Him, "How can a man be born when he is old? Can he enter a second time into his mother's womb and be born?"
5 Jesus answered, "Most assuredly, I say to you, unless one is born of water and the Spirit, he cannot enter the kingdom of God.
6 "That which is born of the flesh is flesh, and that which is born of the Spirit is spirit.
7 "Do not marvel that I said to you, 'You must be born again.'

8 "The wind blows where it wishes, and you hear the sound of it, but cannot tell where it comes from and where it goes. So is everyone who is born of the Spirit."

Nicodemus said, "We know you are a teacher come from God" Why? Because "no one can do these signs that you do unless God is with him." This same ruler of the Jews, following the crucifixion of Jesus Christ, appears again, but this time, openly.

John 19:39-42 (NKJ)
39 And Nicodemus, who at first came to Jesus by night, also came, bringing a mixture of myrrh and aloes, about a hundred pounds.
40 Then they took the body of Jesus, and bound it in strips of linen with the spices, as the custom of the Jews is to bury.
41 Now in the place where He was crucified there was a garden, and in the garden a new tomb in which no one had yet been laid.
42 So there they laid Jesus, because of the Jews' Preparation Day, for the tomb was nearby.

Earlier, when Jesus was speaking to Nicodemus, He spoke of renewal, being born again, not of the flesh (water) but of the Spirit. Notice above in John 3:8 how life becomes "directed" as the wind. When you choose to be filled with God's Holy Spirit, you choose to be directed.

Romans 8:14 (NKJ)
14 For as many as are led by the Spirit of God, these are sons of God.

The root of the word Spirit is pneuma, meaning wind, breeze or the movement of air. Have you ever wondered how God can be everywhere at once? Understand as you see the breeze moving the leaves around you that the Holy Spirit is just like that. An ever- present "possibility" in nature (you don't know where it comes from or where it is going).

The Holy Spirit is either an ever-present possibility or an ever-present reality in you. The refreshment of the Holy Spirit, its cleansing comfort as it "lifts" you into the presence of the Father, is as the most pleasant, reassuring breeze you have ever experienced. God is constantly present, whether in you or not. Never let a leaf move in your presence or a breeze cover you again, without acknowledging His Presence. It is a wonderful reminder of His love.

God is not always "in the wind." Destructive winds are not the same as the Holy Spirit's moving. The forces of nature are at God's disposal but learn to differentiate between the times that His Hand is healing and when it is not. Listen to this incident involving Elijah.

1 Kings 19:10-14 (NKJ)
10 So he said, "I have been very zealous for the LORD God of hosts; for the children of Israel have forsaken Your covenant, torn down Your altars, and killed Your prophets with the sword. I alone am left; and they seek to take my life."
11 Then He said, "Go out, and stand on the mountain before the LORD." And behold, the LORD passed by, and a great and strong wind tore into the mountains and broke the rocks in pieces before the LORD, but the LORD was not in the wind; and after the wind an earthquake, but the LORD was not in the earthquake;
12 and after the earthquake a fire, but the LORD was not in the fire; and after the fire a still small voice.
13 So it was, when Elijah heard it, that he wrapped his face in his mantle and went out and stood in the entrance of the cave. Suddenly a voice came to him, and said, "What are you doing here, Elijah?"
14 And he said, "I have been very zealous for the LORD God of hosts; because the children of Israel have forsaken Your covenant, torn down Your altars, and killed Your prophets with the sword. I alone am left; and they seek to take my life."

I believe that when God said to Elijah that He was not "in the wind, fire and earthquake" that He was teaching us that there are events that are special dispensations of His power which serve no other purpose than showing a man that He is present and can cause such events. These are different than the course of life in which His power is dispensed to bless or to curse.

I suspect such events are not for just "any man," but for one that God is dealing with individually. They are not intended for "others" but for the individual. Why? I speculate, but our God has chosen individuals such as Moses, Isaiah, Ezekiel and Elijah through whom he directly spoke. He often spoke only to them, and even did so with others standing about, who did not hear or understand. I sense that when the wind, earthquakes and fire are experienced by "others" God is in the phenomena and it is not ever a circumstance beyond His control or outside His purposes.

Do you recall the verse that says that not a hair falls from your head that God does not notice? He is in control. We are the clay, He is the potter. He loves His children and provides for them in triumph or in tragedy. "Acts of nature" as they are called implies the absence of God's control. God either causes or allows every act of nature to occur. In the case of Job's troubles, God allowed Satan to "use the forces nature" to accomplish God's greater purpose, a purpose Job did not understand, at first.

There is a "new" dimension to God's methods of intervention. When Jesus Christ did what He did for us, when he suffered and died for our sins, He provided perfect, permanent atonement and God gave Him the responsibility of "judging." But in that same time frame Jesus taught us that His ascension to the Father was accompanied by the Father's sending of the Holy Spirit. It is the Holy Spirit, the breeze that encompasses you and cleanses and fills your heart, that is the essence of Jesus "in you."

The odd thing is that everyone, according to scripture will, whether they think so or not, acknowledge Jesus as the Messiah. That can happen now or at the beginning of the Kingdom Age or at judgment day, but it will happen. When the Messiah returns will you be greeting both a friend and companion, or you will be regarded as a stranger. Listen.

John 15:14-15 (NKJ)
14 "You are My friends if you do whatever I command you.
15 "No longer do I call you servants, for a servant does not know what his master is doing; but I have called you friends, for all things that I heard from My Father I have made known to you.

Philippians 2:9-11 (NKJ)
9 Therefore God also has highly exalted Him and given Him the name which is above every name,
10 that at the name of Jesus every knee should bow, of those in heaven, and of those on earth, and of those under the earth,
11 and that every tongue should confess that Jesus Christ is Lord, to the glory of God the Father.

Here in this next set of verses we find the three dimensions of spirit, "spirit, Spirit and Holy Spirit"

Psalm 51:9-12 (NKJ)
9 Hide Your face from my sins, and blot out all my iniquities.
10 Create in me a clean heart, O God, and renew a steadfast spirit within me.
11 Do not cast me away from Your presence, and do not take Your Holy Spirit from me.
12 Restore to me the joy of Your salvation, and uphold me by Your generous Spirit.

Man has a spirit, and here King David asks that his spirit be steadfast. Then he asks that the Holy Spirit not be taken from him and then he asks that the generous Spirit uphold him. Is there a difference between the Spirit of God and the Holy Spirit? Fundamentally, there is not. But we do know that Jesus clearly taught that the Holy Spirit is an entity that would be "sent" to each one who believed upon Him. Read carefully. This "gift" could not be more clear.

John 14:15-29 (NKJ)
15 "If you love Me, keep My commandments.
16 "And I will pray the Father, and He will give you another Helper, that He may abide with you forever–
17 "the Spirit of truth, whom the world cannot receive, because it neither sees Him nor knows Him; but you know Him, for He dwells with you and will be in you.
18 "I will not leave you orphans; I will come to you.

19 "A little while longer and the world will see Me no more, but you will see Me. Because I live, you will live also.
20 "At that day you will know that I am in My Father, and you in Me, and I in you.
21 "He who has My commandments and keeps them, it is he who loves Me. And he who loves Me will be loved by My Father, and I will love him and manifest Myself to him."
22 Judas (not Iscariot) said to Him, "Lord, how is it that You will manifest Yourself to us, and not to the world?"
23 Jesus answered and said to him, "If anyone loves Me, he will keep My word; and My Father will love him, and We will come to him and make Our home with him.
24 "He who does not love Me does not keep My words; and the word which you hear is not Mine but the Father's who sent Me.
25 "These things I have spoken to you while being present with you.
26 "But the Helper, the Holy Spirit, whom the Father will send in My name, He will teach you all things, and bring to your remembrance all things that I said to you.
27 "Peace I leave with you, My peace I give to you; not as the world gives do I give to you. Let not your heart be troubled, neither let it be afraid.
28 "You have heard Me say to you, 'I am going away and coming back to you.' If you loved Me, you would rejoice because I said, 'I am going to the Father,' for My Father is greater than I.
29 "And now I have told you before it comes, that when it does come to pass, you may believe.

John 15:26 (NKJ)
26 "But when the Helper comes, whom I shall send to you from the Father, the Spirit of truth who proceeds from the Father, He will testify of Me.

John 16:7-15 (NKJ)
7 "Nevertheless I tell you the truth. It is to your advantage that I go away; for if I do not go away, the Helper will not come to you; but if I depart, I will send Him to you.
8 "And when He has come, He will convict the world of sin, and of righteousness, and of judgment:

9 "of sin, because they do not believe in Me;
10 "of righteousness, because I go to My Father and you see Me no more;
11 "of judgment, because the ruler of this world is judged.
12 "I still have many things to say to you, but you cannot bear them now.
13 "However, when He, the Spirit of truth, has come, He will guide you into all truth; for He will not speak on His own authority, but whatever He hears He will speak; and He will tell you things to come.
14 "He will glorify Me, for He will take of what is Mine and declare it to you.
15 "All things that the Father has are Mine. Therefore I said that He will take of Mine and declare it to you.

Here the apostle Paul, further clarified the work of the Holy Spirit in you.

Romans 8:14-16 (NKJ)
14 For as many as are led by the Spirit of God, these are sons of God.
15 For you did not receive the spirit of bondage again to fear, but you received the Spirit of adoption by whom we cry out, "Abba, Father."
16 The Spirit Himself bears witness with our spirit that we are children of God,…

Romans 8:26-28 (NKJ)
26 Likewise the Spirit also helps in our weaknesses. For we do not know what we should pray for as we ought, but the Spirit Himself makes intercession for us with groanings which cannot be uttered.
27 Now He who searches the hearts knows what the mind of the Spirit is, because He makes intercession for the saints according to the will of God.
28 And we know that all things work together for good to those who love God, to those who are the called according to His purpose.

If the Holy Spirit is in you, you are the Temple of God, the place that God abides, and if that Temple sins, you are defiling God's Temple. Listen.

1 Corinthians 6:18-20 (NKJ)
18 Flee sexual immorality. Every sin that a man does is outside the body, but he who commits sexual immorality sins against his own body.

19 Or do you not know that your body is the temple of the Holy Spirit who is in you, whom you have from God, and you are not your own?
20 For you were bought at a price; therefore glorify God in your body and in your spirit, which are God's.

Galatians 5:16-25 (NKJ)
16 I say then: Walk in the Spirit, and you shall not fulfill the lust of the flesh.
17 For the flesh lusts against the Spirit, and the Spirit against the flesh; and these are contrary to one another, so that you do not do the things that you wish.
18 But if you are led by the Spirit, you are not under the law.
19 Now the works of the flesh are evident, which are: adultery, fornication, uncleanness, lewdness,
20 idolatry, sorcery, hatred, contentions, jealousies, outbursts of wrath, selfish ambitions, dissensions, heresies,
21 envy, murders, drunkenness, revelries, and the like; of which I tell you beforehand, just as I also told you in time past, that those who practice such things will not inherit the kingdom of God.
22 But the fruit of the Spirit is love, joy, peace, longsuffering, kindness, goodness, faithfulness,
23 gentleness, self-control. Against such there is no law.
24 And those who are Christ's have crucified the flesh with its passions and desires.
25 If we live in the Spirit, let us also walk in the Spirit.

In the Gospel of John, Chapter 1, verses 1-2, it says, "In the beginning was the Word, and the Word was with God, and the Word was God. He was in the beginning with God".

God is a Triune God. He is God the Father, God the Son and God the Holy Spirit. We have a difficult time, as the creation of God, to grasp the reality of His eternal preexistence, His power to manifest Himself in the flesh and His deliverance of the Holy Spirit to those who believe. But remember that we are the clay and He is the potter. Read on.

Isaiah 64:1-8 (NKJ)
1 Oh, that You would rend the heavens! That You would come down! That the mountains might shake at Your presence–
2 As fire burns brushwood, as fire causes water to boil– to make Your name known to Your adversaries, that the nations may tremble at Your presence!
3 When You did awesome things for which we did not look, you came down, the mountains shook at Your presence.
4 For since the beginning of the world men have not heard nor perceived by the ear, nor has the eye seen any God besides You, who acts for the one who waits for Him.
5 You meet him who rejoices and does righteousness, who remembers You in Your ways. You are indeed angry, for we have sinned– in these ways we continue; and we need to be saved.
6 But we are all like an unclean thing, and all our righteousnesses are like filthy rags; we all fade as a leaf, and our iniquities, like the wind, have taken us away.
7 And there is no one who calls on Your name, who stirs himself up to take hold of You; for You have hidden Your face from us, and have consumed us because of our iniquities.
8 But now, O LORD, you are our Father; we are the clay, and You our potter; and all we are the work of Your hand.

These are truly wonderful verses. Note that ear hasn't heard, nor perceived, and eye hasn't seen any God who acts for the one who waits for Him. Grasp the meaning of those words. Our God "meets" those who rejoice in Him and do righteousness, in spite of our prior attitude. Isaiah then laments over the sins of Israel and finishes by saying, "we are the clay, and You our potter." Earlier Isaiah explained the analogy.

Isaiah 45:9 (NKJ)
9 "Woe to him who strives with his Maker! Let the potsherd strive with the potsherds of the earth! Shall the clay say to him who forms it, 'What are you making?' Or shall your handiwork say, 'He has no hands'?

This last set of verses first describes the stubbornness of the congregation and then prescribes the cure. Heed My words, obey My law. Then we see the gentle, healing touch of the Messiah.

Matthew 12:18-21 (NKJ)
18 "Behold, My Servant whom I have chosen, my Beloved in whom My soul is well pleased! I will put My Spirit upon Him, and He will declare justice to the Gentiles.
19 He will not quarrel nor cry out, nor will anyone hear His voice in the streets.
20 A bruised reed He will not break, and smoking flax He will not quench, till He sends forth justice to victory;
21 And in His name Gentiles will trust,…

Now Isaiah prophesies concerning the coming Kingdom, that wonderful 1000-year period in which Israel will be as a covenant to the people, serving as the host and dispenser of God's righteousness.

Isaiah 49:8-13 (NKJ)
8 Thus says the LORD: "In an acceptable time I have heard You, and in the day of salvation I have helped You; I will preserve You and give You as a covenant to the people, to restore the earth, to cause them to inherit the desolate heritages;
9 That You may say to the prisoners, 'Go forth,' to those who are in darkness, 'Show yourselves.' "They shall feed along the roads, and their pastures shall be on all desolate heights.
10 They shall neither hunger nor thirst, neither heat nor sun shall strike them; for He who has mercy on them will lead them, even by the springs of water He will guide them.
11 I will make each of My mountains a road, and My highways shall be elevated.
12 Surely these shall come from afar; look! Those from the north and the west, and these from the land of Sinim."
13 Sing, O heavens! Be joyful, O earth! And break out in singing, O mountains! For the LORD has comforted His people, and will have mercy on His afflicted.

Now, in the New Testament Peter quotes Isaiah, and declares what I find to be the crux of the matter today. God told Isaiah that He lay in Zion a chief cornerstone and those who reject that cornerstone stumble, being disobedient to the word, the word to which they were appointed. Peter then says to his audience, followers of Jesus Christ, that they "were not a people" but they are now a chosen generation, a royal priesthood who have attained mercy. Listen.

1 Peter 2:6-10 (NKJ)
6 Therefore it is also contained in the Scripture, "Behold, I lay in Zion a chief cornerstone, elect, precious, and he who believes on Him will by no means be put to shame."
7 Therefore, to you who believe, He is precious; but to those who are disobedient, "The stone which the builders rejected has become the chief cornerstone,"
8 and "A stone of stumbling and a rock of offense." They stumble, being disobedient to the word, to which they also were appointed.
9 But you are a chosen generation, a royal priesthood, a holy nation, His own special people, that you may proclaim the praises of Him who called you out of darkness into His marvelous light;
10 who once were not a people but are now the people of God, who had not obtained mercy but now have obtained mercy.

It is the Holy Spirit that directs and guides us. It is the Holy Spirit, I pray, that is placing His Hand upon this book and upon your heart. God wants to pour out His Holy Spirit upon you, right now. You can not be redeemed by obedience to the Law, only. Obedience is wonderful and good but it is the Holy Spirit, by the blood of the perfect Lamb of God, that cleanses you and atones for your sin and enables you to have a new heart.

Acts 2:17-18 (NKJ)
17 'And it shall come to pass in the last days, says God, that I will pour out of My Spirit on all flesh; your sons and your daughters shall prophesy, your young men shall see visions, your old men shall dream dreams.
18 And on My menservants and on My maidservants I will pour out My Spirit in those days; and they shall prophesy.

Holy Spirit – Part 1, and Part 2, from the Scripture Topics section of this website gospelglobalvision.com, gives a more complete scriptural background on the triune God topic. Again, the mystery of God's presence in you shall remain a mystery until it is a reality. Actually, as you read the chapter "God has revealed Himself to every man," you will learn that the truth is in you, but the key to that truth changing your life, forever, begins with your simple confession of faith. Then the mysteries of God will be revealed and then the Word of God will take on meaning. Intellectual assent is worthless, absent a changed life, and a repentant and contrite heart. The revelation of God's truth is only available to those who are cleansed and made ready for rebirth by the redemptive action of our Lord.

CHAPTER 40

FEAR SHOULD BRING US TO OUR KNEES—IT WILL

Fear is a "second best" motivator. The best motivator is true love. True love will give you the courage to act, in defense of one who is loved, in an almost superhuman way. If you take "love" out of the equation, when a calamity is upon you, true fear manifests itself.

It is the lot of humans to experience fear in such a way that even the most macho, powerful people, have gone limp when God displays His power. Those of you who have endured an intense earthquake or witnessed a tidal wave's power or the eruption of a volcano have seen a glimpse of God's power. None of us are "courageous" on such occasions. Listen to the words of an event recorded by Moses.

Exodus 20:18-20 (NKJ)
18 Now all the people witnessed the thunderings, the lightning flashes, the sound of the trumpet, and the mountain smoking; and when the people saw it, they trembled and stood afar off.
19 Then they said to Moses, "You speak with us, and we will hear; but let not God speak with us, lest we die."
20 And Moses said to the people, "Do not fear; for God has come to test you, and that His fear may be before you, so that you may not sin."

We do not like to think of ourselves as fearful. But that does not remove the fact that God's hand can be one of either extreme wrath or of unbelievable, unmerited mercy. You choose which you prefer.

Your sin, and mine, deserves punishment. Being able to say, "I'm sorry, I repent, forgive me God" seems far too simple. Yet, that is precisely what God is offering you as a "prepaid pass to eternity." Who prepaid the pass? How can I get in free given all the sin I have committed? The answer is extremely simple. Grace, the Grace of God, and your faith in the redeeming act of Jesus Christ save you. Jesus, our personal Messiah, One sent from God, took your sins and mine upon Himself, that we might be presented blameless to a Holy Father who will not allow sin to enter into His Presence. Listen.

Isaiah 59:2 (NKJ)
2 But your iniquities have separated you from your God; and your sins have hidden His face from you, so that He will not hear.

When Moses taught God's people about obedience, as they were about to enter into the Promised Land, he made it clear that "fearing God" and teaching his commandments to our children and grandchildren was required. Nothing has changed. Blessings flow from obedience and obedience flows from our faith and "responsive" love. (He loved us first!)

Deuteronomy 6:1-2 (NKJ)
1 "Now this is the commandment, and these are the statutes and judgments which the LORD your God has commanded to teach you, that you may observe them in the land which you are crossing over to possess,
2 "that you may fear the LORD your God, to keep all His statutes and His commandments which I command you, you and your son and your grandson, all the days of your life, and that your days may be prolonged.

Only the High Priest could enter into the Holiest of Holies, into the presence of the Ark of the Covenant. To actually enter into God's Presence requires more than a change of clothing. It requires a new heart, the heart of the Messiah, blameless and pure before the Father. The High Priest went into a tabernacle made by hands. Jesus, only, can carry us into the Holiness of God, into His Presence. We completely under estimate the importance of Holiness. We could never be Holy, in and of ourselves.

The blood of Jesus cleansed you and I of the most horrific sins and of the most childish sins. Your faith, provided you truly repent and turn from your sins and seek with all your heart to love and obey God and to love your neighbor as yourself, has made you whole, clean and presentable to the Father. True love will manifest itself in obedience, worship and service to God and His people. True love moves beyond belief. It consummates itself in action.

Perhaps one of the most pivotal acts of obedience occurred when God tested Abraham, whose faith in God led to a covenant promise which benefits all of Israel to this day. You know the story well. Listen.

Genesis 22:1-18 (NKJ)
1 Now it came to pass after these things that God tested Abraham, and said to him, "Abraham!" And he said, "Here I am."
2 And He said, "Take now your son, your only son Isaac, whom you love, and go to the land of Moriah, and offer him there as a burnt offering on one of the mountains of which I shall tell you."
3 So Abraham rose early in the morning and saddled his donkey, and took two of his young men with him, and Isaac his son; and he split the wood for the burnt offering, and arose and went to the place of which God had told him.
4 Then on the third day Abraham lifted his eyes and saw the place afar off.
5 And Abraham said to his young men, "Stay here with the donkey; the lad and I will go yonder and worship, and we will come back to you."
6 So Abraham took the wood of the burnt offering and laid it on Isaac his son; and he took the fire in his hand, and a knife, and the two of them went together.
7 But Isaac spoke to Abraham his father and said, "My father!" And he said, "Here I am, my son." Then he said, "Look, the fire and the wood, but where is the lamb for a burnt offering?"
8 And Abraham said, "My son, God will provide for Himself the lamb for a burnt offering." So the two of them went together.
9 Then they came to the place of which God had told him. And Abraham built an altar there and placed the wood in order; and he bound Isaac his son and laid him on the altar, upon the wood.

10 And Abraham stretched out his hand and took the knife to slay his son.

11 But the Angel of the LORD called to him from heaven and said, "Abraham, Abraham!" And he said, "Here I am."

12 And He said, "Do not lay your hand on the lad, or do anything to him; for now I know that you fear God, since you have not withheld your son, your only son, from Me."

13 Then Abraham lifted his eyes and looked, and there behind him was a ram caught in a thicket by its horns. So Abraham went and took the ram, and offered it up for a burnt offering instead of his son.

14 And Abraham called the name of the place, THE-LORD-WILL-PROVIDE; as it is said to this day, "In the Mount of The LORD it shall be provided."

15 Then the Angel of the LORD called to Abraham a second time out of heaven,

16 and said: "By Myself I have sworn, says the LORD, because you have done this thing, and have not withheld your son, your only son–

17 "blessing I will bless you, and in multiplying I will multiply your descendants as the stars of the heaven and as the sand which is on the seashore; and your descendants shall possess the gate of their enemies.

18 "In your seed all the nations of the earth shall be blessed, because you have obeyed My voice."

John 3:16-18, 35-36 (NKJ)

16 "For God so loved the world that He gave His only begotten Son, that whoever believes in Him should not perish but have everlasting life.

17 "For God did not send His Son into the world to condemn the world, but that the world through Him might be saved.

18 "He who believes in Him is not condemned; but he who does not believe is condemned already, because he has not believed in the name of the only begotten Son of God.

35 "The Father loves the Son, and has given all things into His hand.

36 "He who believes in the Son has everlasting life; and he who does not believe the Son shall not see life, but the wrath of God abides on him."

Verse 17 speaks to the atoning sacrifice of the Perfect Lamb of God. We simply must believe that God has done what He said He would do. Our sins are paid for and our obedience is required. We must acknowledge God's gift of His only Son.

At some point, our sins deserve punishment and we deserve banishment from the presence of our Holy Father. But as in the story of Abraham, just as the judgment of sin is about to be executed, God intervenes and offers His only begotten Son as a substitute. The Lamb of God is the Messiah, Jesus the Christ and where Abraham did not have to suffer the pain of sacrificing his son, God did suffer that pain. Jesus did not desire to endure the cross, but His obedience resulted in your redemption and mine. Abraham's obedience resulted in the covenant stated in verses 17 and 18.

God says to Abraham,

"Do not lay your hand on the lad, or do anything to him; for now I know that you fear God, since you have not withheld your son, your only son, from Me."

God called Abraham's obedience "fear." I am not sure which comes first, obedience that stems from love or obedience that stems from fear. I suspect it is love that gives us the power to obey and not vice versa. Abraham's love of God included the dimension of fear. Our God is an awesome God and greatly to be feared, says the scriptures. Love God, obey Him and your fear of Him will be as the scripture that says, "Perfect love casts out fear." Listen.

1 John 4:16-18 (NKJ)
16 Love has been perfected among us in this: that we may have boldness in the day of judgment; because as He is, so are we in this world.
17 There is no fear in love; but perfect love casts out fear, because fear involves torment. But he who fears has not been made perfect in love.
18 We love Him because He first loved us.

Given the sacrifice Jesus made for our sins, our relationship with the Father has changed. Where our sins were insufficiently atoned for by the sacrifice of bulls and goats, the perfect Lamb of God has removed our sins from us, as far as the east is from the west, never to be remembered against us again.

Thus, our fear, the dread of punishment deserved, has become reverence reflected in our joy at the Lord's coming. For those that are saved, by the Grace of God, the return of the Messiah will be glorious. Perfect love really will cast out fear. The scriptures say:

James 2:19 (NKJ)
19 You believe that there is one God. You do well. Even the demons believe– and tremble!

Believing in God neither eliminates fear nor prevents judgment. Satan believes in God. Satan certainly fears God and knows that he will be judged by God. Salvation comes to those who repent, who turn from their sins, who obey His word and who acknowledge His Son. Fear only dissipates where forgiveness is assured and forgiveness is only assured if your sins are forgiven, and only One has been given authority to forgive.

Acts 4:11-12 (NKJ)
11 "This is the 'stone which was rejected by you builders, which has become the chief cornerstone.'
12 "Nor is there salvation in any other, for there is no other name under heaven given among men by which we must be saved."

CHAPTER 41

DIE TWICE OR BE BORN TWICE—YOUR CHOICE

You may choose to die twice, or to be born twice. The first death is physical and the second is spiritual. If you experience spiritual death your soul is separated from God, heaven and all things righteous. If you are to be born twice, once physically and again spiritually, you will live eternally. The timing of the second death, if it comes, is on judgment day. The second birth is "of the Spirit." The second birth happens the day that you acknowledge that the Son of God is your personal redeemer and Lord. It is a birth that keeps your name in the Book of Life.

In other words, you make that decision now and your place in eternity is sealed. If you simply decide not to decide, that is a decision in itself and the consequences are whatever they will be, but the Bible says they are not good.

Deuteronomy 30:19-20 (NKJ)
19 "I call heaven and earth as witnesses today against you, that I have set before you life and death, blessing and cursing; therefore choose life, that both you and your descendants may live;
20 "that you may love the LORD your God, that you may obey His voice, and that you may cling to Him, for He is your life and the length of your days; and that you may dwell in the land which the LORD swore to your fathers, to Abraham, Isaac, and Jacob, to give them."

Isaiah 1:18 (NKJ)
18 "Come now, and let us reason together," says the LORD, "Though your sins are like scarlet, they shall be as white as snow; though they are red like crimson, they shall be as wool.

Once you acknowledge that your sins have been atoned for, perfectly, by the shed blood of the Messiah, you spend the remainder of your days, whether brief or long, inscribing things on the only page that matters; the page of life, the record that chronicles your faith, your love of God and your new found capacity to love your fellow man. This side of the page is only available to those who can now stand acceptably before the LORD (See Chapter 31: LIFE – ONE TWO-SIDED PAGE). You stand, not in your own worthiness, but in His, accepting the unmerited gift of the grace of God, with a contrite heart and a humble spirit.

What you and I decide to do, dictates whether the pages of our personal eternity are to be inscribed in God's Holy presence or whether they are to be eternally endured in some very unpleasant place, separated from God's love and the company of His chosen people.

In these following verses, Solomon further distinguishes between life and death. Realize that "finding life" occurs after your spiritual birth. Your choice to ignore your spiritual birth and to go on sinning is a declaration against your own soul and according to the Bible, eternal death awaits.

Proverbs 8:33-36 (NKJ)
33 Hear instruction and be wise, and do not disdain it.
34 Blessed is the man who listens to me, watching daily at my gates, waiting at the posts of my doors.
35 For whoever finds me finds life, and obtains favor from the LORD;
36 But he who sins against me wrongs his own soul; all those who hate me love death."

Listen again to the words of God, recorded by Moses.

Deuteronomy 30:19 (NKJ)
19 ...I have set before you life and death, blessing and cursing; therefore choose life, that both you and your descendants may live.

CHAPTER 42

HOW TERRIBLE WILL IT BE TO BE "SEPARATE" FROM GOD AND THOSE YOU LOVE?

Jesus Christ provided us with one of the most clear scenarios we will ever read about being "in" or "out" of the presence of God. Read this quotation with great care.

Luke 16:19-31 (NKJ)
19 "There was a certain rich man who was clothed in purple and fine linen and fared sumptuously every day.
20 "But there was a certain beggar named Lazarus, full of sores, who was laid at his gate,
21 "desiring to be fed with the crumbs which fell from the rich man's table. Moreover the dogs came and licked his sores.
22 "So it was that the beggar died, and was carried by the angels to Abraham's bosom. The rich man also died and was buried.
23 "And being in torments in Hades, he lifted up his eyes and saw Abraham afar off, and Lazarus in his bosom.
24 "Then he cried and said, 'Father Abraham, have mercy on me, and send Lazarus that he may dip the tip of his finger in water and cool my tongue; for I am tormented in this flame.'
25 "But Abraham said, 'Son, remember that in your lifetime you received your good things, and likewise Lazarus evil things; but now he is comforted and you are tormented.

26 'And besides all this, between us and you there is a great gulf fixed, so that those who want to pass from here to you cannot, nor can those from there pass to us.'
27 "Then he said, 'I beg you therefore, father, that you would send him to my father's house,
28 'for I have five brothers, that he may testify to them, lest they also come to this place of torment.'
29 "Abraham said to him, 'They have Moses and the prophets; let them hear them.'
30 "And he said, 'No, father Abraham; but if one goes to them from the dead, they will repent.'
31 "But he said to him, 'If they do not hear Moses and the prophets, neither will they be persuaded though one rise from the dead.'"

There are so many lessons in this parable. First the rich man knew Abraham was his Father, so he was a rich Jew. It doesn't say the beggar was a Gentile, but the vision of "crumbs from the rich man's table" might well include something more than food. The Gentiles are beneficiaries of God's relationship with the Jews. We literally feed on the crumbs of the feast first served the Jews, but it is Israel who was fed directly. We Gentiles who love God know whom God chose to be His Holy conduit, so to speak.

We Gentiles are neither the root nor the branch. We were, as it says in another place, "grafted" in. We do not have the rich traditions or bloodline of God's chosen people. We, in a sense, feast upon the crumbs, not on the richness of those to whom God gave a special place.

Whether the beggar represents a Gentile or not, it says he died and was carried to Abraham's bosom. It does not say that the beggar, by any external measure, "qualified" to be embraced by Abraham. He is depicted simply as a beggar. Then, in what is for me, a wonderful allegory, the rich man suggests that if the beggar were to "rise from the dead," not only would the rich man's fathers and brothers recognize him as the one who sat at the gate begging, but in doing so, they would now believe in life after death. The rich man felt that if they understood that fact, that it would lead them to acts of faith, which would keep them from enduring such torment. Then

Abraham makes one of the most important statements a Jew could hear in the context of a parable spoken by Jesus.

Luke 16:31 (NKJ)
31 …'If they do not hear Moses and the prophets, neither will they be persuaded though one rise from the dead.'"

I have always thought that "fear" of eternal punishment or eternal separation from God, or eternal separation from your loved ones who love God, or in the case of children whom God loves (let the reader understand), would motivate people to love and obey God. Apparently the fear of punishment, separation, and isolation, does not do it. Let me amend that a little. It does do it, intellectually, but faith is about action, not consent. I have heard many pastors say the following phrase: "People are about 18 inches from being saved. What is in their head must move to their heart." A broken and contrite heart is one ready for healing. When you are completely disgusted with your heart of flesh and all of the sin that it leads you to commit, get a new heart. Accept redemption and renewal or prepare to be separate from those you love, forever.

The parable you just read tells you that it is the rich man who could see and envy the beggar, not that the beggar could see and feel sorrow for the rich man. It says the chasm between those who are "separated" from those who love God cannot be bridged. It looks like the beggar is unaware of the suffering of the rich man. How else could the scriptures be true when they say,

"for the Lamb who is in the midst of the throne will shepherd them and lead them to living fountains of waters. And God will wipe away every tear from their eyes."

If we, in heaven, could see the suffering of our loved ones, every tear would not be wiped away.

If you choose to persist in sin, it looks like your loved ones who are with Jesus will be unaware of your circumstance. You readily know that your unforgiven sin separates you from God but have you considered how painful it will be to be separate from those you love? It is not my intention to convey the message that you should draw near to God in order for you to spend eternity with your loved ones, but that reality is simply an unintended consequence of the choice you have made.

Our earthly family is a great gift of God and the joy that parents feel as they look upon their child is almost inexpressible. Love your family as you love the Lord. Teach them and lead them in paths of righteousness. Pray with them and for them every day and pray that you will all be united in Christ now and forever.

Your children will become "accountable" adults. Show them, by example, how to cope with temptation, to be persons of faith and fidelity. Seek His righteousness in you. Ask daily to be bathed in the freshness and power of the Holy Spirit and thank Jesus daily (constantly) for presenting you to the Father wrapped in His righteousness. Thank God that His thoughts toward you exceed number. Have your every thought and action be "as unto the Lord." Your family will notice and I pray that you will lead them to an eternal reunion.

CHAPTER 43

IF THERE IS ONE GOD—WHY SO MANY DIFFERENT BODIES OF BELIEVERS?

We have just about completed a 2000-year period since the crucifixion, resurrection and ascension of Jesus Christ. This is an age where the gospel has been, or is being spread, to all the nations and a "body of believers" has developed. That "body of believers" is made up of those who believe (and I would say "act on that belief"), that Jesus Christ is indeed the promised Messiah. The definition of the Church, also referred to as the "Bride of Christ," is "the body of believers."

Paul, in his letter to the Romans, clarifies that believers are all "one body." At least that is how he says it is supposed to be. Denominationalism must grieve our Lord.

Romans 12:3-5 (NKJ)
3 For I say, through the grace given to me, to everyone who is among you, not to think of himself more highly than he ought to think, but to think soberly, as God has dealt to each one a measure of faith.
4 For as we have many members in one body, but all the members do not have the same function,
5 so we, being many, are one body in Christ, and individually members of one another.

It is most unfortunate that man has chosen to claim "special knowledge" that permits him to say, "God has revealed new information to me, beyond the scope of the Holy Scriptures, thus some of what you believe is incorrect." I once heard a man say, "If it is new, it is not true and if it is true, it is not new." The Biblical basis for such a statement is referenced by the Scriptures. Listen.

Deuteronomy 4:2 (NKJ)
2 "You shall not add to the word which I command you, nor take anything from it, that you may keep the commandments of the LORD your God which I command you.

Then Jesus tells us how much "editing" of God's Word one can do.

Matthew 5:17-18 (NKJ)
17 "Do not think that I came to destroy the Law or the Prophets. I did not come to destroy but to fulfill.
18 "For assuredly, I say to you, till heaven and earth pass away, one jot or one tittle will by no means pass from the law till all is fulfilled.

Man has historically felt the urge to press "new revelations" upon their listeners, perhaps in an effort to establish themselves as "seers and prophets" that have an inside track to God, the Father. As a result, their pride in their "discoveries" leads them to convene followers who they can then convince that the Holy Spirit, the Father, has revealed to them "insider information" that requires some "adjustments" to your faith and theirs. These adjustments create sects and memberships that are exclusive and different.

Most often they are "almost right," that is, much of which they believe is in agreement with the Scriptures. That is why they are attractive and dangerous. The closer they are to being right, the more attractive they are, thus they are a powerful lure. Those who are very distant from the Scriptures, i.e. satanic worshippers, are not likely to effectively recruit someone grounded in the truth of the Scriptures. I suggest you avoid those who have added to or subtracted from the truth of the Holy Scriptures.

Listen to how angry Jesus was with those who claim with their lips to be "near to God" but whose hearts are far from God.

Matthew 15:7-9 (NKJ)
7 "Hypocrites! Well did Isaiah prophesy about you, saying:
8 'These people draw near to Me with their mouth, and honor Me with their lips, but their heart is far from Me.
9 And in vain they worship Me, teaching as doctrines the commandments of men.'"

What was it that Jesus focused on? He focused on the teachings of the commandments of men as if they were the commandments of God. Read these next verses and understand that the church is the Body of Christ and there is only one body.

Ephesians 1:22-23 (NKJ)
22 And He put all things under His feet, and gave Him to be head over all things to the church,
23 which is His body, the fullness of Him who fills all in all.

Even though there is only one body, the body of believers, that body is made up of very different parts. Each part is important and has an important role. No part is more important than the other. Listen.

1 Corinthians 12:1-27 (NKJ)
1 Now concerning spiritual gifts, brethren, I do not want you to be ignorant:
2 You know that you were Gentiles, carried away to these dumb idols, however you were led.
3 Therefore I make known to you that no one speaking by the Spirit of God calls Jesus accursed, and no one can say that Jesus is Lord except by the Holy Spirit.
4 There are diversities of gifts, but the same Spirit.
5 There are differences of ministries, but the same Lord.
6 And there are diversities of activities, but it is the same God who works all in all.

7 But the manifestation of the Spirit is given to each one for the profit of all:

8 for to one is given the word of wisdom through the Spirit, to another the word of knowledge through the same Spirit,

9 to another faith by the same Spirit, to another gifts of healings by the same Spirit,

10 to another the working of miracles, to another prophecy, to another discerning of spirits, to another different kinds of tongues, to another the interpretation of tongues.

11 But one and the same Spirit works all these things, distributing to each one individually as He wills.

12 For as the body is one and has many members, but all the members of that one body, being many, are one body, so also is Christ.

13 For by one Spirit we were all baptized into one body– whether Jews or Greeks, whether slaves or free– and have all been made to drink into one Spirit.

14 For in fact the body is not one member but many.

15 If the foot should say, "Because I am not a hand, I am not of the body," is it therefore not of the body?

16 And if the ear should say, "Because I am not an eye, I am not of the body," is it therefore not of the body?

17 If the whole body were an eye, where would be the hearing? If the whole were hearing, where would be the smelling?

18 But now God has set the members, each one of them, in the body just as He pleased.

19 And if they were all one member, where would the body be?

20 But now indeed there are many members, yet one body.

21 And the eye cannot say to the hand, "I have no need of you"; nor again the head to the feet, "I have no need of you."

22 No, much rather, those members of the body which seem to be weaker are necessary.

23 And those members of the body which we think to be less honorable, on these we bestow greater honor; and our unpresentable parts have greater modesty,

24 but our presentable parts have no need. But God composed the body, having given greater honor to that part which lacks it,

25 that there should be no schism in the body, but that the members should have the same care for one another.
26 And if one member suffers, all the members suffer with it; or if one member is honored, all the members rejoice with it.
27 Now you are the body of Christ, and members individually.

In this next quotation we find a very clear admonition. Do not be children, tossed to and fro and carried about with every wind of doctrine, tricked by men, by their cunning and plotting.

Ephesians 4:11-16 (NKJ)
11 And He Himself gave some to be apostles, some prophets, some evangelists, and some pastors and teachers,
12 for the equipping of the saints for the work of ministry, for the edifying of the body of Christ,
13 till we all come to the unity of the faith and of the knowledge of the Son of God, to a perfect man, to the measure of the stature of the fullness of Christ;
14 that we should no longer be children, tossed to and fro and carried about with every wind of doctrine, by the trickery of men, in the cunning craftiness of deceitful plotting,
15 but, speaking the truth in love, may grow up in all things into Him who is the head– Christ–
16 from whom the whole body, joined and knit together by what every joint supplies, according to the effective working by which every part does its share, causes growth of the body for the edifying of itself in love.

I realize that my Jewish friends are dismayed by the constant references to the Messiah, but understand this. The Messiah you await will function in exactly the same role as the Messiah who has come. He will be your Deliverer. You will become one with the Body of Christ and all believers will be united. Read the following verses very carefully. They are the perfect truth and full of wisdom and guidance. We have not been left to "figure this all out by ourselves." The Lord has given us clarity and light. If you are in the dark as you read the following verses, it is because you have not asked that His truth be revealed to you, at least not with a humble and contrite heart, seeking renewal and redemption.

Colossians 1:13-29 (NKJ)
13 He has delivered us from the power of darkness and conveyed us into the kingdom of the Son of His love,
14 in whom we have redemption through His blood, the forgiveness of sins.
15 He is the image of the invisible God, the firstborn over all creation.
16 For by Him all things were created that are in heaven and that are on earth, visible and invisible, whether thrones or dominions or principalities or powers. All things were created through Him and for Him.
17 And He is before all things, and in Him all things consist.
18 And He is the head of the body, the church, who is the beginning, the firstborn from the dead, that in all things He may have the preeminence.
19 For it pleased the Father that in Him all the fullness should dwell,
20 and by Him to reconcile all things to Himself, by Him, whether things on earth or things in heaven, having made peace through the blood of His cross.
21 And you, who once were alienated and enemies in your mind by wicked works, yet now He has reconciled
22 in the body of His flesh through death, to present you holy, and blameless, and above reproach in His sight–
23 if indeed you continue in the faith, grounded and steadfast, and are not moved away from the hope of the gospel which you heard, which was preached to every creature under heaven, of which I, Paul, became a minister.
24 I now rejoice in my sufferings for you, and fill up in my flesh what is lacking in the afflictions of Christ, for the sake of His body, which is the church,
25 of which I became a minister according to the stewardship from God which was given to me for you, to fulfill the word of God,
26 the mystery which has been hidden from ages and from generations, but now has been revealed to His saints.
27 To them God willed to make known what are the riches of the glory of this mystery among the Gentiles: which is Christ in you, the hope of glory.

28 Him we preach, warning every man and teaching every man in all wisdom, that we may present every man perfect in Christ Jesus.
29 To this end I also labor, striving according to His working which works in me mightily.

If you decide to bow your knee now to the One that has been sent to redeem you, do not be deceived by men. Be rooted and built up in Him and let no one cheat you through philosophy and deceit. Turn to the Scriptures only and seek guidance from the Holy Spirit. Do not be distracted from your pursuit of a perfect relationship with Him by men. We have become a world that looks and listens to the words and actions of men and women and have largely ignored the truth of the Scriptures. Men, like myself, are one step from defeat, constantly. Our personal righteousness is truly as filthy rags. All of God's Word is an anchor to our soul. Remove the Word from your life and you are adrift, without certainty. Listen.

Colossians 2:4-10, 18-23 (NKJ)
4 Now this I say lest anyone should deceive you with persuasive words.
5 For though I am absent in the flesh, yet I am with you in spirit, rejoicing to see your good order and the steadfastness of your faith in Christ.
6 As you have therefore received Christ Jesus the Lord, so walk in Him,
7 rooted and built up in Him and established in the faith, as you have been taught, abounding in it with thanksgiving.
8 Beware lest anyone cheat you through philosophy and empty deceit, according to the tradition of men, according to the basic principles of the world, and not according to Christ.
9 For in Him dwells all the fullness of the Godhead bodily;
10 and you are complete in Him, who is the head of all principality and power.
18 Let no one cheat you of your reward, taking delight in false humility and worship of angels, intruding into those things which he has not seen, vainly puffed up by his fleshly mind,
19 and not holding fast to the Head, from whom all the body, nourished and knit together by joints and ligaments, grows with the increase that is from God.

20 Therefore, if you died with Christ from the basic principles of the world, why, as though living in the world, do you subject yourselves to regulations–
21 "Do not touch, do not taste, do not handle,"
22 which all concern things which perish with the using– according to the commandments and doctrines of men?
23 These things indeed have an appearance of wisdom in self-imposed religion, false humility, and neglect of the body, but are of no value against the indulgence of the flesh.

These last 4 verses point specifically to the churches that "add rules" to the Scriptures or require their members to behave in ways that differentiate "their church" from the true Church. There is one set of rules as set out in the Scriptures. Sects are those that not only add to or subtract from the Scriptures, but who generally thrive on the fact that they are "exclusive."

We who love the Father, Son and Holy Ghost are all members of one body and Jesus Christ, because he is the One sent by the Father to redeem our souls, is our Head, our Teacher. The 119th Psalm is perhaps the best book in the Bible to teach you the importance of the Word of God. It is a Psalm full of wisdom and verity. This single verse characterizes the content.

Psalm 119:160 (NKJ)
160 The entirety of Your word is truth, and every one of Your righteous judgments endures forever.

There is one body and One Teacher teaches that body of believers from one resource. There is no "new news." The Word is your light.

Psalm 119:102-105 (NKJ)
102 I have not departed from Your judgments, for You Yourself have taught me.
103 How sweet are Your words to my taste, sweeter than honey to my mouth!
104 Through Your precepts I get understanding; therefore I hate every false way.
105 Your word is a lamp to my feet and a light to my path.

CHAPTER 44

WHY HASN'T "FULFILLED PROPHECY" LED TO REPENTANCE?

Over and over again, God has manifested His power and control to man. Even when the absolute certainty of God's intervention is revealed, even though God was in the very act of exercising His authority and evil was being dealt with very, very harshly, they did not repent. Incredible but true. Listen to a perfect example of how hard the heart of man can be.

Exodus 9:13-35 (NKJ)
13 Then the LORD said to Moses, "Rise early in the morning and stand before Pharaoh, and say to him, 'Thus says the LORD God of the Hebrews: "Let My people go, that they may serve Me,
14 for at this time I will send all My plagues to your very heart, and on your servants and on your people, that you may know that there is none like Me in all the earth.
15 Now if I had stretched out My hand and struck you and your people with pestilence, then you would have been cut off from the earth.
16 But indeed for this purpose I have raised you up, that I may show My power in you, and that My name may be declared in all the earth.
17 As yet you exalt yourself against My people in that you will not let them go.
18 Behold, tomorrow about this time I will cause very heavy hail to rain down, such as has not been in Egypt since its founding until now.

19 Therefore send now and gather your livestock and all that you have in the field, for the hail shall come down on every man and every animal which is found in the field and is not brought home; and they shall die."'"
20 He who feared the word of the LORD among the servants of Pharaoh made his servants and his livestock flee to the houses.
21 But he who did not regard the word of the LORD left his servants and his livestock in the field.
22 Then the LORD said to Moses, "Stretch out your hand toward heaven, that there may be hail in all the land of Egypt– on man, on beast, and on every herb of the field, throughout the land of Egypt."
23 And Moses stretched out his rod toward heaven; and the LORD sent thunder and hail, and fire darted to the ground. And the LORD rained hail on the land of Egypt.
24 So there was hail, and fire mingled with the hail, so very heavy that there was none like it in all the land of Egypt since it became a nation.
25 And the hail struck throughout the whole land of Egypt, all that was in the field, both man and beast; and the hail struck every herb of the field and broke every tree of the field.
26 Only in the land of Goshen, where the children of Israel were, there was no hail.
27 And Pharaoh sent and called for Moses and Aaron, and said to them, "I have sinned this time. The LORD is righteous, and my people and I are wicked.
28 Entreat the LORD, that there may be no more mighty thundering and hail, for it is enough. I will let you go, and you shall stay no longer."
29 And Moses said to him, "As soon as I have gone out of the city, I will spread out my hands to the LORD; the thunder will cease, and there will be no more hail, that you may know that the earth is the LORD'S.
30 But as for you and your servants, I know that you will not yet fear the LORD God."
31 Now the flax and the barley were struck, for the barley was in the head and the flax was in bud.
32 But the wheat and the spelt were not struck, for they are late crops.
33 So Moses went out of the city from Pharaoh and spread out his hands to the LORD; then the thunder and the hail ceased, and the rain was not poured on the earth.

34 And when Pharaoh saw that the rain, the hail, and the thunder had ceased, he sinned yet more; and he hardened his heart, he and his servants.
35 So the heart of Pharaoh was hard; neither would he let the children of Israel go, as the LORD had spoken by Moses.

God revealed to Pharaoh his role. "For this purpose I have raised you up, that I may show My power in you, and that My name may be declared in all the earth." and then told him why he was going to be dealt with harshly. "As yet you exalt yourself."

This same Pharaoh who behaved as though he was entitled to power in and of his own hand, stated that he had changed his mind, after seeing God's power. And Pharaoh sent and called for Moses and Aaron, and said to them, "I have sinned this time. The LORD is righteous, and my people and I are wicked."

This confession was insincere, as you can read. Once the rain, hail and thunder ceased, "he sinned yet more; and he hardened his heart." Is this a pattern in the lives of those who exalt themselves? Are they humbled by circumstance only to "rise again?" Wouldn't you think that God's manifest power, demonstrated clearly to them would change their hearts? Has God revealed His power to you? If so, do you now acknowledge Him as your Lord? The fact that man acknowledges His power one moment and returns to sinful ways the next is a phenomenon that is hard to explain.

We usually attribute the failure to repent to wicked people, bent on self exaltation. But listen to Nehemiah as the stubbornness of Israel is discussed.

Nehemiah 9:6-36 (NKJ)
6 You alone are the LORD; you have made heaven, the heaven of heavens, with all their host, the earth and everything on it, the seas and all that is in them, and You preserve them all. The host of heaven worships You.
7 "You are the LORD God, who chose Abram, and brought him out of Ur of the Chaldeans, and gave him the name Abraham;

8 You found his heart faithful before You, and made a covenant with him to give the land of the Canaanites, the Hittites, the Amorites, the Perizzites, the Jebusites, and the Girgashites– to give it to his descendants. You have performed Your words, for You are righteous.

9 "You saw the affliction of our fathers in Egypt, and heard their cry by the Red Sea.

10 You showed signs and wonders against Pharaoh, against all his servants, and against all the people of his land. For You knew that they acted proudly against them. So You made a name for Yourself, as it is this day.

11 And You divided the sea before them, so that they went through the midst of the sea on the dry land; and their persecutors You threw into the deep, as a stone into the mighty waters.

12 Moreover You led them by day with a cloudy pillar, and by night with a pillar of fire, to give them light on the road which they should travel.

13 "You came down also on Mount Sinai, and spoke with them from heaven, and gave them just ordinances and true laws, good statutes and commandments.

14 You made known to them Your holy Sabbath, and commanded them precepts, statutes and laws, by the hand of Moses Your servant.

15 You gave them bread from heaven for their hunger, and brought them water out of the rock for their thirst, and told them to go in to possess the land which You had sworn to give them.

16 "But they and our fathers acted proudly, hardened their necks, and did not heed Your commandments.

17 They refused to obey, and they were not mindful of Your wonders that You did among them. But they hardened their necks, and in their rebellion they appointed a leader to return to their bondage. But You are God, ready to pardon, gracious and merciful, slow to anger, abundant in kindness, and did not forsake them.

18 "Even when they made a molded calf for themselves, and said, 'This is your god that brought you up out of Egypt,' and worked great provocations,

19 Yet in Your manifold mercies you did not forsake them in the wilderness. The pillar of the cloud did not depart from them by day, to

lead them on the road; nor the pillar of fire by night, to show them light, and the way they should go.

20 You also gave Your good Spirit to instruct them, and did not withhold Your manna from their mouth, and gave them water for their thirst.

21 Forty years You sustained them in the wilderness, they lacked nothing; their clothes did not wear out and their feet did not swell.

22 "Moreover You gave them kingdoms and nations, and divided them into districts. So they took possession of the land of Sihon, the land of the king of Heshbon, and the land of Og king of Bashan.

23 You also multiplied their children as the stars of heaven, and brought them into the land which You had told their fathers to go in and possess.

24 So the people went in and possessed the land; you subdued before them the inhabitants of the land, the Canaanites, and gave them into their hands, with their kings and the people of the land, that they might do with them as they wished.

25 And they took strong cities and a rich land, and possessed houses full of all goods, cisterns already dug, vineyards, olive groves, and fruit trees in abundance. So they ate and were filled and grew fat, and delighted themselves in Your great goodness.

26 "Nevertheless they were disobedient and rebelled against You, cast Your law behind their backs and killed Your prophets, who testified against them to turn them to Yourself; and they worked great provocations.

27 Therefore You delivered them into the hand of their enemies, who oppressed them; and in the time of their trouble, when they cried to You, you heard from heaven; and according to Your abundant mercies you gave them deliverers who saved them from the hand of their enemies.

28 "But after they had rest, they again did evil before You. Therefore You left them in the hand of their enemies, so that they had dominion over them; yet when they returned and cried out to You, you heard from heaven; and many times You delivered them according to Your mercies,

29 And testified against them, that You might bring them back to Your law. Yet they acted proudly, and did not heed Your commandments, but sinned against Your judgments, 'Which if a man does, he shall live by them.' And they shrugged their shoulders, Stiffened their necks, and would not hear.

30 Yet for many years You had patience with them, and testified against them by Your Spirit in Your prophets. Yet they would not listen; therefore You gave them into the hand of the peoples of the lands.
31 Nevertheless in Your great mercy you did not utterly consume them nor forsake them; for You are God, gracious and merciful.
32 "Now therefore, our God, the great, the mighty, and awesome God, who keeps covenant and mercy: do not let all the trouble seem small before You that has come upon us, our kings and our princes, our priests and our prophets, our fathers and on all Your people, from the days of the kings of Assyria until this day.
33 However You are just in all that has befallen us; for You have dealt faithfully, but we have done wickedly.
34 Neither our kings nor our princes, our priests nor our fathers, have kept Your law, nor heeded Your commandments and Your testimonies, with which You testified against them.
35 For they have not served You in their kingdom, or in the many good things that You gave them, or in the large and rich land which You set before them; nor did they turn from their wicked works.
36 "Here we are, servants today! And the land that You gave to our fathers, to eat its fruit and its bounty, here we are, servants in it!

First we see God leading and protecting, over and over again, only to see Israel do things like build a golden calf that they could worship. No people on earth have seen the affirmation and leading of God like Israel. Yet, no people, given as much attention and affirmation as Israel, has continued to struggle with obedience, in the way that Israel has struggled. Read the last 5 verses above and ask yourself if you see any truth in those verses.

When the end of this world comes, as we know it, there will be seven bowls of God's wrath poured out upon the earth (Revelation, chapter 16). The bowls of wrath will produce phenomenon much like the judgments against Pharaoh. Listen to the description of the seventh bowl of wrath.

Revelation 16:15-21 (NKJ)
15 "Behold, I am coming as a thief. Blessed is he who watches, and keeps his garments, lest he walk naked and they see his shame."

16 And they gathered them together to the place called in Hebrew, Armageddon.
17 Then the seventh angel poured out his bowl into the air, and a loud voice came out of the temple of heaven, from the throne, saying, "It is done!"
18 And there were noises and thunderings and lightnings; and there was a great earthquake, such a mighty and great earthquake as had not occurred since men were on the earth.
19 Now the great city was divided into three parts, and the cities of the nations fell. And great Babylon was remembered before God, to give her the cup of the wine of the fierceness of His wrath.
20 Then every island fled away, and the mountains were not found.
21 And great hail from heaven fell upon men, each hailstone about the weight of a talent. Men blasphemed God because of the plague of the hail, since that plague was exceedingly great.

Even then, men blasphemed God, acknowledging His power but not accessing his Grace or His forgiveness. What does it take to have a person repent? Surely it is not "more evidence" of God's power. One might ask, how could anyone choose to suffer and die when they could choose life? Listen.

Deuteronomy 30:19-20 (NKJ)
19 "I call heaven and earth as witnesses today against you, that I have set before you life and death, blessing and cursing; therefore choose life, that both you and your descendants may live;
20 "that you may love the LORD your God, that you may obey His voice, and that you may cling to Him, for He is your life and the length of your days; and that you may dwell in the land which the LORD swore to your fathers, to Abraham, Isaac, and Jacob, to give them."

It is God's will that you choose life. You need an "Enabler," a power beyond your flesh to deliver you from the temptations of the flesh and the power of sin. That "Enabler" is the Spirit of God, in you. Go to the chapter "The Holy Spirit" to more fully grasp how to have victory over sin, by the power of God, but understand that when you fully grasp the meaning of the fulfilled promise of a "Deliverer," you are going to need to repent in order to be redeemed. The Messiah said the following words:

John 12:31-43 (NKJ)
31 "Now is the judgment of this world; now the ruler of this world will be cast out.
32 "And I, if I am lifted up from the earth, will draw all peoples to Myself."
33 This He said, signifying by what death He would die.
34 The people answered Him, "We have heard from the law that the Christ remains forever; and how can You say, 'The Son of Man must be lifted up'? Who is this Son of Man?"
35 Then Jesus said to them, "A little while longer the light is with you. Walk while you have the light, lest darkness overtake you; he who walks in darkness does not know where he is going.
36 "While you have the light, believe in the light, that you may become sons of light." These things Jesus spoke, and departed, and was hidden from them.
37 But although He had done so many signs before them, they did not believe in Him,
38 that the word of Isaiah the prophet might be fulfilled, which he spoke: "Lord, who has believed our report? And to whom has the arm of the Lord been revealed?"
39 Therefore they could not believe, because Isaiah said again:
40 "He has blinded their eyes and hardened their hearts, lest they should see with their eyes, lest they should understand with their hearts and turn, so that I should heal them."
41 These things Isaiah said when he saw His glory and spoke of Him.
42 Nevertheless even among the rulers many believed in Him, but because of the Pharisees they did not confess Him, lest they should be put out of the synagogue;
43 for they loved the praise of men more than the praise of God.

Re-read the last two verses and understand that stepping out from tradition to a personal relationship with your Savior will, as a Jew, place you at odds with many persons. The estimate of the quality of your life is not dependent on the praise of men. There are Jews for Jesus who are Torah observant and who find no contradiction in their decision. There are Jews for Judaism who say the Messiah has not come and that Jesus was not the Christ. Someone is wrong. You decide, based on the evidence. Remember, "evidence" can be ignored and prophecy fulfilled does not mean your life will be changed because of that evidence. The Messiah anticipated your need to understand how difficult it would be for you to follow Him. Listen.

Matthew 10:26-39 (NKJ)
26 "… For there is nothing covered that will not be revealed, and hidden that will not be known.
27 "Whatever I tell you in the dark, speak in the light; and what you hear in the ear, preach on the housetops.
28 "And do not fear those who kill the body but cannot kill the soul. But rather fear Him who is able to destroy both soul and body in hell.
29 "Are not two sparrows sold for a copper coin? And not one of them falls to the ground apart from your Father's will.
30 "But the very hairs of your head are all numbered.
31 "Do not fear therefore; you are of more value than many sparrows.
32 "Therefore whoever confesses Me before men, him I will also confess before My Father who is in heaven.
33 "But whoever denies Me before men, him I will also deny before My Father who is in heaven.
34 "Do not think that I came to bring peace on earth. I did not come to bring peace but a sword.
35 "For I have come to 'set a man against his father, a daughter against her mother, and a daughter-in-law against her mother-in-law';
36 "and 'a man's enemies will be those of his own household.'
37 "He who loves father or mother more than Me is not worthy of Me. And he who loves son or daughter more than Me is not worthy of Me.
38 "And he who does not take his cross and follow after Me is not worthy of Me.
39 "He who finds his life will lose it, and he who loses his life for My sake will find it.

The power to obey God faithfully is beyond the reach of most men. We try, and we find examples such as Abraham where his faith was counted unto him as righteousness, but for the most part, our faith is too weak, the power of the flesh, too strong. The power to "not sin" is beyond the reach of every man. Again, listen to the words of Jesus Christ regarding why He came. He came to empower you, by the gift of the Holy Spirit. Listen.

Luke 24:44-47 (NKJ)
44 Then He said to them, "These are the words which I spoke to you while I was still with you, that all things must be fulfilled which were written in the Law of Moses and the Prophets and the Psalms concerning Me."
45 And He opened their understanding, that they might comprehend the Scriptures.
46 Then He said to them, "Thus it is written, and thus it was necessary for the Christ to suffer and to rise from the dead the third day,
47 "and that repentance and remission of sins should be preached in His name to all nations, beginning at Jerusalem.

Jesus came that His Name might lead to your repentance and mine and that His shed blood might provide for the remission of your sins and mine. And where did Jesus say that repentance and remission of sins should first be preached? "Beginning at Jerusalem." Listen to this quotation of "empowerment."

John 14:12-28 (NKJ)
12 "Most assuredly, I say to you, he who believes in Me, the works that I do he will do also; and greater works than these he will do, because I go to My Father.
13 "And whatever you ask in My name, that I will do, that the Father may be glorified in the Son.
14 "If you ask anything in My name, I will do it.
15 "If you love Me, keep My commandments.
16 "And I will pray the Father, and He will give you another Helper, that He may abide with you forever–
17 "the Spirit of truth, whom the world cannot receive, because it neither sees Him nor knows Him; but you know Him, for He dwells with you and will be in you.
18 "I will not leave you orphans; I will come to you.

19 "A little while longer and the world will see Me no more, but you will see Me. Because I live, you will live also.

20 "At that day you will know that I am in My Father, and you in Me, and I in you.

21 "He who has My commandments and keeps them, it is he who loves Me. And he who loves Me will be loved by My Father, and I will love him and manifest Myself to him."

22 Judas (not Iscariot) said to Him, "Lord, how is it that You will manifest Yourself to us, and not to the world?"

23 Jesus answered and said to him, "If anyone loves Me, he will keep My word; and My Father will love him, and We will come to him and make Our home with him.

24 "He who does not love Me does not keep My words; and the word which you hear is not Mine but the Father's who sent Me.

25 "These things I have spoken to you while being present with you.

26 "But the Helper, the Holy Spirit, whom the Father will send in My name, He will teach you all things, and bring to your remembrance all things that I said to you.

27 "Peace I leave with you, My peace I give to you; not as the world gives do I give to you. Let not your heart be troubled, neither let it be afraid.

28 "You have heard Me say to you, 'I am going away and coming back to you.' If you loved Me, you would rejoice because I said, 'I am going to the Father,' for My Father is greater than I.

Do not underestimate the power and purpose of the gift of the Holy Spirit. Our personal unworthiness prevents us from easily moving to the view that we can have the "Mind of Christ" in us or that we are referred to as priests and as saints, but that is exactly what the Word says. This transformation is a miracle, made possible by God. We do not escape the liability of the flesh as long as we are housed in this body, but God knows our weaknesses and temptations. Memorize this verse. It is the absolute truth.

1 Corinthians 10:13 (NKJ)
13 No temptation has overtaken you except such as is common to man; but God is faithful, who will not allow you to be tempted beyond what you are able, but with the temptation will also make the way of escape, that you may be able to bear it.

The reason that prophecy fulfilled has not led to repentance is that "evidence" only convicts if the person viewing that evidence knows they are guilty and then chooses to repent. It is always about "choice," the exercise of personal volition. Choose to escape from temptation and sin, from the power of Satan in your life. Reread the verse above and claim it as you face every decision.

CHAPTER 45

THE FRUIT OF RIGHTEOUSNESS—A FIG TREE DOES NOT GIVE OFF OLIVES!

It is clear that the millennium is the promised restoration of the Kingdom, for the faithful remnant of Israel, and only God knows how great a remnant that will be. You may, up to now, have well pleased God and exercised the faith of Abraham, Isaac and Joseph or you may feel you are uncertain of your position with God. No man can judge the heart of another man. The Holy Scriptures teach, however, that you can know a man by his fruits. You can also know your own heart by examining your own "fruit." Listen to God's Word.

Matthew 7:7-23 (NKJ)
7 "Ask, and it will be given to you; seek, and you will find; knock, and it will be opened to you.
8 "For everyone who asks receives, and he who seeks finds, and to him who knocks it will be opened.
9 "Or what man is there among you who, if his son asks for bread, will give him a stone?
10 "Or if he asks for a fish, will he give him a serpent?
11 "If you then, being evil, know how to give good gifts to your children, how much more will your Father who is in heaven give good things to those who ask Him!
12 "Therefore, whatever you want men to do to you, do also to them, for this is the Law and the Prophets.

13 "Enter by the narrow gate; for wide is the gate and broad is the way that leads to destruction, and there are many who go in by it.
14 "Because narrow is the gate and difficult is the way which leads to life, and there are few who find it.
15 "Beware of false prophets, who come to you in sheep's clothing, but inwardly they are ravenous wolves.
16 "You will know them by their fruits. Do men gather grapes from thornbushes or figs from thistles?
17 "Even so, every good tree bears good fruit, but a bad tree bears bad fruit.
18 "A good tree cannot bear bad fruit, nor can a bad tree bear good fruit.
19 "Every tree that does not bear good fruit is cut down and thrown into the fire.
20 "Therefore by their fruits you will know them.
21 "Not everyone who says to Me, 'Lord, Lord,' shall enter the kingdom of heaven, but he who does the will of My Father in heaven.
22 "Many will say to Me in that day, 'Lord, Lord, have we not prophesied in Your name, cast out demons in Your name, and done many wonders in Your name?'
23 "And then I will declare to them, 'I never knew you; depart from Me, you who practice lawlessness!'

James 3:11-12 (NKJ)
11 Does a spring send forth fresh water and bitter from the same opening?
12 Can a fig tree, my brethren, bear olives, or a grapevine bear figs? Thus no spring can yield both salt water and fresh.

How do you and I feel when we find ourselves bearing the "wrong" kind of fruit? If we say that we love God, yet we are saying and doing things that make us appear to be totally out of sync with God's expectations of us, what has happened? I believe the answer is that we have chosen, at least for the moment, to revert to the power of the flesh. Our inconsistency reminds us of our situation. We are "in the flesh," yet wish to be filled with the Holy Spirit. It is a dilemma that has only one solution. We must "die to the flesh" so that God's Spirit can live in us. We must crucify the flesh, constantly, so that the Spirit may fill us. We must not yield to the temptation to let our minds and our mouths serve Satan.

Listen to what the Holy Scriptures have to say about the fruit one should bear if you say that you love God.

Proverbs 11:30-31 (NKJ)
30 The fruit of the righteous is a tree of life, and he who wins souls is wise.
31 If the righteous will be recompensed on the earth, how much more the ungodly and the sinner.

Proverbs 8:17-21 (NKJ)
17 I love those who love me, and those who seek me diligently will find me.
18 Riches and honor are with me, enduring riches and righteousness.
19 My fruit is better than gold, yes, than fine gold, and my revenue than choice silver.
20 I traverse the way of righteousness, in the midst of the paths of justice,
21 That I may cause those who love me to inherit wealth, that I may fill their treasuries.

Proverbs 12:12-15 (NKJ)
12 The wicked covet the catch of evil men, but the root of the righteous yields fruit.
13 The wicked is ensnared by the transgression of his lips, but the righteous will come through trouble.
14 A man will be satisfied with good by the fruit of his mouth, and the recompense of a man's hands will be rendered to him.
15 The way of a fool is right in his own eyes, but he who heeds counsel is wise.

Proverbs 18:20-21 (NKJ)
20 A man's stomach shall be satisfied from the fruit of his mouth, from the produce of his lips he shall be filled.
21 Death and life are in the power of the tongue, and those who love it will eat its fruit.

Isaiah 57:19-21 (NKJ)
19 "I create the fruit of the lips: peace, peace to him who is far off and to him who is near," says the LORD, "And I will heal him."
20 But the wicked are like the troubled sea, when it cannot rest, whose waters cast up mire and dirt.
21 "There is no peace," says my God, "for the wicked."

Jeremiah 17:7-10 (NKJ)
7 "Blessed is the man who trusts in the LORD, and whose hope is the LORD.
8 For he shall be like a tree planted by the waters, which spreads out its roots by the river, and will not fear when heat comes; but its leaf will be green, and will not be anxious in the year of drought, nor will cease from yielding fruit.
9 "The heart is deceitful above all things, and desperately wicked; who can know it?
10 I, the LORD, search the heart, I test the mind, even to give every man according to his ways, according to the fruit of his doings."

Jeremiah 32:17-19 (NKJ)
17 'Ah, Lord GOD! Behold, You have made the heavens and the earth by Your great power and outstretched arm. There is nothing too hard for You.
18 'You show lovingkindness to thousands, and repay the iniquity of the fathers into the bosom of their children after them– the Great, the Mighty God, whose name is the LORD of hosts.
19 'You are great in counsel and mighty in work, for your eyes are open to all the ways of the sons of men, to give everyone according to his ways and according to the fruit of his doings.

Galatians 5:19-26 (NKJ)
19 Now the works of the flesh are evident, which are: adultery, fornication, uncleanness, lewdness,
20 idolatry, sorcery, hatred, contentions, jealousies, outbursts of wrath, selfish ambitions, dissensions, heresies,

21 envy, murders, drunkenness, revelries, and the like; of which I tell you beforehand, just as I also told you in time past, that those who practice such things will not inherit the kingdom of God.

22 But the fruit of the Spirit is love, joy, peace, longsuffering, kindness, goodness, faithfulness,

23 gentleness, self-control. Against such there is no law.

24 And those who are Christ's have crucified the flesh with its passions and desires.

25 If we live in the Spirit, let us also walk in the Spirit.

26 Let us not become conceited, provoking one another, envying one another.

Psalm 92:12-15 (NKJ)

12 The righteous shall flourish like a palm tree, He shall grow like a cedar in Lebanon.

13 Those who are planted in the house of the LORD Shall flourish in the courts of our God.

14 They shall still bear fruit in old age; They shall be fresh and flourishing,

15 To declare that the LORD is upright; He is my rock, and there is no unrighteousness in Him.

One can ask, moment by moment, what sort of fruit is my life bearing. Every time you find yourself angry, depressed, anxious, impatient, unkind and every other sort of ill mood, just think about the fruit you are bearing. You are sending the wrong signal to yourself and to others if you are allowing yourself to yield bad fruit, fruit that makes Satan smile at your circumstance. Failure of that sort should motivate you to claim the power of the Holy Spirit in you so that you can have victory over sin. Just focus on verse 15 of Psalm 92 above and then enjoy the reality of Galatians 5:22-23.

CHAPTER 46

REPENT—SERVE THE LORD—NOT SATAN

Your diligence in pursuit of the Lord should be like that of a father who can not take his eyes off his newly born child. That is true, unconditional love. If you expect to spend eternity with God, and I pray that you do, how can you reasonably not seek Him, right now?

A loving Father is saying to His children, get your priorities straight. Time is running out. Prophecy is being fulfilled before your very eyes. Prepare yourself to enter into My presence and in the interval, serve Me, worship Me, and obey Me. Keep the commandments, not out of fear, which, given the consequences of judgment would be a reasonable thing to do, but keep the commandments out of love and obey in His strength, not yours.

Choose this day, this moment, who you will serve. Listen.

Deuteronomy 4:39-40 (NKJ)
39 "Therefore know this day, and consider it in your heart, that the LORD Himself is God in heaven above and on the earth beneath; there is no other.
40 "You shall therefore keep His statutes and His commandments which I command you today, that it may go well with you and with your children after you, and that you may prolong your days in the land which the LORD your God is giving you for all time."

God is calling Israel, the nation, and you the Jew, "this day"!

Deuteronomy 26:15-19 (NKJ)
15 'Look down from Your holy habitation, from heaven, and bless Your people Israel and the land which You have given us, just as You swore to our fathers, "a land flowing with milk and honey."'
16 "This day the LORD your God commands you to observe these statutes and judgments; therefore you shall be careful to observe them with all your heart and with all your soul.
17 "Today you have proclaimed the LORD to be your God, and that you will walk in His ways and keep His statutes, His commandments, and His judgments, and that you will obey His voice.
18 "Also today the LORD has proclaimed you to be His special people, just as He has promised you, that you should keep all His commandments,
19 "and that He will set you high above all nations which He has made, in praise, in name, and in honor, and that you may be a holy people to the LORD your God, just as He has spoken."

I have quoted some of these next verses before in this presentation, but I suggest you read them, again and again, until the truth sinks in. Pray for discernment.

Deuteronomy 30:1-20
1 "Now it shall come to pass, when all these things come upon you, the blessing and the curse which I have set before you, and you call them to mind among all the nations where the LORD your God drives you,
2 "and you return to the LORD your God and obey His voice, according to all that I command you today, you and your children, with all your heart and with all your soul,
3 "that the LORD your God will bring you back from captivity, and have compassion on you, and gather you again from all the nations where the LORD your God has scattered you.
4 "If any of you are driven out to the farthest parts under heaven, from there the LORD your God will gather you, and from there He will bring you.
5 "Then the LORD your God will bring you to the land which your fathers possessed, and you shall possess it. He will prosper you and multiply you more than your fathers

6 "And the LORD your God will circumcise your heart and the heart of your descendants, to love the LORD your God with all your heart and with all your soul, that you may live.
7 "Also the LORD your God will put all these curses on your enemies and on those who hate you, who persecuted you.
8 "And you will again obey the voice of the LORD and do all His commandments which I command you today.
9 "The LORD your God will make you abound in all the work of your hand, in the fruit of your body, in the increase of your livestock, and in the produce of your land for good. For the LORD will again rejoice over you for good as He rejoiced over your fathers,
10 "if you obey the voice of the LORD your God, to keep His commandments and His statutes which are written in this Book of the Law, and if you turn to the LORD your God with all your heart and with all your soul.
11 "For this commandment which I command you today, it is not too mysterious for you, nor is it far off.
12 "It is not in heaven, that you should say, 'Who will ascend into heaven for us and bring it to us, that we may hear it and do it?'
13 "Nor is it beyond the sea, that you should say, 'Who will go over the sea for us and bring it to us, that we may hear it and do it?'
14 "But the word is very near you, in your mouth and in your heart, that you may do it.
15 "See, I have set before you today life and good, death and evil,
16 "in that I command you today to love the LORD your God, to walk in His ways, and to keep His commandments, His statutes, and His judgments, that you may live and multiply; and the LORD your God will bless you in the land which you go to possess.
17 "But if your heart turns away so that you do not hear, and are drawn away, and worship other gods and serve them,
18 "I announce to you today that you shall surely perish; you shall not prolong your days in the land which you cross over the Jordan to go in and possess.
19 "I call heaven and earth as witnesses today against you, that I have set before you life and death, blessing and cursing; therefore choose life, that both you and your descendants may live;

20 "that you may love the LORD your God, that you may obey His voice, and that you may cling to Him, for He is your life and the length of your days; and that you may dwell in the land which the LORD swore to your fathers, to Abraham, Isaac, and Jacob, to give them." (NKJ)

Repent is a theme throughout the Bible. Why? I believe that repentance is the whole issue. You can not serve the Lord and serve Satan, simultaneously. To repent is to decide that the war for your spirit is over. It is, interestingly, given God's power, your decision. You could be compelled to obey but as any father knows, that sort of obedience makes your son as a puppet, not a man. God teaches us over and over that we must "choose."

Jeremiah 25:5-6 (NKJ)
5 "They said, 'Repent now everyone of his evil way and his evil doings, and dwell in the land that the LORD has given to you and your fathers forever and ever.
6 'Do not go after other gods to serve them and worship them, and do not provoke Me to anger with the works of your hands; and I will not harm you.'

Ezekiel 14:6-8 (NKJ)
6 "Therefore say to the house of Israel, 'Thus says the Lord GOD: "Repent, turn away from your idols, and turn your faces away from all your abominations.
7 "For anyone of the house of Israel, or of the strangers who dwell in Israel, who separates himself from Me and sets up his idols in his heart and puts before him what causes him to stumble into iniquity, then comes to a prophet to inquire of him concerning Me, I the LORD will answer him by Myself.
8 "I will set My face against that man and make him a sign and a proverb, and I will cut him off from the midst of My people. Then you shall know that I am the LORD.

Repent literally means to "turn," to turn from what you are, in this case, to what you could be. Ezekiel says above that anyone who "sets up his idols in his heart and puts before him what causes him to stumble into iniquity," and then seeks the advice of a prophet concerning the Lord, you will receive an answer from God Himself.

Do you have any "idols in your heart?" What is an idol except anything that you revere more than you revere God? If you could "chronicle every thought and action for one day," in what proportion of that day would God be present? Said differently, if God was "auditing your every thought and action," what would the Auditor have seen this day? Read the following Psalm carefully. This is how well God knows you!

Psalm 139:1-18 (NKJ)
1 O LORD, You have searched me and known me.
2 You know my sitting down and my rising up; you understand my thought afar off.
3 You comprehend my path and my lying down, and are acquainted with all my ways.
4 For there is not a word on my tongue, but behold, O LORD, You know it altogether.
5 You have hedged me behind and before, and laid Your hand upon me.
6 Such knowledge is too wonderful for me; it is high, I cannot attain it.
7 Where can I go from Your Spirit? Or where can I flee from Your presence?
8 If I ascend into heaven, You are there; if I make my bed in hell, behold, You are there.
9 If I take the wings of the morning, and dwell in the uttermost parts of the sea,
10 Even there Your hand shall lead me, and Your right hand shall hold me.
11 If I say, "Surely the darkness shall fall on me," even the night shall be light about me;
12 Indeed, the darkness shall not hide from You, but the night shines as the day; the darkness and the light are both alike to You.
13 For You formed my inward parts; you covered me in my mother's womb.
14 I will praise You, for I am fearfully and wonderfully made; marvelous are Your works, and that my soul knows very well.

15 My frame was not hidden from You, when I was made in secret, and skillfully wrought in the lowest parts of the earth.
16 Your eyes saw my substance, being yet unformed. And in Your book they all were written, the days fashioned for me, when as yet there were none of them.
17 How precious also are Your thoughts to me, O God! How great is the sum of them!
18 If I should count them, they would be more in number than the sand; when I awake, I am still with You.

Psalm 56:8 (NKJ)
8 You number my wanderings; put my tears into Your bottle; are they not in Your book?

The following verses have always intrigued me. They place in perspective how omnipresent our God really is. How often do you think to yourself, "God is present, the Holy Spirit is present, right this second?"

I have stated earlier that the "breeze," when it moves a tree or when you feel its gentle healing, comes from the root word "pneuma." Pneuma is the root word for Holy Spirit. Never let the breeze move around you again without acknowledging the Holy Spirit's presence. The hairs of your head are numbered and not one falls apart from His knowledge. And sometimes you think God doesn't care, He isn't present, and He isn't listening. That is wrong, very wrong thinking. Understand and believe the following verses. If you fail to repent, you fail, according to the scriptures, to enter into God's presence, peace and eternity.

Matthew 10:29-30 (NKJ)
29 "Are not two sparrows sold for a copper coin? And not one of them falls to the ground apart from your Father's will.
30 "But the very hairs of your head are all numbered.

Proverbs 15:3 (NKJ)
3 The eyes of the LORD are in every place, keeping watch on the evil and the good.

Then God tells us that what He sees, He will judge. Repentance is the key to reform.

Ezekiel 18:30-32 (NKJ)
30 "Therefore I will judge you, O house of Israel, every one according to his ways," says the Lord GOD. "Repent, and turn from all your transgressions, so that iniquity will not be your ruin.
31 "Cast away from you all the transgressions which you have committed, and get yourselves a new heart and a new spirit. For why should you die, O house of Israel?
32 "For I have no pleasure in the death of one who dies," says the Lord GOD. "Therefore turn and live!"

2 Corinthians 5:10 (NKJ)
10 For we must all appear before the judgment seat of Christ, that each one may receive the things done in the body, according to what he has done, whether good or bad.

Acts 2:38-39 (NKJ)
38 ...Peter said to them, "Repent, and let every one of you be baptized in the name of Jesus Christ for the remission of sins; and you shall receive the gift of the Holy Spirit.
39 "For the promise is to you and to your children, and to all who are afar off, as many as the Lord our God will call."

Acts 8:22-23 (NKJ)
22 "Repent therefore of this your wickedness, and pray God if perhaps the thought of your heart may be forgiven you.
23 "For I see that you are poisoned by bitterness and bound by iniquity."

Isaiah 57:15-19(NKJ)
15 For thus says the High and Lofty One who inhabits eternity, whose name is Holy: "I dwell in the high and holy place, with him who has a contrite and humble spirit, to revive the spirit of the humble, and to revive the heart of the contrite ones.
16 For I will not contend forever, nor will I always be angry; for the spirit would fail before Me, and the souls which I have made.

**17 For the iniquity of his covetousness I was angry and struck him; I hid and was angry, and he went on backsliding in the way of his heart.
18 I have seen his ways, and will heal him; I will also lead him, and restore comforts to him and to his mourners.
19 "I create the fruit of the lips: peace, peace to him who is far off and to him who is near," Says the Lord. "And I will heal him."**

If you read only this topic, it is enough. It is the entire message. Nothing else matters. If you decide to respond to God's love, if you decide that you have erred greatly up to this moment, then with a humble and contrite heart, stop reading and start praying.

Ask God to forgive you of every sin you have ever committed, by acknowledging Jesus as your personal "Atoner," the Redeemer, and the One who died for your sins. Ask for the total cleansing of your soul. Ask for a new heart, one free from the shackles of your past, one committed to spending whatever days you have left, seeking and serving your Lord.

Ask to be filled, constantly, with the presence and power of the Holy Spirit, with that refreshing, clean breeze of God that surrounds you, now and forever. Then go, as a person dying of thirst, to His Holy Word. Listen to what God wants to teach you. Never intentionally sin again.

And as you commit yourself to His Hands, understand this. Satan will have lost a lover. Satan is not a good loser. As long as you were his slave (I doubt you ever thought of it that way), he could ignore you. You were right where he wanted you, so why waste any energy on you. His goal is to destroy the faith of those who dwell in the security of the Father, the Son and the Holy Spirit.

If you decide to repent, to be born again, you are changing teams. You will have become Satan's enemy and he has no other more important agenda than to try to destroy your new found faith. You can not fight Satan. His power exceeds anything you can intellectually grasp. He is the prince and the ruler of this earth, this temporary testing ground. Only by the power and the presence of the Holy Spirit in you can you resist the temptation he is going to deliver to your doorstep.

How can I speak with such certainty? First, I have been there and so has every Christian. Listen to these verses.

Matthew 12:43-45 (NKJ)
43 "When an unclean spirit goes out of a man, he goes through dry places, seeking rest, and finds none.
44 "Then he says, 'I will return to my house from which I came.' And when he comes, he finds it empty, swept, and put in order.
45 "Then he goes and takes with him seven other spirits more wicked than himself, and they enter and dwell there; and the last state of that man is worse than the first. So shall it also be with this wicked generation."

I say this to you with all certainty. Satan wants to own you and your heart. Listen to God's Word.

Luke 22:31 (NKJ)
31 And the Lord said, "Simon, Simon! Indeed, Satan has asked for you, that he may sift you as wheat.

1 Peter 5:8-9 (NKJ)
8 Be sober, be vigilant; because your adversary the devil walks about like a roaring lion, seeking whom he may devour.
9 Resist him, steadfast in the faith, knowing that the same sufferings are experienced by your brotherhood in the world.

He will stop at nothing to bring you down. I believe that Satan's greatest moments of joy are when he publicly defeats a strong Christian, making that Christian look and feel like a complete idiot. How could a person who has been redeemed somehow fall back into the evil hand of Satan and serve him? The answer is that we who are saved misestimate the power of the flesh, the power of Satan. He can be rebuked, but neither by you nor I. Only the power of the Holy Spirit is greater than the power of Satan. Never vow that you can handle any temptation Satan can deliver. You simply can not overcome his power on your own. Flee, literally, from his lure sensing that the entrapment he offers is just that. It is a trap and it is one that can ruin your life, your marriage, your relationships and perhaps, short of acceptable repentance, your eternity.

The Bible has a classic verse that describes this phenomenon in a very visual way. The verse I refer to comes at the end of a very telling lesson by Peter. You know people who have experienced this kind of temptation and who have misled others in the process. Listen.

2 Peter 2:1-22 (NKJ)
1 But there were also false prophets among the people, even as there will be false teachers among you, who will secretly bring in destructive heresies, even denying the Lord who bought them, and bring on themselves swift destruction.
2 And many will follow their destructive ways, because of whom the way of truth will be blasphemed.
3 By covetousness they will exploit you with deceptive words; for a long time their judgment has not been idle, and their destruction does not slumber.
4 For if God did not spare the angels who sinned, but cast them down to hell and delivered them into chains of darkness, to be reserved for judgment;
5 and did not spare the ancient world, but saved Noah, one of eight people, a preacher of righteousness, bringing in the flood on the world of the ungodly;
6 and turning the cities of Sodom and Gomorrah into ashes, condemned them to destruction, making them an example to those who afterward would live ungodly;
7 and delivered righteous Lot, who was oppressed by the filthy conduct of the wicked
8 (for that righteous man, dwelling among them, tormented his righteous soul from day to day by seeing and hearing their lawless deeds)–
9 then the Lord knows how to deliver the godly out of temptations and to reserve the unjust under punishment for the day of judgment,
10 and especially those who walk according to the flesh in the lust of uncleanness and despise authority. They are presumptuous, self-willed. They are not afraid to speak evil of dignitaries,

11 whereas angels, who are greater in power and might, do not bring a reviling accusation against them before the Lord.
12 But these, like natural brute beasts made to be caught and destroyed, speak evil of the things they do not understand, and will utterly perish in their own corruption,
13 and will receive the wages of unrighteousness, as those who count it pleasure to carouse in the daytime. They are spots and blemishes, carousing in their own deceptions while they feast with you,
14 having eyes full of adultery and that cannot cease from sin, beguiling unstable souls. They have a heart trained in covetous practices, and are accursed children.
15 They have forsaken the right way and gone astray, following the way of Balaam the son of Beor, who loved the wages of unrighteousness;
16 but he was rebuked for his iniquity: a dumb donkey speaking with a man's voice restrained the madness of the prophet.
17 These are wells without water, clouds carried by a tempest, for whom is reserved the blackness of darkness forever.
18 For when they speak great swelling words of emptiness, they allure through the lusts of the flesh, through lewdness, the ones who have actually escaped from those who live in error.
19 While they promise them liberty, they themselves are slaves of corruption; for by whom a person is overcome, by him also he is brought into bondage.
20 For if, after they have escaped the pollutions of the world through the knowledge of the Lord and Savior Jesus Christ, they are again entangled in them and overcome, the latter end is worse for them than the beginning.
21 For it would have been better for them not to have known the way of righteousness, than having known it, to turn from the holy commandment delivered to them.
22 But it has happened to them according to the true proverb: "A dog returns to his own vomit," and, "a sow, having washed, to her wallowing in the mire."

A person reverting to the service of Satan is as one eating his vomit. If that doesn't clarify the situation for you, little else will! Sin may look very attractive. See it for what it is. A trap set for you by the expert, one who takes pleasure in your defeat.

One of the reasons you must study those verses very carefully is that it will help you understand how powerful the lure of sin is. Even some of the strongest believers have fallen victim to the power of Satan. Thank God for the Holy Spirit, the power and presence of Christ in you as you reside in this cauldron of sin. Is it any wonder that the earth and all the things in it will pass away? It is Satan's domain, except at the beginning, Eden, and at the end, Eden restored. Listen to Ezekiel's teaching on this matter:

Ezekiel 36:33-36 (NKJ)
33 'Thus says the Lord GOD: "On the day that I cleanse you from all your iniquities, I will also enable you to dwell in the cities, and the ruins shall be rebuilt.
34 "The desolate land shall be tilled instead of lying desolate in the sight of all who pass by.
35 "So they will say, 'This land that was desolate has become like the garden of Eden; and the wasted, desolate, and ruined cities are now fortified and inhabited.'
36 "Then the nations which are left all around you shall know that I, the LORD, have rebuilt the ruined places and planted what was desolate. I, the LORD, have spoken it, and I will do it."

Then Isaiah further clarifies what is coming:

Isaiah 51:3 (NKJ)
3 For the LORD will comfort Zion, he will comfort all her waste places; he will make her wilderness like Eden, and her desert like the garden of the LORD; joy and gladness will be found in it, thanksgiving and the voice of melody.

I will offer a word of strong advice regarding Satan. Do not spend time studying and investigating all the ways in which he manifests himself in cults and in ideologies. Satan is not a subject to be "understood thoroughly" but instead, flee, literally from any sign of his presence. Listen to several quotes that make this point perfectly.

Genesis 39:6-12 (NKJ)
6 …And Joseph was handsome in form and appearance.
7 And it came to pass … that his master's wife cast longing eyes on Joseph, and she said, "Lie with me."
8 But he refused and said to his master's wife, "Look, my master does not know what is with me in the house, and he has committed all that he has to my hand.
9 "There is no one greater in this house than I, nor has he kept back anything from me but you, because you are his wife. How then can I do this great wickedness, and sin against God?"
10 So it was, as she spoke to Joseph day by day, that he did not heed her, to lie with her or to be with her.
11 But it happened about this time, when Joseph went into the house to do his work, and none of the men of the house was inside,
12 that she caught him by his garment, saying, "Lie with me." But he left his garment in her hand, and fled and ran outside.

1 Corinthians 6:15-20 (NKJ)
15 Do you not know that your bodies are members of Christ? Shall I then take the members of Christ and make them members of a harlot? Certainly not!
16 Or do you not know that he who is joined to a harlot is one body with her? For "the two," He says, "shall become one flesh."
17 But he who is joined to the Lord is one spirit with Him.
18 Flee sexual immorality. Every sin that a man does is outside the body, but he who commits sexual immorality sins against his own body.
19 Or do you not know that your body is the temple of the Holy Spirit who is in you, whom you have from God, and you are not your own?
20 For you were bought at a price; therefore glorify God in your body and in your spirit, which are God's.

1 Timothy 6:9-14 (NKJ)
9 But those who desire to be rich fall into temptation and a snare, and into many foolish and harmful lusts which drown men in destruction and perdition.

10 For the love of money is a root of all kinds of evil, for which some have strayed from the faith in their greediness, and pierced themselves through with many sorrows.
11 But you, O man of God, flee these things and pursue righteousness, godliness, faith, love, patience, gentleness.
12 Fight the good fight of faith, lay hold on eternal life, to which you were also called and have confessed the good confession in the presence of many witnesses.
13 I urge you in the sight of God who gives life to all things, and before Christ Jesus who witnessed the good confession before Pontius Pilate,
14 that you keep this commandment without spot, blameless until our Lord Jesus Christ's appearing,

2 Timothy 2:22 (NKJ)
22 Flee also youthful lusts; but pursue righteousness, faith, love, peace with those who call on the Lord out of a pure heart.

See sin for what it is. Sin is Satan's tool to bring you down. When the allure of sin is at your doorstep, you can analyze it, gaze at it, consider it or flee from it. You can not, in and of your own strength, resist it. Those who study the powers of evil are drawing near to that which you should avoid, assiduously.

I suppose it is obvious, but if not, understand this. False idols take on all sorts of external appearance. Whether it is palm reading, channeling, spiritism, astrology or black magic, it matters not. They are all efforts to have your life and decisions directed by some power other than the Holy Spirit in you. Spiritism, mysticism and all sorts of "seers" exist today. Read these quotations carefully. God will be very angry with those who practice such things.

Leviticus 20:26-27 (NKJ)
26 'And you shall be holy to Me, for I the LORD am holy, and have separated you from the peoples, that you should be Mine.
27 'A man or a woman who is a medium, or who has familiar spirits, shall surely be put to death; they shall stone them with stones. Their blood shall be upon them.'"

1 Chronicles 10:13 (NKJ)
13 So Saul died for his unfaithfulness which he had committed against the LORD, because he did not keep the word of the LORD, and also because he consulted a medium for guidance.

2 Chronicles 33:1-7 (NKJ)
1 Manasseh was twelve years old when he became king, and he reigned fifty-five years in Jerusalem.
2 But he did evil in the sight of the LORD, according to the abominations of the nations whom the LORD had cast out before the children of Israel.
3 For he rebuilt the high places which Hezekiah his father had broken down; he raised up altars for the Baals, and made wooden images; and he worshiped all the host of heaven and served them.
4 He also built altars in the house of the LORD, of which the LORD had said, "In Jerusalem shall My name be forever."
5 And he built altars for all the host of heaven in the two courts of the house of the LORD.
6 Also he caused his sons to pass through the fire in the Valley of the Son of Hinnom; he practiced soothsaying, used witchcraft and sorcery, and consulted mediums and spiritists. He did much evil in the sight of the LORD, to provoke Him to anger.
7 He even set a carved image, the idol which he had made, in the house of God, of which God had said to David and to Solomon his son, "In this house and in Jerusalem, which I have chosen out of all the tribes of Israel, I will put My name forever;

Jeremiah 10:2-5 (NKJ)
2 Thus says the LORD: "Do not learn the way of the Gentiles; do not be dismayed at the signs of heaven, for the Gentiles are dismayed at them.
3 For the customs of the peoples are futile; for one cuts a tree from the forest, the work of the hands of the workman, with the ax.
4 They decorate it with silver and gold; they fasten it with nails and hammers so that it will not topple.
5 They are upright, like a palm tree, and they cannot speak; they must be carried, because they cannot go by themselves. Do not be afraid of them, for they cannot do evil, nor can they do any good."

Isaiah 8:18-20 (NKJ)

18 Here am I and the children whom the LORD has given me! We are for signs and wonders in Israel from the LORD of hosts, who dwells in Mount Zion.

19 And when they say to you, "Seek those who are mediums and wizards, who whisper and mutter," should not a people seek their God? Should they seek the dead on behalf of the living?

20 To the law and to the testimony! If they do not speak according to this word, it is because there is no light in them.

Isaiah 19:2-3 (NKJ)

2 "I will set Egyptians against Egyptians; everyone will fight against his brother, and everyone against his neighbor, city against city, kingdom against kingdom.

3 The spirit of Egypt will fail in its midst; I will destroy their counsel, and they will consult the idols and the charmers, the mediums and the sorcerers.

Ezekiel 13:9-10 (NKJ)

9 "My hand will be against the prophets who envision futility and who divine lies; they shall not be in the assembly of My people, nor be written in the record of the house of Israel, nor shall they enter into the land of Israel. Then you shall know that I am the Lord GOD.

10 "Because, indeed, because they have seduced My people, saying, 'Peace!' when there is no peace…

Ezekiel 13:17-18, 23 (NKJ)

17 "Likewise, son of man, set your face against the daughters of your people, who prophesy out of their own heart; prophesy against them,

18 "and say, 'Thus says the Lord GOD: "Woe to the women who sew magic charms on their sleeves and make veils for the heads of people of every height to hunt souls! Will you hunt the souls of My people, and keep yourselves alive?

23 "Therefore you shall no longer envision futility nor practice divination; for I will deliver My people out of your hand, and you shall know that I am the LORD."'

Micah 5:12-13 (NKJ)

12 I will cut off sorceries from your hand, and you shall have no soothsayers.

13 Your carved images I will also cut off, and your sacred pillars from your midst; you shall no more worship the work of your hands;

Acts 19:13-20 (NKJ)

13 Then some of the itinerant Jewish exorcists took it upon themselves to call the name of the Lord Jesus over those who had evil spirits, saying, "We exorcise you by the Jesus whom Paul preaches."

14 Also there were seven sons of Sceva, a Jewish chief priest, who did so.

15 And the evil spirit answered and said, "Jesus I know, and Paul I know; but who are you?"

16 Then the man in whom the evil spirit was leaped on them, overpowered them, and prevailed against them, so that they fled out of that house naked and wounded.

17 This became known both to all Jews and Greeks dwelling in Ephesus; and fear fell on them all, and the name of the Lord Jesus was magnified.

18 And many who had believed came confessing and telling their deeds.

19 Also, many of those who had practiced magic brought their books together and burned them in the sight of all. And they counted up the value of them, and it totaled fifty thousand pieces of silver.

20 So the word of the Lord grew mightily and prevailed.

The following quote covers more ground than simply this subject of false idols, but you should see this in the context of "independence from God."

Isaiah 47:8-15 (NKJ)

8 "Therefore hear this now, you who are given to pleasures, who dwell securely, who say in your heart, 'I am, and there is no one else besides me; I shall not sit as a widow, nor shall I know the loss of children';

9 But these two things shall come to you in a moment, in one day: the loss of children, and widowhood. They shall come upon you in their fullness because of the multitude of your sorceries, for the great abundance of your enchantments.

10 "For you have trusted in your wickedness; you have said, 'No one sees me'; your wisdom and your knowledge have warped you; and you have said in your heart, 'I am, and there is no one else besides me.'
11 Therefore evil shall come upon you; you shall not know from where it arises. And trouble shall fall upon you; you will not be able to put it off. And desolation shall come upon you suddenly, which you shall not know.
12 "Stand now with your enchantments and the multitude of your sorceries, in which you have labored from your youth– perhaps you will be able to profit, perhaps you will prevail.
13 You are wearied in the multitude of your counsels; let now the astrologers, the stargazers, and the monthly prognosticators stand up and save you from what shall come upon you.
14 Behold, they shall be as stubble, the fire shall burn them; they shall not deliver themselves from the power of the flame; it shall not be a coal to be warmed by, nor a fire to sit before!
15 Thus shall they be to you with whom you have labored, your merchants from your youth; they shall wander each one to his quarter. No one shall save you.

Jesus is the one who has defeated the power of Satan. Listen to the words of James, the half brother of Jesus (Mary had additional children but the additional children were fathered by Joseph, not the Holy Spirit).

James 4:1-10 (NKJ)
1 Where do wars and fights come from among you? Do they not come from your desires for pleasure that war in your members?
2 You lust and do not have. You murder and covet and cannot obtain. You fight and war. Yet you do not have because you do not ask.
3 You ask and do not receive, because you ask amiss, that you may spend it on your pleasures.
4 Adulterers and adulteresses! Do you not know that friendship with the world is enmity with God? Whoever therefore wants to be a friend of the world makes himself an enemy of God.
5 Or do you think that the Scripture says in vain, "The Spirit who dwells in us yearns jealously?"

6 But He gives more grace. Therefore He says: "God resists the proud, but gives grace to the humble."
7 Therefore submit to God. Resist the devil and he will flee from you.
8 Draw near to God and He will draw near to you. Cleanse your hands, you sinners; and purify your hearts, you double-minded.
9 Lament and mourn and weep! Let your laughter be turned to mourning and your joy to gloom.
10 Humble yourselves in the sight of the Lord, and He will lift you up.

Jesus' victory over death, is our victory over death as well. The only kind of death that matters is spiritual death. Physical death is as nothing, if it means you are transitioning to perfection, to eternal life in a perfect place where sin does not exist. The following verses should help you understand God's perspective on death.

Isaiah 57:1-2 (NKJ)
1 The righteous perishes, and no man takes it to heart; merciful men are taken away, while no one considers that the righteous is taken away from evil.
2 He shall enter into peace; they shall rest in their beds, each one walking in his uprightness.

Listen to the point again. The righteous, when they die, is taken away from evil and shall enter into peace. We grieve, properly, but they who die in Christ, joyfully celebrate their redemption.

We who love God will not die twice! We are born twice, once of the water, at physical birth and once of the Spirit. Being born again is to be born of the Spirit.

If your spirit is to dwell in eternity with other evil spirits, separated from those who love God and from whom God loves, then you have completely misunderstood God's will for you. He would that no man perish.

2 Peter 3:9 (NKJ)
9 The Lord is not slack concerning His promise, as some count slackness, but is longsuffering toward us, not willing that any should perish but that all should come to repentance.

But you have volition. You are in charge. Who can you possibly blame for not responding to God's love? Repent, I pray and respond to His love. His eyes are upon you this moment and the eternal kingdom and His eternal peace awaits you. The angels are standing on tiptoes to see you knock at the door and come in.

Luke 15:10 (NKJ)
10 "Likewise, I say to you, there is joy in the presence of the angels of God over one sinnerwho repents."

Your name is in the Book of Life. Do not blot it out. It is God's perfect will that you be His child, under His care and protection, forever.

CHAPTER 47

THE WORD—THE VERY ESSENCE OF TRUTH— A PERMANENT PROMISE

It seems impossible to please God if one will not heed His word nor obey His law. Do you heed His word? Today, most men listen far more to men than to God. In fact, reading these comments and excerpts is a very poor substitute for being fed directly from the Word of God. There is a wonderful verse that sums up the times in which we live.

2 Timothy 4:1-4 (NKJ)
1 I charge you therefore before God and the Lord Jesus Christ, who will judge the living and the dead at His appearing and His kingdom:
2 Preach the word! Be ready in season and out of season. Convince, rebuke, exhort, with all longsuffering and teaching.
3 For the time will come when they will not endure sound doctrine, but according to their own desires, because they have itching ears, they will heap up for themselves teachers;
4 and they will turn their ears away from the truth, and be turned aside to fables.

Here you have what should be regarded as an emergency announcement. "The time will come when… they will turn their ears away from the truth." And to whom will they listen? Men; teachers who will tell them what is pleasing to their ears. I have quoted Hebrews 4:12 before. Go back and read it again. If you completely understand the full meaning of that verse, you will never value the musings of man over or equal to the Word of God. Get into the Word, every day.

Please do not get angry at what I am about to say, but ask yourself if it is not true. Most Jews do not study the Word of God, diligently. Many spend more time reading the words of man than of God. Since I am venturing out on to thin ice, I might as well speak plainly about religious ritual.

The concept of "appeasing God" by ritual strikes a very strong chord with me. The Gentile churches and the synagogues must make the acquisition, by grace, of God's Holy Spirit their primary mission. Getting people to pattern their lives in acceptable ritual, in a completely honorable pattern, by all external appearances, can lead to a "comfort level" in which "works or good deeds" become a seductive entrapment.

It permits people in churches and synagogues to feel "Okay," to do the right thing and to "fit in." Those feelings may or may not spring from the perspective of "I live, yet not I, but Christ lives in me." Crucifying the "flesh" and living "in the Spirit" are foundational elements, which enable ritual and works to be "dynamic," in that one's entire life is "handed over" to the control of the Holy Spirit and the meaning of John 3:8 hits home.

John 3:8 (NKJ)
8 "The wind blows where it wishes, and you hear the sound of it, but cannot tell where it comes from and where it goes. So is everyone who is born of the Spirit."

To yield control, to become a tool in the Hand of God, to sense his constant direction, is to forfeit everything of the flesh, those things most of us spend a lifetime accumulating such as identity, assets, status, physical strength and prowess, political and social power, a "reputation," individuality, intelligence and self reliance.

No wonder the step is so large that few will take it. To die to self is an act of contrition and humility that seems available only to the most "broken" who have exhausted their own personal reserves of strength and integrity, whose lives are almost over, either figuratively or physically.

Thank God this is not true. Instead, God teaches us that His love, His constant Spiritual Presence, His power, His mercy and grace, were all made possible by the redeeming sacrifice of Jesus, who atoned for the sins of every person, who when He died and rose again, exemplified my resurrection, my renewal, made possible by Him, my Judge and my Redeemer.

Jesus promised me He would send the Counselor, the Comforter, the Holy Spirit, to renew me, teach me and fill me, constantly, with His Presence. He promised to be my Advocate before the Father. I say these things as personally as possible, because religion is not about ritual, but it is about a relationship. A personal relationship between you and the Father, made possible by Jesus, enhanced and made manifest by the Holy Spirit in you.

Again, listen to His Holy Word.

Psalm 119:8-16(NKJ)
8 I will keep Your statutes; Oh, do not forsake me utterly!
9 How can a young man cleanse his way? By taking heed according to Your word.
10 With my whole heart I have sought You; Oh, let me not wander from Your commandments!
11 Your word I have hidden in my heart, that I might not sin against You!
12 Blessed are You, O LORD! Teach me Your statutes!
13 With my lips I have declared all the judgments of Your mouth.
14 I have rejoiced in the way of Your testimonies, as much as in all riches.
15 I will meditate on Your precepts, and contemplate Your ways.
16 I will delight myself in Your statutes; I will not forget Your word.

Listen again, because you must grasp this, to a prophecy that will make you very sorry that you did not take full advantage of the opportunity at hand. It is a prophecy yet to be fulfilled, but when it does occur, you will greatly lament the fact that you did not read the Word when it was abundantly in your midst.

Amos 8:11-13 (NKJ)
11 "Behold, the days are coming," says the Lord GOD, "That I will send a famine on the land, not a famine of bread, nor a thirst for water, but of hearing the words of the LORD.

12 They shall wander from sea to sea, and from north to east; they shall run to and fro, seeking the word of the LORD, but shall not find it.
13 "In that day the fair virgins and strong young men shall faint from thirst.

We will literally not be able to hear the Words of the Lord when the great tribulation begins. The Antichrist, the one who introduces 3½ years of peace and safety, who cooperates in the restoration of the Temple and the reinstitution of sacrifice, will, during the last 3½ years of the tribulation, ban the Word, destroy it and cause all who read it to either die or to deny their Lord. It is time, now, to store the Word in your heart that you might not sin against the Lord.

People tell me they do not have time to read and study God's Word. Let's look at a solution to that problem. Do you know who wants to talk to you at 4 a.m. in the morning? In most cases, No one! At that time of day, no one wants to talk to you, but God does. Try praying this prayer. God, awaken me at 4 a.m. if you want me to read your Word. When He does awaken you, get up, step out into the early morning air, look to the heavens, lift your hands to Him in prayer, then find a good place to read and read with the passion of one who knows that the Word you hold in your hand will forcibly be taken from you. Also pray that 5-6 hours sleep will count as 8 hours and that God will strengthen you in more ways than spiritually.

Listen to what His Word says about sleep.

Proverbs 6:4-11 (NKJ)
4 Give no sleep to your eyes, nor slumber to your eyelids.
5 Deliver yourself like a gazelle from the hand of the hunter, and like a bird from the hand of the fowler.
6 Go to the ant, you sluggard! Consider her ways and be wise,
7 Which, having no captain, overseer or ruler,
8 Provides her supplies in the summer, and gathers her food in the harvest.
9 How long will you slumber, O sluggard? When will you rise from your sleep?
10 A little sleep, a little slumber, a little folding of the hands to sleep–

11 So shall your poverty come on you like a prowler, and your need like an armed man.

Proverbs 20:13 (NKJ)
11 Do not love sleep, lest you come to poverty; open your eyes, and you will be satisfied with bread.

1 Thessalonians 5:5-6 (NKJ)
5 You are all sons of light and sons of the day. We are not of the night nor of darkness.
6 Therefore let us not sleep, as others do, but let us watch and be sober.

Yes, we need sleep, but not so much that there is no time left for God's Word in our daily lives. One of the greatest assurances of God's Word being critical to your well being is presented by King David.

2 Samuel 22:29-34 (NKJ)
29 "For You are my lamp, O LORD; the LORD shall enlighten my darkness.
30 For by You I can run against a troop; by my God I can leap over a wall.
31 As for God, His way is perfect; the word of the LORD is proven; he is a shield to all who trust in Him.
32 "For who is God, except the LORD? And who is a rock, except our God?
33 God is my strength and power, and He makes my way perfect.
34 He makes my feet like the feet of deer, and sets me on my high places.

The psalmist teaches it most simply and perfectly.

Psalm 119:103-105 (NKJ)
103 How sweet are Your words to my taste, sweeter than honey to my mouth!
104 Through Your precepts I get understanding; therefore I hate every false way.
105 Your word is a lamp to my feet and a light to my path.

Why, assuming you believe in God, would you not eagerly assimilate the Holy Scriptures, as one who is starving to know Him, one who seeks to be blessed by Him, as one who earnestly prays that you shall spend eternity with Him? I recommend that you go to www.solascriptura.com and read the topic, "The Word." It is a rich collection of wonderful scriptures about the Word which I assembled.

At some point, every knee will bow and every tongue "should" confess that Jesus Christ is Lord. That includes saints and sinners. Whether you hope to worship Jesus Christ, the Messiah, in the Kingdom or now, you should consider the possibility that denying Jesus is a risk not worth taking. Listen to what the scriptures say.

Matthew 10:27-39 (NKJ)
27 "Whatever I tell you in the dark, speak in the light; and what you hear in the ear, preach on the housetops.
28 "And do not fear those who kill the body but cannot kill the soul. But rather fear Him who is able to destroy both soul and body in hell.
29 "Are not two sparrows sold for a copper coin? And not one of them falls to the ground apart from your Father's will.
30 "But the very hairs of your head are all numbered.
31 "Do not fear therefore; you are of more value than many sparrows.
32 "Therefore whoever confesses Me before men, him I will also confess before My Father who is in heaven.
33 "But whoever denies Me before men, him I will also deny before My Father who is in heaven.
34 "Do not think that I came to bring peace on earth. I did not come to bring peace but a sword.
35 "For I have come to 'set a man against his father, a daughter against her mother, and a daughter-in-law against her mother-in-law';
36 "and 'a man's enemies will be those of his own household.'
37 "He who loves father or mother more than Me is not worthy of Me. And he who loves son or daughter more than Me is not worthy of Me.
38 "And he who does not take his cross and follow after Me is not worthy of Me.
39 "He who finds his life will lose it, and he who loses his life for My sake will find it.

Such language needs no comment. That is why you must go directly to the Word of God. In these next verses, Jesus cried it out, telling the Jews that believing upon Him was a matter of extreme urgency, then and now.

John 12:44-50 (NKJ)
44 Then Jesus cried out and said, "He who believes in Me, believes not in Me but in Him who sent Me.
45 "And he who sees Me sees Him who sent Me.
46 "I have come as a light into the world, that whoever believes in Me should not abide in darkness.
47 "And if anyone hears My words and does not believe, I do not judge him; for I did not come to judge the world but to save the world.
48 "He who rejects Me, and does not receive My words, has that which judges him– the word that I have spoken will judge him in the last day.
49 "For I have not spoken on My own authority; but the Father who sent Me gave Me a command, what I should say and what I should speak.
50 "And I know that His command is everlasting life. Therefore, whatever I speak, just as the Father has told Me, so I speak."

If the "Word" is going to judge you, wouldn't it be a good idea to know what the Word says. I capitalized the "W" because of the following quote.

John 1:1-5 (NKJ)
1 In the beginning was the Word, and the Word was with God, and the Word was God.
2 He was in the beginning with God.
3 All things were made through Him, and without Him nothing was made that was made.
4 In Him was life, and the life was the light of men.
5 And the light shines in the darkness, and the darkness did not comprehend it.

The word of God will bring you to the place it brought King David when he said:

1 Chronicles 16:8-36 (NKJ)
8 Oh, give thanks to the LORD! Call upon His name; make known His deeds among the peoples!
9 Sing to Him, sing psalms to Him; talk of all His wondrous works!
10 Glory in His holy name; let the hearts of those rejoice who seek the LORD!
11 Seek the LORD and His strength; seek His face evermore!
12 Remember His marvelous works which He has done, his wonders, and the judgments of His mouth,
13 O seed of Israel His servant, you children of Jacob, His chosen ones!
14 He is the LORD our God; his judgments are in all the earth.
15 Remember His covenant forever, the word which He commanded, for a thousand generations,
16 The covenant which He made with Abraham, and His oath to Isaac,
17 And confirmed it to Jacob for a statute, to Israel for an everlasting covenant,
18 Saying, "To you I will give the land of Canaan as the allotment of your inheritance,"
19 When you were few in number, indeed very few, and strangers in it.
20 When they went from one nation to another, and from one kingdom to another people,
21 He permitted no man to do them wrong; yes, He rebuked kings for their sakes,
22 Saying, "Do not touch My anointed ones, and do My prophets no harm."
23 Sing to the LORD, all the earth; proclaim the good news of His salvation from day to day.
24 Declare His glory among the nations, his wonders among all peoples.
25 For the LORD is great and greatly to be praised; he is also to be feared above all gods.
26 For all the gods of the peoples are idols, but the LORD made the heavens.
27 Honor and majesty are before Him; strength and gladness are in His place.
28 Give to the LORD, O families of the peoples, give to the LORD glory and strength.

29 Give to the LORD the glory due His name; bring an offering, and come before Him. Oh, worship the LORD in the beauty of holiness!
30 Tremble before Him, all the earth. The world also is firmly established, it shall not be moved.
31 Let the heavens rejoice, and let the earth be glad; and let them say among the nations, "The LORD reigns."
32 Let the sea roar, and all its fullness; let the field rejoice, and all that is in it.
33 Then the trees of the woods shall rejoice before the LORD, for He is coming to judge the earth.
34 Oh, give thanks to the LORD, for He is good! For His mercy endures forever.
35 And say, "Save us, O God of our salvation; gather us together, and deliver us from the Gentiles, to give thanks to Your holy name, to triumph in Your praise."
36 Blessed be the LORD God of Israel from everlasting to everlasting And all the people said, "Amen!" and praised the LORD.

I realize that I am one of those "Gentiles" from whom David said you should be saved. The definition of a Gentile is any one who is not a Jew. Even the preservation of that fact and the breadth of its application distinguish Israel from all others.

In David's time, the Gentiles were, for the most part, not worshippers of God. In fact, most Gentiles today probably do not think of themselves as worshippers of the God of the Jews. Many mistakenly feel that they are "nothing like the Jews." That is sad but perhaps no more so than Jews who feel they are nothing like the Christians. Christians need to be reminded that Israel is at the very center of God's plan for the nations and people of this earth and Jews should see the Christian's as brothers, either now or later.

If you study the scriptures diligently you will come to the understanding that God's chosen people, the Jews, are still God's chosen people. I, as a Gentile, have been "grafted" in, included as a branch but never as the "root. Listen to these two Old Testament quotations.

Isaiah 11:10 (NKJ)
10 "And in that day there shall be a Root of Jesse, who shall stand as a banner to the people; for the Gentiles shall seek Him, and His resting place shall be glorious."

Isaiah 49:6 (NKJ)
6 Indeed He says, 'It is too small a thing that You should be My Servant to raise up the tribes of Jacob, and to restore the preserved ones of Israel; I will also give You as a light to the Gentiles, that You should be My salvation to the ends of the earth.'"

God chose Israel. This book to Jews everywhere is intended to provoke you to perform "due diligence," to cause you to investigate what may be new possibilities.

I write to you, somewhat in ignorance of your culture and traditions, thus if I have unintentionally offended, forgive me. I think you must know by now that I am for you and not against you. In honesty, no one who truly loves God can be against God's people, any of them.

This next quotation starts with a very difficult set of verses for a Jew "on hold." It makes it clear that you must deal with the question of "Who is the Messiah" if you want the manifestation of the Holy Spirit in your life, right now. It is His Spirit that witnesses to your spirit and teaches you all things. One thing it will teach you is that love, a type of love that only God can place in your heart, will be a distinguishing feature of your "new life."

1 John 4:1-21 (NKJ)
1 Beloved, do not believe every spirit, but test the spirits, whether they are of God; because many false prophets have gone out into the world.
2 By this you know the Spirit of God: Every spirit that confesses that Jesus Christ has come in the flesh is of God,
3 and every spirit that does not confess that Jesus Christ has come in the flesh is not of God. And this is the spirit of the Antichrist, which you have heard was coming, and is now already in the world.
4 You are of God, little children, and have overcome them, because He who is in you is greater than he who is in the world.

5 They are of the world. Therefore they speak as of the world, and the world hears them.
6 We are of God. He who knows God hears us; he who is not of God does not hear us. By this we know the spirit of truth and the spirit of error.
7 Beloved, let us love one another, for love is of God; and everyone who loves is born of God and knows God.
8 He who does not love does not know God, for God is love.
9 In this the love of God was manifested toward us, that God has sent His only begotten Son into the world, that we might live through Him.
10 In this is love, not that we loved God, but that He loved us and sent His Son to be the propitiation for our sins.
11 Beloved, if God so loved us, we also ought to love one another.
12 No one has seen God at any time. If we love one another, God abides in us, and His love has been perfected in us.
13 By this we know that we abide in Him, and He in us, because He has given us of His Spirit.
14 And we have seen and testify that the Father has sent the Son as Savior of the world.
15 Whoever confesses that Jesus is the Son of God, God abides in him, and he in God.
16 And we have known and believed the love that God has for us. God is love, and he who abides in love abides in God, and God in him.
17 Love has been perfected among us in this: that we may have boldness in the day of judgment; because as He is, so are we in this world.
18 There is no fear in love; but perfect love casts out fear, because fear involves torment. But he who fears has not been made perfect in love.
19 We love Him because He first loved us.
20 If someone says, "I love God," and hates his brother, he is a liar; for he who does not love his brother whom he has seen, how can he love God whom he has not seen?
21 And this commandment we have from Him: that he who loves God must love his brother also.

Israel as a nation has been "on hold." Job tells you what happens when a stump smells water. The Messiah is the fountain of life. He is the Living Water.

Job 14:7-9 (NKJ)
7 "For there is hope for a tree, if it is cut down, that it will sprout again, and that its tender shoots will not cease.
8 Though its root may grow old in the earth, and its stump may die in the ground,
9 Yet at the scent of water it will bud and bring forth branches like a plant.

2 Kings 19:27-31 (NKJ)
27 'But I know your dwelling place, your going out and your coming in, and your rage against Me.
28 Because your rage against Me and your tumult have come up to My ears, therefore I will put My hook in your nose and My bridle in your lips, and I will turn you back by the way which you came.
29 'This shall be a sign to you: you shall eat this year such as grows of itself, and in the second year what springs from the same; also in the third year sow and reap, plant vineyards and eat the fruit of them.
30 And the remnant who have escaped of the house of Judah shall again take root downward, and bear fruit upward.
31 For out of Jerusalem shall go a remnant, and those who escape from Mount Zion. The zeal of the LORD of hosts will do this.'

Listen to this exhortation, placed in the Holy Scriptures, for you, by God.

Acts 2:16-41 (NKJ)
16 "But this is what was spoken by the prophet Joel:
17 'And it shall come to pass in the last days, says God, that I will pour out of My Spirit on all flesh; your sons and your daughters shall prophesy, your young men shall see visions, your old men shall dream dreams.
18 And on My menservants and on My maidservants I will pour out My Spirit in those days; and they shall prophesy.
19 I will show wonders in heaven above and signs in the earth beneath: blood and fire and vapor of smoke.
20 The sun shall be turned into darkness, and the moon into blood, before the coming of the great and awesome day of the Lord.
21 And it shall come to pass that whoever calls on the name of the Lord shall be saved.'

22 "Men of Israel, hear these words: Jesus of Nazareth, a Man attested by God to you by miracles, wonders, and signs which God did through Him in your midst, as you yourselves also know–

23 "Him, being delivered by the determined purpose and foreknowledge of God, you have taken by lawless hands, have crucified, and put to death;

24 "whom God raised up, having loosed the pains of death, because it was not possible that He should be held by it.

25 "For David says concerning Him: 'I foresaw the Lord always before my face, for He is at my right hand, that I may not be shaken.

26 Therefore my heart rejoiced, and my tongue was glad; moreover my flesh also will rest in hope.

27 For You will not leave my soul in Hades, nor will You allow Your Holy One to see corruption.

28 You have made known to me the ways of life; you will make me full of joy in Your presence.'

29 "Men and brethren, let me speak freely to you of the patriarch David, that he is both dead and buried, and his tomb is with us to this day.

30 "Therefore, being a prophet, and knowing that God had sworn with an oath to him that of the fruit of his body, according to the flesh, He would raise up the Christ to sit on his throne,

31 "he, foreseeing this, spoke concerning the resurrection of the Christ, that His soul was not left in Hades, nor did His flesh see corruption.

32 "This Jesus God has raised up, of which we are all witnesses.

33 "Therefore being exalted to the right hand of God, and having received from the Father the promise of the Holy Spirit, He poured out this which you now see and hear.

34 "For David did not ascend into the heavens, but he says himself: 'The Lord said to my Lord, "Sit at My right hand,

35 Till I make Your enemies Your footstool."'

36 "Therefore let all the house of Israel know assuredly that God has made this Jesus, whom you crucified, both Lord and Christ."

37 Now when they heard this, they were cut to the heart, and said to Peter and the rest of the apostles, "Men and brethren, what shall we do?"

38 Then Peter said to them, "Repent, and let every one of you be baptized in the name of Jesus Christ for the remission of sins; and you shall receive the gift of the Holy Spirit.
39 "For the promise is to you and to your children, and to all who are afar off, as many as the Lord our God will call."
40 And with many other words he testified and exhorted them, saying, "Be saved from this perverse generation."
41 Then those who gladly received his word were baptized; and that day about three thousand souls were added to them.

Romans 13:9-14 (NKJ)
9 For the commandments, "You shall not commit adultery," "You shall not murder," "You shall not steal," "You shall not bear false witness," "You shall not covet," and if there is any other commandment, are all summed up in this saying, namely, "You shall love your neighbor as yourself."
10 Love does no harm to a neighbor; therefore love is the fulfillment of the law.
11 And do this, knowing the time, that now it is high time to awake out of sleep; for now our salvation is nearer than when we first believed.
12 The night is far spent, the day is at hand. Therefore let us cast off the works of darkness, and let us put on the armor of light.
13 Let us walk properly, as in the day, not in revelry and drunkenness, not in lewdness and lust, not in strife and envy.
14 But put on the Lord Jesus Christ, and make no provision for the flesh, to fulfill its lusts.

Finally, listen to this plea, written expressly to the Jews, by a Jew. Read it as though it was addressed to you personally, for in truth, it is!

Hebrews 12:1-29 (NKJ)
1 Therefore we also, since we are surrounded by so great a cloud of witnesses, let us lay aside every weight, and the sin which so easily ensnares us, and let us run with endurance the race that is set before us,
2 looking unto Jesus, the author and finisher of our faith, who for the joy that was set before Him endured the cross, despising the shame, and has sat down at the right hand of the throne of God.

3 For consider Him who endured such hostility from sinners against Himself, lest you become weary and discouraged in your souls.

4 You have not yet resisted to bloodshed, striving against sin.

5 And you have forgotten the exhortation which speaks to you as to sons: "My son, do not despise the chastening of the Lord, nor be discouraged when you are rebuked by Him;

6 For whom the Lord loves He chastens, and scourges every son whom He receives."

7 If you endure chastening, God deals with you as with sons; for what son is there whom a father does not chasten?

8 But if you are without chastening, of which all have become partakers, then you are illegitimate and not sons.

9 Furthermore, we have had human fathers who corrected us, and we paid them respect. Shall we not much more readily be in subjection to the Father of spirits and live?

10 For they indeed for a few days chastened us as seemed best to them, but He for our profit, that we may be partakers of His holiness.

11 Now no chastening seems to be joyful for the present, but painful; nevertheless, afterward it yields the peaceable fruit of righteousness to those who have been trained by it.

12 Therefore strengthen the hands which hang down, and the feeble knees,

13 and make straight paths for your feet, so that what is lame may not be dislocated, but rather be healed.

14 Pursue peace with all people, and holiness, without which no one will see the Lord:

15 looking diligently lest anyone fall short of the grace of God; lest any root of bitterness springing up cause trouble, and by this many become defiled;

16 lest there be any fornicator or profane person like Esau, who for one morsel of food sold his birthright.

17 For you know that afterward, when he wanted to inherit the blessing, he was rejected, for he found no place for repentance, though he sought it diligently with tears.

18 For you have not come to the mountain that may be touched and that burned with fire, and to blackness and darkness and tempest,

19 and the sound of a trumpet and the voice of words, so that those who heard it begged that the word should not be spoken to them anymore.
20 (For they could not endure what was commanded: "And if so much as a beast touches the mountain, it shall be stoned or shot with an arrow."
21 And so terrifying was the sight that Moses said, "I am exceedingly afraid and trembling.")
22 But you have come to Mount Zion and to the city of the living God, the heavenly Jerusalem, to an innumerable company of angels,
23 to the general assembly and church of the firstborn who are registered in heaven, to God the Judge of all, to the spirits of just men made perfect,
24 to Jesus the Mediator of the new covenant, and to the blood of sprinkling that speaks better things than that of Abel.
25 See that you do not refuse Him who speaks. For if they did not escape who refused Him who spoke on earth, much more shall we not escape if we turn away from Him who speaks from heaven,
26 whose voice then shook the earth; but now He has promised, saying, "Yet once more I shake not only the earth, but also heaven."
27 Now this, "Yet once more," indicates the removal of those things that are being shaken, as of things that are made, that the things which cannot be shaken may remain.
28 Therefore, since we are receiving a kingdom which cannot be shaken, let us have grace, by which we may serve God acceptably with reverence and godly fear.
29 For our God is a consuming fire.

Hebrews 13:14-16 (NKJ)
14 For here we have no continuing city, but we seek the one to come.
15 Therefore by Him let us continually offer the sacrifice of praise to God, that is, the fruit of our lips, giving thanks to His name.
16 But do not forget to do good and to share, for with such sacrifices God is well pleased.

Mark 16:15 (NKJ)
15 And He said to them, "Go into all the world and preach the gospel to every creature.

Time may be very short. Use whatever resources God has given you, whether they are physical, mental, or spiritual, to serve Him. Not out of fear, which would be a logical thing for the unsaved to do, but out of love and appreciation for His love to you. In humility and contrition, submit your will to His will, your spirit to His Spirit that His joy, peace and eternal salvation might be a "gift" realized, an engagement consummated.

2 Corinthians 5:17 (NKJ)
17 Therefore, if anyone is in Christ, he is a new creation; old things have passed away; behold, all things have become new.

Psalm 51:1-19 (NKJ)
1 Have mercy upon me, O God, according to Your lovingkindness; according to the multitude of Your tender mercies, blot out my transgressions.
2 Wash me thoroughly from my iniquity, and cleanse me from my sin.
3 For I acknowledge my transgressions, and my sin is always before me.
4 Against You, You only, have I sinned, and done this evil in Your sight– that You may be found just when You speak, and blameless when You judge.
5 Behold, I was brought forth in iniquity, and in sin my mother conceived me.
6 Behold, You desire truth in the inward parts, and in the hidden part You will make me to know wisdom.
7 Purge me with hyssop, and I shall be clean; wash me, and I shall be whiter than snow.
8 Make me to hear joy and gladness, that the bones You have broken may rejoice.
9 Hide Your face from my sins, and blot out all my iniquities.
10 Create in me a clean heart, O God, and renew a steadfast spirit within me.
11 Do not cast me away from Your presence, and do not take Your Holy Spirit from me.
12 Restore to me the joy of Your salvation, and uphold me by Your generous Spirit.|
13 Then I will teach transgressors Your ways, and sinners shall be converted to You.

14 Deliver me from bloodshed, O God, the God of my salvation, and my tongue shall sing aloud of Your righteousness.
15 O Lord, open my lips, and my mouth shall show forth Your praise.
16 For You do not desire sacrifice, or else I would give it; you do not delight in burnt offering.
17 The sacrifices of God are a broken spirit, a broken and a contrite heart– these, O God, You will not despise.
18 Do good in Your good pleasure to Zion; build the walls of Jerusalem.
19 Then You shall be pleased with the sacrifices of righteousness, with burnt offering and whole burnt offering; then they shall offer bulls on Your altar.

I pray that God will use this book to bring glory to Himself. You are God's Glory when you seek Him and serve Him. Our worship of Him fulfills His purpose. God delights in our obedience and enables us, by His Grace, to have faith. The kind of faith that moves mountains, something He is about to do.

James 4:8 (NKJ)
8 Draw near to God and He will draw near to you.

May our God richly bless you and keep you in His Hand forever.

EPILOGUE

GOT ETERNITY?

Are you certain that death is the end?

We all face two deaths, one physical and one spiritual. We cannot avoid physical death but we can avoid spiritual death. Those who feel that you are spiritually dead are wrong, at least for the present, because your choices remain before you.

Spiritual death comes, in this lifetime and for eternity, when you decide that you are simply flesh and that you reject the notion that God exists. Spiritual death accompanies a belief that you have no spirit and that when you die, you die. You are spiritually dead if God's Spirit has not embraced, enveloped and apprehended you. That is a big concept, to be sure, but His Spirit has either filled your heart, witnessing to your spirit, or it has not.

For the time being, we are trapped, as it were, in the flesh but most of us logically aspire to be with God as eternal spiritual beings. What drives us to seek to discover whether we have a spiritual side to our being? Well for one reason, death is a certainty. You say you do not fear death, you have had a lot of fun and you have enjoyed an abundance of God's blessings. Still, you sense or you are certain that death is not the end, it is the beginning.

We want to satisfy our inner desire to be like God, a desire He has placed upon our hearts (call it a conscience but it is much more complex than that, Romans 1:18-22, Romans 2:14-16, Hebrews 8:10-11, James 1:21,

Colossians 1:20-23) but we also have fleshly instincts (sex, pride, selfishness and so on) that lead us to disobey God's laws.

The spirit of man will live on. The question is, will your spirit be united with the Spirit of God or be separated from His Spirit because of your failure to seek a personal relationship with Him? On the other hand, if you do acknowledge that there is life after death, are you obedient enough to make it into the Kingdom of God?

The answer is, no, you are not obedient enough to make it into the Kingdom of God, nor is anyone else. God's word says that He will not countenance sin. An uncleansed, sinful person will not stand in His midst. No man has ever been perfectly obedient. The Scriptures say that sin is sin and that there is no hierarchy of sin. If you say that you have only stolen something while another person killed someone, you are both in the same place because you have committed a sin for which atonement is required. This is why arrogance and self-righteousness have no place in our lives. We all need to be forgiven for huge sins and small sins. It is very easy to forgive others if you understand what the forgiveness of Christ has done for you. We are never to judge another man's sin or his salvation. We can observe his actions and see if he bears the kind of fruit he espouses but even then we can not judge the condition of his heart. You can and you should pray for sinners. The salvation of a sinner is a joy to observe. The Scriptures say ...there will be more joy in heaven over one sinner who repents than over ninety-nine just persons who need no repentance. Luke 15:7

Why are you telling me these things?

This message is a personal appeal, not sponsored by or affiliated with any organization. If you do not believe God exists or you do not believe that you have a spirit that will continue to exist after death, this information will seem to be or is in fact, irrelevant. Just set it aside. You may, at some point, want to rethink your position. If you do believe (or are not sure) God exists and that the spirit of those who have died before you are with the God that created them, then you should end up being encouraged and hopefully motivated to develop a closer personal relationship with God. In either case this message is intended to encourage you. I pray that you will find it worth reading and where possible, Lord willing, it may change your life now as well as the eternal destination of your soul.

As to my motivation, God's word says… " Go into all the world and preach the Gospel to every creature. He who believes and is baptized will be saved; but he who does not believe will be condemned." Mark 16:15-16. It is the last part of that verse that has my attention. I can not remain silent if any of His children, including you, is in danger of being separated from the love of God and all those that love God, forever. I am not saying you are in danger. None of us are to judge the condition of another man's soul, but if you are not sure of your personal relationship with God, then read on.

Since I have sent out over a million copies of this message, I have some experience with initial questions and responses. Let me clear up a few of them now. If you received this message in the mail, I received your mailing address as part of a zip code directory of addresses which can be purchased by any person. No one asked me to send this message to you personally. Everyone in your area received this booklet. The booklet has a non-profit stamp on it because I complied with the Postal Services criteria for such status. I am the President of a California Corporation called The Sola Scriptura Project, a non-profit organization. I collect no fees, salaries or reimbursements from anyone. Proceeds of any kind (book sales, donations, etc.) go directly to the Sola Scriptura Project. With disclaimers aside, let's get to the issues.

I believe the Bible is the inerrant Word of God, thus the term "Sola Scriptura" which means "Only the Scriptures". I accept, by faith, that it is God's Holy Word. "As for God, His way is perfect; The word of the LORD is proven; He is a shield to all who trust in Him. For who is God, except the LORD? And who is a rock, except our God?" 2 Samuel 22:31-32 Please focus on the phrase, "The word of the LORD is proven" Prophecy fulfilled is one of the most important verifications of the Holy Scriptures being the word of God.

If death is a certainty, how can I choose life?

God understands where you are in your thinking at this very moment and how you got there. In spite of all the good reasons that you may not have secured a personal relationship with Him, He still holds an open hand to you. That fact, in itself, is a miracle. If you have, for your entire life, failed to honor God and acknowledge Him before men, He still patiently waits for you. He also knows, this second, what your final response is going to be. Because God is omniscient, He sees the beginning and the end of your life. You make the decisions but God knows, in advance, what you will decide. Some refer to this as predestination because God knows if you will respond to His call, thus your final circumstance is known by God. But focus on this quotation of Jesus by the Apostle John. "You did not choose Me, but I chose you and appointed you that you should go and bear fruit..." John 15:16

First, God loved you and has called you. Then you choose to respond or not. As of right now, you have made a choice. The ramifications of your choice are of eternal significance. Listen to what God said about the consequences of your choice. "I call heaven and earth as witnesses today against you, that I have set before you life and death, blessing and cursing; therefore choose life, that both you and your descendants may live; that you may love the LORD your God, that you may obey His voice, and that you may cling to Him, for He is your life and the length of your days..." Deuteronomy 30:19-20

The choices you have made, that matter most, are reflected in your personal answer to these questions. Is there a God? Is the Bible the Word of God? Is Jesus Christ who He said He was? Is Satan a "fallen angel", given an earthly kingdom, that he might challenge the authority of God? Are Satan and his band of renegade angels a powerful group of evil spirits, constantly tempting you? Did God create man in His own image? Does man have a soul, a spiritual side of his being? The choices to believe or not remain before you, even if you think you have already decided.

Satan, the ruler of this world, John 16:11 was present in the Garden of Eden, tempting man to disobey God. The fact that Adam and Eve were disobedient was no surprise to God. It set in motion a series of historical events played out by both the obedient and the disobedient. The struggle continues today.

You may not want to hear what I am about to say because you may feel guilty about being caught up in a modern phenomenon that defies logic. Why on earth would people use God's name in vain and speak the name of Jesus as an exclamation mark or worse. Our culture now says "Oh my G-d" in the most unholy circumstances, attaching no sense of honor to God in what they are saying. God's name is Holy, Jesus' name is Holy and He is your only means of redemption. Your heart should ache when their names are dishonored, especially by innocent children who are imitating adults.

Satan, your accuser, wants you to fail.

Satan's role in all of this (the evil spirit) is to tempt you to sin and to be able to accuse you before the Father. I believe you would agree that sin abounds and seems to be worsening with time.

Sin, embedded in the very flesh of man, is the tool Satan uses as he seeks to control man. God hates sin. Our sin actually grieves Him, according to the Scriptures. He loves righteous, virtuous, loving behavior. God, who revealed His true nature and His expectations through Jesus Christ, the Embodiment of God, has provided that sacrifice is the means by which we are cleansed of sin. This may be one of the most difficult, yet significant concepts for any of us to grasp. Atonement for sin is a requirement of God. You and I can not enter into the presence of God, our Holy Father, as "sinners". Our sin must be atoned for in a manner acceptable to God. Only Jesus who took our sins upon himself can present us holy and blameless before God. When we pray to the Lord, we do not do so in our righteousness but instead we do so in the righteousness of Jesus.

Satan does not want man to worship and obey God nor to enter into eternity as His Saints. Satan's agenda is to have man fail in his efforts to serve God. The Scriptures teach that God has given Satan a large range of opportunity to try and bring man down. Satan would snatch you, this moment, from any further serious consideration of what I am saying to you. As you can learn in the first two chapters of the Book of Job, Satan is permitted by God, to tempt you and to try to defeat you.

If you accept the possibility that what I have described is true, also understand that God has made a wonderful provision for those who may have spent their whole lives being deceived by Satan. Satan's message basically says, "Come, eat of the fruit of the tree of knowledge. Surely you shall not die. For God knows that in the day you eat of it your eyes will be opened and you will be like God, knowing good and evil." Ever since that line worked on Eve, its influence has continued.

Satan's modern message is "Eat, drink and be merry, for tomorrow you die". If physical death was the "end", Satan's message would make death an escape from responsibility, a quiet resting place for eternity, i.e. dust unto dust. But no, you will find Satan made a fool of you, just as he did Adam and Eve, and you will have bought into an eternal separation from God and those who love Him and serve Him. Please read Luke 16:19-31. That is a powerful passage that should serve as a wake up call. Your spirit will live on, either joyfully blessed or forever burdened. And what gain did sin provide? What is the long term reward? Sin is always deadly in retrospect. When we serve evil we are fully aware of our guilt before God. If you choose to persist in sin, your prayer should be that there is no eternal Father and that you are only flesh, not spirit and flesh.

The Scriptures teach that God provided a final, excruciatingly painful sacrifice to allow the sins of man to be forgiven. He sent His only Son into the world, born of a virgin, to live a sinless life, to proclaim the Word, to suffer at the will of some of His own people because they rejected His claim of being "equal to God", and to die a humiliating death on the cross. Thus Jesus became the means by which believers are reconciled to God. There is no need for further sacrifice. Christ has taken on the sins of the world and because of His resurrection and His promised return, those who worship God and confess that Jesus Christ is Lord, will spend eternity with Him.

The Messiah came that you might be reunited with God. You were His child at birth, innocent and unaccountable, and He desires that you be His child now. Your innocence, as an adult, can not be "achieved". It is a gift from God. When we acknowledge our sin to Him, and ask for cleansing and turn from the sin that separated us from God in the first place, we return, as an innocent child, to His eternal care and love. We were born God's children, even if we have not been serving Him. God is like any loving father, waiting for his child to return.

One of Satan's roles is to prevent us from understanding that message, or better yet, if we do understand it, to have us become "religious". Satan would have us believe that ritual, ceremony, good deeds, obeying the laws of man and God, will reconcile us with God. These are certainly appropriate behaviors but it is possible to do these things and still not experience a heartfelt, personal relationship with Jesus. Many well intentioned people strive for righteousness, to be like Jesus, but find they are impotent in the face of stress. They give in, getting caught up in lying, drunkenness, pornography, drugs, infidelity, jealousy and self worship and as a result they feel very unsaintly and very unworthy.

Heaven, a reward for high achievers?

Neither good deeds nor merit badges can help us earn salvation. If our "works" could deliver us into a personal relationship with the Holy Father, then Jesus Christ would have never needed to go the cross. We could have "earned" grace. Grace is defined as receiving unmerited favor from God. We do not deserve His forgiveness and the power of His Presence in our lives. Sin, in spite of our good deeds, deserves punishment but we have received grace because of what Christ did on the cross.

Christ would not have needed to go to the cross if man could "redeem himself" and know that God exists. If you have "proof", and a means of reconciliation, you do not need faith. The crucifixion of Jesus was a major turning point in the history of man (B.C. / A.D.). If one fails to grasp what God did for those who believe on Him, at the cross, one fails to understand atonement and forgiveness.

Since we are all sinners, admittedly I am sure, and since God will not and can not countenance sin (look upon or be in the presence of sin), God provided a solution. His sinless Son went to the cross on our behalf and now we can stand in the presence of God completely forgiven. If you are still suffering from guilt, which makes you feel unworthy, you are carrying a burden you need not carry. The Scriptures say:

"The LORD is merciful and gracious, slow to anger, and abounding in mercy. He will not always strive with us, nor will He keep His anger forever. He has not dealt with us according to our sins, nor punished us according to our iniquities. For as the heavens are high above the earth, so great is His mercy toward those who fear Him; As far as the east is from the west, so far has He removed our transgressions from us." Psalm 103:8-12

To be forgiven, one need only ask. The act of confessing your sins and having them erased forever seems far too simple, yet the world is full of guilt-ridden persons who in their heart of hearts know that their sin has separated them from God.

God's Word, the enduring light: The Truth

The Word of God is our only reliable guideline in trying to understand God's will for our lives. It is an absolute treasure of inspiration, wit, instruction and advice. We dedicate our lives to certain principles, disciplines and activities. Do they include time with God's Word? What evidence will we offer when we are asked whether our lives demonstrated that we love God with all our heart, mind and soul? If you want to get to know God, read His Word! A Bible on a shelf, unstudied, may as well not exist.

No man, aside from Jesus, who existed from the beginning and will exist to the end (I am the Alpha and the Omega, the beginning and the end), has ever seen God. We who believe God exists do so on the basis of "evidence". We see in all that was created, God's complex and perfect plan. The beauty and power of what was created is in God's hands and He controls all forces of nature. Man often gets angry at God's allowing tragedy to occur. The Scriptures teach that which was created with the potential for perfection, was desecrated by sinful man. God's Eden will be restored and Satan, at that time, and in that place, will be restrained.

Eventually there will be a New Jerusalem, perfect in every way. This world, (our testing ground and Satan's domain) and everything in it will be destroyed. Heaven will be a place of joy and peace for God's children, only, not for Satan or Satan's allies. It was not God's will that man would fail to abstain from sin, but God did and does give us a choice. Sin leads to judgment, sometimes by God directly and sometimes by the laws of nature or the laws of man. Man has choices and some of them lead to bad consequences, even when innocent yet unaccountable people are involved. One does not want to ever be in the position of harming a child or someone whose mental state is as a child. God loves the children and would have us exhibit the faith that a child exhibits in those they trust.

God went so far as to point toward very specific prophetic events, which did occur, in His effort to help us with our faith. But what is faith? The Scriptures say, "Now faith is the substance of things hoped for, the evidence of things not seen." Hebrews 11:1. In other words, faith is a product of observing God's wonderful manifestations of Himself and His plan, then "believing" and acting on that belief.

God wants to reconcile you to Himself. He created you in His own image. He loves you. He knew you before you were in your mother's womb. Psalm 139:13-16 "For You formed my inward parts; You covered me in my mother's womb. I will praise You, for I am fearfully and wonderfully made; …Your eyes saw my substance, being yet unformed. And in Your book they all were written, the days fashioned for me, when as yet there were none of them." Abortion, in the light of the Scriptures, is a very bad choice; forgivable but not consistent with what you just read. Ask the Holy Spirit to lead you and give you His counsel in this matter.

God's expectations (requirements) of His children.

If you do not know the definitions of the following words, please study and understand them: OMNIPOTENCE, OMNIPRESENCE and OMNISCIENCE. No god is as our God. Simply said, God is all powerful, always present and knows all things. He is in control. He sees you now, He is present with you now and He knows all things, including the choices you will ultimately make. God gave you volition, the right to choose. You are not a puppet but volition is fraught with risks. It makes you accountable for your choices and it makes the shepherds who lead us very accountable for the counsel given.

God has two key commandments which are imbedded in the 10 Commandments. Jesus said to him, "'You shall love the LORD your God with all your heart, with all your soul, and with all your mind.' This is the first and great commandment. And the second is like it: 'You shall love your neighbor as yourself.' On these two commandments hang all the Law and the Prophets." Matthew 22:37-40.

If you love God, you should, in all humility and contrition, decide to repent (to turn away from your sins), be baptized, be obedient and to seek His will for your life. In the Scriptures, He asked us to recognize and acknowledge who Jesus was, why He came and what action we are to take. The action required is basically incredible. If we accept Jesus Christ as the propitiation (stand in) for our sins, confess our sins and turn away from those sins, God will cleanse us, draw us near to Him in this life and promise us eternal life.

We honor Christ, our sins are forgiven and we are "in the kingdom". What price did we pay? Confession, a changed life and a decision to worship Him and to honor and obey His Word; what price did God pay? Even yet I can not stand to see one of my children or grandchildren suffer. I would always rather suffer in their place. God sent His Son to save us, while we were yet sinners. The passion endured by Jesus was for you and me. John 3:16 "For God so loved the world that He gave His only begotten Son, that whoever believes in Him should not perish but have everlasting life".

Life is extremely short if you measure it against eternity. The span of our life can not be mathematically compared to eternity. One is finite (has a point at which it ends), the other is infinite (has no end point). Life is a very short test (since you are reading this, the test isn't over), but if we fail the test, we are eternally separated from God. The Scriptures teach that when we accept Christ we become a "new creation, behold old things pass away and all things become new" 1 Corinthians 5:17. Accepting Christ means discarding the dominance of the "flesh" in our life. We can not do that easily. Understand this; when you decide to cling to Jesus, Satan will have lost control of a soul, your soul! He then attacks with "seven other spirits more wicked than him and they enter and dwell there; and the last state of that man is worse than the first" Luke 11:26. Do not vow to love God and then go back to serving Satan. It takes spiritual strength, the power and presence of Christ in you, to deal with sin. Is there some powerful sin that won't let go of you? God will, by the presence of the Holy Spirit, empower you to resist and to defeat that sin. Pray unceasingly for deliverance from sin and take steps to avoid sin.

Do you recall the story of Noah and how God brought the flood to destroy all but the righteous few (Noah, his 3 sons and wives, 8 people)? How sinful could the people in Noah's time have been? Do you think they had invented more ways to sin than we have in these days? I doubt it. In our time, sin abounds. Measure it any way you want, but God could not be happy with what is going on. I doubt that an hour goes by in which ideas, words, publications, and broadcasts do not bring sin into our homes. An unfiltered Internet connection is one of Satan's most potent new weapons. Take personal and political steps to stop the uninvited solicitation and advocacy of sin. Your children and many of you are tempted by Satan, daily. Flee from such material and commit yourself to taking steps to escape from its influence.

Will there be another great judgment? The Scriptures say "yes". The world will fall into such sinful disarray, that only a "remnant" will be pleasing to God (hopefully more than 8 people). When God sent Jesus to us, it was to reconcile ourselves to Him. Jesus was not only the solution to our need for forgiveness, but through Him the Father provided the gift of the Holy Spirit. When Christ was crucified, He said that unless I go to heaven to be with the Father, the Holy Spirit, the Helper, the Counselor, the Comforter, could not come.

The Holy Spirit, God's love and power in you.

We can not, of our own power, overcome the influence of sin, by adhering to God's law. That is where the Holy Spirit is the only answer. Our battle is against an evil spirit, a powerful, deceptive force that can even appear to be "for good". The Scriptures say, "For false christs and false prophets will rise and show great signs and wonders to deceive, if possible, even the elect" Matthew 24:24. If you do not study the Bible I do not know how you will be able to identify false teachers and leaders who will guide you into bad decisions and alliances.

I am convinced that many today suffer failure in their effort to "do the right thing", not because they do not understand how to define righteous behavior, but because they do not understand the gift of the Holy Spirit. To believe in God and to believe in Jesus is good. But the Scriptures teach that the devil also knows whom God and Jesus is, and trembles. A relationship with the Father, Son and Holy Ghost is not an "intellectual assent". It is more than saying "yes, I believe God exists". It is the acceptance of a new heart and a new start. It is that moment in which you are born again and the Holy Spirit and your spirit are made as one, united as intended by God, forever. When that happens, The Spirit of God and our spirit become intertwined. We are no longer captives of the flesh, our physical nature.

If we are in Christ, these are the characteristics our new nature should reveal: Love, joy, peace, patience, kindness, goodness, faithfulness, gentleness and self-control Galatians 5:22. Read those over carefully. Which of us would not want those words to characterize our nature and the quality of our daily experiences? Try listing the opposite characteristics and you will see what I mean, i.e. angry, depressed, anxious, impatient, unkind, without faith, lacking in self-control, etc.

Telling people about your faith helps you sustain your commitment. You will find that every moment of every day allows you to experience God's presence. The Scriptures say that His thoughts toward you exceed number Psalm 40:5. Not a hair falls from your head of which He is unaware Matthew 10:27-31. You will learn that your thoughts and actions can be "as unto the Lord" Colossians 3:23-25. He knows your thoughts and observes your actions. You never are doing a good or bad deed privately. If you claim Jesus as your Savior, His desire is to empower you to be His good and faithful servant.

We are not able to intellectualize our way into an understanding of God's word. The wisdom and discernment we can gain from the Scriptures is beyond the reach of any that are not earnestly seeking a relationship with Him. In 1 Corinthians 1:18 it says, "For the message of the cross is foolishness to those who are perishing, but to us who are being saved it is the power of God". A pastor I know once said that man is about 12 inches from being saved, the distance from his head to his heart. God wants you to know Him and to respond to His call but He knows, even this moment if you will love Him in return for the love He has shown you. No one is forced to respond. God gave man volition, the power to choose.

A stern but loving warning

If you want to serve Christ, you will be "out of step" with the deteriorating standards of this world. If you are actively serving Christ, Satan is after your soul. You and I, in our own flesh, can not conquer sin. We are taught in 1 Corinthians 10:13, "No temptation has overtaken you except such as is common to man: but God is faithful, who will not allow you to be tempted beyond what you are able, but with the temptation will also make the way of escape, that you may be able to bear it". This world is Satan's playground. We are "in" it but do not have to be "of" it. We can, through the power of the Holy Spirit, endure any temptation (always from the devil, never from God) and come out the other side, victorious. God allows us to be tested, but God does not "tempt" His children.

I believe that the most dangerous religious sects are those whose claims include a great deal of truth. One of Satan's best tools is a very attractive religion that almost has it right. That usually means they have added to or subtracted from the Holy Scriptures, some key elements of truth. Listen to what God's Word says: Deuteronomy 4:2 "You shall not add to the word which I command you, nor take anything from it, that you may keep the commandments of the LORD your God which I command you."

Do not cling to a group that claims new, additional truth has been revealed to them, especially if it supersedes or conflicts with Scripture. God's Holy Word is the whole truth.

What is so terrific about Christianity is that what you are asked to do makes sense. Don't sin, love God, love your neighbor, obey, out of love, all of the commandments and when you stumble, and we will, ask for forgiveness and renewed strength. There are, according to Scriptures, two judgments. First the judgment based upon our acceptance of Christ, which places us in the kingdom and second the judgment of believers.

Just because Jesus is willing to continually forgive us, don't think there is no judgment of continual sin. Jesus asks us to "repent", which means to turn from our sin. We are not to continue doing that which Jesus went to the cross to cleanse us of. Think about it. Are we asking Him to go to the cross, again and again, for our sins? Not a logical request. Jesus wants to strengthen us, to give us the gift of the Holy Spirit and to help us deal with temptation, a circumstance that will not go away in this life.

As to the position that Jesus Christ is the only way to God, the Scriptures leave no alternative. "..there is no other name under heaven given among men by which we must be saved." Acts 4:12 Christ said, "I am the way, the truth and the life. No one comes to the Father, except through Me." John 14:6 That may seem harsh to those who seek to know God by other means, however, that is what the Scriptures say. It has been said that you can think that Jesus was a lunatic, a liar or the Lord. He did not offer the option of being considered "only" a good guy, a righteous man, a teacher, and a prophet. As of this moment, you have made a choice. The ramifications of your choice are of eternal significance. There is no way except for the shed blood of Jesus, covering your sins and mine, to enter into the presence of God.

Apprehending eternity: Finish well!

I pray that you consider the following commitment. We all make time for those things in life that are important to us. In Jesus' life, he frequently separated Himself from the people to spend time with God. We have the gift of the Scriptures, something of pivotal importance. Please consider reading the Bible, at least a few minutes, every day. Read in a quiet place of peace if possible. What could be more important than spending time with God? We faithfully listen to a lot of other communications and many of them are a complete waste of our time.

God wants you to listen to His Word and to talk to Him, bringing all of your needs, the needs of your family and friends and your desires to Him. The answers may not always be yes but they will always fit perfectly into His plan for your life. Learn to be patient and to wait upon the Lord. He knows your needs and His Spirit intervenes for you in ways that you do not even perceive Romans 8:26-27.

If you start reading, for instance, in the Gospel of John or in the Psalms for 5 minutes each day, I can promise you it will go well beyond 5 minutes. The Holy Scriptures is a great treasure. The Scriptures say: Your word I have hidden in my heart that I might not sin against You. Psalm 119:11.

Some of the Psalms are the most beautiful words ever written and the wisdom of Proverbs and Ecclesiastes is unmatched. Go to a Bible, highlight key verses, look up parallel references and join a fellowship support group. Pray that God will direct you to a Bible centered church. Although Christianity is a very personal thing, it flourishes when it is shared. Let the love of God and the Light within you, shine before men. Let the joy of your salvation be evident to all. Be an encourager, a witness and an ambassador for Christ. The Great Commission that Christ called us to is "To go into all the world and preach the gospel." Mark 16:15

Perfection in Christ eludes us all. We strive, we endeavor to serve, we seek His will for our lives and we commit our resources and our family to His care, but the Christian walk is a journey, full of challenges. Listen to the words of the apostle Paul. "Not that I have already attained, or am already perfected; but I press on, that I may lay hold of that for which Christ Jesus has also laid hold of me. Brethren, I do not count myself to have apprehended; but one thing I do, forgetting those things which are behind and reaching forward to those things which are ahead, I press toward the goal for the prize of the upward call of God in Christ Jesus." Philippians 3:12-14, NKJ

I meet many people who think that their history of sin has indelibly "tattooed" them, that they are beyond God's reach and God's love. If that is you, you are a perfect example of why Jesus went to the Cross. God promises to forgive murderers, terrorists, sodomists, homosexuals, pornographers, child molesters, liars and thieves, cheaters, prideful persons and on and on. The Scriptures tell us that God hates the sin but loves the sinner. Jesus came to pay the price for such sins and to reconcile all who will repent, not a select few, but all. Listen and understand: Luke 23:39-40 "Then one of the criminals who were hanged blasphemed Him, saying, "If You are the Christ, save Yourself and us." But the other, answering, rebuked him, saying, "Do you not even fear God, seeing you are under the same condemnation? And we indeed justly, for we receive the due reward of our deeds; but this Man has done nothing wrong." Then he said to Jesus, "Lord, remember me when You come into Your kingdom." And Jesus said to him, "Assuredly, I say to you, today you will be with Me in Paradise."

Jesus just taught you a key principle; finish well! None of us deserve to have a lifetime of sin wiped away, but that is the offer. While you are finishing well, listen to some wonderful promises of Jesus: "I have come that they may have life and that they may have it more abundantly". John 10:10 Peace I leave with you, My peace I give to you; not as the world gives do I give to you. Let not your heart be troubled, neither let it be afraid. John 14:27 The Apostle Paul said: I have been crucified with Christ; it is no longer I who live, but Christ lives in me; and the life which I now live in the flesh I live by faith in the Son of God, who loved me and gave Himself for me. Galatians 2:20

Additional resources and encouragement:

I compiled a web site of Family Bible Studies, Daily Devotions and Topical Readings, www.solascriptura.com that may be helpful. I also authored the "End Times" web site that you are currently visiting "Israel – The Chosen or the Enemy". Both web sites have feedback buttons that send your comments or concerns directly to me. You are able to use those links to comment on this message as well. Feedback is more than welcome.

I pray that God will richly bless you and your family, forever.

Bruce Caldwell, Ed. D.